LIBRARY LIT. 5 – The Best of 1974

edited by

BILL KATZ

and

ROBERT BURGESS

The Scarecrow Press, Inc.
Metuchen, N.J.   1975

ISBN 0-8108-0808-0
Library of Congress Catalog Card Number 78-154842

CONTENTS

Introduction   v

Part 1.   LIBRARIES AND LIBRARIANS

Thinking the Unthinkable About Libraries: A Theory
    of the No-Growth Collection (Daniel Gore)   1
Evidence of Erosion of a Resource Due to Population
    Growth: Case of the Public Library (Raymond
    Jackson)   12
Behavior in Libraries (Peter Jordan)   23
An American Experience (Toyo S. Kawakami)   36
Ideals and Axioms: Library Architecture (Jane Holtz
    Kay)   44
Books and Beds: Libraries in Nineteenth and
    Twentieth Century American Hotels (Manuel D.
    Lopez)   57
Peacocks and Posers: Librarianship as a Profession
    (Judith McPheron)   90
The Bargaining Economics of Libraries: The Mean-
    ing for Libraries and the Library Profession
    (Donald G. Mercer)   95
Unions and Libraries: The Spheres of Intellect and
    Politics (Roger E. Michener)   110
Business Libraries: Role and Function in Industrial
    America (Mildred S. Myers and William C.
    Frederick)   132

Part II.   TECHNICAL SERVICES/READERS' SERVICES

Cataloging Philosophy (Sanford Berman)   147
Fifty Years of Young Adult Reading, 1921-1971
    (Margaret Hutchinson)   153
Four Misconceptions of Machine Fanatics in Judging
    Direct Human-Computer Interaction (Janice M.
    Ladendorf)   194
The Library Resources, Inc., Library of American

Civilization Demonstration at the George Washington
University Library (Paul A. Napier, Annette D.
Steiner and Rupert C. Woodward)   201
Inter-library Loans: The Experience of the Center for
Research Libraries (Gordon Williams)   238

Part III.   COMMUNICATION AND EDUCATION

The Information Explosion (Wilfred Ashworth)   247
Education for Cataloging (J. Balnaves)   267
To Each Generation Its Own Rabbits (Dennis Flanagan)   276
Literature Bedeviled: A Searching Look at Filmstrips
(Ethel L. Heins)   285
Johnny Still Can't Read (Daniel Melcher)   293
Dumped from a Wharf into Casco Bay: The Historical
Records Survey Revisited (Leonard Rapport)   315
The Effect of Literary Awards on Children's Book
Recommendations (Dorothy J. Schmidt and
Jeanne Osborn)   326
The First and Last Frontier of Communication: The
Map as Mystery (Wilbur Zelinsky)   338
Disestablishing the School, and the Public Library
(Leo N. Flanagan)   349

Part IV.   THE SOCIAL PREROGATIVE

Social Responsibility and Libraries (Arthur Curley)   363
Some Insight into Access: The Problems of Prison
Libraries (Agnes M. Griffin)   390
Libraries and the First Amendment after Nixon
(Nat Hentoff)   395
Black Book Reviewing: A Case for Library Action
(Ann Allen Shockley)   407
The Marginal Man (S. Simsova)   415

EPILOGUE

A Computer Analysis of Library Postcards (CALP)
(Norman D. Stevens)   427

Notes on Contributors   435

INTRODUCTION

This fifth annual collection, like its predecessors, brings together 30 articles judged by the jurors to be the "best" published between November 1973 and November 1974. What purpose does this yearly anthology serve?

Principally, it recognizes lively writing on subjects of current and continuing importance to the library profession. And to judge by the complaints of library school students who must read the favorites their professors include on reading lists, this encouragement is still in order.

Perhaps the definition of "best" is most amply clarified by an example from this year's choices: Berman's "prose-poem." Poetry critics might not choose it for a selection of the best poetry of 1974, but this year's jurors found: 1) that it had been suggested for inclusion by several persons; 2) that it had elicited considerable comment when published, and more when reprinted in Library Journal; 3) that it was one of several on its subject under consideration for inclusion, indicating a high current professional interest in the topic of subject headings; and 4) that discussion ran high among the jurors before it was voted in, comments ranging from "best selection for this year" to "a little Berman goes a long way."

Humor has been but rarely included in the previous four volumes. We have been waiting for a "scholarly" contribution from the Molesworth Institute which could be selected, and we have one this year. Certainly the serious work of this renowned organization should have recognition in this series. We encourage even the profession's most dedicated critics and polemicists to put their tongues in cheek and give us more to choose from another year.

Your help in discovering items for consideration for next year is indeed welcome. The final selections this year were made while Senior Editor Bill Katz was on sabbatical.

v

The penalty for all the pleasures of London is the risk of not agreeing with the final result.

The jurors this year were Norman Horrocks, Editor, Journal of Education for Librarianship and Director, School of Library Service, Dalhousie; Ann Prentice, Assistant Professor, School of Library and Information Science, Albany; Gerald R. Shields, Assistant Professor, School of Information and Library Studies, Buffalo and former Editor, American Libraries; and the constant in the five juries to date, Eric Moon, President, Scarecrow Press. Their reading of some 75 articles under considerable time pressure, their skill in analyzing content for "meat" and their ready recognition of good writing has made it possible for the Associate Editor to maintain the high standards of previous volumes. Special thanks to Sherry Gaherty, who helped this year again with permissions and a myriad of other details.

Robert S. Burgess
Albany, New York
December, 1974

Part I

LIBRARIES AND LIBRARIANS

THINKING THE UNTHINKABLE
ABOUT LIBRARIES: A THEORY
OF THE NO-GROWTH COLLECTION*

Daniel Gore

> All the rivers run into the sea; yet the sea is not
> full.
> --Ecclesiastes 1:7

When Abraham Lincoln was asked how long a man's
legs should be, he replied "Long enough to reach the ground."

One feels comfortable with such an answer: it makes
sense, it conforms to reality, it doesn't strain the imagination.

When one asks a librarian how large a library should
be, the invariable answer is "Larger. And with provision
for further expansion fifteen years hence."

One used to feel comfortable with that answer too, because it made sense of a sort (at least to academicians, who
intuitively know there is no such thing as enough books), and
it certainly conformed to the only reality we have known
since the foundation of the Alexandrian Library 2300 years
ago. Libraries have always grown until fire, flood, or fighting put an end to them.

But lately the answer has begun to weigh upon the

---

*This article appeared, in somewhat amended form, as "Ze-
ro Growth for the College Library," in College Management,
Aug. -Sept. 1974, pp. 12-14. It is reprinted by permission
of the author and publisher. © 1974 by Macmillan Professional Magazines, Inc. All rights reserved.

imagination, at least of those who pause to reflect upon the
consequences of the observed geometric growth rate in academic libraries in the 20th century.

For several decades now academic library collections
have been doubling every 15 years or so. University libraries that held several hundred thousand volumes in the 1930's
hold several million today, and at that rate many of them
would become, in just fifty more years, about the size of
the Library of Congress today--a library of such gargantuan
dimensions it calls upon the resources of a whole nation to
sustain it.

The budgets of some present day university libraries
exceed the total institutional budgets of some small colleges.
Yet some of those colleges have libraries whose growth rates
will, if maintained over the next 50 years, bring them up to
the multimillion-volume levels of the great university libraries.

Is anyone prepared to believe that the nation will ever
support a hundred university libraries the size of today's
Library of Congress, whose annual budget is approaching a
hundred million dollars?

Or that colleges fifty years hence will be able to devote to their libraries the constant-dollar equivalent of their
current total institutional budget?

The imagination collapses under so ponderous a pros-
pect, and one turns away from this problem, as from so
many others, with the soothing conviction that the next generation will surely solve it--especially since they will have
the benefit of four times as many books as we have today to
guide them in their thinking.

A dilemma arises here, for the library buildings we
have today just won't hold four times their present content,
and the money won't be available to expand them. During
the last decade more than a billion dollars' worth of new
academic library buildings were constructed in the U.S., and
paid for mainly with federal money. Library expansion on
that scale had never been seen before, nor are we likely to
see it again in our generation. The building boom is over.
But in a few hundred years most of those buildings will be
filled to capacity, as will their associated storage facilities,
and relatively little federal or other funding is in sight to

provide the usual remedy of more space. So the problem
of coping with the geometric growth of academic libraries
just will not wait for the next generation to solve it. We
will have to solve it for them.

One solution that has been tried, and proved a failure,
is miniaturization, through microfilming or computer storage,
or any other technique. While certain results are achieved
by those measures--for example vast and probably useless
expansion of total resources, and reduction of data-retrieval
times--they contribute nothing to the solution of the physical
growth problem. The highest growth rates in the history of
academic libraries have occurred precisely during the 30-
year period when microtechnology was on the ascendant.
That microtechnology has had no effect on the space problem
is partially accounted for by the fact that librarians typically
acquire publications in microformat only when, for whatever
reason, they cannot or will not acquire them on paper. Microform collections have thus generally developed not as substitutes for something bulkier, but as collections that simply
would not have existed in any form had they not been available in microform. (The use that is actually made of general microform collections is notoriously low, so low that
one suspects that in most cases far more economical methods
could be provided for delivering their content to a patron, if
and when the demand arose. Replacing journal backruns with
micro-equivalents, for example, is in most instances economic folly. Demand on most journal backruns in nearly all
libraries is so near zero that one should simply remove
them--perhaps to some regional lending center--and be done
with them completely.)

The solution to the growth problem will be found, I
believe, not in the development of new technology to shore
up the cracking foundations of the ever-climbing Tower of
Babel, but in thinking carefully about that most perplexing
question, How large should a library be?

Such answers as have been given fall into three categories. First there is the heroic-impulsive, or Alexandrian
answer, so called because it arose with the formation of the
Alexandrian Library in 300 B.C., almost coincidentally with
the origin of the peculiarly Western attitude that bigger means
better, and that limits are inherently bad. The Alexandrian
answer is simply that the library should acquire everything
and keep it forever, lest something of inestimable value perish from the earth through negligence or misvaluation. The

Alexandrian librarians are said to have collected hundreds of thousands of scrolls while that library existed. But despite their heoric efforts, and those of all succeeding generations of librarians, only 500 titles from classical antiquity have survived.

Rarely do libraries play a significant role in the long-term survival of books. In short-term preservation, yes; long-term survival, no. The Bible exists today not because librarians preserved it for 2,000 years, but because scribes, and then printers, endlessly reproduced it.

Though the historical outcome of the Alexandrian approach to preservation is not reassuring, college and university faculties are instinctively Alexandrian in their view of the library. The sheer magnitude of numbers at least forces them to give up the idea of acquiring everything--50 million books published since Gutenberg; 400,000 new ones each year, plus some 300,000 new serials volumes--but nothing will persuade them to give up a volume once it has been acquired.

More recently there is the Philosophical answer, which stipulates that an academic library should be large enough to hold whatever books are needed to support the curriculum, to support research where graduate programs are conducted, and to permit some "recreational reading." The Philosophical answer has the merit of plausibility, but gives no clue as to the actual size of the library required, beyond the relative indication that a larger library will be required to support a "larger" curriculum. The Philosophical answer avoids any forthright mention of what will happen to the collection if, say, a segment of the curriculum is simply dropped, or course content is updated in such a way that much of the existing collection proves to be either irrelevant or erroneous. Proponents of the Philosophical view studiously avoid offending the Alexandrians by tacitly pretending that the reason for bringing a book into a library is also a reason for keeping it there forever. To pretend that is to pretend that the curriculum today is precisely that of the last century, although of course "larger." But one is tempted to pretend almost anything rather than risk the hissing cry of "Philistine!" from the Alexandrians who, while prepared to concede that a curriculum must change, and that courses once offered need not be offered forever, nonetheless insist that the library that "supports" the curriculum must forever be the same library, only larger. The Philosophical answer by default amounts to agreeing that an academic library shall always be larger.

Finally there is the Scientific answer, which has the
virtue of providing exact numbers of volumes required, by
means of a formula based on such variables as enrollment,
size of faculty, number of graduate fields, etc. The principal value of the Scientific answer is that it may favorably
impress a fiscal officer who is not disposed to pry too deeply
into your bedrock scientific formula, and discover that the
whole thing miraculously floats upon a bottomless swamp of
pure impressionism. It should be noted that the Scientific
answer applied only to questions of "How small may a library
properly be?" It is calculated to frighten administrators into
believing their library is too small, and is thus couched exclusively in terms of minimums. It resolutely ignores the
question, "How large should a library be?" as its proponents
assume that anyone in his right mind knows a library should
be just as big as it possibly can be, and always growing
bigger.

The Alexandrian, the Philosophical, and the Scientific
approach to libraries all require that they always grow larger,
world without end. [1] So potent and pervasive is this trinity,
one would not dare speak out against it unless its ultimate
outcome were both manifestly absurd, and close at hand. Now
that race car drivers are publicly declaring that speed limits
are needed on the Indy 500, it may be permissible for a librarian to propose that size limits are needed for libraries.

If we put aside our Alexandrian prejudices for a moment, and ask what is the main function of an academic library, rather than how large it should be, I think we will
get general agreement that its primary function is to provide
books[2] for readers who want to read them now. (No suggestion is intended that academic libraries have no proper archival, or preservational role. Undoubtedly they do, but the
proportion of their holdings devoted to that function is insignificant in relation to the space problem.) Though we may
fret ourselves in a high-minded way about the imagined needs
of our patrons in the 21st century, the needs we must actually fill are those of the student standing on the other side of
the circulation desk, plaintively asking to be told why he so
rarely finds the books he needs to read. The answer usually
has nothing to do with the size of the collection; or, rather,
it is not because the collection is too small.

When we suspend the perplexing question of collection
size and ask instead questions about performance rates in relation to necessary functions, some unexpected results ensue,

one of them being that by making your collection smaller you
can actually provide more and better service.

Let us first ask what is an acceptable performance
rate with regard to recorded holdings. To an Alexandrian
the required rate is 100%--that is, the library should own,
and the catalog record, every book that every patron, present or future, may ever ask for. To achieve that ideal rate
you will have to own some 50, 000, 000 books, and add about
400, 000 new ones every year, plus 300, 000 new serial volumes.

If you will agree to a rate less than 100%, some surprising things happen. Several years ago the Yale Library
discovered it owned about 90% of the books its patrons wanted
to see, yet it owned only 2, 500, 000 titles, or 5% of the total
that might be asked for. By falling off the Alexandrian ideal
by a mere 10%, the Yale Library could forego the purchase
of 47, 500, 000 books--and the construction of a building twice
the size of the Empire State to hold them.

Consider now another measure of library performance: the availability rate, by which I mean the rate of success in finding on the shelves a book you want that the catalog says the library owns. Recent inquiries into this phenomenon indicate that an availability rate around 50% may be
the norm. Assume now that you can find entries in the catalog for 90% of the books you want to see, and that you will
find 50% of those actually on the shelves. The net result is
a performance rate of 45%, which is dismal, but not because
the library is too small. The cause lies elsewhere, and the
remedy is not to add more titles to the collection.

During the 1960's R. W. Trueswell, now Chairman of
the Industrial Engineering Department at the University of
Massachusetts, published a series of statistical studies of library inventory phenomena, showing that a very small proportion of an academic library's collection accounts for nearly
all the use. [3] He makes the intriguing suggestion that 40% of
a collection may account for 99% of the recorded use; and, if
that be so, then at least half the collection may be removed
without perceptibly affecting the availability of books that
people will actually read. Trueswell's astonishing predictions
so offend the Alexandrian temperament that they have met
with the most devastating possible response from the library
profession: they have been ignored.

Corollary to the proposition that most books in a large library are rarely or never used is the proposition that a small percentage of books are always in very heavy demand, and thus frequently unavailable when you want to borrow them. Hence in most libraries you are likely to fail nearly half the time to find the book you want, though the library owns it. The demand is too heavy for the supply, and libraries usually give no systematic attention to the problem. One library that did--the University of Lancaster's--discovered that when measures were taken to improve the availability rate from 60% to 86% by shortening the loan period of high-demand books, the per capita use rate more than doubled. [4] Had they instead doubled the number of titles in the collection, the availability rate would have been imperceptibly affected.

At the moment one can find very little data to answer these three essential questions regarding an academic library's performance:

1) What percentage of books wanted by patrons are recorded in the catalog? (The Holdings Rate).
2) What percentage of wanted books recorded in the catalog are available on the shelves? (The Availability Rate).
3) What percentage of all books a patron wants are available to him on the shelves? (The Performance Rate: Holdings Rate times Availability Rate).

From the patron's standpoint the third question is the one that really matters, and the librarian's problem is to decide what combination of Holdings and Availability Rates will yield the best results with the available resources.

Though scant, data now available on these matters are sufficient to make it worthwhile for any library to begin testing certain hypotheses aimed at improving Performance Rates while reducing collection size. I will present an illustration here to show what is realistically possible, using estimates which, though they certainly will not apply exactly to any one library's situation, should prove close enough to suggest a suitable point of departure.

Assume a university library with the following characteristics:

Collection size	1,000,000 vols.
Current additions	50,000 vols/yr.

Enrollment	20, 000 students
Holdings Rate	90%
Availability Rate	50%
Performance Rate	45%

The Performance Rate in this library is quite poor, but probably typical of such libraries. A decision is made to improve it, by going the traditional route of adding to the holdings. Consider now the result that will be obtained by the most extreme imaginable application of the Alexandrian ideal: by some miracle you create a library holding every book under the sun, and add to it everything that is published everywhere, as it comes off the press. Your library now holds 50 million volumes, and each year you add 700, 000 new ones. Your Holdings Rate climbs to 100%, but your Availability Rate remains 50%, for you have done nothing to affect it. The Performance Rate (the product of Holdings and Availability Rates) thus moves up from 45% to 50% and, though you have spent two billion dollars on the project, your patrons perceive things to be far worse than they were before, because they now have to walk ten times as far to suffer about the same number of disappointments as before.

The tenure of university librarians over the last fifteen years parallels in brevity that of university presidents, because they sought to improve Performance Rates by zealously attending to Holding Rates while ignoring the availability problem. Nothing really happened, except that their libraries got bigger and they got other jobs.

Keeping in mind the Trueswell predictions regarding collection size and Performance Rates, and the University of Lancaster's experience with Availability Rates, let us now consider how we may radically improve Performance Rates by drastically cutting collection size.

Using Trueswell's simple statistical criterion for predicting which books in the collection will receive little or no use in the future, we remove 500, 000 of them at one fell swoop. The Holdings Rate now drops from 90% to 85%. Why so little? Because the Holdings Rate applies to books that people will want to read, and you have statistically contrived to leave practically all of those books in the library.

At the same time, by statistical methods we identify those books whose predictable demand is so great that one or more added copies will be needed to achieve a certain pre-

dictable Availability Rate. By computer simulation we determine that 100,000 added copies will bring the Availability
Rate to 95%, which is the best we can afford.

   We have now a collection of 600,000 volumes, a Holdings Rate of 85%, and an Availability Rate of 95%. Although
the collection has been reduced by 40%, the Performance Rate
has climbed from a dismal 45% to a sterling 81%. Though
the library has shrunk in size, everyone miraculously perceives that it has grown enormously, because suddenly, for
the first time, they find books when they want them. Per
capita use rates will probably double, while collection maintenance costs plummet.

   And the new building that was going to be needed five
years hence will never be needed, because the number of
volumes required to maintain any specified Performance Rate
will remain constant (assuming enrollment does) as the years
go by. While the titles held by the library will change from
year to year, as patron demand shifts from one book to
another, the total number of volumes remains constant. The
intake rate of new volumes may be any figure you like (or
can afford), because the outflow rate will exactly equal it, if
you are firm in your resolve not to attempt minor improvements in your Holdings Rate by vastly expanding the number
of different books in your collection.

   The Alexandrians will be tragically depressed by all
this, and curse you both loud and deep for your rampant
philistinism.   But even they will make the astounding discovery that the books they actually want to read are, as if
by magic, suddenly available when they wish to read them.
As the opportunities multiply for them actually to read the
books they've always wanted to, but never could because the
library was so big, their lifelong frustrations with the library
will diminish, and eventually they may forget what a wicked
trick you played on them.

   As for that 15% deficiency in your Holdings Rate,
much of that can be made up, if you wish, by overhauling
your acquisitions and processing operations, so all new Eng-
lish-language imprints will reach your library on or around
publication date, and be available for circulation a day or so
after you receive them. [5] Demand for books is at its peak
when they are new.   Yet academic libraries are notorious
for average delays of a year or longer in making them available.   Eliminating that delay could largely offset the 5%

Holdings Rate drop that resulted from the removal of 500, 000
unused books.

Much of the remaining deficiency in your effective
Holdings Rate can be compensated for by participation in an
efficient interloan network. Such networks are developing
rapidly around the nation, and are exhibiting Performance
Rates in the range of 80%, with average delivery times of
five days or less.

By these two measures your effective Holdings Rate
can be brought at least to 95%, and your Performance Rate
to a spectacular 90%. And all of this will cost you substantially less than you would spend to achieve a 45% Performance Rate going the traditional exponential growth route.
Collection maintenance costs do not usually show up in an
academic library's budget, but they are there all the same.
They consist of such things as lighting, heating, cooling,
janitorial service, and the capital and depreciation costs of
real estate. Assuming standard stack capacity of 15 volumes per square foot, average annual maintenance costs are
about twenty cents per volume. Total maintenance costs of
course grow exponentially so long as the collection does. A
million-volume library today has annual collection maintenance costs of $200, 000. If the collection doubles every fif-
teen years, those costs will climb, in forty-five years, to
$1, 600, 000 per year.

With what you save in maintenance costs by creating
a no-growth collection, you can easily afford a full-scale,
rapid-delivery interloan service, to keep your effective Holdings Rate even higher than it was with an exponentially growing collection. You can even buy a Gutenberg Bible every
year with a portion of the savings left over, or a Shakespeare
First Folio if there are no sellers of the Bible that year.
That should convince the Alexandrians that you are not a
Philistine after all, but a person of discriminating judgment
who prefers to spend his money on things of permanent value
--things you just can't get from anybody on interloan.

What to do with the half million volumes you discarded
and the 50, 000 per year you will discard hereafter? Regional and national storage centers are the obvious answer,
since they can, by eliminating multiple copies of discards
that will flow in from many libraries, cut aggregate storage
space requirements by 90% or more.

All multiples of more than two or three (or whatever figure turns out to be operationally prudent) will be pulped, so that new books can be made without laying forests waste.

"Unto the place from whence the rivers come, thither they return again. " That is why, according to Ecclesiastes, the sea is never full. And that is why, once your library has reached a certain size, it need never be full again. How large should that library be? Large enough to satisfy a Performance Rate that is substantially better than what you now have, but always less than 100%, which nobody can afford.

When that size is reached, based on your own judgment of what is a satisfactory Performance Rate, you have a no-growth collection, and the means for keeping it that way. Your head and your bookstacks are out of the clouds, and your feet have reached the ground.

Notes

1. The Philosophical and Scientific schools may mention, sotto voce, the appropriateness of superficial weeding. But nothing of consequence ever comes of it. Weeding at significant levels occurs only through theft, which unfortunately removes precisely, and only those volumes that should not be weeded.

2. I use the term in its extended sense, for convenience, to cover anything a library may supply: books, journals, cassettes, etc.

3. The principal study is R. W. Trueswell, Analysis of Library User Circulation Requirements, Final Report (January, 1968). N. S. F. Grant GNO 435.

4. Michael K. Buckland, "An Operations Research Study of a Variable Loan and Duplication Policy at the University of Lancaster, " in Operations Research, ed. Don R. Swanson and Abraham Bookstein (Univ. of Chicago Press, 1972), 97-106.

5. An economical method for accomplishing this, tested and proved in some thirty college and university libraries to date, is described in my paper "In Hot Pursuit of FASTCAT, " Library Journal, Sept. 1, 1972, pp. 2693-95.

EVIDENCE OF EROSION OF A RESOURCE DUE TO POPULATION GROWTH: CASE OF THE PUBLIC LIBRARY*

Raymond Jackson

The modern theory of public expenditure has historically focused on determining the optimal supply of goods and services to be provided by the public sector with less attention devoted to developing rules and procedures concerning their use. Once the public good is supplied, however, persons and institutions acting individually without restrictions may erode its economic value by producing what James Buchanan calls "public bads."[1] In order to avoid this erosion a complete theory of the public sector involves problems of efficient use of the goods, service or facility as well as the appropriate expenditure. According to Buchanan, the conservation of private property can normally be trusted to the workings of the market but the conservation of public property requires explicit public policy.[2]

Examples of this erosion process can readily be found in the land resources supplied by the public sector for recreation. Krutilla and Knetsch note the ecological damage done by an even greater number of visitors to Yosemite, the Grand Canyon's south rim and the geothermal sights of Yellowstone.[3] Such over-utilization threatens the long-run survival of the resource and explicit restrictions limiting use are required for their conservation. The usual economic solution is to restrict entry by fees in order to limit demand to the optimal number of users. Unfortunately for outdoor recreational facilities dollar values for marginal benefits and marginal costs cannot readily be determined because of the nonmarket character of both benefits and costs. The optimal number of visitors in an economic sense is difficult to calculate and a "rule-of-thumb" approach might be more suitable.

*Reprinted by permission of the author and publisher from Land Economics, February 1974, pp. 70-75.

In the above examples of intensive use, "capacity" could be
defined as the ecological danger point where the long-run existence of the resource is jeopardized with user fees then
set to limit the number of visitors during any time period to
capacity.

Another example of the production of "public bads" in
the natural resource area concerns the current essentially
free entry into the lobster industry. Frederick Bell has
empirically tested a model showing a decline in the steady-
state lobster catch along the northeastern coast when the
number of traps set exceeds a certain limit thus leading to
adverse effects on the growth of the species.[4] Due to the
absence of a carefully developed plan for the exploitation of
this common-property resource, Bell shows that the industry
literally destroys itself through overinvestment as the price
of lobster increases. A non-optimal but perhaps workable
solution would be to permit entry as long as there is an increase in the long-run sustainable yield.

The absence of adequate public policy in the use of
highways also leads to individual behavior producing "public
bads. " A. A. Walters' model of traffic congestion shows
that the number of cars flowing off a highway increases as
the number of entrants increases but declines after the number of entering cars exceeds a certain level.[5] A "rule-of-
thumb" approach for public facilities, such as highways, is
to allow the number of users to increase as long as total output is also increasing. When total output measured in some
economically meaningful sense falls, such as vehicles-per-
hour in the Walters example, with an additional user then the
"capacity" is reached and further admission should be restricted.

This paper develops a model of library use which
demonstrates that continued population growth in the area
served leads to an erosion in the stock of books and eventually diminishes rather than increases total circulation. In
this case a "rule-of-thumb" solution to library membership
might be set at the point where additional members cause
circulation to decline. Further population growth can create
a situation where the rate of loss through use exceeds the
rate of addition through purchase. The library's capital stock
is thus eroded and endangered in a manner analogous to the
threatened destruction of the resource stock of recreational
areas. The public library experience can be extended to
other facilities in the public sector, such as housing develop-

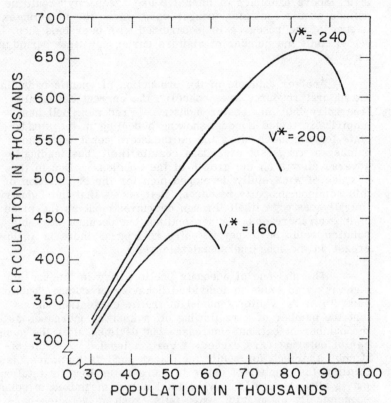

Figure 1--Total Circulation As Population Increases,
Given Target Stocks of 160,   200 and
240 Thousand Volumes

ments and educational institutions, where concern with an
adequate expansion of supply has led to a lack of policy regarding use.   This situation may lead to an erosion of facilities and a reduction in the value of their services producing
the common complaint about the decline in the quality of public services despite rising expenditures and taxation. [6]

A Model of Library Use

During each time period volumes are added to the
stock of books through purchase decisions but the stock is

reduced as volumes are lost, misplaced, misshelved, stolen
or never returned. The steady-state stock depends on the
rate of addition by purchase and the rate of loss. In order
to estimate the number of volumes added through purchase
we assume that without losses imposed by use, the stock of
books would increase following the logistic growth curve

$$(1) \quad V_t = \frac{V^*}{1 + be^{-gt}}$$

where V_t = volumes on hand at time t, V^* = the target stock
of volumes set as the long-run goal for the library, and b
and g are parameters. Differentiating equation (1) with respect to t yields an addition to the stock arising from purchase of

$$(2) \quad \frac{dV}{dt} = g(V^* - V_t)\frac{V_t}{V^*}$$

Though the above logistic curve was used by Bell as
part of a biological growth model, the decision rule suggested
by (2) seems to make sense intuitively when applied to the
growth of a library's stock through purchase.[7] When the
number of books on hand V_t is low the difference between
the target V^* and V_t is great but only a relatively small
fraction, V_t/V^* of V^* - V_t, can be ordered. When the library is near capacity V^* - V_t is small but a large fraction
of this difference can be purchased. While (2) is the increment to the stock through purchase during t there is a decline due to losses arising from use. This reduction is assumed to be proportional to the size of the population M_t
served by the library and is written as θM_t. Subtracting
θM_t from equation (2) allows the net change in the number
of volumes on hand for time period t to be written as

$$(3) \quad \frac{dV}{dt} = g(V^* - V_t)\frac{V_t}{V^*} - \theta M_t$$

The output of the library during a specified time
period, as measured by total circulation, should be proportional to 1) the size of the community served, 2) the educational level of the population, and 3) the quality of the library. Denoting E_t as the educational level and measuring
library quality as V_t/V^*, the number of volumes on hand as
a fraction of the target number, suggests a total circulation
function C_t of the form

$$(4) \quad C_t = \beta E_t M_t \frac{V_t}{V^*}$$

where β is the proportionality constant.

Equations (3) and (4) comprise the model describing
the relationship of population size to the stock of books and
total circulation. The steady-state solution to the stock of
books can be found by setting $dV/dt = 0$ or where the addition to the stock through purchase exactly offsets the erosion
due to population pressure. Setting (3) to zero yields an expression relating the target stock V^* to the steady-state stock
V_t of

$$(5) \quad V^* = \frac{V_t^2}{V_t - \dfrac{\theta M_t}{g}}$$

Substituting V^* into the circulation equation (4) produces an
equation of circulation per capita, C_t/M_t, that can be written
as

$$(6) \quad \frac{C_t}{M_t} = \beta E_t - \beta \frac{\theta}{g} E_t \frac{M_t}{V_t}$$

Equation (6) says that the steady-state circulation per capita
is an increasing function of the community's educational level
E_t and a decreasing function of an intersecting term, M_t/V_t,
the number of people in the community for each book on hand
at the library. The coefficient of E_t should therefore be
positive and $E_t(M_t/V_t)$ is expected to have a coefficient with
a negative sign.

Empirical Test of the Model

The parameters of the model θ/g and β are estimated
for the years 1951, 1961 and 1971 from equation (6) using
cross-sectional data. Data were collected for those libraries
in Massachusetts serving city populations of between 20,000
and 120,000 people. The sample attempts to include libraries characterized as medium-sized with similar services,
costs, and delivery systems.[8] Hence rural libraries and
those located in large, high-density urban areas were excluded since no attempt is made to build into the model variables to describe the special characteristics of systems located within sparsely populated areas or those operating
multi-branch facilities within major cities.

Information on circulation C_t and volumes V_t for 1951, 1961 and 1971 was obtained from annual reports of the Massachusetts Board of Library Commissioners. [9] Population data M_t is estimated as the population reported in the census years 1950, 1960 and 1970. [10] The educational level of the community, E_t, is measured as the percentage of adults over the age of 25 finishing high school as reported in the above census years. Applying ordinary least squares to estimate circulation per capita from (6) yields the following results (figures in parentheses are t-statistics):

$$1951 \quad \frac{C_t}{M_t} = \frac{1.69 + .127 \, E_t - .096 \, E_t}{(1.9) \quad (6.6) \quad\quad (-2.6)} \frac{M_t}{V_t}$$
$$R^2 = .65$$
$$\text{obs.} = 44$$

$$1961 \quad \frac{C_t}{M_t} = \frac{1.20 + .173 \, E_t - .128 \, E_t}{(1.1) \quad (7.9) \quad\quad (-3.0)} \frac{M_t}{V_t}$$
$$R^2 = .71$$
$$\text{obs.} = 47$$

$$1971 \quad \frac{C_t}{M_t} = \frac{-1.11 + .168 \, E_t - .106 \, E_t}{(-1.1) \quad (11.0) \quad\quad (-6.5)} \frac{M_t}{V_t}$$
$$R^2 = .74$$
$$\text{obs.} = 64$$

In each year the coefficients of E_t and $E_t(M_t/V_t)$ have the expected signs and are statistically significant at the 5 percent level or better. The model did not include a constant and the results support this formulation since the constant term is statistically insignificant at the 5 percent level in each case though barely so for 1951. The parameter β of the model is directly given from (6) as the coefficient of E_t in the regression equation. The parameter θ/g is not found directly but the coefficient of $E_t(M_t/V_t)$ is $\beta(\theta/g)$. Using the results for β an estimate of θ/g can be made since θ/g is simply the regression coefficient of $E_t(M_t/V_t)$ divided by β. The model's parameters for each year have the following values:

$$1951 \quad \beta = .127 \quad \theta/g = .756$$

$$1961 \quad \beta = .173 \quad \theta/g = .739$$

$$1971 \quad \beta = .168 \quad \theta/g = .634$$

As an illustration of the effects of population growth on a library system the estimates of β and θ/g for 1971 will be used to relate total circulation C_t and population M_t. Setting equation (3) to zero yields a steady-state stock of books V_t equal to

$$(7) \quad V_t = \frac{V^* + \sqrt{(V^*)^2 - 4\dfrac{\theta}{g} M_t V^*}}{2}$$

recalling that V^* is the target the community has set for the library's stock. [11] Substituting this expression into (6) total circulation can be expressed as a function of population as

$$(8) \quad C_t = \beta E_t M_t - \frac{2\beta\dfrac{\theta}{g} E_t M_t^2}{V^* + \sqrt{(V^*)^2 - 4\dfrac{\theta}{g} M_t V^*}}$$

Table I shows the results of calculations of total circulation made using equation (8) as population increases with 1971 values of $\beta = .168$ and $\theta/g = .639$. The educational level E_t is fixed at 70 percent of the population over the age of 25 finishing high school or $E_t = 70$. Total circulation is presented for target library stocks V^* of 160, 200 and 240, 000 volumes with population M_t varied selectively within the intersecting range for each target. Note that as population grows, total circulation also rises at first but the increment becomes less and less due to the decline in the steady-state stock of books.

Population pressure, in a sense, erodes the resource and as it continues growing, circulation reaches a maximum and then starts falling. The positive contribution of a greater number of users to total circulation is offset by the negative effects of a decline in the steady-state number of volumes on hand. Capacity in terms of users could be defined as the population level maximizing circulation. Finally, population pressure becomes so intense that no real steady-state stock is possible and the resource is ultimately destroyed. This critical point is indicated in Table I by an asterisk and corresponds to a population level where, from equation (7), $M_t \geq 4(g/\theta)V^*$. Figure 1 sketches the full relationship between population and circulation partly tabulated in Table I and clearly illustrates the eventual negative effect of in-

Table I—Estimated Circulation and
the Steady-State Stock of Books*

Population	Circulation (Vols/Yr)	Steady-State Stock (Vols)
Target = 160,000 Volumes		
40,000	377,600	128,400
44,000	401,200	124,000
48,000	420,500	119,000
52,000	434,200	113,500
56,000	440,000	106,800
60,000	431,300	97,700
*62,000	—	0
Target = 200,000 Volumes		
50,000	472,000	160,500
54,000	496,000	156,000
58,000	516,700	151,400
62,000	533,400	146,200
66,000	545,100	140,400
70,000	550,000	133,500
74,000	543,600	124,800
78,000	507,500	110,600
*80,000	—	0
Target = 240,000 Volumes		
70,000	622,000	181,200
74,000	638,000	176,000
78,000	651,300	170,300
82,000	658,700	163,800
86,000	658,900	156,300
90,000	646,900	146,600
94,000	599,300	130.000
*96,000	—	0

Given β = .168, θ/g = .634, E_t = 70 and V
Targets of 160, 200 and 240 Thousand Volumes.

—

creased population size on total circulation. The critical
population size threatening the long-run viability of the library is just beyond the highest population value plotted for
each target stock of books. The capacity of the resource
might be understood in Figure 1 as that population size producing the peak circulation.

Implications

     This paper has demonstrated that population growth can lead to a decline in the output obtained from a resource and finally, after a certain point, to an end to the resource's economic usefulness. A model of erosion has been applied and successfully tested for a library system though policy implications are important to other goods and services provided by the public sector, particularly those concerning land resources. An increase in population can erode natural resources and deteriorate public facilities as well as reduce library volumes. The rate of recuperation of a natural resource such as park land or the annual maintenance expense for the public facility is analogous to the purchase of additional volumes by the library. At some point an increase in the number of users will cause a decline in the annual economic output of a public sector resource just as it leads to a decline in circulation at the library. As a "rule-of-thumb" for public policy, the number of users could be restricted in order to avoid this inefficient stage of operation. At some further point along the path of population growth is the eventual destruction of the resource just as the library's stock of books is eventually destroyed when the annual erosion due to use exceeds additions through purchase.

     Evaluations of current policies toward the use of public sector resources should therefore not necessarily associate an expansion in the number of users with an increase in economic benefit. Public administrators should also be alert to the danger associated with a growth in use since erosion may reduce the economic value of the resource or even threaten its survival. [12] Policies ignoring conservation by permitting continued unrestricted entry or entry at nominal cost cannot be defended as being in the short-run or long-run public interest. The case for limiting the number of users is particularly strong for land resources due to their unique character. In the library case eventual destruction of the resource through erosion caused by population pressure could be averted by raising V^*, the target stock of books, but in the natural resource situation an increase in the target stock of these facilities may be, as in the case of wilderness areas, fishing grounds, redwood forests, sand dune waterfront and other common-property resources, literally impossible. In other public sector concerns, such as housing, transit, education, or the arts, resources could be maintained by increased expenditures but without appropriate rules concerning use, individualistic choice produces "public bads" and the additional expenditures will yield a disappointing increment to social welfare.

Notes

1. James M. Buchanan, "Public Goods and Public Bads," in John P. Crecine (ed.), Financing the Metropolis (Beverley Hills: Sage Publications, 1970), pp. 51-56.

2. Ibid., p. 69.

3. John Krutilla and Jack Knetsch, "Outdoor Recreation Economics," Annals of the American Academy of Political and Social Science, May 1970, pp. 63-70.

4. Frederick Bell, "Technological Externalities and Common-Property Resources," Journal of Political Economy, January 1972, pp. 148-158.

5. A. A. Walters, "The Theory and Measurement of Private and Social Cost of Highway Congestion," Econometrica, October 1961, pp. 676-699.

6. For a further analysis of the need, in some cases, for bureaucratic organizations to constrain individualistic choice, see Vincent Ostrom, The Intellectual Crisis in American Public Administration (University, Alabama: University of Alabama Press, 1973), pp. 56-73.

7. Bell, op. cit., p. 149.

8. See H. W. Winger, "Characteristics of the Medium Size Public Library," in Leon Carnovsky and Howard Winger (eds.), The Medium Sized Public Library: Its Status and Future (Chicago: University of Chicago Press, 1963).

9. Massachusetts Board of Library Commissioners, Annual Reports, Boston, 1951-1971.

10. U. S. Bureau of the Census, Census of Population. General Social and Economic Characteristics. Washington, D. C., Government Printing Office, 1950-1970.

11. Only the positive sign for the square-root term is relevant since it yields $V_t = V^*$ when $M_t = 0$ and results

in the desired relationship $dV_t/dM_t \geq 0$ implying a
decline in the steady-state stock with increased population.

12. Unfortunately, current traditions in public administration
regarding efficiency may lead administrators to over-
look the underlying causes of the problem and thus
fail to develop constructive proposals. See Ostrom,
op. cit., pp. 33-47 and pp. 124-129.

BEHAVIOUR IN LIBRARIES*

Peter Jordan

There appear to be two ways in which librarians approach the question of behaviour in libraries and, in particular, reader behaviour. On the one hand there is the view that things happen instinctively and the "correct" behaviour is discovered without the interference of anybody else--"things sort themselves out. " If you take this view you would hardly believe the question is worth discussing and would only think about it if very obviously deviant behaviour such as rowdiness, discussed recently by the Branch & Mobil Libraries Group,[1] took place in the library. Compared with the need to sort out specific problems such as those thrown up by computerisation or local government re-organisation, reader behaviour seems to be of little interest and of no urgency-- indeed esoteric--the sort of thing a library school lecturer would be thinking about!

The second view treats reader behaviour as a far more worthwhile topic to be studied closely; just as the sociologist and the psychologist are basically interested in understanding and explaining why people behave the way they do in society, so the librarian is answering the question why people behave the way they do in libraries.

Why should he be concerned?

All libraries exist for a purpose or purposes. Increasingly, with the introduction of management techniques such as MBO, librarians are beginning to define specific objectives which they wish to meet and behaviour of both readers and staff can prevent such objectives being achieved. A very common element in behaviour is the noise produced by

*Reprinted by permission of the author and publisher from New Library World, January-February 1974, pp. 11-13, 36-37.

it and one can easily think of examples both of noise and
silence preventing objectives being met.   A recent report
on a Yorkshire Polytechnic Library contains the following, "the noise level is intolerable. At times the library cannot be used for its true purpose owing to talking students. "

Over thirty students and staff at Leeds took part in a
library observation exercise in two central public libraries
(one small and one large), several branch libraries and in
one departmental and two subject libraries of the Polytechnic,
and I would like to offer some evidence about behaviour from
this exercise as well as from other material which I have
come across.

This was in no sense a random sample of libraries--
merely an exercise taking place in various types of library
and focussing on behaviour.   We can in no way generalise
from the finding, but they do suggest areas which individual
libraries could pursue in their own situations.   One must also
bear in mind that observation alone has problems as a social
investigation method.   In particular one has to infer the
meaning of the behaviour and this may not be accurate--a
reader may look as though he is asleep but really he is
thinking hard about a problem.

An important aspect of this study was that of teaching
students to discover as far as they can, the truth about a social situation and not to accept second-hand accounts by interested parties.   For example most annual reports contain
figures on issues, inter-loans, noteworthy reference queries
--that is selected items which display the library in a way
the librarian prefers.   How many annual reports list the
number of people who fall asleep in the library, the number
who were seriously disturbed by noise, the number who left
in disgust at the shabby treatment they received, or the
number who came once only, and discovered the library was
just not for them?

A basic problem in observation is what to observe.
Erving Goffman, in Behaviour in Public Places, [2] focuses on
the individual in his main and subordinate involvements. There
are obviously difficulties in observing individual readers or
staff in this way and therefore we looked at the dominant and
subordinate behaviour in a particular library or part of a library.

Dominant Behaviour

This varied as one might expect depending on the type
of library or department.   In the Commercial and Technical
Library it was studying and consultation of reference books;
in the reference library, study and discussion by readers in
groups; in the lending library, returning books, browsing,
reading books and circulating the return trolleys.   It is interesting to note how there are changes through time.   In
one Polytechnic subject library it was reported that around
twelve o'clock the place became noisy as students made lunch
arrangements, the noise continued as students left for and
returned from lunch.   One can see similar changes in public
libraries for example when children come out of school and
staff are prepared to tolerate certain behaviour at certain
times of the day but not at others.

Linked with this toleration is the affecting of involve-
ment--pretending dominant behaviour.   Goffman cites "urban
public libraries where staff and the local bums may reach a tacit
understanding that dozing is permissible as long as the dozer
first draws out a book and props it up in front of his head. "[3]

One or two perceptive observers saw that more detail
than "studying" or "choosing books" was required.   For example one noted that the majority of readers wandered about
the library looking lost.

Two aspects of dominant staff behaviour were particularly remarked upon.   The noise made by them was noticed
in some departments.   One person described how they
"tramped up and down the library, dropped books and generally created a good deal of havoc. "   Goffman makes an interesting point about manual staff--"in an office building or
library where a rather strict decorum may obtain, the maintenance crews may see the occasion quite differently: they
may work in profane clothing, run down the hallway when a
quick repair is required, enter rooms at will, shout easily
down the hall, plug a portable radio into the outlet nearest
their work, and maintain a level of conversational loudness
quite prohibited to the office staff. "[4]

Secondly the amount of involvement with readers varied tremendously among the libraries and not necessarily in
the way you would expect.   In a large reference library readers were seen to leave in disgust after waiting for attention

whilst in two of the Polytechnic subject libraries the service
was prompt and helpful.   The lack of involvement by staff
was seen to be closely associated with indications of staff/
reader separateness such as distinctive clothing, large barrier
like counters (one department had three) behind which staff
"hide. " The interesting question of how staff can identify
with student needs in an academic library by being student-
like themselves might be raised here.

Subordinate Behaviour

        In a library a good deal of behaviour, as mentioned
already, is not publicised, although it is not dominant behaviour.

        A few people were observed to be day dreaming, some
were conversing whilst a sort of ritual dance went on in a
reading room as the users moved from one vertically displayed newspaper to another.   One non-mover was seen to be
asleep standing up.   "Deviant" behaviour of this sort was
seen most frequently in the two newspaper reading rooms and
one wonders how much the common antagonism to these
places is caused by the undesirable behaviour in them. I will
look shortly at why this behaviour occurs and point out how
facilities provided can determine the behaviour.   An interesting piece in the Camden Newsletter for May 1973 suggests
that the attitude towards squatters given in a staff instructions: "In conclusion, I have little doubt that squatters are
not residents and therefore Camden, as a library authority,
has no duty to make library facilities available to them, "
hides the true motive--"the staff instruction appears to have
no clear motive, even its precise intention is a little ambigu-
ous, it isolates but does not define, a group of people for exclusion from the library.   How do we know who is a squatter
and who is a bona fide Camden resident?   It is an irony of
the instruction that we can only tell if a person comes into
the former category, if he is so good as to inform us of his
doubtful origin.   In other words, to disqualify someone, we
require from him more information openly volunteered than
is normally offered by the majority of readers.   It is a
puzzling situation. "[5]

        The treatment afforded the squatter is very similar to
that afforded the mentally ill which Goffman writes about so
perceptively in Stigma[6] and Asylums. [7]   The biographies of
these people are revealed to several others compared with

the "normal" person who can keep his private affairs to himself if he wishes.

Library Atmosphere

Librarians would, I think, find it profitable to ask themselves about the atmosphere in their own libraries. The students asked themselves what sort of occasion a library visit was--e. g., informal or formal. It is useful to see the library visit in the context of visits to other public places and to ask how it is different and in what way. A number of clues are available, for instance dress and speech (is the library a social meeting place, does conversation drift to a certain level until readers realise they are talking too loudly?). Once again differences were found among the libraries visited. Whilst the Polytechnic subject libraries had a relaxed atmosphere with users talking in normal voices one newspaper reading room was described as unfriendly and miserable and in one central lending library people were said to wander around the shelves looking afraid and unsure. One observer claimed that the readers assumed a "library face" when they entered the building--a particular expression suitable for the use of a public library. This is certainly one area where images presented by some librarians differ from the truth as seen by observers, e. g., Janet Hill and Geoffrey Smith in a recent "Woman's Hour" broadcast on libraries, Ray Pahl and subsequent correspondence in the Assistant Librarian in 1969. [8]

Reasons for Library Behaviour: Social

A very important factor inclined to be ignored is the exclusion factor. Many people rarely enter libraries voluntarily largely as a result of their socialisation. Significant others in their lives--parents, teachers, peer groups--have either never encouraged library use or never been able to motivate it in them. In Tony Parker and R. Allerton's The Courage of His Convictions[9] a criminal's reminiscence is quoted, "I can remember before now on more than one occasion, for instance, going into a public library near where I was living and looking over my shoulder a couple of times before I actually went in just to make sure no one who knew me was standing about and seeing me do it. " Luckham, [10] Groombridge[11] and others have shown how dominant the middle classes are in using public libraries and of course they

are especially dominant in gaining places in higher education
and therefore using academic libraries. A question that must
be asked, especially in public libraries, is whether the behaviour expected of readers is that appropriate to a middle
class residence. The greater informality in the academic libraries observed seemed to be due to the age of users, the
attitude of staff and their close acquaintance with regular
users more appropriate in a public branch library rather
than a central library.

Socialisation by the Library Staff and Other Readers

        In our exercise we found little evidence of direct staff
influence on reader behaviour though it was hypothesised that
staff behaviour affected reader behaviour. A recent report
on a Yorkshire Polytechnic library connects the two recommending that "a silence rule must be enforced--the greatest
defect for me is constant talking by library staff as well as
library users. " An item in the Lancaster University Library Gazette gives specific instructions to staff:

> ### Noise in the Library
>
> There is recent evidence from Liverpool that most
> of the noise which disturbs readers comes from--
> guess whom?--LIBRARY STAFF!
>
> Would you all please remember this and try to cut
> down unnecessary conversation and disturbance. In
> particular:
>
> (1) DON'T CLATTER AROUND WHEN SHELVING.
>
> (2) DO TALK IN WHISPERS IN ALL READER
>   AREAS.
>
> (3) IF YOU WORK IN AN OFFICE (AND THIS
>   PARTICULARLY APPLIES TO THE RESEARCH
>   OFFICES ON A FLOOR AND TO ASSISTANT
>   LIBRARIANS' OFFICES ON B AND C FLOORS)
>   DON'T RAISE YOUR VOICE DURING PERSONAL
>   OR TELEPHONE CONVERSATIONS--KEEP
>   YOUR OWN (AND YOUR VISITORS') NOISE
>   LEVEL DOWN.
>
> (4) In the staff room DON'T SHOUT OR SCREAM

WITH LAUGHTER, however funny your friends'
stories may be--the Reference Area is only
just outside the door.

(5) DO DISCOURAGE YOUR VISITORS FROM
     WALKING ROUND THE LIBRARY MAKING
     REMARKS IN STENTORIAN VOICES.

(6) DO ASK READERS TO BE SENSIBLE ABOUT
     THEIR OWN NOISE AND CONVERSATIONS.

Although children making a noise were seen to be
ignored in our exercise it is probably in dealing with children
that the librarian personally exercises most constraint on
reader behaviour. It is most important in public and school
libraries for the librarian to work out carefully the objectives
of his library and to be certain that the constraints he imposes on the children do not conflict with them. He should
also remember that the objectives of the library must be very
closely associated with the objectives of the school itself. An
interesting example was recently described to me in which a
school librarian preferred to allow children to behave more
freely in the library than they were permitted to do in their
classrooms but this was frowned upon by teachers as it con-
flicted with the general views of the school on discipline.

What we did find was that other readers exercised
more constraint than staff. Readers in the reference library
quickly showed their disapproval of noise made by others--
usually by the expression on their faces.

An interesting constraint has been discovered in the
study of periodical use in public libraries now being carried
out at Leeds Polytechnic with a DES grant. Overwhelmingly
periodical use is dominated by men. In the reading rooms
scarcely a woman was seen and the student did in fact observe women coming to the door of a reading room and turning away probably influenced by the sight of a dingy room full
of middle-aged and elderly men.

Physical Constraints

It is often forgotten, particularly in older buildings
where there is not the impetus to rethink the library's activities afforded by the planning of a new building, that the lay-
out of the furniture, especially shelves, readers' advisers'

desks, chair and tables is an important determinant of behaviour in the library. Specific activities such as story
hours, charging and discharging are usually catered for but
the more unobtrusive activities tend to be overlooked. Are
readers expected to sit down or stand up in a lending library
when they are choosing books? Why were users of a newspaper reading-room expected to stand up to read the papers
as if they were in a gents lavatory? If tables and chairs are
provided what are users encouraged to do? In some new
buildings long comfortable seats have been provided without
tables. With nowhere to put their books, readers have tended
to recline on these "sofas." Librarians dislike them, because, they say, they are extravagant of space but also, I
suspect, that lying on a couch is not thought to be a library-
like posture. Similarly some children's librarians allow
children to lie on the floor reading, others do not. If it is
thought desirable is a suitable floor surface provided?

        A good deal of attention has been paid to the layout of
libraries in order to isolate noisy areas from less noisy
ones. An interesting example is the Cambridge University
study by Marples and Knell. [12]

        We have worked on these lines in the Leeds Poly-
technic Department of Librarianship library and it does seem
to work. We have a lounging area, a semi-noisy study area,
and a quiet study area. Surveys have shown the lounge area
(with comfortable chairs) hardly to be used at all but the
semi-noisy area is heavily used and a good deal of noise is
made. Students seem to want to talk about their work as
they do it--they also talk about many other things. It did
appear from our observations that friends sat opposite each
other rather than next to each other for ease of conversation.
Any physical barriers to conversation would affect sitting positions. It has been found both by students in our own library and, I understand, by the Cambridge University Library
Management Unit that for study purposes, carrel-type facilities are the first to be filled then users sit at tables by
themselves. It is only as a last resort that readers sit next
to others at tables. It has been thought that even simple divisions providing a small amount of privacy would at least
cause fewer readers to claim that a reading room is "full"
even though there are still a fair number of vacant seats.

        The physical appearance of the library was also men-
tioned by observers as a constraint. For example, the im-
posing Victorian entrance of a large city library was thought

not to be attractive to some people. In this library also
turnstiles were remarked upon by everyone who watched as
readers negotiated bags over them or contemplated climbing
three flights of stairs to the reference library as an alternative to an unreliable lift. These are all examples of exclusion factors which could prevent some people from entering
the library and thus exclude the behaviour they would bring
to it.

Perhaps the most important occasion in library behaviour is when the librarian and the reader meet ("the li-
brarian-reader interface" in the jargon). Although contemporary writers like Argyle[13] and Goffman and many other social psychologists are producing material on this subject little
appears directly focussed upon it in our professional press
and yet a recent survey of students who left Leeds one year
ago has shown that they would like more in their courses on
dealing with people. [14]

Our exercise and my own observation as a reader for
a number of years has shown that the treatment given to
borrowers in public libraries by librarians is no better, and
often worse, than that given in most shops. It is often dis-
tinctly inferior, it seems to me, to that given in other professional establishments such as banks. The small amount
of observation in academic libraries showed that treatment
was far superior there. This example was typical of the
public libraries:

> Waiting for a librarian to complete name and ad-
> dress on some extra tickets another librarian
> turned round and rather sharply wanted to know
> 'Have you just joined?'--the tone employed was one
> that could be taken for a personal insult--more of
> a bark than a civil question. Having explained the
> position the same question was again asked in a
> similar offensive tone.

This is little better than the treatment accorded to
Snuffy in Robert Roberts' fine study of Salford life in the first
quarter of the century, The Classic Slum:

> Joining the library sixty years back was, for a
> child, an essay in adventure. Snuffy went, nerves
> tensed, cap in hand, down the long, dark ramp,
> eased himself through the swing doors and tiptoed
> to the counter. Beyond, on a stool, bathed like a

priest in holy calm, sat Mr. Shadlock himself,
deep in the racing handicap book. The boy stood
for a time in respectful silence, then he sighed,
sniffed, shuffled twice, coughed politely through his
hot fingers, and at last, his heart pounding, he
dared to put the question 'P-please, sir, could I
'ave a joinin' form sir?' Mr. Shadlock pursued his
studies. The minutes trod softly by. A gas jet
belched delicately behind its frosted globe. The
wall-clock tittered. Snuffy drew breath and tried
again, but the words stuck in his gullet: a thin,
foolish bleat threaded the silence. He blushed
scarlet, licked his dried lips and turned to go.
Then Mr. Shadlock spoke, suddenly, violently.
'Eh?' Panic-stricken, the boy stuttered into speech,
'P-please, sir, could I-could....' Like a bomb the
Librarian burst among the faltering syllable, 'Out
of it!' he roared.

'Didn't yer tell'im it was for the vicar?' asked his
elder sister later. Snuffy admitted the error. 'You
should allus say it's for the vicar,' Em' counselled,
'or for Mr. Arnott at the 'Duke of York,' or some
nob like that. It's terrible 'ard to get a form off
yer own bat.' After five attempts, however, Snuffy
succeeded.

Most librarians concerned about the poor treatment of
readers would probably say it was due to lack of basic polite-
ness ("the customer is always right") most likely borne out
of an undesirable attitude towards the readers. Whilst I
think this is a sound basic judgement I do believe the librarian should be far more aware than he is at the moment about
the process of interpersonal communications. When a librarian interacts with a reader each participant recognises certain signs which help him to assess the needs of the other--
speech, dress, facial expression, body posture etc. He
should become more adept at recognising these signs but I
think equally important, because we all daily have to recog-
nise such signs in order to manage our lives, he should be
on his guard against misinterpretation of such signs. For
example how can he be made aware how much help a reader
needs to find a particular fact--a wave in the direction of the
reference books, an accompanied journey to the shelves, an
explanation of how the reference work can be used, or the
finding of the information itself? How do we know whether a
reader is satisfied or dissatisfied with our services? The

video-tape made by Brighton Public Library illustrated
to me how little we probably know about our own methods of
dealing with people and the impression we make upon them.
What is the effect, for example, of carrying on a conversation with another member of staff whilst serving a reader at
the counter? Some other professions who depend much more
on interpersonal communication are paying a lot of attention
to it, e.g., Basil Berstein[16] on speech in schools and the
very interesting analysis of classroom language by Dr. R. M.
Coulthard of Birmingham University. [17] For an excellent account of current knowledge in the subject see Michael Argyle's
Penguin The Psychology of Interpersonal Behaviour. The recent survey by the Cambridge University Library Management
Unit into senior and intermediate staff deployment in academic
libraries has shown how the emphasis is still heavily biased
towards duties of a technical nature--(acquisitions, cataloguing and classification, serials and binding preparation). [18]
These occupied the staff for nearly half the time compared
with one quarter on reader service.

Printed Guides

        Printed library guides to public libraries give little
indication of the behaviour expected in the library. It was
suggested by some of the students who examined the guides
that the atmosphere of the library could be suggested by the
tone and style of the guide--Westminster's guide is written
in a strict, abrupt manner whereas Barry's is welcoming.

        Academic libraries do pay more attention to the sub-
ject. Hull University's guide contains seven pages on be-
haviour--regulations which would normally appear as a notice
in a public library in a not very prominent position.

        The classic "silence" notice is seldom seen in librar-
ies now and generally admonitory notices are less prevalent.
This does mean however, that those notices which do appear
reflect a special emphasis on that aspect of behaviour. One
newspaper reading room we observed is still in the past with
notices about loitering, litter, smoking and retaining a newspaper longer than ten minutes.

        It is also most interesting to observe how libraries
are portrayed by the media, e.g., in TV, comedy shows, in
comics. Do these affect users' behaviour in libraries? What
do you think of this extract from Walt Disney's Now I Know
comic?

Libraries are places where you may borrow books.
Sometimes libraries are very large and sometimes
they are only quite small.

It is nice going into a library because it is always
very quiet inside. No one is allowed to run or
shout or even talk loudly. It looks as though our
Disney friends have not read the notice. Can you
read what it says?

Elmer Elephant was so interested in the book he
was looking at that he didn't see Miss Clementine
Crocodile's tail. I wonder who is going to clear
up the mess!

What kind of library do you have in the place where
you live? Do you borrow books? I hope that the
people who visit your library are not as naughty as
the Disney folk who borrow books from Naboombu
Library! I think Elmer should go home and read
his books in bed.

We may get a good laugh out of such writing but if we
believe libraries are not like that where do the writers get
their ideas from and do they have any effect on others? One
puzzler to end with. If you decide silence is not appropriate
in your library how do you encourage noise?

Notes

1. Service Point, no. 3, May 1973, p. 13.

2. Goffman, E. Behaviour in Public Places, 1963.

3. op. cit. , p. 55.

4. op. cit. , p. 20.

5. Camden Newsletter, May 1973, p. 1 and 2.

6. Goffman, E. Stigma, 1963.

7. Goffman, E. Asylums, 1961.

8. Pahl, R. "Friendly Library. " Assistant Librarian,
     June 1969.

9. Parker, A. and Allerton, R. The Courage of His Convictions, 1962.

10. Luckham, B. The Library in Society, 1971.

11. Groombridge, B. The Londoner and His Library, 1964.

12. Marples, D. L. and Knell, K. A. Circulation and Library Design: the Influence of Movement on Library Design, 1971.

13. Argyle, M. The Psychology of Interpersonal Behaviour, 2nd ed., 1972; and Argyle, M., ed. Social Encounters, 1973.

14. Jones, N. and Jordan, P. One Year Later: a Survey of Students Who Completed Their BA (Librarianship) in 1972, 1973 (unpublished).

15. Roberts, R. The Classic Slum, 1971.

16. Bernstein, B. Class, Codes, and Control. Vol. 1, 1971, vol. 2, 1973.

17. Coulthard, R. M. "The Analysis of Classroom Language." Social Science Research Council Newsletter, no. 19, June 1973.

18. Smith, G. C. K. and Schofield, J. L. "A General Survey of Senior and Intermediate Staff Deployment." Journal of Librarianship, vol. 5, no. 2, April 1973.

AN AMERICAN EXPERIENCE*

Toyo S. Kawakami

After Pearl Harbor was attacked in December, 1941, the long smoldering resentment against Oriental immigrants on the West Coast broke out in open hostility towards the Japanese. Within a few months, after the start of the war, 112, 000 Japanese were removed from the Pacific coast states and herded into concentration camps. This was done by executive order of February, 1942, and military procedures.

Of these Japanese, some 70, 000 were the Nisei, the second generation, born U. S. citizens, and the others were their parents, the Issei, the first generation, ineligible for U. S. citizenship. My family was but one out of the thousands exiled from our homes to isolated, barbed-wire enclosures in dreary sections of California, Idaho, Arizona, Wyoming, Colorado, Utah and Arkansas for the duration of the war.

In March hurried preparations were begun for the evacuation. Liquidation of property, in many instances at great sacrifice, proceeded at a rapid rate, and opportunists took advantage of the bewildered Japanese. Even our family, with so little, found strangers entering our house to look for bargains and Mother sold the kitchen stove, dining room table and chairs for five dollars.

Father and I packed our valued book collection in cartons to be stored with a friend. Our losses were, in comparison to other Japanese, not as heavy. Yet this forced exodus meant sudden uprooting, parting from friends, abandoning possessions we could not keep, and adjusting elsewhere to a life we could not begin to imagine.

Ours was a large family, including Mother and Father, my three sisters and five brothers (one of them was then

*Reprinted by permission of the author and publisher from OLA Bulletin (Ohio Library Association), April 1974, pp. 4-8.

serving in the Army), my six-month-old son and myself.
We were among the first to leave Berkeley in April, 1942.
We were allowed to take bedding and linens, necessary clothing, sufficient number of eating utensils, and essential personal belongings, but limited to what each individual could
carry himself, generally hand luggage. Because my brothers
offered assistance, I included an extra duffle bag of baby
clothes.

Assembly Centers

        The assembly centers, located on fair grounds or race
tracks, served as corrals, before the evacuees were sent to
more permanent camps. Our assembly center was the Tanforan Race Track in San Bruno, a few miles south of San
Francisco. On departure day, the Berkeley Japanese gathered together at a church and were taken by chartered buses,
under military guard, to Tanforan, where we stayed for six
months. At the race track entrance, we were searched for
contraband before housing was assigned to us. Because of
the size of our family, we were allowed two horse stalls as
living quarters.

        Swinging half-doors divided each horse stall into two
rooms. The rear room had formerly sheltered a horse, and
the walls were marked by deep hoof-prints, wisps of hay
white-washed into the cracks, and a pervasive odor that was
accentuated on muggy days. We had no furniture, except
army cots, so Father made several stools and a table from
scrap lumber deposited where barracks were still being built.

        Curfew was imposed, and roll call was held twice
daily, morning and evening. Civil liberties were at a minimum, and the race track was securely guarded, surrounded
by watch towers manned by armed sentries. Searchlights
played around the camp at night. Here we were initiated into communal living, enduring inconveniences of tight quarters,
hiking distances to uncurtained showers, and doorless lava-
tories, interminable waiting in lines at the mess hall and
post office, and answering to family numbers instead of sur-
names.

        One night, very late, when I was on my way to the
latrine, I heard a sentry call out, but kept walking, until I
heard a shot go over my head. A spotlight was turned on
me and as quickly turned away. I then hastened along, but
on unsteady legs.

38

Churches Established

Protestant, Catholic, Seventh Day Adventist, and Buddhist churches were established early to bolster the morale of the internees. Another support to morale was the opportunity to work, and wages were set at eight dollars a month for the unskilled, twelve for the skilled, and sixteen for the professional (doctor, teacher, and administrative assistant). Subsequently, in Utah, the salary scale was increased to twelve, sixteen, and nineteen dollars. In addition, a clothing allowance of several dollars a month was given to each worker.

Schools were started for children and adults, and volunteer evacuee teachers, I among them, were employed. The graduates from nearby universities taught their major subjects in the high school under the grandstand. Without any current textbooks, we made use of old ones discarded by outside schools. The teachers wrote their own outlines and lesson plans and distributed lavender ditto copies to their students.

Rumors began to seep through the assembly center in August that we would be moved to a permanent camp in Utah. The second camps were called relocation centers or projects, and ten were established under the War Relocation Authority, a civilian body. Bulletins on how to prepare for the moving appeared, but no one knew until September when the actual moving would occur. Again there were the stir and unrest of packing and crating. Everything had to be packed and tagged before inspection by the Army two days before departure.

The first group that left for Utah was the advance work group of more than two hundred volunteers to prepare for the induction of those to follow. Among them was my brother William, a bacteriologist on the sanitary engineering crew. Since our horse stall was closest to the fence and the gate to the train, our stable roof provided a convenient place for watching. People came from far ends of the race track to climb on the roof and see friends off with hand-printed bon voyage signs.

Relocation--Topaz

The Central Utah Relocation Project, usually called

Topaz after a mountain in the west, came into existence on
September 11, 1942, with the arrival of the first internees.
The camp was situated several thousands of feet above sea
level, so winters were extremely cold and long, with the
snows falling in early autumn and ending in late spring.

The camp stretched out in blocks, comparable to ordinary city squares, and each block contained twelve barracks,
a laundry-latrine building, a dining hall, and a recreation
hall.   The laundry and mess hall faced each other down the
center of the block.   The resident barracks, six in a row,
were lined along both sides of the block and sandwiched the
two center buildings.

The volunteer advance group worked at the receiving
stations, as one contingent after another came from the assembly center.   My family went to Utah the end of October,
and we were greeted on arrival by my brother, and a small
band of Boy Scouts, standing ankle-deep in the alkali dust and
tooting their horns in the heat.   Their banner, held over-
head, read: "Welcome to Topaz, the Jewel of the Dessert!"

We had become accustomed to seeing barracks at Tanforan, but we found this new camp desolate and bleak, where
hundreds of identical, black tar-papered ones squatted in
rows, block after block.   The camp contained forty-two city
blocks in an area of one square mile, guarded by barbed-
wire fence and sentry posts and an encampment of military
police.

Each barracks was divided into rooms, the small end
rooms for couples and the larger middle rooms for family
units.   Our family had the two center rooms, but in order to
go from one room to the other, we had to go outside and
enter the other room by another door.   With only army cots
in the rooms, the evacuees again resorted to making furniture
out of scrap lumber.   Eventually, through ingenious ways,
the rooms acquired a more home-like atmosphere.

There were about 8,500 of us in Topaz, mainly from
the San Francisco Bay region.   Since we realized that we
would remain interned until the end of the war, we settled
into the daily routine of living, coping with smothering dust-
storms, work schedules, mess hours, and devising what leisure activities we could.   After teaching in the high school
and also supervising the Basic English Department for adult
learners, I was transferred to the public library.

The Library

Although the Topaz Public Library originated on October 2, 1942, it was not officially opened until December,
1942, when fifty-five crates of books, seventy-seven cartons
of magazines, and supplies in boxes made from dismantled
shelves came from Tanforan. The library was organized by
two professional librarians with the assistance of a book-
binder. The Tanforan collection consisted of about five thousand books, gifts from personal friends and from California
schools, colleges and public libraries.

At first, the library was located at Recreation Hall 32
and encountered delays in getting the roof tarred, cast iron
stoves installed for heating, walls and ceilings sheetrocked
for insulation. The vastly different climate in Utah sometimes necessitated the closing of the library in the afternoon
because of the bitter cold.

Throughout October and November books and magazines were donated by residents, until the library's holdings
numbered almost seven thousand books and several thousand
issues of periodicals.

Other Libraries

Besides the Topaz Public Library, there were the
grammar school and high school libraries. Within the Community Services Division, the school libraries were under the
Education Section and the public library under Community
Activities. The public library was dependent upon minimal
fees and donations to purchase needed supplies and books.
From this meager income was started the rental collection
of current best sellers. The charge of five cents a week
for each book and quick turnover enabled the ordering of
more titles.

The public library moved to another barracks in Block
16. Half the space, totalling twenty by one hundred feet,
contained adult fiction and nonfiction, and the other held the
children's section and magazines. One small end room was
used for bookbinding, the other for office and cataloging, and
mess hall tables with attached benches, filled the reading
area.

The library opened in its new location on December 1,

1942, and the next day presented a concert of classical recordings. The response of the audience was so enthusiastic
that concerts were given every Wednesday evening. Program
notes, with information about the selections, composers, and
the following week's expectations, were mimeographed for
those attending the concerts. Library notes and book reviews
appeared in Topaz Times, the camp newspaper.

Teachers brought elementary school classes for orientation, and high school students crowded into the library to
study. One high school class was assigned the topic of
juvenile delinquency, and the staff discovered afterwards that
every article about this subject had been ripped out of the
bound journals. To better library service, staff members
of the school libraries and the public library formed a Library Council to discuss mutual problems and plans.

Interlibrary Loans

A rotating collection of selected titles was borrowed
from the Salt Lake County Library at Midvale, Utah, and
shelved in a special section; these books added variety. In
January, 1943, interlibrary loan service was granted by the
college libraries of Utah and the University of California at
Berkeley, so the scope of the public library was extended
considerably.

The camp librarians took care of the correspondence
with college libraries, payment of postal and insurance
charges, receiving and return of requested books until the
library closed. Every week librarians walked blocks to take
books to the patients in the hospital.

Since many Issei were unable to read in English, a
Japanese branch library was opened in February. All the
books in this library were on personal loan, to be returned
to the rightful owners when the camp closed. At first the
circulation of Japanese books was limited to just those par-
ticipating, but later the books were made available to non-
lenders also.

Towards the end of February gravel was laid down
for a pathway from the unpaved road to the library, so people
could come to the building without slipping in mud or slush.
As attendance reached about four hundred fifty persons a day,
the library was kept open in the evenings. Current pamphlets were obtained to augment the often outdated reference books.

To brief the evacuees
on world news, the Reports
Division sent weekly news-
maps for posting on the library bulletin board. Outside
newspapers were received,
among them the Oakland
Tribune and the San Fran-
cisco Chronicle, for many
evacuees were from those two
cities.

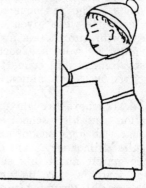

Library Grows

Bookend--Topaz Public Library

The library paid for
its first magazine subscriptions, fourteen in all, but later
War Relocation Authority funds increased them to fifty-two.
The rental collection also grew, and the bright covers from
new books decorated the library walls. Occasionally amuse-
ment was caused by inadvertent arrangement of the book
jackets, as when A Tree Grows in Brooklyn was paired with
Behind the Rising Sun. Since these books had been made
possible from fees paid by the camp residents, they were
sold, just before the library closed, at greatly reduced
prices, and the money from this sale benefited the Topaz
Scholarship Fund.

For Christmas, 1943, the library had unusual decora-
tions, designed by a graduate engineering student. Under his
direction, hundreds of snowflakes were cut from silver paper,
threaded onto thumb tacks and hung from the ceiling, between
billowy clouds of pale pink and blue crepe paper. He made
wheels of wood, in graduated diameters, bore holes into the
sides, inserted dry willow branches and covered them with
green crepe paper.

Using patterns the engineering student created, the
staff members made geometric ornaments out of colorful bits
of paper and fabrics. These were fastened to the branches,
and he suspended the circles of wood, narrow to the widest,
from the ceiling to make a mobile Christmas tree that swayed
and turned gently, delighting the beholders.

On February 22, 1944, a No Fine Day was held, and
missing books quietly returned to their shelves. The following month brought several days of a heavy blizzard, which

resulted in no attendance, so staff members spent the time shelf-reading, mending and cataloging.

Merger

In June, 1945, when relocation out of camp was being accelerated, and schools had finally closed, the Topaz Public Library merged with the school libraries and became part of the newly formed Community Library. While on its own, the library had survived because of its users, and in turn, had kept cultural interests alive for the evacuees.

As the year 1945 turned towards autumn, camps began to close, and the evacuees began leaving to start life outside. As more residents left and the blocks became depleted, I thought of the events that had brought us to Topaz.

Because some members of our family had relocated to Cincinnati for schooling or work, the last of us joined them at the end of October in Ohio. My son was now past his fourth birthday. He had never seen a concrete building, an ordinary house, a city, a lawn, a park, a bush in bloom, and people of other color. I saw the outside world with the fresh sight of a wondering child and accepted our release as he did.

IDEALS AND AXIOMS:
LIBRARY ARCHITECTURE*

Jane Holtz Kay

"Libraries Are Fun!" said a cardboard sign above the
checkout desk.

"Amuse me," I scowled darkly, silently.

"Your Public Library Tells It Like It Is," said a
second mobile pink message swinging at eye level.

"How is 'it'?" I wanted to grump back.

The signs were dangling innocuously enough from
strings secured to the ceiling of a new library in Foxboro,
Mass., during one spring's National Library Week. But--as
I wanted to jabber back at the signs--I was not visiting the
library to have "fun" or even to read and study. (Library
visits, need I say, may be fulfilling, helpful, a delight, or
any one of a number of adjectives, but ... "fun" ... well, I
could only compare what had happened to Manhattan when
they tagged "Fun" onto that "City.") The jovial signs stirred
memories of childhood during World War II when anyone who
dared think libraries were "fun" was sent to the yard post-
haste to pursue such hedonistic pleasures in more appropriate
places.

So much for my puritan past, I sighed, adieu. Libraries were now supposed to be Fun. My purpose that cold
day some half dozen years ago was to discover--not judge--
what libraries were and thus armed, comment on how their
architecture filled, or did not fill, that function.

A Foxboro neighbor of the library on the Common had

*Reprinted by permission of the author and the American
Library Association from American Libraries, May 1974,
pp. 240-246. Copyright 1974 by the ALA.

alerted me. The journalistic Paul Revere had called the
Boston Globe one morning to report an "ultra-modern" building in the center of the old town.   From his voice and my
experience, I could predict that his "ultra-modern" was likely
to be as "ultra" as the other objects to which the assembly-
line word was fixed (automobiles, refrigerators, toasters,
and so forth sprang to mind).   This, as the case would turn
out, meant that the library would be more or less straight-
forwardly new.   It would simply be a contemporary structure
untamed by some Colonel Sanders "colonial" paste-up over
the workaday interior.

I was right.   The Foxboro library was somewhat heavy
in mass but attractive enough.   It was also about as radical
as baked beans as it sat there squaring the corner of the
town's Common.   The Common, the historic grassy square
that had reached a polite standoff with the latterday commerce on one side, still shaped an urban and even poetic
center here as in so many New England towns.   Around its
green edges clung an architecture mix of church, houses,
store.   The new structure carried on its literary duties quite
properly there.   The library wore conservative modern dress
as church and houses had each worn the "modern" garb of
their day.   Only later did I learn the struggle for that style.
When the Foxboro town fathers had told the architect they
wanted him to build a "colonial building" to match the "colonial buildings" on the other sides of the Common, the architect asked what they meant.   Find him one to fit the label.
Sure enough, what the committee dubbed "colonial" had been
constructed three-quarters of a century after the label.   So
emboldened, the architect built to the order of the day. Hence,
my caller's "ultra. "

That was my initiation into the subject of the library
as architecture.

My initiation into the library as womb began at an
earlier age, of course.   It started, I suppose, as many other
book lovers' did: the day my mother stalwartly plunked me
in the middle of the weekly circle of Story Hour.   Story Hour
was Friday afternoons and I still remember the scene.   The
smell of oak walls.   The late afternoon sunlight filtering in
dusty streaks through the planes.   The air, chilled or spring,
breezing in through the open windows.   (Are there any windows that open out there today?) And, of course, the sweet,
lilting voice of the librarian reading the tale of Bartholomew
Cubbins and however many hats he had.   I remember it with
all my senses.

Remarkably, for me, the scene has not changed. In
this mobile "Nation of Strangers, " I happen to be raising my
children where I was raised. They have sat in the same
magic circle. But barely. Even now, my town library is
expanding into new quarters. Briefly, the golden oak bookcases of the children's room remain. For a while, still, I
can fancy myself big as Gulliver as I squat beside the picture
books and Early Readers with my children. I am all the
ages of my life, young and grown-up alike there. The library rooms carry layers of association, as do all old places.
Of heritage, if you will. Indeed, all architecture is continuity, onion layers of growth and decay, life and death, the
sense of generation. Like literature, architecture is tradition
and innovation. New design forms--like new literary modes
--evolve from the old, reflect the mores, move and stir to
new words/forms. Civilization, in literature or in architecture, is evolution. In the most mundane sense, my daughters
love my mother's battered Uncle Wiggily (though their library
doesn't stock it as serious enough) and the new Maurice
Sendak alike. Perhaps old buildings, old books, are a bit
too pungent. They hold their own rather brazenly for the
technocrats, refusing to slot into the pedagogy or technology
a la mode. But both old and new have place. Or should one
have to write this for keepers of books? One would think
not. Yet only last week, I drove to a 19th-century library
in Wellesley. Handsomely quirkish, it is an eccentric collection of bits and pieces of design, a rascal even in its
time, and it is in danger. I am told it is quite impractical,
too small; its fate is uncertain. Everywhere expansion is inevitable. Other libraries share its uncertain state. But
makers of libraries, of all people, should know the special
sense of place and time old works possess. We can whip
Uncle Wiggily into print again when fashion comes its way;
we get no second chance if we level these rich and human libraries now deemed impractical.

"Of all people, " I have just written. There it is then,
too: the nostalgia, the sense of specialness, the feeling for
the library as home, if not bastion. For as I dwelt on the
abstract form and purposes of the library from time to time
in my critical chores, I gradually uncloaked a sneaking possessiveness in my view of the libraries I was visiting. I
found that of all the structures I entered--the city hall of
handsome muscularity, the elegant museum, the cramped
housing, the high rise that went sleek into the night--which-
ever ... it was always libraries that inspired the strongest
feelings of ownership and identity. I became an instant user.

For good or ill, I could not judge these "second homes" de-
tachedly.   Try as I might to side with administrator or
architect, my criticism is always more personal than the
neutral eye should allow.

      Yet I fancy I am not alone in that identifying.   For,
as I began to consider the article to be written here on library architecture, I realized how many others share this
possessiveness.   I recalled, for instance, a friend in medical
school seven or eight years ago telling me about Harvard's
Countway Medical Library.   I found the structure rather
striking; it even won an AIA award.   But he was stewing in
his own juices about the alphabetical shelves that split, somewhere between, say "m" and "n" causing him to walk a half
block in his pursuit of a book.   I remember him writing a
jingle to the effect, strummed to the tune of "The 'M' That
Got Away."   He said he was going to mail it to the architect.
I supplied the name, Hugh Stubbins.   I doubt that he mailed
it, but, still, I can't picture him or anyone being provoked
to song, by a high rise or medical building.   For, again, of
all the glass and wood, brick and plastic, big and little,
monumental and tiny structures that make up a world of public places, the library is most home.

      I do not mean merely that one could, or should, nest
embryolike in its folds and corners.   The "cozy" nesting element seems out for those who opt for vast and open spaces
for flexibility and ease of surveillance, I guess.   I mean that
of all the institutions that house us, it is the library that belongs most to the user.   At school, the authority of teacher
lingers in the corridors; the student seeks release from it,
the adult is not invited.   The shop is the private possession
of the shopkeeper.   The church serves mostly its own membership.   Each of us does have traffic with city and town
halls but only for fleeting bureaucratic instants.   As for the
once great public spaces--the streets and plazas that were
the meeting places in European or older American cities and
towns--they quickly disappear.   We have spent the last half-
century driving out and flattening what remains behind. Cities
and suburbs lack community.   How few public places can we
visit to read or indeed for absolutely no purpose whatsoever?
Save for the rare community center, where else but the library can we enter and belong as simple citizens, without
card or commitment?

      I suppose this is a big burden for libraries.   It is un-
fair to think of them as Adult Drop-in Centers.   Society can

not, should not, put the burden of community on one place.
As a critic, I know that; as a library-goer, I feel otherwise.
But as both architecture critic and user, I have found libraries far more influential than those who make them know.
Perhaps all buildings are so. The Hidden Dimension, social
anthropologist Edward Hall called his book recording how
"personal space" shapes human behavior. But light, form,
aesthetics as well as calculated plan and placement of book
reading room, card catalog, tell what use and meaning the
library architecture will produce in ways we do not consider.

        At least they have influenced me, and not, alas, al-
ways to the good.   For, in truth, after childhood, I recall
most school libraries as places to be shunned.   Not books,
of course: only their "containers. "

        There was, to begin, my public high school, the pro-
verbial one, placed dead center on an axis of goings and
comings.   It might just as well have posted that "Fun" sign
above its main door.   An adolescent book-lover and none too
comfortable with idle chatter, I looked for an oasis. I found
an open noisy social hall.   Perhaps the librarian took comfort in the crowds of potential readers; but the atmosphere
did not realize that potential.   I cannot remember where the
books I wanted were in the library; I can picture the librarian fussing over the candy wrappers lying outside the door.

        Next came college: here, too, I do not know how pro-
fessional librarians viewed the place, since rehoused.   To
me their missionary zeal in making an equitable distribution
of the goods--reserve books--sought by the avaricious learners (or grade-seekers) of Radcliffe overrode any other spirit
in the place.   I can still feel the execrable wooden seats, so
hard no poor splinter would dare emerge; I see the long tables
and a study hall blessed with a circulation pattern calculated
so that every arrival clamored for attention.   Instead, I opted
for the fiction living room, struggling in a half-sit, half-
kneel position to overcome the softness of the few hard-won
lounge seats.   As for Harvard's impressive Widener Library:
as a freshman, I wandered through its vast stadium awash in
a sea of maleness dotted by tables long as life rafts, and
never returned.   In those days of blatant Consciousness I
chauvinism, Harvard's smaller undergraduate library, La-
mont, was closed to women.

        So it went until thesis time when--and now, to illus-
trate the potency of libraries, I make this confession--I chose

my honors thesis subject on the decision not to tolerate the
conditions herein described.   In the next months, I trundled
some few dozen texts by city-planner/humanist/critic Lewis
Mumford back to my dormitory bed; secured my honors, and
somewhere en route made Mumford's passions my own. (Such
is the coincidence called personal history.)   But if today I
chide my 21-year-old self as frivolous in her scholarship, is
she so removed from her more disciplined descendant--from
all human nature?   I am still the reporter who chose research subjects for the chance to spend long hours tucked in
the splendid mysteries composed by H. H. Richardson in his
famous Thomas Crane Memorial Library across the street
from a first newspaper job at The Quincy Patriot Ledger; and
(shall I admit it?) I am a writer and critic who will neglect
an article because it demands intolerable hours of dizziness
peering down on the dread microfilm.

        I dare not abstract from the microcosm of me to call
these influences good or evil for society as a whole.   Only
to point up their potency; to say how loudly our buildings
speak.   Maybe we want--or wanted 15 years ago--to winnow
out the less serious among our scholars: let those of monkish
discipline concentrate their darnedest, the libraries of the
fifties were saying to me.   Today what do they say?   The
closed-in carrels now adopted finally speak of study as a
more private pursuit.   But what are those empty lofts and
vast glass expanses saying?   That surveillance and expansion
come first?   That now is ephemeral so why plan when facing
the amorphous, indefinite future to which we are hostage?
And the empty shell stacks placed like warehouses?   They
say, as consultant Keyes Metcalf puts it, that knowledge is
expanding, that growth is no longer on an arithmetic curve
but "an exponential one. "   I understand how they reassure librarians that no one will catch them short of space.   Tomorrow will be bigger, they are saying.   Well, fine, if that's
what society wants.   That is not the whole message, however.
These structures tell me that architecture is space packaging:
a box.   They must tell the ecologists among us that growth is
our most important product, at the expense of quality.   Well,
is it?   Society is questioning bigness elsewhere; even the
business schools pause now and then before the notion of an
ever grosser Gross National Product.   Library architecture
can go for growth; must do so, I'm told.   If at least we made
these calculations consciously.   But do we really consider the
implications of these acts of design or is it that indecision,
lack of goals and ideals become hardened into the placeless
places we see?   In truth, the influence of these structures is

an incomplete equation. The reckoning of architect and librarian so often forgets a digit: the human user.

Which brings us in a way both personal and (I hope)
architectural to the assignment at hand ... the design of libraries.

In the month or so since I have expanded these
thoughts, I have surveyed some literature on the subject,
chatted with administrators and architects, visited again the
places traced in the above saga of Libraries I Have Known.
I have on my desk, for instance, a down-to-earth book by
Ralph E. Ellsworth called Academic Library Buildings. Its
cover depicts a library aloft; poised like a bird's nest upon
a tree-shaped trunk of concrete. The structure reminded me
a bit of the Viennese ferris wheel of "Third Man" fame,
powered more for vista than pragmatic purpose. I recalled,
too, architect John Johansen's prize-winning Clark University
Library in Worcester, another sculpture drawn to excess; I
was distressed, more recently, by Philip Johnson's heavy library addition, upstaging the magnificent Boston Public Library by McKim, Mead and White. I went then to the more
restrained and more effective new brick library at Phillips
Exeter Academy in New Hampshire by Louis Kahn, a much-
admired designer: like others before me, I couldn't find the
door. Yes, I can see why librarians look at such gymnastics
as architectural exhibitionism. I who enjoy the exhibition
was weary of the game. It saddens me that these excesses
lead to programming out the other side of the coin: their
virtues. The rare American architect ventures to talk of
whimsy, of mystery, of richness, when even grace and proportion get such bad names.

Finally, to frost the cake of conspicuous architectural
consumption, I went to visit New York University's new Bobst
Library in Washington Square.

It is, of course, the spectacle of spectacles. The
atrium of library fame has entered the age of the pharaohs.
One's mind may not bend permanently from gazing up to its
roof atop the 150-foot atrium, nor from peering down the 12
stories upon a floor "strikingly paved with marble in a black,
gray and white checkered pattern adapted from the floor of
Andrea Palladio's sixteenth century church of San Georgio
Maggiore in Venice." Mine, however, boggled. Where oh
where did it end? Somewhere in the box at the start of this
architectural maze stood your gentle reader. Our glum little

Thurber man was looking forlornly for the object lost in all
this--the book.

I rushed to the more mundane literature of the pragmatists and administrators.   I had energy reports from EFL
and conference reports on library environments; a classic
pamphlet on lighting from Keyes Metcalf and a thick book on
Library Buildings by the ALA.   I steeped myself in suggestions that "Total reader space should be apportioned as follows: study-carrels--60 percent; group study rooms that may
also serve as rooms for the use of audiovisual equipment, 15
percent; flat-top tables--8 percent; lounge furniture--17 percent." I could not muffle concern that the ruggedly individualistic extra inches of some long-legged lounger might not
wreck the whole formula by bringing--heaven help us!--the
17 percent for lounging up to a disastrous 17. 1! I could not
suppress the feeling that good architecture is the rule of the
specific as well: the specific site, the specific problem,
specific individuals.   The statistics were tiring, the undeviat-
ing large ground floors, the formula layouts wearied me, too.

Yet these functionaries were right in a way.   Who
will deny the need for the general rule? Only an intrepid
soul would argue that "moving a book from stack to reader
is not substantially different from the process of supplying
goods to customers from a warehouse inventory."   Logic
wins: the pragmatists will beat you to intellectual submission.
For a time.   For a while, then, I was even willing to side
with the coldest of the numerologist.   It is just as silly to
get dewy-eyed about the future of the book as one's ancestors
did over the end of parchment, I nodded.   Despite my own
enduring vertigo by microfilm, I began to defer to the judgments on change and technology.   Yes, I finally sighed, if by
some lucky accident, the book survives, it is really because
it is a fantastic--er--machine.   Ladies and gentlemen: the
new knowledge container! Portable! Storable! Susceptible
to instant information retrieval, center or end! The minimal consumer of space and energy!

For days, I ricocheted from pragmatics to aesthetics.
One day, I cheered for rugs but less because I enjoyed
squatting on the rug in Harvard's Graduate School of Design
library than for their acoustical properties; I accepted steel
cabinetry and wasteland lofts as ambassadors against "Future
Shock." I even allowed--almost--the need for the whirring
Xerox machine I discovered stationed like a gray uniformed
invader, in the oaky aristocracy of my Richardson Library.

"The old idea of the library as a secluded room, in which a
few scholars could browse at leisure among dusty volumes,
has given way to the idea that it is essentially a vehicle of
popular education. " Architectural Record wrote these words
in 1910, at the start of the library movement.   Could one
say otherwise in 1974?   Another day, another chat, however,
and I was back with the aestheticians; I would even allow
Philip Johnson, our architectural Bourbon, his marble, his
vaunted space, even his looming structure over Washington
Square because, in a sense, he paid for it.   "Mr. Johnson
is not only an architect of distinction who believes in elegance, but he is a very good money raiser, " former head
of that library Charles Gosnell opined at a conference recorded in Library Buildings.   And because elegance is its
own reward, I find Johnson's eclectic turn to this spartan
monument and his philosophy a counting of angels on the head
of the pin of aesthetics.   Still, far from me to put down aspirations to beauty and hadn't Elmer Bobst, donor of $11
million of that $25 million museum, rejected a cheaper
model?   "Some donors, " said Gosnell, "like to have distinctive architecture. "   Who can argue?

So the pendulum swings, but no more so in library
design than on the larger landscape.   Extremism is the architectural order of the day everywhere: on the one hand, the
opters for efficiency--whether for commercial or public-
spirited motives; on the other, the defenders of aesthetics
and ego trips.   The polarities never seem to find the happy
middle as if the extremes were right or mutually exclusive.
One no more wants a handsome building that demands a jog
from "m" to "n" than a "functional" one whose grimness
causes kids to put on their bowling alley manners.   Just as
good administering and efficiency is not cut-rate construction,
so good architecture is not a paste-on billboard for the architect to use as canvas.   On both sides, building design is a
listening/learning event.   Space becomes more than a container for books and the duties of book "keepers"; more too
than a sculptural void.

By this definition, library architecture--all architecture, in fact--needs a shakeup of axioms.   A case in point
this winter is our view of contemporary architecture as a
ravenous consumer of energy.   Buildings, according to the
American Institute of Architects, gobble one-third of the U.S.
total energy; and of that one-third, they waste 30 to 40 percent.   Libraries are not super-hogs like high rises.   Still,
the ill-sited closed window species, heated and then cooled,

sealed and then ventilated, riding roughshod over the clim-
atic and topographical dictates of the environment appear
everywhere. 95 to 96 percent of all new libraries are air-
conditioned. Who'll bet that more than 10 percent of those
have windows that open? Whatever happened to lighting
switches next to book stacks ... gone the way of the single
switch of our office buildings.

Everywhere, libraries have adopted lighting standards
set by the men who sell them: the Society of Illuminating Engineers. Keyes Metcalf, the former Harvard library head
who began as an errand boy and at 85 continues his consulting errands at an amazing tilt, goes back 75 years to when
lighting standards were set at one-and-a-half-foot candles.
It's been creeping up ever since, he says. "In 1905, the
U. S. Post Office decided that their postal clerks had to read
letters and so forth so that they needed four-foot candles. In
1930, it was seven-and-a-half-foot candles. In 1940, the
sweatered consultant sitting on the sofa of his low-60-degree-
heated house goes on, "I was chairman of a subcommittee on
scientific aids to learning. We were worried about eye fa-
tigue with microfilm. We decided that 17-foot candles would
be adequate for anybody." The other day Mr. Metcalf saw a
booklet recommending 100-foot candles. Its authors: the Society of Illuminating Engineers.

My Richardson Library may be a bit Dickensian with
its reddish carved wainscotting, its somber cork floor, the
few fine light fixtures, and the leaded windows letting in the
soft light. But I was neither blinded by glare nor groping
through darkness. Refinement, care in placement, taste,
even drama can do with light what no mere wattage standard
even suggests. Ill-thought-out lighting standards are simply
symptomatic. As fossil fuels shrink and the ethic turns to
what Ian McHarg calls Design with Nature, we may turn back
a bit to the parsimony of past libraries which didn't try to
outmuscle or technologize the real world away.

Another dispensable axiom, as has been hinted, is the
axiom of open space. This Utopia of a universal--totally
flexible space fit for all activities in all times--probably
came from the architects, imported via the International Style.
Architects have tempered their endorsement of the glass box
and all-purpose room more than many libraries. Death to
inner columns--the bane of expansion and flexibility--goes the
credo. As libraries dismissed the rigidity of inner columns,
however, they forfeited their contouring of space into a more

amenable place. At what price providing for the future? economics? indeterminate space? There must be better ways.
In the name of grandness, I suppose, libraries boast wide
entrances; in the name of security, one enters these many
portals only to squeeze into check-in and check-out lines.
Contradiction is costly; so is shortsighted planning: we skimp
where we might be rich; are lavish were we could be economical.   "We get pressure from all sides to make the reading room one big room so supervision is possible from one
place, " says architect William Warner. His firm's splashily
delightful Bancroft School won an ALA-AIA-NBC award. He
has fought for color and cubbyholes, for levels of space and
"a loft so you can go away. " For identity. Besides service,
we need "breaking up the space, " as he puts it: a focus and
shape, touches of color and texture, attention to the architectural cliché that "god is in the details. " Somewhere between the problems of staff and the problems of human scale
lies the ideal: the design of a library house that is not a
warehouse. Some architects like Warner can manage to in-
ject a bit of joy in the process. Warmth is a goal; firm-
ness, commodity, and delights are the words architects like.
Indeed, I would maintain that it is the search for these missing "extras" that make big donors settle on monuments; that
made the Foxboro town fathers think that only mimicking the
past would supply the human spirit they sought.

     Our presidential libraries are the most flagrant ex-
ample of the corruption of the misguided search for something "extra. " Sometimes sprawlingly folksy and pseudo-his-
torical, sometimes tombic (the new LBJ Memorial Library
by Skidmore, Owings and Merrill), theirs is All Glory architecture. It pines mindlessly for the past or goes for gross-
ness of scale. It dishonors our President and, as in the
case of the John F. Kennedy Memorial Library designed for
Cambridge by I. M. Pei, may even manage to disrupt a whole
community.

     In a brighter light, the decade-old award done jointly
by the American Library Association, the American Institute
of Architects, and the National Book Committee at least approaches the problem professionally. Admittedly, the awards
now seem time-bound: I do not picture a 1974 jury enthusing
about a structure as "pristinely simple, the interior monumental, the exterior an elegant statement and dramatization
... " at least not in a New Haven street. Another 1960s library bears the screen-like camouflage of the mode of the
day; still another borrows the arches now frowned on as

phony historicism. Also: I think the award-givers, like librarians as a whole, need to reconsider whether a tower library is, in fact, a center and focus or a disruption of campus scale.   I suspect that like the Beaux Arts palace library,
this heightened form will pass from favor.   And, as said,
they need to ponder about the extremes of windowless walls
or glassy ones.   Looking over the awards and generalizing
from New England, I would second-guess that more additions
and renovations merit the award attention.   An overview of
architecture as a whole tells me too that libraries suffered
from the myopic vision of the tower-in-the-park.   They neg-
lected to relate to streets and neighborhoods.   I would put
community posture and siting way up in the roster of prizes.

     Still, if the photos do not overwhelm they appear to
be quality structures.   For myself, I applaud the notion of
juries as standard-setters.   Architecture by competition, both
before and after the design, is a good tool.   It contrasts with
the untempered or one-sided client/architect view; it may
mitigate the promiscuous praise of, say, a Library Journal
listing I now see before me.   The journal's 12 pictures and
outlines cheer for a pyramid-like structure that reminds me
of an Apex discount store-cum-parking lot.   They praise the
super-scale overhang and heavy formalism of a library that
is set, mind you, "in a native pine forest." In one indis-
criminate breath, the pages endorse a mock colonial copycat
and Philip Johnson's behemoth mentioned in Boston, along
with half a dozen more attractive libraries.   I single this out
as no worse in its way than some endorsements in architectural magazines; it is an indicator of the need for standards.
Who will set standards?   As I hesitate to either laud or con-
demn these photographs without a visit and talk on site, so I
question the ALA awards made without first-hand inspection.
Better these awards, however, than the dozen descriptive
photos that lift the language of press releases.   The need is
independent evaluation: from the architect, from the administrator, and also from Thurber's little man.

     Perhaps this is a good time in the history of libraries
and the history of architecture to do so: to pause for thought
and rethought about the ideals and axioms listed.   Library
building has slowed.   Constricted funds must bring questions
about goals.   Architecture, too, is in flux and chaos; the
rationalism and expressionism of the decade past have battled
to an aesthetic standstill even in the somewhat arcane annals
of design fashion.   No single mode prevails.   Architects have
begun to look for integration in siting, not showmanship; li-

brarians to the full spectrum of human needs.   Buildings do
speak; so do people with wants that bump and jostle, clamor
and whisper, too.   Now is a good time for listening to them
all.

BOOKS AND BEDS: LIBRARIES IN
NINETEENTH AND TWENTIETH CENTURY HOTELS*

Manuel D. Lopez

The number and popularity of hotel libraries reached
its height during the 1920's; however, that aspect of hotel life
had sporadic predecessors for at least fifty years.   It is
possible that a bookish inn-keeper or post house manager,
after deciding that a particular traveler was a kindred spirit,
shared his personal library of an evening.   Such a courtesy
would have been simply a personal favor.   Historically, travelers have hoped for protection from the elements, sought to
avoid becoming victims (sometimes by even their hosts) and
were grateful for basic creature comforts.   To achieve these
objectives other travelers have advised the following qualities
as necessary: "have always the eyes of a falcon, the ears
of an ass, the face of an ape, the mouth of a hog, the
shoulder of a camel, the legs of a stag, and see that you
never want two bags very full, that is one of patience and
another of money. "[1]

Obviously, one did not expect on a journey to find sol-
ace for the soul or refreshment for the mind--at least not in a
caravansary as one historian of American hotel life observes,
"The West had more hotels and fewer comforts than any
place in the world. "[2]   Yet the first extensive published information about hotel libraries focuses upon the library of
the What Cheer Hotel, Sacramento Street, San Francisco.
Originally a boarding house in 1852, the hotel was established
upon the European plan.   The proprietor, R. B. Woodward,
"a smart Yankee, " immigrated from Rhode Island and established his hotel upon some unique principles: women, in-
toxicants and gaming tables were rigidly excluded from the
premises, no credit, no boarders.   In contrast to the other
outstanding San Franciscan hotels, the clientele was largely
composed of the "honest miner, " farm hands, stockmen and

*Reprinted by permission of the author and publisher from
The Journal of Library History, July 1974, pp. 196-221.

travelers concerned with economy.   The charge for a bed
was two dollars a week and meals were available in the res-
taurant for an average of twenty cents--beef steaks, chops,
cutlets, sausages, fishes, etc., 10 cents, soups, entrees,
roast joints, 10 cents. [3]   Over 4000 meals of plain but quality
food were served a day. [4]   The other conveniences offered by
the hotel included a laundry and a department where a man
could have his clothes mended and generally repaired.   Free
to guests was a boot blackening room where the traveler
could clean and shine his footwear.   Connected to the hotel
was an art gallery containing sculpture and paintings imported
from Rome at a cost of about $20, 000.   Complementary to
the art gallery was a museum (45 x 14) established in 1859
of which it was said that "for variety and all that goes to
make up a museum, no collection in the state can compare
with the museum of the R. B. Woodward's What Cheer
House. "[5]   Apparently this was not an exaggeration as the
right wall contained over six hundred preserved birds from
all over the world as well as twenty-five specimens of animals.   Indian artifacts and hand crafts from the South Seas,
the North West Coast and Sandwich Islands occupied the left
hand wall.   Located at the rear of the museum were the cabinets housing the sea shells from the Sandwich Islands, the
coast of California and the Society and Friend Islands.   Specimens of minerals were also displayed, as well as a collection of Australian, European and American butterflies and
insects.   The collection of eggs--from Ostrich to Humming-
bird's--numbered twelve hundred.   The resources of the
museum also included a collection of pickled reptiles and fish
as well as a display of units of money ranging from Roman
coins and medals to Indian Wampum.

        Entrance to the Museum was through the Library and
Reading Room, which, "although large, is the best patronized
and the most crowded of any in this extensive establishment. "[6]   The library was established because Mr. Woodward
believed that hotels should provide for more than just physical needs.   Traveling East, encouraged and aided by the
publishing firm of Harper Brothers, he purchased some fifteen hundred books, of "good moral tendency, " attempting to
provide for the diverse tastes and needs of his guests.   Considering his clientele, the hundred volumes on bee-raising,
gardening, horticulture, stock raising, vine-growing, etc.
seem appropriate.   There were some four hundred volumes
of fiction including titles by Cooper, Dickens, Mrs. Bremer,
Irving, Hawthorne, Marryat, Scott and Thackeray.   The one
hundred and fifty historical works were matched by an equal

number of biographies and the collection was given additional
balance with poetry, drama, translations of the classics, an
extensive section on travels and voyages as well as a number
of practical, religious and miscellaneous titles.   By 1859,
the collection had grown to three or four thousand volumes
occupying the south side and west wall of the library. [7]

The book collection was supplemented by such journals
as Harper's Magazine, the Overland Monthly and other magazines published in California, the East Coast and Europe.
The cost of newspapers--from California and the principal
ones from the East Coast and Europe--amounted annually, in
gold, to over $1200. [8]

One contemporary describes the use of the library:
"From early morning until shutting-off time comes at night
this reading room is filled with guests, and it's really interesting to see their absorption.   The seats are ranged closely,
side by side, and there sit the bookworm miners ... quiet
as the regulations demand, bound up in a biography ... or
reading of adventures which recall their own wild experiences. "[9]   Three years later it is noted, "The house has its
library--a rather good one, by the way, and tolerably well
patronized.... "[10]   The library of the What Cheer House received no more note than that and, apparently while still fulfilling a definite function, was not considered worthy of additional comment.   It is ironic that the history of libraries,
institutions that collect, organize and preserve records, is
extremely deficient in its own historical primary and secondary sources.   Unfortunately, the final disposition of the Library of the What Cheer House is both a victim and example
of this situation.   If there was a catalog or written record
of the titles in the library, it is not extant.   Nor is there
any explanation available concerning the "regulations" of the
library.

Substantive evidence of another hotel library does not
occur for thirty-two years until the publication of the "Catalogue" of the Hotel Touraine, Boston.   Except for what can
be gleaned from the catalogue, there is no information concerning the origin, span of existence or policies concerning
the library.   There is an indication of a life span of at least
twenty-two years when the present tense is used in a 1922
article[11] in reference to this library.

The catalogue itself is 19.5cm x 14cm, of sky blue
paper with the legend Hotel Touraine Library: Catalogue[12] on

the cover, followed by one blank leaf.   There is no title page
or table of contents.   Page two begins the alphabetic author
and title listing that continues until page ninety-seven.

At the top of page two the reader is informed, "Guests
who desire to have books sent to their rooms, will please
apply to the office. "   In contrast to the What Cheer House
Library, guests were not confined to a reading room and the
regulations were somewhat more permissive.   The organization of the catalogue presents a number of questions.   A
Supplement section begins on page ninety-seven and continues
to page one hundred and fifteen.   As in the first section,
authors and titles are listed in one alphabet.   This is followed by a six-page unnumbered section entitled New Books,
the books simply listed by title and not in any apparent order.
The final unnumbered two-page section, New Books, again
simply lists titles in no apparent order.   A possible explanation for the failure to incorporate the Supplement and both
New Books sections into the main body of the catalogue would
be the expense of hand-set type.   Costs must have been a
consideration, as neither the author or title entries present
any information concerning publisher, edition or date of imprint.   The number of volumes is noted, but with few exceptions no indication of translator is made. [13]   The entries in
the catalogue also lack descriptive notes or annotations.

If the catalogue is a realistic representation, the book
collection was quite substantial, almost formidable.   Titles
including the writings of Louisa M. Alcott (9); Balzac (40);
Philip Brooks (10); Edward Bulwer (23); Thomas Carlyle
(8); a three-volume collection of the Poetical Works of Geoffrey Chaucer; S. L. Clemens (16); Cooper (32); F. M. Crawford (26); two translations of Dante; Richard Harding Davis
(13); Dickens (17); Doyle (12); George Eliot (11); Goethe (13);
Hardy (14); W. D. Howells (30); Henry James (21); Kipling
(11); George McDonald (24); Marryat (14); George Meredith
(14); William Morris (7); M. Olephant (5); Walter Pater (7);
Poe (4); Charles Reade (12); John Ruskin (35); W. Clark
Russell (12); George Sand (11); Scott (25); Henryk Sienkiewicz
(6); F. Hopkinson Smith (6); Smollett (5); R. L. Stevenson
(29); F. R. Stockton (14); H. B. Stowe (13); Thackeray (15);
Thoreau (11); Tolstoi (9); Trollope (11); Jules Verne (9); Mrs.
Humphry Ward (6); Charles Dudley Warner (15); Mary E.
Wilkins (6); Zola (5).

For those embarking on the Grand Tour twenty-two
titles by Karl Baedeker were available; other non-fiction titles

included a twenty-five-volume Encyclopaedia Britannica, the
American Commonwealth Series (13); the American Statesman
Series (24), four works by Charles Darwin, fourteen by T.
H. Huxley and thirteen by John Tyndall. In addition, the
collections included histories of Boston, New England, the
United States and foreign countries. Titles such as, How to
Know Wild Flowers and H. M. Stanley's How I Found Livings-
ton, while not a significant part of the collection, are evi-
dence that an attempt was made to provide for a variety of
tastes and moods.

A second catalog of a hotel library was published in
1904 by the Hotel St. Francis, San Francisco, [14] and its half
title page informs,

> Books may be borrowed by guests and retained one
> week.   The librarian will grant an extension of
> time on application.   Books not returned when due
> will be charged to the account of the guest.
> The Library is free for the use of guests only.

This policy statement allows some obvious inferences:
that the hotel was not about to subsidize the bibliographic
needs of its patrons beyond its portals; that the use of the
library was not without regulation, controls and records; a
specific individual, "the librarian," was the responsible hotel
staff member in charge, in contrast to the "office" of the
Hotel Touraine, and the attractions of the library extended
beyond the premises, necessitating the final admonition.

The catalog itself is quite attractive, with a heavy,
somewhat glossy red paper cover (15.4cm x 22cm).   The
first leaf is blank and the second bears the legend Hotel St.
Francis Library with the above policy statement positioned
immediately below.   This is followed by the title page:

> Hotel St. Francis
> Library Catalogue
> Californiana
> Miscellaneous

Then a Foreword on the next page, the one-half title page
and then the catalogue begins on page nine.   The numbered
pages are 9-59, followed by a colophon finishing with a blank
leaf.

The Foreword expresses an awareness of typography

and printing and a collector's appreciation for monographs
published in and about California. While this catalogue has
a foreword, an advance over that of the Hotel Touraine, it
lacks a Table of Contents. The Catalogue of the Hotel St.
Francis is in two parts: "Californiana" and "Miscellaneous";
actually, both terms are misleading. The first section (pp.
5-24) is not limited to California but encompasses a variety
of publications (including annual reports of companies); titles
about Oregon, Vancouver, Arizona, Colorado, Utah, the other
Western States, British Columbia, Mexico, Hawaii; Canadian
folklore and folk life. Histories, travels, literary criticism
and books on Japanese and Chinese art and history are also
part of the "Californiana" section.

"Miscellaneous" (pp. 25-59) is devoted to literature,
current fiction and non-fiction. While the publications of
L. M. Alcott are not listed, the titles of the following authors
are: Balzac (93); Edward Bulwer (29); T. Carlyle (12); S. L.
Clemens (18); Cooper (32); F. M. Crawford (7); Dickens (26);
Doyle (17); George Eliot (13); Goethe (20); Kipling (20); Marryat (24); Poe (1); Charles Reade (17); Ruskin (45); Scott (28);
F. H. Smith (14); Smollett (5); R. L. Stevenson (43); Thackeray (28); Tolstoi (23); Trollope (12); Charles Dudley Warner
(1). A sixteen-volume Encyclopedia Americana and the
American Statesman Series, twenty-eight titles, is representative of the non-fiction; the works of Darwin and T. H. Huxley are not listed.

Each of these sections has its own alphabetic author/
title form of entry. Other than to indicate that a title has
two or more volumes, no information is provided concerning
publisher, edition, translator, or date of publication. There
are no annotations or notes concerning the contents of the
books.

Following the 1906 earthquake, the Hotel St. Francis
was gutted by fire. When it reopened, its Tapestry Room
served as a reading room (23 x 32). [15] There is no indication of a library or a record of books being available to
guests.

The year that the Hotel St. Francis published its catalogue, E. M. Statler, who was to become America's foremost
hotelman, [16] opened his Inside Inn, a temporary hotel, on the
grounds of the St. Louis Fair. This was his second such
venture; the first was a wooden structure, with a capacity for
5,000 guests a night, erected in Buffalo, N.Y., to serve the

visitors to the Pan American Exposition.   Due to careful and
new business practices and the incorporation of the labor-
saving devices, Mr. Statler made a small profit in contrast
to the other concessionaires that had financial losses resulting from rains, cold weather, the distraction of nearby Ni-
agara Falls and, finally, the assassination of President Mc-
Kinley that closed the Exposition.

Different circumstances, refinements of procedures
and innovations employed at Buffalo as well as the addition
of others made the Inside Inn a financial success and Mr.
Statler a profit of $361, 000.   His goal was to own his own
permanent hotel.   Realization of that ambition, which evolved
into a chain of hotels, is paralleled, chronologically, by the
proliferation of hotel libraries between 1917 and 1927 and is
inextricably associated with E. M. Statler's influence on the
American hotel industry and its history.

He built his first hotel in Buffalo, New York and
stunned the hotel industry by having circulating ice water and
a bath in every room as well as providing other conveniences
and services at nominal rates.   He continued to make modifications and add innovations--all to enhance the quality of the
guest's day and night.   While "Service" was his basic philosophy, which was reified by his personal observation of
guests and situations; his approach also included adopting or
adapting any useful concept and he was a consistent exponent
of the free exchange of ideas and solutions in the industry.

Described as a constant reader, usually of essayists
or commentators on human relations or conduct of life, the
following quotation illustrates both the man and his philosophy: "Our use of electric lamps on the heads of our beds or
on the somnoes at the side of the beds was suggested through
the use of a room in another hotel where the light was very
convenient for reading in bed--a habit which I have enjoyed
for many years. "[17]   The value of such a statement could be
questioned, particularly when it is made by an expert in public relations.   However, Mr. Statler's commitment to books
seems to be substantiated by the floor plans of his hotel
apartment indicating a library (16' 6-1/2" x 13' 5") only
slightly smaller than his parlor.

The floor plans of the second Statler--Cleveland, October 18, 1912--do not specify a particular area for a hotel library, [18] nor does the article of 1912 by the architects
George B. Posts & Sons refer to a library. [19]   However, the

following year, E. M. Statler, in an article, places the library in the area of the "Men's Club, " a grill room and bil-
liard room. [20] The next year, in June, 1914, it is noted,
"One of the liveliest sessions the Library has ever seen was
the auction sale of choice seats for the Hermit Club performances, "[21] and Mrs. Brainerd was identified as the Librarian
who, because of an injury, was replaced by Mrs. Gene
Dorn. [22] Obviously, some modifications were made to accommodate this addition of a new feature of Statler hotels.

A third Statler opened in Detroit, February, 1915 and
the library (27 x 44)[23] was not an afterthought in this instance.   Located on the Ballroom floor, its Elizabethan design
was emphasized by oak paneled walls and woodwork.   Oak
furnishings and a ceiling of dull antique gold completed the
room.   The bookcases had leaded glass doors and any excitement generated by their contents was probably subdued by the
black and grey carpets that were complemented by heavy
velvet hangings of a similar color.

The establishment of this library caused one editor of
a hotel trade paper to observe, "Many hotels and hoteliers
have affected the library stunt but gingerly and perfunctorially
and letting it go at practically that--virtually without informing or admonishing and electrifying the patronage who only by
chance comes to see or hear of the mental provision or preserve. "[24] Failure of "informing or admonishing and electrifying" was not the Statler organizational style, and he goes
on to explain that the "feature of a generous and glorious library" is being emphasized by the Statler-Detroit management.   Part of the campaign was a printed catalogue of the
library that had been sent to editors of hotel trade papers.
It can also be inferred from his comments that copies of the
catalogue were available in each hotel room.   He says the
catalogue is, "a handsome and attractive octavo book of
cream paper and brown binding, clearly and neatly printed,
and divisioned into glance indexes of authors, titles, and
classifies the latter with appealing comments or a pat quotation. "[25]

The book collection undoubtedly merited its own catalogue, as another trade paper editorial states, "The library
in Hotel Statler, Detroit is--to judge by its catalogue; just
received by us--a masterpiece of literary discretion. "[26] The
emphasis on this "feature of the house" was not short-termed.
Five years later, the Statler Salesmanship was still informing
its employees and the hotel industry about this aspect of

Statler service: One article has the lead: "Prince Caetani
Gets Library Catalogue. Italian Ambassador Guest in our
Detroit House, Admires this Particular Feature of Statler
Service." It points out that the Prince had specifically commented on the library service, and quotes his letter, "I wish
particularly to thank you for the copy of the Library Catalogue...."[27]

   In contrast to the Detroit situation, when the St. Louis
Statler opened November 11, 1917, a library of 1500 volumes, [28] "where guests can obtain books without charge, "[29]
was located at the St. Charles Street end of the mezzanine
lobby and arranged in large bookshelves of Italian walnut. [30]
Thick carpets, a fireplace and comfortable furnishings completed this "Men's Lounge"; however, the library was not in
a separate room. A library was also added to the Buffalo
Statler by simply accommodating book cases in the mezzanine
lounge. However, the promise that, "The Statler-Detroit departure [the catalogue] will be paralleled as expediently as
possible in the Buffalo, Cleveland and St. Louis sister houses
and the Pennsylvania...."[31] was not fulfilled until 1919. At
least three library catalogues for Statler hotels--Buffalo, and
St. Louis and the Hotel Pennsylvania--were copyrighted that
year. It was appropriate that the book collection of the Hotel
Pennsylvania was the largest and most sophisticated of the
Statler libraries, as that enterprise, sincerely described by
the New York Times as "the World's largest tavern," was
spectacular, at least in size (2, 200 rooms, 2, 200 baths) and
the volume of people, food, mail and telephone calls it could
accommodate. It was equally impressive in terms of convenience and facilities. In contrast to the general decor,
Italian Renaissance colors and styles, the library was Jaco-
bean, with dark oak paneling, a fireplace and recessed book
shelves protected by leaded glass doors. English embroid-
ered linen drapes completed the furnishings. [32] Like most
Statler libraries it was located on the first mezzanine floor.

   The printed catalogue of the library placed in every
room made the contents of the library easily accessible. Considering that it represented the library of one of the finest
hotels in the world, and in contrast to the colorful library
catalogues of the Hotel Touraine and the Hotel St. Francis,
it was rather unpretentious. Of a convenient size (17. 4cm x
11. 4cm) with a brown binding, the cover carried, in a recessed oblong, this legend:

The Hotel Pennsylvania
Library
An Annotated Catalogue

In the foreword, E. M. Statler asserts, "Few things in the
Statler hotels have afforded more satisfaction to our guests
than the libraries, " and the importance of this service is indicated by the routine of the Hotel Pennsylvania's housekeep-
er.   Before a vacant room could receive her approval for
occupancy, she had to check what was for the standard hotel
room unusual equipment of some 60 items, in proper order
for quantity: telephone memo pad, room and meal rate card,
doctor card, servidor book, city maps, post cards, pen
points, both stub and fine, calendar, library catalogue, etc.,
the library catalogue ranking tenth in order of importance.

    The Preface to this catalogue merits reproduction, as
it is, with minor changes, substantially the preface used in
the catalogues published in 1919 for the Statler Hotels in
Buffalo, New York and St. Louis.

Books--At Your Service

    The books listed and described in this Catalog are
here for your use and pleasure.
    Few things in the Statler Hotels have afforded more
satisfaction to our guests than the libraries.   For
books can always offer something to make up for
the absence of familiar faces, in a strange city,
and can turn to pleasure and profit many an evening or Sunday which would otherwise be lost or
lonesome.

A Book For Any Mood

    There is no pretension that this Library has any
book you can ask for--but it is believed that you
will find here something to match any mood or
please any taste.   There may or may not be something on your specialty, but assuredly you will find
'something good to read, ' whether you want solid
fare or playful fiction, a poem or a jest, a thoughtful essay or a detective story.   And if you are so
fortunate as to have 'the gift of tongues, ' and feel
for a French or Spanish or Italian volume, you will
find a catholic selection from the three literatures
--which is not limited, any more than the English
section, to the classics.

Perhaps a word should be said in explanation of the absence of 'standard sets' and many shelves-full of the books which it is supposed 'no gentle-man's library is complete without.' The plain fact is that most of those are not the books that are asked for by the guest of a hotel--who, for an evening's reading, is more apt to call for Steven-son or Mark Twain or W. W. Jacobs than for Sr. Walter Scott or James Fenimore Cooper or Dickens. You will find much of the best of the 'standard authors' in this collection, but it will be some of their most readable and most-liked works rather than 'sets' embracing everything they wrote.

The Library--Or Your Room

The Library is on the Mezzanine Floor, on the opposite side of the building from the elevators. It is a comfortable room, and you are invited to make use of it--the Librarian will be pleased to help you find 'something to read.' If, on the other hand you will prefer the comfort of your own room, tel-ephone for the book you want and it will be sent up to you; this Catalog is intended to make it easy for you to select a book without visiting the Library.

No Charge, Of Course

There is no charge of any kind for the use of books--provided, of course, they are returned to the Library before you leave. The Librarian makes a memorandum of any volume issued to your room, and credits you with its return when you send it back.

We Hope You'll Enjoy Them

This introduction accomplished, may we hope that the Library will be a source of pleasure to you during your stay with us, that you will feel free to use it--and even, that you may number among the pleasant acquaintances made under this roof some book to which your memory will recur at times with a kindly thought for the day on which the acquaintance was made. It is in the hope of just such happenings that the Library is made a part of Hotel Pennsylvania's service to you.

E. M. Statler [Signature]

Considering that Statler Service, while catering to individual needs, was in reality based upon the development of
efficient routines and procedures combined with standardized
furnishing and equipment, the reasonable expectation regarding these library catalogues would be a high degree of uni-
formity.   Superficially, this seems to be the situation: all
three have the same kind and color binding; all are copyrighted in the same year, 1919; and all were produced by
Gies & Co., a firm of lithographers and printers that was
located at 111 Swan Street, Buffalo, New York.   But a closer
examination produces evidence to the contrary: the Hotel
Pennsylvania catalogue measures 17.4cm x 11.4cm, that of
St. Louis 17.9cm x 11.2cm and the Buffalo catalogue is
17.9cm x 10.9cm.

In contrast to the previous hotel library catalogues,
the Statler catalogues are a little more sophisticated, as they
have a Table of Contents, each one incorporating the same
idiosyncracy.   The fiction section, the final section of the
catalogue, is listed first, followed by the non-fiction section
which is subdivided alphabetically by category: Fine Arts;
Biography; Drama and theatre; Economics, etc., Games,
sports, amusements; General Literature, essays, etc.; History, travel, and adventure; Music; Nature, natural history,
agriculture; Poetry; Reference; Religion; Science.   The inclusion of general literature etc., poetry, drama and theatre
in a non-fiction section is a little startling.

The individuality of the catalogues is manifested by
even the most superficial examination of their tables of contents.   The final section in that of the Hotel Pennsylvania is
Books in Foreign Languages: French--Novels (78 authors,
185 titles), Poetry (16 poets, 17 titles), Theatre (29 dramatists, 52 titles), General Literature (28 authors, 38 titles);
Spanish--Novels (27 authors, 64 titles), Poetry (15 poets,
17 titles), Theatre (13 dramatists, 20 titles), General Literature (20 authors, 29 titles); Italian--Novels (47 authors, 73
titles), Poetry (10 poets, 13 titles), Theater (6 dramatists,
15 titles); General Works (46 authors, 53 titles).   Such a
collection would be appropriate for a large cosmopolitan city;
in contrast, the other catalogues do not list any foreign
language titles.

The Buffalo catalogue has a unique section in its table
of contents, Mythology and Folklore, containing three authors
and five titles.   It must be noted that all three authors and
their works were located in various sections of the Hotel

Pennsylvania catalog and one of the authors and his work was
found in the St. Louis collection.

The catalogue of the Hotel Pennsylvania has another
distinguishing feature. Its History, Travel and Adventure
section has a four-page subsection devoted to the Great War.
Perhaps it is here that the absolute exclusion of German
language books from the Books in Foreign Languages should
be noted.

While all three catalogues are deficient regarding publisher, edition, translator or date of publication, in contrast
to their predecessors (Hotel Touraine, St. Francis, not Detroit) each entry is annotated and identical in all three catalogues, an approach that would seem practical and efficient.
The evidence for one editor or compiler is diminished by a
number of exceptions. For example, in the section on Poetry,
Walt Mason's Horse Sense is described in the Hotel Pennsylvania catalogue as: "A book by an American poet philosopher,
who writes rhymes that look like prose."

The same annotation is used in the Buffalo catalogue
but the one in the catalogue of the St. Louis collection is a
little more extensive, "His verses--typographically disguised
as prose--are familiar to every newspaper reader--and are
more widely read in America than the rhymings of any other
writer."

Another example is: Gulick, L. The Efficient Life.
"Practical health talks for busy men. The well-known director of physical education in New York City cannot write a
dull book, and this one is of great practical value." (Hotel
Pennsylvania).

Gulick, Luther. The Efficient Life. "Useful in helping people how they may improve whatever degree of efficiency they individually possess." (St. Louis).

The entry for the author's name and the annotation for
the Buffalo catalogue are identical to that in the St. Louis one.

Not only does the annotation in the Hotel Pennsylvania
catalogue differ, but also the manner in which the author's
name is cited. All three annotations for William J. Henderson's What Is Good Music are identical but he is cited differently (Wm. J.) in the Hotel Pennsylvania list from the identical entries in the catalogues of Buffalo and St. Louis (Wm.

James). Apparently, there is no conscious relationship between the variations of entry and/or differences in annotations.

More significant differences may be revealed by a review of the contents of the three hotel libraries. The total
number of volumes in the Hotel Pennsylvania is three thousand, and fifteen hundred volumes in the St. Louis collection.
The number of volumes for the Buffalo collection is not available; however, extrapolating from the ratio of titles (fiction
and non-fiction) to known totals in the other two collections
would indicate a one-third duplication, [33] thus giving the 1919
Buffalo collection fifteen hundred volumes.

The fiction category of the three collections was compared with the fiction best seller lists for the period 1895 to
1918, [34] the year prior to the copyright date of the printed
catalogues. While fiction constituted approximately one-third
of the collections of St. Louis and Buffalo, it constituted
something less than one-fourth of the Hotel Pennsylvania collection. Best seller titles in the St. Louis and Buffalo collections were approximately one-fifth of the collection, while
the Hotel Pennsylvania catalogue has a total of fourteen per
cent. There were sixty-eight best seller titles, representing
fifty-eight authors, duplicated in all three hotel libraries.

Mrs. Sarah Renfrew, [35] a Statler librarian, informs
us that book selection for the Statler Hotel libraries "has been
largely governed by public approval" with no attempt to "keep
abreast of the present day press." She also states that each
Statler library was a subscriber to the Literary Guild, a
book club started in 1927. Maintaining a scrap book of local
newspaper clippings containing Statler publicity was also one
of the duties of Statler librarians. Apparently there was no
attempt to standardize book selection among the libraries.

The hotel library which received the most acclaim,
publicity and recognition from the hotel industry was created
for the second hotel E. M. Statler built in Buffalo. Opened
on May 19th, 1923, the hotel fronted on five of the city's
principal streets, and had 1,100 rooms. Its nineteen stories,
dominating the sky line, made it the tallest building in the
state, outside New York City. It was also the largest hotel
between New York City and Chicago. As guests of Mr. Statler, over 200 hoteliers from all parts of the country came
for the opening, by steamer from Detroit and Cleveland and
by special cars from St. Louis, Chicago and Toronto. The

cars for the Boston delegation were attached, at Albany, to
the special train provided for the 125 New York hotel men.
Special traffic regulations were instituted and the Mayor of
Buffalo, Frank X. Schwab, declared a civic holiday.

Unlike the Hotel Pennsylvania, the use of the materials in this structure was not constrained by the limitations
imposed by war.   The exterior design was Georgian and the
tapestry brick was laid in an English cross-bone pattern.
The interior favored the Renaissance--Italian and Spanish, with
rich blues, greens and reds.   Tapestries, silks, velvets, and
oriental rugs provided accents for the walnut furniture based
on a medieval Italian design.   Raphaelistic decoration and
metal work in antique gold and polychrome contributed to the
current concept of luxury.   Walls and columns were constructed of four kinds of imported marble--Botticino, Traver-
tine, Levanto and the black and gold.

There were several exceptions to the style of decoration, for example, the Chinese Room and the Georgian Room,
but the Mezzanine Lounge reflected the dominant theme with
its rich colors, Italian motifs, walnut furniture upholstered
in reds, greens and blues and a gilded iron railing.   The
Library (13 x 44)[36] located to the rear left of the Mezzanine,
was in sharp contrast. [37]   Oak paneling, a greenish blue car-
pet of salt and pepper design and hand-blocked English linen
draperies created a subdued and restful atmosphere.   At each
end of the room was a fireplace of English Renaissance style,
and the oak and walnut furniture was dominated by the central ceiling light, an illuminated geographical globe bordered
by signs of the zodiac.   Behind leaded glass doors the books
were arranged, by category, on the recessed shelves. [38]
Frank Bering, the manager of the Hotel Sherman, Chicago,
commented, "The library was the most homelike atmosphere
I have ever seen in a hotel, "[39] and The Hotel World stated,
"The hotel's library on the mezzanine floor is one of the
most beautiful rooms in the building and its carefully made
collection of approximately 2, 000 volumes covers enough
branches of literature to provide books for almost any mood,
studious or otherwise. "[40]   Fred Muller, steward for the
Blackstone and Drake Hotels, Chicago, concluded his evaluation of the new Statler with, "that gem of the house, the library. "[41]

The second edition of the Catalogue of the Hotel Statler, Buffalo (1923) is not substantially different in format and
arrangement, from the first, with one exception: it does not

include a section on Mythology and Folklore. The collection
of 1,324 titles allocates about one-third of 2,000 volumes for
the duplication of titles. There is an emphasis on non-fiction. In this category, the previous collection had 535 titles;
the new collection, with twenty-five percent more volumes,
had 631 non-fiction titles, an increase of about twenty percent. Best seller titles did not dominate the collections, as
they totalled only about one-fifth of the fiction. Each collection had less than fifty percent of the possible 207 best seller
titles. For the same period, 1895-1918, the second Buffalo
library collection had a diminished number of best seller
titles despite an increase of over two hundred fiction titles.
The 1923 catalogue, for the period of 1919-1922, lists only
eight best seller titles out of a possible 39 titles.

Concerned about the hotel industry's over-expansion,
Mr. Statler protected his investment by opening a combination
hotel and office building in Boston on March 10th, 1927.
Three thousand guests including Mayor Nichols of Boston and
Governor Fuller of Massachusetts attended the opening. It
was reported that the Governor was impressed with the library, its 3,000 volumes and the availability of its catalogue
in every hotel room. [42] As usual, the library (15 x 44)[43]
was located on the mezzanine floor, was Georgian in style
with rich carpets and hangings, and had a vaulted parchment
ceiling, a fireplace and scones of brass and pewter. [44] Miss
Mary Fox was the Librarian. A Mr. King, in a Boston
Transcript editorial, states that "he is favorably impressed,
to the point of bubbling enthusiasm with the new Hotel Statler
library in Boston," and continues that it "must be conceded
a very high rating."[45] He also finds the catalogue (180
pages), the selection of titles, the arrangement and the annotations impressive. "Were there ever more intelligent book
notes--far outrunning any natural anticipation one might
possess concerning the real librarianship which a hotel might
be expected to show, or to take pains about. The whole undertaking is astonishing and most gratifying...."[46]

While the library received its just accolades, it was
the innovation of a radio in every room, adding a new dimension to Statler service, that made the Boston Statler
unique. The hotel industry was stunned. Convinced that
radio was the greatest entertainment medium yet developed,
Mr. Statler had, at the cost of $50,000, provided every guest
of the Boston Statler with a radio in his room. The following year, at an expense of $750,000, radios were installed
in the guest rooms of every Statler Hotel. The Statler

traveller could now listen to the favorites: Amos and Andy,
Ben Bernie, the Happiness Boys, Jack Pearl, Joe Penna and
Rudy Vallee and the Statler concept of service had provided
a resource, other than the library, which the patron could
use to "turn to pleasure and profit many an evening or Sunday which otherwise would be lost or lonesome."

While E. M. Statler was incorporating new services
that might compete with or overshadow his hotels' libraries,
his competitors were emulating his pre-radio bibliographic
success. On May 2, 1927 the Stevens Hotel in Chicago
opened pridefully as the world's largest hotel. The library
was located in a suite on the fourth floor[47] and according to
Miss Gertrude M. Clark, who organized the service, had the
ultimate goal of twenty thousand volumes[48] but opened with
an initial collection of three thousand books. Less than half
were reported as fiction; Miss Clark's selection policy was
to exclude "strictly technical books and to select only what
might interest the general reader or what will be so comprehensive that it will contain something on what is sought."[49]
The policies regarding "sets" are similar to those outlined
in the prefaces of the Statler library catalogues. This is also
true of the policies regarding guests' use of the library and
their freedom to take a desired book to their room, however,
similarities do not include a catalogue being printed for this
library. The Hotel Stevens Library[50] had several unique
features. Thirty magazines and ten out-of-town newspapers
were available in a separate room of the library suite.
Maintaining a clippings file of reviews of current dramatic
performances in Chicago was a projected service.[51] The library contained a few juvenile books but most of that literature was located on the floor devoted to the hotel nursery and
children's playroom.

The Hotel Stevens library attempted, like the Statler
libraries, to serve a broad spectrum of guests; in contrast,
the library of the Hotel McAlpin in New York was actually
created for a more specific clientele, the business community, despite the statement, "The library ... will be of general service and convenience for the guests of the McAlpin
and for visitors of the Hotel."[52] As of September, 1922, the
library was to be established on the mezzanine floor "in a
course of a few months." Three years after the publicity
and distribution of the catalogues of the Statler libraries, Mr.
Boomer, managing director of the Hotel McAlpin, proceeded
to establish a hotel business library. An article describing
the projected library suggests the motivation and, perhaps

unintentionally, the reason for the lack of additional information about the venture: "That a practical businessman and his
promotion expert should see in books a vehicle for a new
form of hotel promotion is an indication of the increased appreciation of the prestige that can be gained and the interest
aroused by putting books to practical use in a new way. "[53]
In the Dale Carnegie tradition, the selection of titles for the
library was used for hotel advertisement. Trade paper editors were solicited for their recommendations regarding the
names of leaders of industry and commerce. Mr. Boomer
sent a questionnaire to two thousand businessmen, representing twenty different fields of manufacturing, finance, etc.,
asking them to list ten books of first importance in their area
of business. The editors of trade papers were also requested
to submit their recommendations. After the suggestions were
compiled, the library was to consist of ten titles for twenty-
six aspects of commerce and industry. If the project was
completed, it would have resulted in a business library of
only 260 titles, limited in its appeal to the hotel's guests,
and because of its nature requiring constant revision. This
library differs considerably from other hotel libraries not
only in its diminutive size and its limitations concerning content, but also in the projected policy of its value to guests
and visitors to the hotel. [54]

        Another refinement of the hotel library concept was
instituted by Joseph Huckins, Jr. of the Huckins hotel chain
of Arkansas, Texas and Oklahoma. He established in the
Lee-Huckins Hotel, Oklahoma City, a reference library only
for the use of the hotel's employees, stating, "I believe our
employees can become more efficient if they have ready opportunity to 'find out' about things through a reference library
maintained by the hotel. "[55] To avoid loss, misplacement and
inadvertent dispersal, all books, regardless of original format, were to be placed in a large-size binding.

        The concept of hotel libraries was subjected to a
broad spectrum of implementation, resulting from diverse
motives and designed for a variety of clienteles. The establishment of a library by an individual, a community, or
an organization always is a matter of pride as, depending
upon the creators, it implies the surplus economic resources
to support a library, and the leisure to enjoy it. It is also
a concrete manifestation of a belief in the future, in the intrinsic value of the collection, and in the continued existence
of the clientele the library serves. Consequently, when libraries are established it is usually a matter of public record;

on the other hand when libraries are dissolved it is usually
accomplished quietly for the obvious reasons. The over-expansion of the hotel industry, the Depression, the competition
of radio, movies and the mass production of inexpensive
books, all contributed to the decreasing appeal of the hotel
library. It has been stated that the dissolution of a library
is not usually a newsworthy event; however, Mr. Theodore
Krueger, Manager of the Hotel Statler, Buffalo, used that
very situation to burnish the Statler image. In 1941, the
Victory Book Campaign was soliciting books for the Armed
Services libraries. On behalf of the Statler Hotels, Mr.
Krueger donated the entire library of the Hotel Statler to this
particular war effort. Today, the bookcase doors are cur-
tained and the "library" is now the "Grover Cleveland, " a
private dining and meeting room.

        With the elimination of hotel libraries, usually the
reading resources of hotel guests were limited to the Gideon
Bible, [56] the offerings of the lobby newsstand or those of the
nearest all-night drug store. The exceptions to this situation have
been provided by Hilton hotels, where the Hilton Bedside
Books have been placed in every hotel room since 1952. To
date seven volumes, totalling between 900, 000 and 1, 000, 000[57]
copies, have been printed and distributed. Attractive in format, the books, which can also be purchased at the desk for
one dollar, contain selections to catch the attention of the
most casual reader. They are anthologies of poetry, essays,
and fiction--almost miniature libraries, as indicated by the
Preface:

            For those quiet moments in your hotel room--
        before the start of the day's activities, between en-
        gagements, when you're ready for bed but not quite
        ready for sleep--we are pleased to offer these
        varied entertainments in good reading, The Hilton
        Bedside Book, Volume Seven.
            We hope that the wide diversity of reading pleas-
        ure contained in this selection of fiction, prose
        and poetry will echo the reading tastes of our
        guests, offering not everything for all of you, but
        something for each of you.
            You can play the role of detective on several
        vital cases, and test your own ideas on human
        physiology against the findings of experts Montagu
        and Darling. There's the vicarious thrill of help-
        ing a tenderfoot fisherman try to land his first
        giant gamefish. And a nostalgic 1920's visit to

America's most human humorist, Robert Benchley.
You'll hear the wild cry of a prehistoric sea-
monster, and the not so different sound of a steam
locomotive in the reminiscences of a country boy's
love affair with trains.

Straight or mixed, here are suspense, nostalgia,
humor and adventure; myth, history, poetry, and
fantasy; prehistoric and present-day animals; places
faraway in time and in space; rogues, reticent
ladies, sportsmen, and scientists.

Browser or borrower, may you find enjoyment!

Conrad N. Hilton,   Barron Hilton,
Chairman   President
                Hilton Hotels Corporation

Such one-volume "libraries" do not need a catalogue,
but the illusion of historical continuity is aided by the Preface of the Hilton Bedside Book which seems reminiscent of
an introduction to catalogues for hotel libraries that no longer
exist.

Notes

1. John Florio, Second Fruites XCIII (1591); other variations
    of this sentiment are by Torriano, Piazza Universale,
    p. 157 (1666); Thomas Nashe, Works (Grosart) v. 141
    (1594); T. Gainsford, Rich Cabinet, fo. 147 (1616);
    Fynes Moryson, An Itinery, iii, i, 49 (1617); John
    Taylor the Water Poet, A Short Relation of a Long
    Journey (1652); John Ray, English Proverbs, p. 296
    (1678); Franklin, Poor Richard's Almanack, 1737.

2. Richard Van Orman, A Room for the Night (Bloomington
    and London: Indiana University Press, 1966), p. 34.

3. "A California Caravansary," Harper's Magazine, XXXIV
    (April, 1867), p. 604.

4. Ibid. , p. 606.

5. "The Museum at the What Cheer House," Hutchings'
    California Magazine, IV, No. 12 (June, 1860).

6. "Library of the What Cheer House, San Francisco,"
    Hutchings' California Magazine, IV, No. 1 (July, 1859).

7. Ibid.

8. "A California Caravansary, " p. 606.

9. Ibid.

10. "Caravansaries of San Francisco, " Overland Monthly, V
    (August, 1870), p. 180.

11. "Hotel McAlpin Adds a Business Library," Publishers'
    Weekly, CII (September 23, 1922), p. 1006.

12. Boston: A. Mudge & Son, 1902.

13. "Dante Alighieri, Divine Comedy, translated by H. W.
    Longfellow, 3 vols. "; "Dante Alighieri, Divine Comedy
    and the New Life. Translated by C. E. Norton. 4
    vols. "

14. Hotel St. Francis, San Francisco, Library, Library
    Catalogue; Californiana; Miscellaneous (San Francisco:
    Printed for the Hotel St. Francis, 1904), 59 pp.

15. American Architect and Architecture, XCV, no. 1739
    (April 21, 1909), pl. 2.

16. For biographies of E. M. Statler, see: Rufus Jarman,
    A Bed for the Night (New York: Harper & Brothers,
    1950); Floyd Miller, Statler (New York: The Statler
    Foundation, 1968); Lesley Hughes Browder, Jr. ,
    E. M. Statler, "Hotel Man of the Half Century" (Mas-
    ter's Thesis, Cornell University, 1959).

17. E. M. Statler, "Exchanging Ideas on Hotel Manage-
    ment, " Hotel Management, I, No. 1 (February, 1922),
    p. 7.

18. E. M. Statler, "The Hotel Statler, Cleveland, Ohio, "
    The Architectural Review, II, n. s. 1913, p. 102.

19. "The Hotel Statler, Cleveland, Ohio, " Architecture and
    Building, XLIV 1912, pp. 496-502.

20. Statler, "The Hotel Statler, Cleveland, Ohio, " p. 101.

21. Statler Salesmanship, II (June, 1914), p. 44.

22. Ibid., III (January, 1915), p. 58.

23. For photographic view of the library, see: Architectural
    Record, XXXVII (April, 1915), p. 235; for floor plans
    see p. 230.

24. Editorial, Western Hotel and Travel, reprinted in Statler
    Salesmanship, IX (January/February, 1918), p. 264.

25. Ibid.

26. Editorial, Hotel Gazette, reprinted in Statler Salesman-
    ship, IX (January/February, 1918), p. 263.

27. "Prince Caetani Gets Library Catalogue," Statler Sales-
    manship, XVIII (May /June, 1923), p. 22.

28. "Hotel Statler to be Opened to Public Saturday," St.
    Louis Post-Dispatch, November 6, 1917, p. 2.

29. "Guests Throng New $3,000,000 Hotel Statler," St.
    Louis Post-Dispatch, November 11, 1917, p. 3.

30. For photographic view of the library see: Statler Sales-
    manship, IX (November, 1917), p. 224; Architecture
    and Building, L (February, 1918), pl. 34. For floor
    plans see: Architectural Forum, XXVIII (February,
    1918), p. 34.

31. Editorial, Western Hotel and Travel, ibid.

32. For photographs of the library see: Architectural Forum,
    XXX, No. 4 (April, 1919), pl. 58: The Independent,
    May 8th and 15th, 1920, p. 203. For floor plans
    see: Architectural Forum, ibid., p. 96.

33. Hotel Pennsylvania, 3,000 volumes, 1365 titles (711 non-
    fiction, 654 fiction): St. Louis, 1500 volumes, 1,000
    titles (485 non-fiction, 515 fiction).

34. Alice Payne Hackett, Fifty Years of Best Sellers, 1895-
    1945 (New York: R. R. Bowker Co., 1945). A more
    extensive analysis is offered by Claud Cockburn,
    Bestseller: The Books that Everyone Read, 1900-1939
    (London: Sidgwick & Jackson, 1972), pp. 1-17.

35. Sarah Renfrew, "Hotel Statler Library," Special Librar-

ies, XXII (May-June, 1931), p. 159-160.

36. For floor plans see: Hotel Monthly, June, 1923, p. 31; Architectural Forum, XXXIX (July, 1923), p. 12.

37. For view of entrance to library from the Mezzanine see: Hotel Monthly, June, 1923, p. 40.

38. For photographs of the library see: Hotel World-Review and Hotel Management, June 9, 1923, p. 16; Architectural Forum, XXXIX (July, 1923), p. 14; Statler Salesmanship, XVIII (May/June, 1923), p. 42; Hotel Bulletin, June 23, 1923, p. 464-R.

39. "Hotel Statler III of Buffalo, N. Y., 1, 100 Rooms, " Hotel Monthly, June, 1923, p. 23.

40. Hotel World, June 9, 1923, p. 22.

41. "Hotel Statler III...," p. 26.

42. Statler Salesmanship, XXV, Boston Opening Number, 1927, p. 35.

43. American Architect and Architecture, CXXXII (July 5, 1927), p. 20.

44. For photograph see: Statler Salesmanship, XXV, Boston Opening Number, 1927, p. 46.

45. "Editorial, Boston Transcript, " reprinted in Statler Salesmanship, ibid., p. 47.

46. Ibid., p. 48.

47. For floor plans see: Benjamin B. Shapiro, "Structural Design of the Stevens Hotel, " Architectural Forum, XLVII (August, 1927), p. 110.

48. Henry J. B. Haskins describes the capacity of the library at 15, 000 volumes. "The Stevens Hotel, Chicago, " ibid., p. 102.

49. H. H. Slawson, "Unique Travelers' Library in New Chicago Hotel, " Publishers' Weekly, XCI (June 18, 1927), p. 2326.

50. For photograph of the library see: Slawson, p. 2327.

51. Ibid.

52. "Hotel McAlpin Adds a Business Library," Publishers'
     Weekly, CII (September 23, 1922), p. 1006.

53. Ibid.

54. This proposed library was not the Hotel McAlpin's first
     experience with libraries. In a description of the
     then-to-be-constructed hotel in Architects and Build-
     ers' Magazine, XLIII (February, 1911), p. 212, a
     library 30' x 40' was to be located on the mezzanine
     floor. For the floor plan see: "Hotel McAlpin, New
     York," Architecture and Building, XLV (February,
     1913), p. 44. When the Annex was added to the
     hotel, the sixth story was "the women's floor," and
     contained a library, a special parlor, hair dressing
     rooms, a seamstress' room, and children's play-
     room. Ibid., LIII (August, 1918), p. 53.

55. "A Hotel Reference Library," Special Libraries, X
     (1919), p. 75.

56. The Gideons is one of the oldest interdenominational
     laymen's evangelistic organizations. Founded in
     1899, they began placing the Holy Bible in every
     hotel guest room in 1908. Thus far, nearly two
     million Bibles have been distributed.

57. Personal letter, Ralph E. Shikes of Editorial Projects,
     Inc., New York, publishers of the Hilton Bedside
     Books.

COMPARISON OF BOOK CATALOGS

Non-fiction books in the libraries of the Hotel Pennsylvania,
Hotel Statler, St. Louis and the Hotel Statler, Buffalo (1919).
Starred titles are also listed in the 1923 Hotel Statler Li-
brary Catalogue.

ART, ARCHITECTURE, ARTS AND CRAFTS, AND
     COLLECTING

Caffin, Chas. H.   American Masters of Sculpture

Kimberly, W. L. *How to Know Period Style in Furniture
Moore, Mrs. N. Hudson. The Collector's Manual
Poore, H R.   *Pictorial Composition and the Critical Judge-
     ment of Pictures
Reinack, S. *Apollo
Sturgis, Russell. The Appreciation of Pictures

BIOGRAPHY, MEMOIRS, LETTERS AND REMINISCENSES

Allen, A. V. G.   *Phillips Brooks--His Life and Letters
Chestnut, Mary B. A Diary from Dixie
Gilder, Richard Watson.   Grover Cleveland
Dewey, George. *Autobiography
Jones, F. A.   *Thomas A. Edison: Sixty years of an Inven-
     tor's Life
Franklin, Benjamin. *Autobiography
Clemens, Samuel L.   *Joan of Arc
Keller, Helen. *Story of My Life
Rothschild, Alonzo. *Lincoln, Master of Men
Lucas, E. V. The Gentlest Art
Lee, Sidney. *William Shakespeare
Stevenson, Robert Louis.   *Letters
Balfour, Graham. *Life (R. L. Stevenson)
Washington, Booker T. Up from Slavery
Pennell, Elizabeth Robin.   *James A. McNeill Whistler

DRAMA AND THE THEATRE

Burton, Richard. *How to See a Play
Dickinson, T. H.   *The Case of American Drama
Hale, Edward Everett, Jr.   *Dramatists of Today
Hamilton, Clayton
          *Studies in Stagecraft
          *The Theory of the Theatre, and Other Principles of
               Dramatic Criticism
Matthews, Brander
          *The Development of the Drama
          *A Study of the Drama
Nathan, George Jean.   Another Book on the Theatre

ECONOMICS, BUSINESS, SOCIOLOGY, POLITICAL SCIENCE,
     ETC., ETC.

Blackford, Katherine and Arthur Newcomb.   The Job, the
     Man, and the Boss
Brandeis, Louis D.   Business--a Profession
Fiske, Amos. *The Modern Bank

Fowler, Nathaniel C., Jr.
        *How to Save Money
        *Practical Salesmanship
George, Henry.   *Progress and Poverty
Gulick, Luther.   *The Efficient Life
Hagerty, James Edward.   Mercantile Credit
Hatfield, H. R.   *Modern Accounting
Hungerford, Edward.   *The Modern Railroad
Johnson, Emory R.
        American Railway Transportation
        *Ocean and Inland Water Transportation
Johnston, Alexander.   *A History of American Politics
Kaufman, Herbert.
        *The Clock That Had No Hands
        Do Something, Be Something
Maxwell, William.   *Salesmanship
Mills, James Cooke.   Our Inland Seas
Moody, Waller D.   Men Who Sell Things
Parsons, T.   *The Laws of Business
Pratt, Sereno S.   *The Work of Wall Street
Prendergast, William A.   *Credit and Its Uses
Taussig, Frank W.   *The Principles of Economics

GAMES, SPORTS AND AMUSEMENTS

Brewster, E. T.   *Swimming
Daly, Maurice and W. W. Harris.
        *Daly's Billiard Book
        Dick's Game of Patience; or Solitaire with Cards
Foster, R. F.   *Foster's Complete Hoyle
Haultain, Arnold.   *The Mystery of Golf
Henshall, James A.   *The Book of Black Bass
Kephart, Horace.   *The Book of Camping and Woodcraft
Little, Raymond D.   *Tennis Tactics
Vardon, Harry.   *The Complete Golfer

GENERAL LITERATURE, ESSAYS AND BELLES-LETTRES

Benhan, William G.   *The Laws of Scientific Hand Reading
Bennett, Arnold.
        *How to Live on Twenty-four Hours a Day
        *The Human Machine
        Literary Taste
        *Mental Efficiency, and Other Hints to Men and Worms
        Married Life
Black, Hugh.
        *Friendship
        *The Practice of Self Culture

Burroughs, John. *The Breath of Life
Cabot, Richard C. *What Men Live By
Call, Annie Payson.
    *The Freedom of Life
    *Power Through Repose
Clemens, Samuel L. *Is Shakespeare Dead?
Conwell, R. H. *Acres of Diamonds
Crothers, Samuel McCord. *The Gentle Reader
Emerson, Ralph Waldo
    *The Conduct of Life
    *Essays
Finck, Henry T. Food and Flavor
Fisher and Fisk. *How to Live
Fosbrake, Gerald E. *Character Reading Through Analysis
    of the Features
Grahame, Kenneth. Pagan Papers
"Grayson, David" (Roy Stannard Baker)
    *Adventures in Contentment
    *The Friendly Road
    Adventures in Friendship
Holmes, Oliver Wendell. *The Autocrat of the Breakfast
    Table
Ibsen, Henrik.
    Brand
    *A Doll's House
    *The Wild Duck
    *The Lady from the Sea
    *Ghosts
    *The Warriors at Helgeland
    *An Enemy of the People
    *Hedda Gabler
    *The Master Builder
    Little Eyolf
    John Gabriel Borkman
    When We Dead Awaken
    *Peer Gynt
Keller, Helen. *Optimism
Kirk, Eleanor. *The Influence of the Zodiac Upon Human
    Life
Kung, George Frederick. *Folk-lore of Precious Stones
Lamb, Charles. *The Essays of Elia
Lee, Gerald Stanley. Crowds
Maeterlinck, Maurice.
    *The Blue Bird
    Death
    *The Life of the Bee
Mitchell, Donald G. Reveries of a Bachelor

Palmer, George Herbert. *Self-cultivation in English
Payot, Jules. *The Education of the Will
Perry, Bliss.
    *The American Mind
    *A Study of Prose Fiction
Repplier, Agnes. *Americans and Others
Roosevelt, Theodore. *The Strenuous Life
Saintsburg, George. *A Short History of English Literature
Schauffler, Robert Haven. *The Joyful Heart
Shakespeare, William. *Works
Shaw, George Bernard.
    *Man and Superman
    *Misalliance
    *Fanny's First Play
    *The Dark Lady of the Sonnets
    *Plays Pleasant and Unpleasant
    Three Plays for Puritans
    *Doctor's Dilemma
    John Bull's Other Island
Stevenson, Robert Louis.
    *Essay on Travel, and the Art of Writing
    Familiar Studies of Men and Books
    *Lay Morals and Other Papers
    *Memories and Portraits
    *Virginibus Puerisque
Thompson, Vance. *Drink and Be Sober
Thoreau, Henry David.
    *Autumn
    *Summer
    *Winter
    *A Week on the Concord and Merrimac River
Van Dyke, Henry.
    *Days Off
    *Fisherman's Luck
    *Little River

HISTORY, TRAVEL, GEOGRAPHY & ADVENTURE

Baring, E. J. Round the World in Any Number of Days
Hopkins, Albert A. *The Scientific American Handbook of
    Travel
Slocum, Joshua. *Sailing Alone Around the World
Cobb, Irvin S. *Europe Revised
Dreiser, Theodore. *A Traveler at Forty
Mencken, H. L. Europe After 8:15
Collier, Price. *England and the English from an American
    Point of View

Dickens, Charles.   *A Child's History of England
Green, John Richard.   *A Short History of the English
       People
Howells, William.
       *Certain Delightful English Towns
       *Seven English Cities
Lucas, E. V.   *A Wanderer in London
McCarthy, Justin.   *A Short History of Our Own Time
Marks, Jeanette.   *Through Welsh Doorways
Boulger, D. C.   *Belgian Life in Town and Country
Hough, P. M.   *Dutch Life in Town and Country
Lucas, E. V.   *A Wanderer in Holland
Motley, John Lathrop.   *The Rise of the Dutch Republic
Barker, Edward H.   *France of the French
Carlyle, Thomas.   *The French Revolution
Lucas, E. V.   *A Wanderer in Paris
Lynch, Hannah.   French Life in Town and Country
Stevenson, Robert Louis.   *Travel with a Donkey in the
       Cevennes
Collier, Price.   Germany and the Germans, from an
       American Point of View
Dawson, W. H.   German Life in Town and Country
Sidgwick, Mrs. Alfred.   Home Life in Germany
Howells, William Dean.
       *Italian Journeys
       Tuscan Cities
       Venetian Life
Hutton, Edward.   *Cities of Lombardy
Lucas, E. V.   *A Wanderer in Florence
Smith, F. Hopkinson.   *Gondola Days
Villari, Luigi.   Italian Life in Town and Country
Frank, Harry A.   *Four Months Afoot in Spain
Hay, John.   *Castillian Days
Howells, William Dean.   *Familiar Spanish Travels
Brochner, Jesse J.   Danish Life in Town and Country
Brown, Mrs. Demetro Vaka.   *Haremlik
Garnett, L. M. J.   *Turkish Life in Town and Country
Heidenstam, G. von.   Swedish Life in Town and Country
Mahaffy, J. P.   *Rambles and Studies in Ancient Greece
Palmer, F. H. E.
       Austro-Hungarian Life in Town and Country
       Russian Life in Town and Country
Story, A. T.   *Swiss Life in Town and Country
Bacon, A. M.   *Japanese Girls and Women
Bard, Emile.   *Chinese Life in Town and Country
Clement, E. W.   Handbook of Modern Japan
Collier, Price.   The West in the East, from an American

Point of View
Compton, Herbert.   *Indian Life in Town and Country
Kennan, George.   Tent-Life in Siberia
Knox, George William.   *Japanese Life in Town and Country
Landon, A. Henry Savage.   An Explorer's Adventures in
     Tibet
Van Dyke, Henry.   *Out-of-Doors in the Holy Land
Breasted, J. H.   *History of Egypt
Duchaillu, Paul.   Equatorial Africa
Edward, Amelia B.   *A Thousand Miles Up the Nile
Loti, Pierre.   Egypt
Roosevelt, Theodore.   *African Game Trails
Stanley, Henry M.   In Darkest Africa
Catlin, George.   *The Boy's Catlin
Griffith, W. L.   *The Dominion of Canada
Wallace, Dillon.   The Long Labrador Trail
Allen, James Lane.   *The Blue Grass Region of Kentucky
Channing, Edward and M. F. Lansing.   The Story of the
     Great Lakes
Dodge, T. A.   *A Bird's-eye View of Our Civil War
Drake, Samuel A.
          *The Making of the Great West
          *Making the Ohio Valley States
Elson, Henry W.   *History of the United States
Hale, Mrs. Louis.   *We Discover New England
Hosmer, James Kendall.   A Short History of the Mississippi
     Valley
Hough, Emerson.   *The Story of the Cowboy
Hungerford, Edward.   The Personality of American Cities
Inman, Henry.   The Old Santa Fe Trail
Johnson, Clifton.
          *From the St. Lawrence to Virginia
          Highways and Byways of the Great Lakes
          *Highways and Byways of New England
          *Highways and Byways of the Mississippi Valley
          Highways and Byways of the South
Kephart, Horace.   *The Southern Highlander
Lodge, Henry Cabot.   *The War with Spain
Lummis, Charles F.   *A Tramp Across the Continent
Muir, John.   *Our National Parks
Page, Thomas Nelson.   *The Old South
Powell, Alexander.   *The End of the Trail
Roosevelt, Theodore.   *Ranch Life and Hunting Trail
Stevenson, Robert Louis.
          *Across the Plains
          *In the South Seas
          *The Silverado Squatters

Stockton, Frank R.   *The Buccaneers and Pirates of Our
        Coast
Street, Julian.   *Abroad at Home
Thwaites, Reuben Gold.
        *Down Historic Waterways
        *On the Storied Ohio
Boyce, William D.   *Illustrated South America
Bullard, Arthur.   *Panama, the Canal, the Country and the
        People
Frank, Harry A.   *Zone Policeman 88
Hayward, Walter B.   *Bermuda Past and Present
Ober, F. A.   *A Guide to the West Indies and Panama
Roosevelt, Theodore.   *Through the Brazilian Wilderness
Ruhl, Arthur.   *The Other Americans
Bulcy, E. C.   Australian Life in Town and Country
LeRoy, James A.   *Philippine Life in Town and Country
Shackleton, Sir Ernest H.   The Heart of the Antarctic

MUSIC

Goepp, Philip H.   *Symphonies and Their Meaning
Henderson, William James.   *What Is Good Music?
Krehbiel, Henry E.   *How to Listen to Music
Schauffler, Robert Haven.   *The Musical Amateur
Upton, George P.
        *Standard Concert Guide
        Standard Concert Repertory
        *Standard Operas

NATURE, NATURAL HISTORY, AGRICULTURE, ETC.

Bostock, F. C.   *The Training of Wild Animals.
Burkett, C. W.   *Agriculture for Beginners
Dickinson, Mary C.   *The Frog Book
Ditmars, Raymond L.   *The Reptile Book
Doubleday, Mrs. Frank N.
        *Bird Neighbors
        *Birds That Hunt and Are Hunted
        *Nature's Garden
Holland, W. J.
        *The Butterfly Book
        *The Moth Book
Hornaday, W. T.   *American Natural History
Howard, Leland O.   *The Insect Book
Jordan, David and B. W. Everman.
        *American Food and Game Fishes
Keeler, Harriet L.   *Our Native Trees and How to Identify
        Them

McFarland, J. H.   *Getting Acquainted with Trees
Marshall, Nena L.   *The Mushroom Book
Rogers, Julia E.   *The Tree Books
Sharp, Dallas Lore.
        *The Lay of the Land
        The Whole Year Round

POETRY

Adams, Franklin P.
        By and Large
        Tobogganing on Parnassus
Braley, Berton.   Songs of the Workaday World
Browning, Mrs. Elizabeth Barrett.   *Poems
Bryant, William Cullen.   *Poems
Burns, Robert.   *Poems
Byron, Lord   *Poems
Drummond, W. H.   *The Voyageur
Field, Eugene.   *Poems
Keats, John.   *Poems
Kipling, Rudyard.   *Collected Verse
Longfellow, Henry Wadsworth.   *Poems
Lowell, James Russell.   *Poems
Mason, Walt.   *Horse Sense
Omar Khayyam.   *Rubaiyat
Palgrave, Francis T.   *The Golden Treasury of Songs and
        Lyrics
Poe, Edgar Allan.   *Poems
Quiller-Couch, A., ed.   *Oxford Book of English Verse
Riley, James Whitcomb.   *Complete Works
Shelley, Percy Bysshe.   *Poems
Stedman, Edmond Clarence.   *American Anthology 1787-1900
Tennyson, Alfred.   *Poems
Van Dyke, Henry.   *Poems
Whitman, Walt.   *Poems
Whittier, John Greenleaf.   *Poems

REFERENCE

Angeli, A. and J. McLoughlin.   *Spanish-English and English-
        Spanish Dictionary
Bartlett, John.
        *Familiar Quotations
        *Cassell's New French-English and English-French
            Dictionary
Crabbe, George.
        *English Synonyms
        *Everyman's Encyclopedia

Fernald, James C.
    *A Working Grammar of the English Language
    *Heath's German-English and English-German Dic-
        tionary
Robert, Lieut. -Col. H. H.   *Rules of Order for Deliberative
    Assemblies
Robert, Helen L.   The Cyclopedia of Social Usage
Roget, P. M.   *Thesaurus of English Words and Phrases
*Scottish Clans and Their Tartans
*Webster's New International Dictionary
*Who's Who
*Who's Who in America

RELIGION

Abott, Lyman.   *The Evolution of Christianity
Brinton, D. G.   *Religions of Primitive Peoples
Clarke, J. F.   *Ten Great Religions
Coe, George A.   *The Religion of a Mature Mind
Eddy, Mary Baker.   *Science and Health, with Key to the
        Scriptures
Gladden, Washington.   *Applied Christianity
Mathews, S.   *The Church and the Changing Order
Wilcox, Elia Wheeler.   *New Thought, Common Sense and
        What Life Means to Me

SCIENCE, ELECTRICITY, ETC.

Atkinson, Philip.   Electricity for Everybody
Darwin, Charles.
        *The Descent of Man
        *On the Origin of Species by Means of Natural Selec-
            tion
Hudson, Thomas J.   *The Law of Psychic Phenomena

PEACOCKS AND POSERS:
LIBRARIANSHIP AS A PROFESSION*

Judith McPheron

Much has been written in the recent and not-so-recent past about librarians and professionalism. It is what we should all be striving for, the ultimate good, our coming of age. In library school, I would estimate that at least thirty per cent of class time was devoted to the subject, and we were all urged and admonished to become that wonderful and ineffable thing, the Professional. There was voluminous and hazy discussion as to exactly what that meant, but on one point they all agreed: it meant service, of a high order, to mankind.

Also mentioned at various times were intellectual rigour, organizations, education, and a literature of one's own. All sounds nice and rosy, like a bunch of genteel secular nuns, but I think there is a nastier business lurking around the corner. We seem to have been sold, and are continuing to sell each other a bill of goods. What we aspire to is not only the higher good of mankind, but bourgeois respectability and comfort, and a sense of insularity and class solidarity which keeps us forever separate from that seamy bunch, the workers.

In America, the notion of professionalism defines itself not so much as a life's work one is committed to, but as an economic and social class. The two groups that are generally acknowledged as "professional" by the public are doctors and lawyers, and I think that no one can make the mistake that it is because they are dedicated to mankind, but because of their incomes and attendant social status. Medical and legal services are often virtually unobtainable for the poor, who need them more than anyone, and if they are, the dis-

---

*Reprinted by permission of the author and the Association of Assistant Librarians from the Assistant Librarian, July 1974, pp. 116-118.

comfort and difficulty connected with them are prohibitive.
So while we speak of our seemingly good reasons for professionalism, it is in reality this group of doctors and lawyers with whom we want to ally ourselves, want to emulate.
All of our motives cannot be good.

In countries where there is no defined, established
upper class, an unofficial élite soon arises, but even if unofficial, not casual. This is the situation we are now stuck
with here, and so there are all sorts of groups besides librarians chomping at the bit to be let in, and be so acknowledged publicly. It is this feeling which kept teachers from
organizing for so long, and which keeps a large portion of
the "intelligentsia" from openly criticizing the social structure. No one who has accepted the title of professional, or
who aspires to it, can be anything but quiet, careful and conservative, because his entire status rests on these qualities.
He is not simply a member of a moneyed class, but a leading conserver of the status quo, one who is seen as a step
above others, not through hereditary position, but through his
own achievements. So it is not surprizing that the American
Medical Association has always been strongly against medical
reform, just as Bar associations have been very slow to cen-
sure members who perform unethically (Watergate not excepted).

Showy Clothing and Bought Hair-do's

The crazy thing about the aspirations of librarians is
that they are going for the social status, not the money.
They attempt, through their tedious meetings, organizations,
publications, to convince the country and themselves that they
"know what they're doing; "have special and highly trained
skills and knowledge that other people don't, have a "classi-
ness" which distinguishes the true professional. I am not
arguing with the claim of special knowledge, but plumbers
and electricians have a speciality too, and they make as much
money. What I am arguing with is the attempt of a group of
people to con themselves and to let those with the power and
the money continue to con them.

It is this ability to be conned that often marks the
middle class mentality. Their fondest wishes are not to become millionaires, but to be seen as special, better, separate, more worthy than other groups of people, namely the
working class. There are many men who are revolted by the

92   Library Lit. -74

idea of people seeing them in working clothes, operating
machinery or whatever, and so would rather take a white
collar job which pays less and bores them, but which gives
them the aura of respectability and working with their "heads"
not their hands. And librarians are falling into the same
trap, even if they don't realize it. In many libraries, the
"professional" work is clearly separated from the "non-professional, " even though much of both kinds of work is simply
clerical. The librarians are willing to come early, stay
late, and do all sorts of extra jobs if only they can be called
"professional" and not be confused with those others, the library workers. They want everyone to know that they are
dedicated, that money considerations don't influence their
willingness to work, and that their special education and
training entitles them to membership in a secret sort of fraternity, where gentility, respectability and service to mankind reign supreme.

        This is not to say that some real dedication does not
exist, but that it should not exist as a way of furthering
class rivalries and snobbishness. Recently I attended a library organization meeting which seems a good example of
all I am talking about. First, we were charged a fee for
attending and lunch which was exorbitant. No one complained
about this at all; it would have seemed petty and "unprofes-
sional, " and would have indicated the truth that many of us
could not really afford it. Professionals always have ready
pocket money to spend for organizational meetings, "business" lunches, etc. Second, it looked rather like a businessmen's ball, everyone dressed to the teeth in expensive
conservatively showy clothing, jewelry and bought hair-do's.
Everything was "tasteful, " nothing of even the slightest importance was talked about, amiability was rampant, and
everyone was comfortable in his fraternity. When one librarian tried to object to the silliness and wastefulness of
the proceedings, and the organization in general, he was
quickly censured, and told that the article he had attempted
to pass out (unsuccessfully; the officers of the organization
made sure no one could get a copy) was in "bad taste. " One
would expect that in a group of people dedicated to the service
of mankind, human freedom, and particularly, intellectual
freedom, shrieks of defiance and unbelief at this behaviour
would have gone out instantly. Quite to the contrary, I have
never been in such a large group of people which was so
quiet, placid, comfortable. In short, no one said anything,
and the librarian was made to feel a bit of a crank. Our
brotherhood was clearly declared at that moment--not with

the unruly, unkempt classes of "lower" workers, but with the
American Medical Association.

Distaste of the Working Class

This same set of attitudes is making things rough for
those who do not identify themselves with the élite.   When
the formation of labour unions for librarians is mentioned, it
is hushed as the most vulgar sort of radicalism.   This seems
hard to believe as the country has been unionized for so long.
It indicates, rather, I think, distaste at the idea of being
identified with the working class.   Doctors and lawyers,
after all, do not unionize.   This is the most obvious example
of self-conning, because while so many librarians are really
underpaid, they would rather accept that condition than con-
junction with people "beneath" them, and so of course, their
genteel and timid requests for better pay go unanswered.
And those who do not share these attitudes are considered
"dangerous. "

It is not by chance that those "non-professional" workers in libraries are not finding it so difficult to organize,
although they too are feared as an infection.   They simply do
not have the imagined status to lose.   Our refusal to align
ourselves with library workers of all sorts also says something about our notions of service.   Although there is a big
move on to serve a public not before connected with libraries,
the working and lower classes, and it spawns much impas-
sioned rhetoric, one wonders at its ultimate sincerity if we
cannot even see that we have a lot more in common with
"non-professional" library workers, who share similar
knowledge, than we do with doctors and lawyers.   It seems
to me that the first step in extending ourselves to the public
at large is to identify ourselves correctly with our own workers, and with workers in general.   Then we will not be re-
enacting the melodrama of the landed rich who deign to offer
assistance to the poor from on high, but will be equals talking together, giving something we have special knowledge of
and receiving their special skills and knowledge in kind.

Finally, we should see that the idea of "professionalism" is just a way of mystifying knowledge, of keeping people
separate and ignorant of what others do and how, and encouraging a social set-up where people find it acceptable to
think that they are better than others, and have a greater
share of wealth and benefits.   While we have not completely

been accepted as "professionals" yet, we still have a chance
of moving away from these attitudes, and declaring ourselves
on the side of equality and social justice.

THE BARGAINING ECONOMICS OF LIBRARIES:
THE MEANING FOR LIBRARIES AND
THE LIBRARY PROFESSION*

Donald G. Mercer

Those who wish to improve libraries must learn to
bargain effectively. But this, as will be shown, is far from
being easy. Considerable skill, of a type that most librarians are unlikely to have, is required. Without this skill librarians may find it difficult to defend their realm. This is
most unfortunate. Conservative American attitudes of the
kind typified by Milton Friedman, formerly an economic ad-
visor to President Nixon, are probably inimical to the interests of tax-supported libraries and are probably attractive
to conservative elements in Canada. This could mean that
the librarians of Alberta in particular would have to cope
with a movement which would put libraries into the private
sector of the economy on a sink or swim basis. Even if this
does not happen, the fact remains that bargaining likely to
affect libraries is going on in Alberta and elsewhere. If they
are to defend their interests, librarians must learn to bargain.

It would be difficult to overestimate the importance of
bargaining and the bargaining unit for both are the agents of
economic and social change. Within the bargaining unit conflicting claims are considered and eventually a decision,
which often supersedes a previous ruling, is made and is accepted, in most instances, by all initially concerned. As
new rulings appear, conditions change and this affects other
groups who must, if they are to maintain their position, resort to bargaining as well. The process described here
affects the whole of society. Neither libraries not librarians
are exempt.

*Reprinted by permission of the author and publisher from
Library Association of Alberta Bulletin, January 1974, pp.
10-20.

Bargaining is a complex multi-faceted phenomena involving a number of dependent variables. The variables are
linked by information flows, many of which are generated by
different individuals or groups of individuals within the bargaining unit. These flows, usually released when it is most
advantageous to do so, link the variables together.

In order to understand bargaining, each variable must
be considered separately. It must be identified and its significance assessed with respect to a particular problem at a
particular time. The assessment given here is a preliminary
one subject to modification should new information become
available. The bargaining variables are enumerated in what
seems to be the order of importance given a long-term viewpoint:

1. Goodwill

While financial power is required for immediate day-
to-day survival, goodwill is required for long-term survival.
Goodwill, which implies acceptance and the desire to patronize a particular entity even though competitors are at a
particular instance in time equally good, requires salesmanship, a marketable product, the ability to change with the
time, and, in the long run, demonstrate leadership in the
product area.

Monopolies, being sheltered from the effects of competition, are under less pressure to develop goodwill. Statutory monopolies, of which libraries are a type, are under
still less pressure. Therein lies their safety in the face of
change, but therein also lies their greatest danger. Because
of the blind faith and trust placed by people in statutory
bodies, [1] and because there are often artificial barriers to
entry into the business being conducted by the statutory monopolies, [2] these bodies often lose their innovative talents
through lack of usage.

It is necessary to recognize that new forms of competition threaten the goodwill variable on which libraries have
always relied. Libraries are no longer seen as being leaders in the business of supplying needed information. They
are unable to compete with the new data manipulation systems. Their position as a source of entertainment and as a
supplier of news has been usurped by radio and television.
To a considerable extent, those that patronize libraries do so

in order to fulfill the dictates of the teaching staff in the
universities or in the schools.   But even this market is likely
to decline if alternatives to academic education as a method
of providing useful and realistic training for life are developed.

If there is a decline in goodwill, it must inevitably
have an adverse effect on the financial power of libraries,
the sine qua non of daily operations.   Should the demand for
the type of library service now known decline (or remain
stable as population increases in the area served) the validity
of claims made for funds will decrease.   Both budgets and
salaries will decrease as administrators and politicians see
the reality behind the claims being made.   The inference is
obvious: The time for change is now.

2.   Financial Power

As every individual consumer is aware, little can be
done in the world without money which may be regarded as a
claim on certain unspecified resources.   When money is
spent, a decision is made to buy this rather than that.   Removing the inflation factor, the more money available, the
greater the claim over resources and the greater the number
of options available.   Liquidity, which refers to cash or easy
access to cash, often by means of a good credit rating, is
an important, but not the only, aspect of financial power.

For libraries, the source of financial power is the
funding authority, the town council for example.   The link
with the real consumer market place, where information is
bought and sold, is, in most instances, indirect and tenuous.
This means that the money needed for sheer existence, development, and successful product marketing depends less
upon ability, direct consumer satisfaction, and the offering
of a societally useful service than upon the attitudes of those
actually funding libraries.

3.   Vested Interests in the Results of Bargaining

There are two levels of interest here.   The first is
that of an institution.   The second is that of particular individuals.   It is this factor which helps to explain the often
noticeable dichotomy between the interests of individuals and
institutions. [3]   In any event, to be aware of vested interest is
an essential key to long-term survival.

Librarians do have a vested interest in the outcome:

If libraries disappear, so do they. Since the outcome is
really the result of a series of bargains repeated over time,
the awareness of what is at stake must be maintained at all
stages. The danger is that librarians, being sheltered because they work for a statutory monopoly, will become indifferent to the problems of the day, especially if, as is so
often true with female librarians, their spouse happens to be
the real breadwinner in the family unit. Indifference with
respect to the outcome is a major factor contributing to the
loss of any bargain or series of bargains.

4. Bargaining Ability

People are born every day who, because of the factors
of heredity and environment, develop strong bargaining capabilities both for themselves and for the institutions with
which they become associated. Good bargainers have the
ability to assess the strengths and weaknesses of the other
bargainers so that the appropriate tactics may be employed.
They have the ability to find and then make use of information to the discomfort of their opponents. But there is a
danger. It is possible that this bargaining ability can be
used by individuals with a vested interest to crush the initi-
ative of those with more creative ability which, in the long
run, is a practice detrimental to the interests of any organization trying to survive. Even so, the battles will be lost
without bargaining ability.

5. Connections and Influence

While this variable relates more to individuals than to
institutions, it must be remembered that institutions are
composed of people having connections and influence at various levels and to varying degrees. The level, the influence,
and the intensity of the connection become highly significant
especially when compared with the connections possessed by
people on the opposite side of a bargaining situation.

Connections and influence become even more significant when the creative talents demanded by open market competition become less important as is almost invariably true
with sheltered monopolies, especially those of the statutory
kind. Indeed, when dealing with statutory monopolies, the
phrase connections and influence implies, as the reader probably realizes, politics of the most intensive kind. Rewards,
which are really allocated resources, go to the best politicians who are not necessarily the hardest workers or the

best qualified.   In brief, politics usually explains the why of
who gets what.

It is true that connections and influence will help librarians who are often in the unenviable position of having to
persuade municipal, university, or provincial administrations
that their money requests are realistic and that the library
really is an efficient unit in which the value of services
rendered exceeds the cost.   Unfortunately, however, connections and influence become weakened in the face of trouble,
the apparent failure of libraries, and the image of success
possessed by competitors.

6.   Constituency

Representatives on bargaining units must respect and
adhere to the views of their constituents.   This is particularly the case for those sheltered from the pressures and
immediacy of the market place.   Note that some bargaining
representatives may have more than one constituency.   Under
this circumstance, conflicts of interest can occur so as to
decrease the effectiveness of a bargainer in promoting a particular cause.

Constituency is important because it is related to connections and influence or politics for those that prefer the
more familiar term.   Unfortunately constituency both within
and beyond the library is likely to be based on a system of
mutual admiration and protection that is oblivious to the
realities of the situation being faced by the institution.

7.   The Number of Bargainers in a Bargaining Unit

The greater the number of bargainers in a unit, the
more the time which must be spent in lobbying, the greater
the possibility for the application of divide and conquer tactics, the greater the possiblity of employing emotional arguments to influence the outcome, and the longer the decision-
making process will probably be, simply because the range
of vested interests is apt to be larger than in a smaller unit.

8.   Size

The larger an institution, the greater its predomi-
nance, and the more politically disruptive its disappearance
is likely to be.   This means that a relatively large organization in a small town could probably develop great political

leverage. Just as General Motors is able to influence the
United States Government, so a public library board should
be able to influence the town council. But size can also be
a false feeling of security, especially in the absence of market pressures. If a Ralph Nader can bring General Motors
to its knees, there is always the possiblity that an able citizen who happens to be annoyed can do the same for the local
library.

9. Information

Information, an intangible commodity manufactured on
demand for specific purposes, is often of the utmost importance
in bargaining situations. What is particularly significant is
the manner in which information is manipulated by the members of the bargaining unit. Simply by withholding information, a crucial element in successful decision making, it is
often possible to trap the opposition into the making of incorrect deductions and wrong decisions.

Librarians must take pains to insure that they are as
well informed as the other experts on bargaining units dealing with library matters. Being well versed with respect to
the sources of information, librarians have, or ought to have,
an initial advantage. Just as important, however, is the
ability to utilize this information.

Diagram 1 illustrates the essential nature of the bargaining unit, be it dealing with libraries or anything else.
As can be seen, the decisions of the unit result from initial
inputs in the form of the variables attributable to each member and from subsequent negotiations. During the negotiations information from within and without the unit is being
manipulated continuously and plays a key role.

Diagram 2 illustrates the significance of the time and
timing, both of which are important in bargaining for several
reasons. First, it is possible, given sufficient time, to persuade members of the bargaining unit during a particular bargain, or between bargaining sessions, with a view to affecting
the nature of the final decision or decisions. Second, time
and timing are important with respect to the release of information, the making of promises, or the issuing of threats.
Third, a given variable may be more important at one time,
less important at another.

Diagram 1 - A stylized bargaining unit

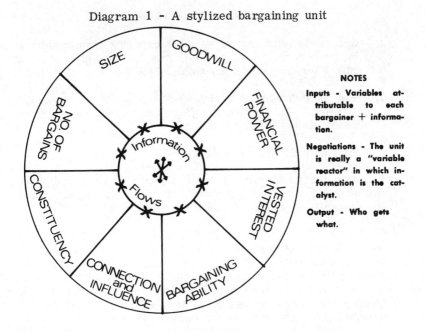

NOTES

Inputs - Variables attributable to each bargainer + information.

Negotiations - The unit is really a "variable reactor" in which information is the catalyst.

Output - Who gets what.

Diagram 2 - The timing of variable manipulation

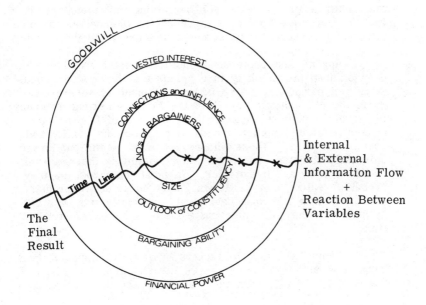

102

Notes to Diagram 2

1. Crucial to less crucial variable ordering from outside to
inside spheres, e.g. goodwill may be related to size but
only after size has been established.

2. The arrangement of variables shown produced a specific
outcome. To produce a different outcome the variables
would occupy different spheres.

3. Information links all spheres.

4. At a particular point in time a lower order variable on
an inner sphere could rise to an outer or higher sphere
where it would be of greater significance.

        Membership on, or even access to, a bargaining unit
is always desired by those whose interests are likely to be
affected by the decisions of the unit. In the past when information was not disseminated as effectively as it is now, and
when it was therefore easier to keep secrets, many individuals did not know that certain bargaining units, whose decisions would affect them, actually existed. Now, however,
thanks in part to television, people are more aware and are
less inclined to accept the narrow limits of expertise and
ownership as prerequisites for bargaining unit membership.
In brief, people either want to represent themselves or to be
effectively represented by someone responsive to their wishes.

        Anyone who takes the trouble to reflect upon what has
been said so far is likely to conclude that in most instances
their own bargaining power is low. Consumer sovereignty,
given the oligopolistic nature of the North American economy,
is largely a myth. [4] Neither the consumer of food nor the
consumer of information can do much about the quality and
cost of services. Those who regard most of the public and
university libraries as organizations inhibiting the retrieval
of information are out of luck. In most instances, as they
probably realize, any criticism, be it constructive or not,
would probably fall upon deaf ears, especially if it was not
in tune with the political climate inside the library at the
time.

        People who turn to experts in order to improve their
bargaining situation are apt to be disappointed, especially if
the consultants rely upon the traditional economic arguments.

Neither the perfect competition and monopoly arguments associated with the static theory of the firm, nor the general assumptions behind econometrics, or even the usual supply-demand analysis explains the process of change in the real world.   The only exception is in the short run but even then the underlying causes of change are human decision. These are the factors which must be studied if events are to be understood, the necessary first step in dealing with them. [5]

Diagram 3, will help to illustrate the argument.   For the reasons already given the situation at E1 is really determined by considerations other than those of price (P) or quantity (Q).   The key question is what were the human factors which determined the shape of the demand and supply curve so that D1 and S1 intersect at E1?   An increase in demand represented by D2 brings about the situation at E2 with an increase in both P and Q and a corresponding increase in revenue (P x Q).   But what really gave rise to this shift or for that matter to any other shift which might occur?   And what gives rise to the appearance of substitutes which probably caused the shift from D1 to D'1?   To answer these questions it is necessary to examine human decisions, the reasons for them, and the final effects of these decisions.

There are other problems with which supply-demand analysis will not cope.   Any firm, a bookstore for example, wants to shift the demand for its services outwards and at the same time increase both revenue (P x Q) and the profits derived therefrom.   But what does this mean in terms of public needs and societal costs?   Who is actually paying for the extra profit and, more specifically, how does the drive for increased profits affect tax-supported libraries?

On the basis of the analysis presented, it would appear that the best survival strategy for libraries would be an all-out attack on any threat to goodwill, an asset which must be preserved and hopefully expanded.   When libraries are generally recognized as being the leaders in their product area, there will be no threat.   To achieve this state of affairs, a co-ordinated five-pronged assault, illustrated in Diagram 4, is the tactic recommended.

Diagram 3 - Supply-demand analysis

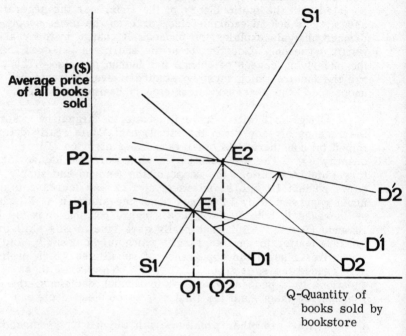

NOTES

1. The shape of the demand curve depends upon the close-
    ness of substitutes for books, e.g. television, the possi-
    bility of actually camping rather than reading about it.

2. The supply curve function depends upon the cost of pro-
    ducing various quantities of books and is probably irreg-
    ular in shape.

3. Library services, which are really information services
    (fiction is often informative), can be close substitutes.

4. D'1 and D'2 are more "elastic" situations in which con-
    sumers are more conscious of price because close sub-
    stitutes are available. Note that unfortunate educational
    experiences may drive people away from books and to-
    wards substitutes. To increase revenue (P x Q) book
    stores must be increasingly innovative as the demand
    curve becomes more horizontal, i.e. competitive pressure
    from libraries encourages bookstores to give consumers
    better service.

Diagram 4 - Assaulting the threat to the libraries

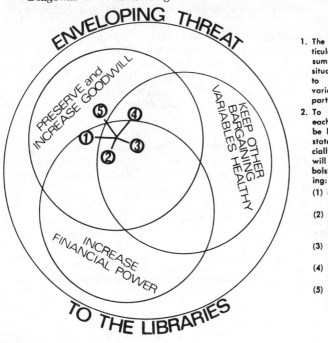

ENVELOPING THREAT

PRESERVE and INCREASE GOODWILL

KEEP OTHER BARGAINING VARIABLES HEALTHY

INCREASE FINANCIAL POWER

TO THE LIBRARIES

NOTES

1. The threat to a particular library is the summation of the situation with respect to the bargaining variables, goodwill in particular.

2. To meet the threat, each variable must be kept in a healthy state. This is especially true for good will which can be bolstered by buttressing:

   (1) research capabilities

   (2) capacity for innovation techniques

   (3) marketing techniques

   (4) bargaining capabilities

   (5) recruiting and in-house training practices

Specifically, libraries should buttress their:

(1) research capabilities. This can be done by gathering information and by doing research with respect to:

   (a) the relationship between all types of libraries and existing educational programmes. Could the current role of the libraries be improved? If so, how?

   (b) current as opposed to ideal teaching practices in libraries. Note that there are reading and learning techniques which are crucial to effective library utilization.

   (c) the schools of Library Science. To whom do these schools report? Are they in any way responsible to the profession? What is being taught and is this realistic in the light of perceived needs? What arrangements have the schools made to monitor the performance of graduates? What has been produced so

far? How good is it? These are some of the
questions which should be asked--and answered.

(d) markets.   Could libraries fill gaps in the information market? Could public libraries provide consumers with the valid, relevant, timely, understandable information needed for wise buying decisions?
There is a need for a consumers' information
service--a need not now filled to the degree necessary.

(e) the nature of information. If the diagram shown below is an acceptable model, the implications could
be studied and inculcated into any library system
being redesigned. _____

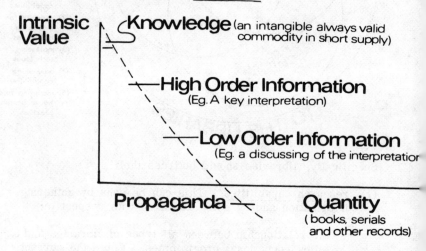

Intrinsic Value

Knowledge (an intangible always valid commodity in short supply)

High Order Information (Eg. A key interpretation)

Low Order Information (Eg. a discussing of the interpretation

Propaganda

Quantity (books, serials and other records)

NOTES

1. On the abscissa, quantity increases geometrically.

2. Intrinsic value is not the same as market value. The
market value of knowledge is probably low, that of advertising usually high.

3. Knowledge is here defined as an intangible commodity
which is always valid and upon which it is always safe
to build.

4. Information is defined as an intangible commodity manu-

factured on demand for a specific purpose, e.g. a library's financial report, the utility of which declines as time passes. High order information often makes hitherto unrecognized but valid connections. (If it is possible to predict the contents of a message, then it is not really information.)

5. Propaganda, of which advertising is a prime example, is defined as filtered information biased in favour of someone or something. It is not a suitable commodity on which to base decisions.

(f) information flows. If better information handling procedures are to be designed, it would be desirable to know who is generating information, how it is disseminated once produced, how stored once disseminated, how retrieved, by whom, and for what purpose.

(2) capacity for innovation. A great threat to creativity always comes from sheltered groups with vested interests. Some of these groups have not been seriously challenged by new concepts for a long time. Thus university faculties would probably resist any innovation which questioned their teaching methods. School and even public libraries would also have to resist pressure from vested interest groups.

(3) marketing techniques. Libraries could ascertain how they are regarded by the community served. Then they could, if it were necessary, implement procedures likely to improve the image.

(4) bargaining capabilities. This could be done by hiring expert bargainers. Hiring is recommended because the better bargainers are probably in private industry where their talents are recognized and rewarded.

(5) recruiting and in-house training practices. It is essential for libraries to hire those with the skills required for survival. Having been hired they must be effectively utilized and encouraged to become even more proficient.

The course for the profession to take follows from what the libraries must do. This is something the library schools cannot ignore; it is their responsibility to supply the correct talent, skill, and personality mix. Unless the schools succeed, goodwill must inevitably decline.

To summarize: It has been suggested that librarians will, if they consider the nature of bargaining, come to understand the process responsible for the economic and social changes which affect all individuals and all institutions. Once the process is understood it then becomes possible to plan a strategy to defend the interests of libraries and librarians. As has been indicated, this strategy is based on the assumption that it is essential to preserve and to increase goodwill, something which always accrues when an entity is seen to be the leader in its field. A multipronged assault on practices detrimental to maintaining and increasing goodwill are the tactics suggested.

If a final word is needed, it would be this: Librarians should follow the advice given by Herrick to the virgins:

> Gather ye rosebuds while ye may
> Old time is still a-flying;
> And this same flower that smiles today,
> Tomorrow will be dying.

Notes

1. Public respect for law and expertise allows enterprises to abuse the monopoly provided by their patent grants. A pertinent example of patent abuse that endangered the strategic position of the Allies in World War II is found in R. A. Solo's study entitled Synthetic Rubber, a Case Study of Technological Development under Government Direction, U. S. Congress, 2nd Session, U. S. G. P. O., 1959. (U. S. Senate. Committee on the Judiciary, Sub-Committee on Patents, Trademarks, and Copyrights, Study No. 18)

2. It is probable that the artificial barriers which discourage entry into most of the professions are not entirely in the public interest.

3. It is interesting to look at administrative decisions with a view to ascertaining whose interests are really being served. Administrators sometimes raise salaries not to reward competence but to ensure loyalty. Note that highly competent but formally unqualified junior personnel are easily threatened if they happen to rock the boat. New appointees often bring their friends with them, an acceptable practice only if their friends

have expertise unavailable in the local area.

4. The consumer is really a helpless prisoner in a dicta-
    torial bargaining situation. The frustration of indi-
    vidual consumers or groups of consumers may help
    to explain alienation, the sine qua non of violence.
    Such violence is usually expensive to society. See:
    Harris, T. A., I'm OK--You're OK. New York,
    Harper & Row, 1969.

5. The arguments with respect to scale economy currently
    in vogue amongst Western economists should be viewed
    with suspicion. The general argument is that up to a
    certain point the greater the volume of production, the
    less the unit cost. But what is the cost to society of
    increasing the volume of production? Has volume
    been increased to satisfy a demand created by infor-
    mation and market manipulation of a socially undesir-
    able kind?

UNIONS AND LIBRARIES: THE SPHERES OF INTELLECT AND POLITICS[1]*

Roger E. Michener

In the realm of libraries the last decade has brought more changes than constancies--some welcome, others not. This flux--through its attendant social uncertainty--has permeated every aspect of librarianship, giving rise among librarians to unprecedented controversy and discussion surrounding the library as a social institution. Most of the changes have been viewed with mixed feelings, but none has been received with greater ambivalence or less rationality than the growth of trade unions in libraries.

This growth, primarily since 1965, may be seen as a revival, for it is the third time that unions and libraries have been brought together over more than half a century. The first time came just after World War I; by 1919 five library unions, all in large Eastern cities, had affiliated with the American Federation of Labor. The second time was during the Depression; by 1939 approximately 700 librarians had unionized at six work locations. [2] The third time was the late 1960s. [3] This third movement, although not yet accorded thorough statistical study like the first two, is clearly the largest.

Grave economic circumstances are usually given as the causes for the first two union movements. The economic hardships, unemployment, low salaries, layoffs, and shutdowns of these periods are seen as sufficient explanation for the growth of unionism following the first war and during the Depression. Historically this explanation has been accepted as adequate, because, as the economic situation improved, the unions collapsed or faded away.

There is no such single explanation for this third union movement in libraries, and the reasons for its growth are

*Reprinted by permission of the author and publisher from Southeastern Librarian, Winter 1974, pp. 15-25.

far from investigative resolution. No quantitative studies yet exist to indicate the extent of library unionization; but when a new pattern of behavior begins to sweep through a social stratum previously resistant to it, responsibility can be ascribed to more than one factor. A burgeoning group of experts on collective bargaining in academic settings point to five main sets of hypotheses or circumstances to explain the rise of unions in libraries.

1. Economic: Universities and libraries have gone from two postwar decades (1945-1965) of prosperity and growth to a period of sudden retrenchment. As the job situation shifted from a seller's to a buyer's market, as the supply of qualified persons outstripped the demand, and as state and private universities were faced with more limited resources, salaries either ceased increasing or raises lagged behind rises in prices. And as universities tried to make do with less funds, some turned to reductions in staff size, accompanied by efforts to increase the work load. [4]

2. Organizational: Accompanying the rapid growth of higher education in the postwar era has been an increase in the size of institutions and in the development (in the public sector) of gigantic multicampus universities with a reduced feeling of collegiality. Inevitably such development led to central and greater bureaucratization and reduced the sense of purpose once shared by librarians and library administrators. [5]

3. Legislative: Legislation enabling bargaining elections and formal representation rights for public employees did not emerge in a major way until the 1960s. In 1962 President Kennedy issued an executive order providing for representation by Federal employees. A majority of states now have followed his step with laws covering their employees. As Joseph Gabarino notes, such "permissive legislation is the key explanation for the burst of academic unionism in the late 1960s and early 1970s."[6] Though some unions were able to secure representational rights prior to passage of such legislation, on the whole, full-fledged collective bargaining has occurred only after the passage of enabling legislation or the establishment of legal precedent. [7]

4. Events of the Last Decade: The sudden growth in the 1960s of egalitarian movements among the intellectually oriented strata--including college students--which related to the civil rights movement and, particularly, to the opposition

to the war in Vietnam, stimulated support for objectives
identified with liberal-left ideology, among them student participation in institutional governance.   This thrust for power
challenged many traditional prerogatives. [8] Ironically, unionism in academe, though supported disproportionately by the
faculty supporters of that ideology, became a conservative
force vis-à-vis student power.   Librarians, concerned about
resisting changes that could potentially undermine them, about
maintaining their status, and about overcoming or reducing
pressures from administrators, followed the faculty.

      5. Internal Discontents: One or another combination
of these circumstances caused librarians to view their institutions with distaste--even some alienation--and to find many
of the conditions of their employment, quite apart from economic questions, unsatisfactory.   They felt, primarily, with
the rise of professionalism in librarianship, that they should
have an expanded voice in the governance of the library.
Once the legislative and economic pre-conditions were established, this desire for influence over the library's administrative and policy decisions is perhaps the important cause
of unionization, and it is certainly its greatest sustaining
force.

      "The highest wisdom," Goethe wrote, "would be to
understand that every fact is already theory. "[9] High wisdom
does not come to most of us, and it is too much to expect
that we should already have evolved a body of theory from
the facts of library unionization.   The five hypotheses, however, come a long way for such a short time, and it is not
too much to expect that assessments for the future can be
made.   Assessments of the emergence of collective bargaining and widespread trade unionism in academic settings too
often revolve around a narrow discussion of the perquisites
of unions and their ideological demands, ignoring totally the
special qualities of academic institutions and libraries.   Libraries have a special effect on the life of the mind; so do
unions.   In speaking of the future, Benjamin Aaron, a widely-
regarded labor lawyer and recently chairman of a special
committee established by the California legislature to advise
it on collective bargaining legislation for public employees,
makes a different sort of assessment with emphasis on the
institution instead of on the union.

            What is missing from this vision of the future
            [when unionism is widespread], or at least dimly
            perceived, is a quality of life in our colleges and

universities in which eccentricity and nonconformity
can still flourish, in which distinguished scholarship is honored despite its lack of 'relevance'--
that mean little word; in which cost-benefit analysis
is not the sole basis on which the value of every
course or degree program is judged; and in which
these institutions, in addition to administering to
the contemporary needs of their students and helping to solve some of the problems faced by the
broader community, remain the guardians and
transmitters of the world's cultural heritage. [10]

The growth of unions in libraries is fifty years old,
but the present growth is unprecedented in its size and proportion to former occurrences. No doubt this growth is
strongly correlated with the recent rise of unionism among
university and college faculties. Unions, now that nearly
twenty-five per cent of the American labor force belongs to
one, are an accepted fact of life. [11] So are the formation
and organization of them, according to laws that establish
rules and procedures for actions which are permissible and
not permissible.

In 1935 the United States Congress passed the National
Labor Relations Act, the Wagner Act. In 1947 the Congress
altered this law, because of the Taft-Hartley amendments,
calling it the Labor Management Relations Act, and in 1959
the Congress again changed the law to the Labor-Management
Reporting and Disclosure Act, because of the Landrum-Grif-
fin amendments. This law, known commonly in legal and
industrial relations circles as "the Act," derives its authority
from the constitutional clause affecting the congressional regulation of interstate commerce, and its general purpose is

...to provide orderly and peaceful procedures for
preventing the interference by [employers or em-
ployees] with the legitimate rights of the other, to
protect the rights of individual employees in their
relations with labor organizations whose activities
affect commerce, to define and proscribe practices
on the part of labor and management which affect
commerce and are inimical to the general welfare,
and to protect the rights of the public in connection
with labor disputes affecting commerce. [12]

This Federal legislation regarding the practices of

collective bargaining affects only those libraries in the private sector of the economy; that is, libraries which are part of a private educational institution or part of an organization subject to the Federal legislation. Despite this limited jurisdiction, those states and municipalities that have authorized collective bargaining for their employees often follow the guidelines established in the Federal legislation and the legal precedents established by court action or the administrative agency provided by the Act, the National Labor Relations Board.

In 1935 the Congress did not envisage that the legislative descendant of the Wagner Act would be used to regulate labor disputes in libraries, but the law is progressive, and subject to continuing interpretation and change. The following discussion of several cases outlines the decisions of the National Labor Relations Board with respect to unions and libraries, and demonstrates the changing character of the law. These cases involve the denial and assertion of jurisdiction of the Act over private universities and libraries, definition of communities of interest and the appropriate constituencies of the units for collective bargaining, and codification of the difficult question of what characterizes a supervisor in libraries.

The National Labor Relations Board rendered an important decision in December 1951. In Trustees of Columbia University[13] the Board reviewed the then recently enacted Taft-Hartley amendments to the National Labor Relations Act and concluded that

> ...the activities of Columbia University affect commerce sufficiently to satisfy requirements of the statute and the standards established by the Board for the normal exercise of its jurisdiction.... [14]

As a discretionary matter, however, the Board declined to assert such jurisdiction because of statements in the House Conference Report[15] that seemed to indicate approval of what the Report believed to have been the Board's pre-1974 practice of declining, in the exercise of its discretion, to assert jurisdiction over certain nonprofit organizations. [16] The Board held that

> ...we do not believe that it would effectuate the policies of the Act for the Board to assert jurisdiction over a nonprofit, educational institution where the activities involved are noncommercial in nature

and intimately connected with the charitable purposes and educational activities of the institution.[17]

   In June 1970 the Board reversed its 1951 ruling with
a benchmark decision that asserted jurisdiction over eleemos-
ynary organizations.   The language of Section 14(c) of the
Act does not compel the Board to assert jurisdiction.   It
does manifest rather a congressional policy favoring assertion
where the Board finds that the operations of a class of employees exercise a substantial affect on commerce.   In Cornell University[18] the Board found extensive evidence at the
hearing to document the claim that educational institutions
have a massive impact on interstate commerce, reflecting
the recent growth of universities, and the Board asserted
jurisdiction over those private colleges and universities whose
operations have a substantial affect on such commerce to insure a uniform application of the national labor policy.

   One of the contenders in this case--the Association of
Cornell Employees-Libraries (ACE)--consisting of approximately 270 nonprofessional, nonsupervisory employees of the
Cornell University Libraries, requested that they be considered a separate unit for the purposes of collective bargaining.
ACE held that the Libraries constituted a separate administrative unit in Cornell's organizational structure and that the
work performed in this separate unit was distinct from the
work of other such employees at the University.   In its ruling against ACE's contention for a separate unit the Board
held:

> Although ACE has acted informally in behalf of the li-
> brary employees in the handling of grievances, it has
> never negotiated a collective bargaining contract for
> them, nor has it been recognized as their bargaining
> representative.   Apart from the fact that these em-
> ployees have organized themselves separately, there
> is little which justifies establishing a separate bargain-
> ing unit for them.   Their work and skills are similar
> to those of many other employees on the Ithaca cam-
> pus, and they enjoy the same working conditions and
> benefits as other Cornell employees.   In view of the
> foregoing, we do not find that the library employees
> possess a sufficiently separate community of interest
> which would warrant establishing the separate unit
> sought by ACE. [19]

The Board defined the appropriate unit, within the meaning
of Section 9(b) of the Act, as: "All nonsupervisory, nonpro-

fessional employees of Cornell University within the State of New York, excluding professional employees and supervisors as defined in the Act. "[20]

The Board, having asserted jurisdiction over new territory and having defined the appropriate nonprofessional unit in this important decision, moved further in two decisions of April 1971. In C. W. Post Center of Long Island University[21] the Board defined the unit and asserted jurisdiction over professional employees working at private, not-for-profit educational institutions; and in Long Island University (Brooklyn Center)[22] the Board clarified further the constituency of the professional unit.

In C. W. Post the petitioner, the United Federation of College Teachers, sought to include librarians in the bargaining unit with faculty, arguing that they shared the same community of interest. The employer, Long Island University, held that librarians should not be included in the same unit with faculty members. This divergence first broached the issue of what constituted professionality for librarians under the law. Insofar as each of the twenty-seven librarians at C. W. Post held the Master of Arts degree in library science, which is widely considered to be the professional degree, the problem of professionality was merely opened and did not become an issue of serious contention. The Board found that the C. W. Post librarians were professional employees within the meaning of Section 2(12) of the Act. Because they engaged in functions closely related to teaching and because they shared many of the same benefits as faculty, the Board declared the librarians to have a community of interest with the faculty and included them in the faculty unit. The Board's discussion defined the following professional unit as appropriate for the purposes of collective bargaining within the meaning of Section 9(b) of the Act.

> All professional employees ... including professors, associate professors, assistant professors, instructors, adjunct professors, adjunct associate professors, adjunct assistant professors, lecturers, professional librarians, guidance counselors, and research associates; but excluding all other employees, student assistants ... and supervisors as defined in the Act. [23]

In the case following, Long Island University (Brooklyn Center), decided on the same day (April 20, 1971), the

Board denied the employer's contention that faculty should be separated from the unit containing librarians and other professional employees of the institution. In denying this position, the Board reiterated its foregoing definition of the appropriate unit and solidified its ruling that professional employees, save those excepted in administrative or supervisory posts, must organize campus-wide.

By adjudicating the rights of clerical workers in Cornell University and those of professional employees in the two Long Island University cases, and, by holding that each separate community of interest--clerical and professional-- must organize throughout a university or college campus, the Board has firmly defined the two distinct units appropriate for collective bargaining within educational institutions and sharply etched the extremities of the communities of interest. Additionally, within the guidelines of the Act, the Board has made it difficult for librarians, professional and nonprofessional, to organize separately and apart from the rest of their campus. Librarians seeking so to organize in all likelihood will have to argue before the Board for the differentiation of professional librarians from faculty, of nonprofessional employees from other personnel similarly employed throughout the institution, and for the uniqueness of the library.

With jurisdiction asserted and constituency of the bargaining units determined, at least for the moment, the important piece of legal business remaining to libraries is the definition of a supervisor within the library setting and within the indicia of Section 2(11) of the Act.

Of all the customs surrounding trade unions, one of the most inviolable is that management and its representatives cannot join. Supervisors are representatives of management, if not management itself, whether they define themselves that way or not, and, as such, they are specifically enjoined from entering the bargaining unit under the Act. Presently, there are two controversies surrounding supervisors. First, in libraries it is understood that there exist three species of supervisor: 1) the professional supervisor of professional employees; 2) the nonprofessional supervisor of nonprofessional employees; and 3) the professional supervisor of nonprofessional employees. It is also understood that the first two species of supervisor are not eligible for union membership in their respective bargaining units. But there is dispute over the professional supervisor of nonpro-

fessional employees. One argument holds that no supervisor
can join any unit. The opposing argument holds that the professional supervisor of nonprofessionals has no conflict with
his community of interest and therefore may join the professional union. It is easy to see why in libraries facing
unionization that this is a central question; the size of the
professional unit is directly affected, and with it the possible
success or failure of a unionization effort.

The second controversy surrounding supervisors is:
how much time does a supervisor have to supervise in order
to be a supervisor for the purposes of collective bargaining?
This is not a trivial question for libraries. Many people in
libraries, while meeting some of the supervisory indicia of
the Act, tend to be more readily described as consultants
than supervisors, given the independent nature of library
work. A section head in a catalog department, for example,
may appear to a junior cataloger more as a reviser and consultant than as a direct foremanesque supervisor, and the
section head may think of himself in that way as well. Both
of these are important questions in unionizing libraries, for
they help determine the size and constituency of the bargaining unit, which may, in turn, determine the life or death of
the union.

In three cases the National Labor Relations Board has
spoken to these two controversies, although in at least one
instance the decision is under appeal. The Board undertook
these matters in Fordham University,[24] where it held,

> ...the AAUP would include, and the Employer
> [Fordham] would exclude, all professional librar-
> ians. While the librarians do not have faculty
> status, it is clear that some of them are profes-
> sional employees and should be included in the unit.
> The record does not contain sufficient evidence to
> determine whether any of them are supervisors.
> Accordingly, any librarian whose status either as
> a professional employee or as a supervisor is in
> dispute may vote subject to challenge. [23]

The Board followed with the important Adelphi University[26] decision in Spring 1972, from which derives the
"Adelphi Rule." In this case a faculty member, who had
some of the indicia of supervisor with regard to his secretary, was in dispute. The Board ruled that he was properly
to be included in a bargaining unit of faculty members since

he spent less than fifty per cent of his time "supervising"
non-unit personnel, and clearly did not "supervise" any persons in the unit sought; he was not to be considered a "supervisor" within the meaning of the Act.   The Board explained:

> ...an employee whose principal duties are of the
> same character as that of other bargaining unit
> employees should not be isolated from them be-
> cause of a sporadic exercise of supervisory author-
> ity over non-unit personnel.   No danger of conflict
> of interest within the unit is presented, nor does
> the infrequent exercise of supervisory authority so
> ally such an employee with management as to cre-
> ate a more generalized conflict of interest of the
> type envisioned by Congress in adopting Section
> 2(11) of the Act.   Moreover, we have made it clear
> that such an employee is considered to be in the
> unit only to the extent that his interests as a non-
> supervisory employee are involved. [27]

The Board codified the "Adelphi Rule" in another decision, New York University, [28] handed down in July 1973.
In this case, rendered more complex by representational
hearings between the American Association of University Professors and the American Federation of Teachers, the Board
decided:

> Unlike faculty, the function of a librarian may
> change with title, and promotion may depend on
> the existence of a vacancy.   Further distinguish-
> ing librarians from faculty are their regular work-
> week; lack of proportional representation in the
> university senate ... and, perhaps more basically,
> the fact that they are not considered faculty.   On
> the other hand, they are a professional group,
> charged with the responsibility for accumulating
> appropriate materials and serving the other mem-
> bers of the university in that respect, and most
> fringe benefits are available to them.   We conclude
> that they possess a sufficient community of interest
> to be included in the unit, as a closely allied pro-
> fessional group whose ultimate function, aiding and
> furthering the educational and scholarly goals of the
> university, converges with that of the faculty, though
> pursued through different means and in a different
> manner.

Their interest in the unit does not, however,
put an end to the matter, as the Employer also
argues for their exclusion, in whole or in part, as
supervisors. Initially we reject the Employer's
contention that all professional librarians possess
supervisory authority over non-unit employees to a
degree requiring their exclusion. The Employer's
brief concedes that eight librarians do not perform
supervisory duties as part of their everyday work.
Additionally, however, as we noted in Adelphi,
supra, the supervisory exclusion is primarily aimed
at situations where this authority is regularly exercised over employees whose inclusion in the unit
is sought by the unit.... Applying this standard
[of the 'Adelphi Rule'] we shall exclude as supervisors only those professional librarians who supervise other employees in the unit or who spend
more than fifty per cent of their time supervising
non-unit employees.

Although testimony was adduced by the Employer
and the AAUP on both the extent and exercise of
the professional librarians' supervisory authority,
there is a basic conflict which the record does not
contain enough detail to resolve. Professional librarians whose supervisory status has not been
stipulated to, or which cannot be resolved by agreement among the parties pursuant to the criteria we
have found applicable, will be permitted to vote
subject to challenge. [29]

These are significant findings that should greatly affect
the growth of unions in libraries. As with all adjudications,
there are persons not content with the decisions of the NLRB,
and in many legal areas controversy continues and litigation
is pending. Nonetheless, this is what has been produced so
far, and it is considerably less cohibiting than what preceded
it. [30]

The labor law was written for industrial contexts, not
libraries: the law has been interpreted, changed, and expanded in light of those industrial contexts. The American
labor movement has firm traditions at this point, and the
precedents and interpretations of the labor law are based in
large measure on those traditions. In expanding jurisdiction
to academic settings the Board has taken care not to disturb
its previous tillage. In its findings for colleges and universities the Board has written decisions that are condign with
its previous work for industrial settings.

The work of factories, however, is not the work of libraries; yet if librarians wish to unionize rapidly and effectively the surest road to success lies in making the actions of labor in libraries congruent to the traditions of the labor movement and the labor law. For purposes of unionization and for recognition under the law, the labor structure in libraries must be made similar to that of the labor structure in industrial settings and factories.

Libraries are not factories. They are secondary intellectual institutions that derive their traditions and dependence from broader normative systems--usually a university or a community--which uphold or support primary intellectual traditions. Nor are those who work in libraries factory workers. While librarians need not be intellectuals, they, like their institutions, must embrace primary intellectual traditions--among them scholarly teaching and research-- contained in the broader system.

One of the important primary intellectual traditions is the freedom of inquiry: to search for truth and to base action on its discovery--academic freedom. It is in the service of this freedom that libraries are most useful; it is in the pursuit of this freedom that librarians, in varying degree, dedicate their efforts. Academic freedom and the purpose of libraries are intertwined, and they are based on intellectual actions, not political actions.

Unions, however, are political, not intellectual--political in the sense of wishing to shift or to wrest power or influence from the present order. The steps taken by unions to organize are political, and the steps taken by management to discourage or limit the growth and strength of a union are also political. When a union enters a library, whatever the merits of unionization may be, it moves the work of a library from an intellectual context into a political arena which subverts the primary intellectual traditions of the institution and which jeopardizes the freedom of inquiry for the scholarly community.

It is my view that when a union forms within a library, whatever the constituency of the parties in interest, that a class struggle between the library administration and a group of library professionals results. Unionization in libraries is the setting for conflict over control on institutional resources with respect to the conditions of employment (the

non-economic issues), and it is the setting for conflict over
a re-distribution of authority. Forming a union in re
the benefits of employment (the economic issues), while important, is considerably less so. In this interpretation,
unions organize for control of institutional power, not exclusively for a greater share of economic resources.

The economic uncertainty of our time may give trade
unionism some appeal to librarians on the basis of bread-
and-butter issues. It has long been an incontrovertible assertion of modern civilization that everyone is underpaid,
that everyone deserves a larger salary and greater benefits
of employment. But people, realistically, do not become librarians or choose to work in libraries because they feel
they will get rich. Simultaneously, they realize that the resources of libraries are limited. In the public sector, it is
usually some other agency of government that determines the
budget. The library can lobby for its fair share in municipal or state allocations, but how great is its influence? In
the private sector, the economic limitations are even more
obvious, and, with the recent abdication of the Federal government in educational spending, the constraints on the private institutions are even greater. Trade unionism may
effectuate salary increases, salary parity, adjustment of in-
equities, and other improvements on bread-and-butter issues,
but it cannot do very much because libraries do not control
large economic resources.

Unions in libraries can achieve only limited success
in improving the benefits of employment. They can cause,
however, significant change in the conditions of employment.
Unions arise in libraries over conflict of the conditions of
employment (however clothed in economic rationales), and
these are political, not economic, matters. A group seeking
larger voice in the administrative affairs and decisions of the
library chooses one of several channels to shift the balance
of power in its favor. A shift in hegemony requires collective action to resolve the conflict of governance. Collectivi-
zation can come in the muted form of what is popularly
called in a tautological slogan "participatory democracy," or
it can come in the harsher form of trade unionism. [31]

The conditions of conflict and dissatisfaction within a
library must be severe and the level of frustration high before a group will undergo a transmutation of identity from
professional to trade unionist, however disguised and palat-
able trade unionism may be made to seem. Once such a

transmutation occurs, a middle-level group of professional
librarians creates a class conflict between an upper-level
group of library administrators for a share of political control over the institution in which the middle-level group en-
lists support from and eventually demands supremacy over a
lower-level group of nonprofessional employees.   The efforts
of a middle-level professional group to form a trade union
for the purposes of obtaining a share in institutional governance is a new turn of events in trade unionism since the
founding of the American Federation of Labor in 1886 and
likewise unique in librarianship.

Let me illustrate both my hypothesis of class conflict
where a middle-level professional group interested in political
questions has engaged in conflict with management, has dominated the nonprofessional worker, and has removed, in large
measure, the traditional bread-and-butter issues of trade
unionism from the arena of conflict, and this new development in the history of trade unionism, by drawing examples
from the experience of the University of Chicago Library.

The union effort arose at Chicago in February 1971
with a group of librarians and support staff asserting that
they held jointly a community of interest, apart from the
university faculty and other university employees, and accordingly seeking recognition from the Library for their union.
The University denied this recognition.   Subsequent legal
action, following the indicia of Section 9(b1) of the Act, saw
this union bifurcated into two groups in accord with the precedents, one for the professionals, the other for the cler-
icals.   At this juncture the union leaders (mostly professionals) decided to hold the case of the clerical workers and
support staff in abeyance, until that of the professionals was
resolved and recognition granted them.   This latter case has
yet to be resolved or recognized, for it turns on the constituency of the unit.   The library administration asserts that
supervisors, quite forbidden by the Act to do so, have joined
the professional bargaining unit.   But who is a supervisor?
The union argues that those persons seen as supervisors by
the library administration are, in fact, not supervisors within the meaning of the Act, nor within the findings of the New
York University case, for these professionals assert that they
have never exercised supervisory responsibility and authority
within the Act's stipulated indicia and therefore 1) were not
supervisors and 2) could join the professional unit that is
striving to organize for the purposes of collective bargaining.
To complicate further this dispute, a non-supervisory, pro-

fessional member of the staff filed a complaint of unfair labor
practice against the Library in which was charged that the
professional union was a "company union" because it contained supervisors. [32]

It seems clear that the professional group acted in a
political manner by excluding the non-professional group from
first chance at collective bargaining, and that by including
controversial people in the unit, that is people who might be
determined to be supervisors, who were also the ones who
organized the unit, the professional group sought not ready
and certain recognition for their union, but a re-distribution
of authority and power, sharing more of it with the library
administration, as a direct result of unionizing.   Matters
more or less rested until 15 June 1973.   On that date, in an
all-library meeting, the administration announced the termination of six vacant positions and the dismissal of six library
employees, four of whom were active or leaders in the
unionization movement.   The reason offered for these terminations was economic necessity; no other issues were involved.

The union responded to these terminations, calling
them "firings," by a series of picket lines and on 25 June it
staged a one-day strike against the Library, which it described as ninety per cent effective.   The heavy majority of
active marching strikers--not employees who arranged not to
come to work for one reason or another--were members of
the clerical union, not the professional one, which further
supports my view of lower-level domination by the middle-
level group.   While unionists were striking in Chicago, others
were striving in Las Vegas at the annual conference of the
American Library Association for recognition of Chicago's
problem.   Several actions were initiated in Las Vegas to
consider the situation at the University of Chicago Library.

The Provost of the University appointed on 27 June a
"Committee to Review Certain Matters Pertaining to the Library," which reported that the actions of the library administration in meeting their budget constraints were by and
large justifiable, that is, the terminations were by and large
justifiable on economic grounds.   The union took exception
to this report.   At the present several legal actions are
under way, and no doubt more are contemplated. [33]   All of
these legal maneuvers are political actions striving to resolve
political questions, and they are divorced from the intellectual purposes of the library.

These actions reflect the struggle of two elements, one seeking greater power, the other striving to retain control, with the third element, the nonprofessional union, subverted to the professional one. Helmut Schelsky, writing on the wider setting of disorder in the German universities, contributed a piece entitled "The Strategy of the 'Conquest of the System': The Long March Through the Institutions" to the Frankfurter Allgemeine Zeitung in which he reached similar conclusions about institutional governance. Professor Schelsky writes:

> The strategy of 'conquest of the system' [Systemüberwindung] ... is bound up with the aim of establishing a system of social supremacy over the workers under a new ruling class. I regard the ideological components of this strategy ... as only a facade which hides a purposeful and realistic machiavellian political strategy of the pursuit of power. Because its fundamental principle consists in turning the basic values of the system into a weapon against the system, the inherent defense mechanism of the system cannot work effectively. Neither can an idealistic value-orientation nor the institutional defenses be effective since these strategists act 'legally' ...

Schelsky continues,

> Simone Weil rendered a judgment on our time when she said: 'Both the ego and the social are idols.' Indeed since the freedom of the individual and social justice are the bases of our society, all that has to be done is to idolize them in order to discredit them and the human reality in which they are embodied. [34]

Libraries will not continue to be institutions for intellectual work if such idolization is permitted, if those within libraries discredit the validity of criteria for intellectual performance, if they reject the obligation to conform with those criteria, and if they supersede them by political criteria in matters of library practice.

In the illustrative case of the University of Chicago Library, the union members, having acted on the bases of political considerations, raised a cry of outrage on the termination of four of their members, which led to a strike. They

stated that they viewed the actions of management as political, that they were frustrated by the political decision that
led to the dismissals.   They declared they had been the un-
toward victims of political decision.   Their cry of outrage
is hypocritical, for they, as well as the library administrators, acted on the bases of political considerations.   In some
sense and to some extent they are right that political considerations were used in their termination.   But if they are
right in that sense and to that extent they have only themselves to thank.   Those who live by politics in universities
will also perish by politics, and the same is true for libraries.

In a certain sense everything is political, quite apart
from the inculcation of particular articles of substantive political belief; but in the same sense everything a human being
does is religious and the more zealous the religious person,
the more emphatically he insists on the subjection of every
action to the discipline of a comprehensive and pervasive
code of religious conduct.   So it is with art: everything we
do has its aesthetic side and aesthetic actions have costs and
repercussions in every other sphere of life.   In this same
sense libraries are political.   In most countries, libraries
are supported by the state, which means that the magnitude
of financial support is a political decision.   Libraries are
also political in the sense that they assist in training people
for the performance of certain roles, important in the functioning of society, and by performing those roles libraries
enable society to be what it is.   There are other ways in
which libraries--and their governing institutions--are political.

Yet there is one way--and the most important and
fundamental of all--in which they are not political.   Libraries contribute to the discovery and teaching of truths that are
true regardless of who rules and how he rules, regardless
of the political standpoints and desires of librarians, researchers, and students, regardless of the desires of politicians, professional or amateur.   Intellectual activities are
categorically different from political activities.   Although
political and intellectual activities are intertwined in innum-
erable Gordian knots, they are not identical.   Political institutions are not intellectual institutions, even though political
institutions have substantive intellectual elements.   Intellectual institutions are not political institutions although they
have many ties with politics.   What is essential in an intellectual institution is not political.   If those who are appointed
to work in libraries and if those who are admitted to study

in them act politically, in disregard of and with harm to cul-
tivating scientific and scholarly truths, they are to that extent not giving their minds to that for which they were appointed or admitted.

The nineteenth and early twentieth centuries have low
standing and are in ill-repute among the bien pensants of
progress. So-called "Victorian" morality, ambition, respectability, inequality are a few of the features of that age
which arouse contemporary disapprobation. Another feature
of that celebrated age of bourgeois society, quand la vie
était belle et douce, that first evoked the animosity of its
collectivist critics was the "separation of the spheres" wherein the economic, the religious, the political, the artistic
were regarded as separate and distinct from each other, each
to be carried on at its appropriate time and each to be regarded as having a body of rules and necessities appropriate
and suitable to itself. Of course, no complete separation of
politics, economics, culture, religion and so forth from each
other was possible. Still, an effort was made to keep the
spheres from each other, and to some extent the effort was
successful. Results were not uniformly beneficial, but genuine achievement and genuine benefit did result from this
effort to delineate the sphere of political action vis-à-vis the
intellectual sphere. That the separation would never be complete was evident; nor was such a complete separation wholly
desirable.

The principle of the separation of the spheres has
much to recommend it. The principle recognizes the plurality of human interests and that each interest and its associated activity have standards and criteria appropriate to
it and not to other interests. Even though we recognize now
that the collaboration or integration of the spheres is as important as their autonomy, we must acknowledge that whether
integrated or autonomous each is distinctive. It is a matter
of urgency that librarians recognize this distinctiveness in
the relations between the spheres of intellect and politics.
Only by recognizing this distinctiveness can the proper balance between them be found and only by so doing can the intellectual purposes of the library be secure. In cases of
unionization, a library, by refusing or neglecting the separation of the sphere, confounds its intellectual role with
political issues. Political actions and counter-actions, however disguised as intellectual deeds or economic constraints,
can be bitterly divisive, sadly sundering a library and causing staff morale and performance to decline. The unhappi-

ness that characterizes a library so divided and rent over
political considerations is a misfortune of the first order and
one that lessens or negates the central purpose of libraries.

Unionization in libraries will continue to grow and
spread among librarians and library staffs for two reasons.
The first is economic, from which all unions have derived
their raison d'être in this country since the 1880s. If the
present state of the job market continues where supply out-
strips demand (in 1971 the number of white-collar and professional employees unable to find work doubled over that of
1970[35]) and professional workers continue to find their formerly advantageous market position eroding, if unable to depend upon scarcity and uniqueness to ensure favorable bargaining positions, librarians will seek job security and benefits through unionization. The present state of the labor law
points in this direction and, as the labor force shifts to a
higher percentage of white-collar workers and a lower one of
blue-collar workers, labor unions will be squeezed for economic survival and forced to unionize public and private institutions. [36]

The second reason unions will continue to grow in libraries is the unabated tendency that came in the 1960s to
disperse the authority of institutional governance, coupled
with internal discontents over the administration of the library which makes such dispersal desirable in the eyes of
unionists. The desire for a re-distribution of authority remains great, and there is nothing to indicate that it will
diminish or that the class conflict resulting between professionals and administrators will abate. Both these reasons
indicate the continued growth of library unions and both un-
derscore the need for recognizing the separation of the
spheres of intellect and politics.

To retain the integrity of the library as an intellectual
institution, to preserve internal harmony, and to prevent dissolution of the library's strengths, (1) librarians, administrators and unionists alike, should adjudicate personnel questions, whether collective or individual, without recourse to
political ideology by insisting on the separation of intellect
and politics; and (2) librarians should undertake to clarify the
liberal conception of intellectual freedom and action apart
from political action for both persons and institutions. In a
difficult time for libraries, financially and organizationally,
when the pressures for a shift in hegemony from administrators to middle-level professionals are greater than before,

only such a clarification can provide the charter for the necessary autonomy and integration of the spheres of intellect and politics, two vital spheres in our lives and in those of our libraries.

Notes

1. This article is adopted from an address entitled "Unions and Libraries: A View from Chicago," given 25 October 1973 at the biennial conference of the Georgia Library Association, Savannah, to the College and University Section.

2. Bernard Berelson, "Library Unionization," Library Quarterly IX (October 1939): 477-510.

3. Melvin S. Goldstein, Collective Bargaining in the Field of Librarianship (Brooklyn, New York: Pratt Institute, 1968); also Joseph S. Hopkins, "Unions in Libraries," Library Journal, October 1, 1969, pp. 3403-7; Karl Nyren, "Librarians and Labor Unions," Library Journal, June 1, 1967, pp. 2115-21; Tracy H. Ferguson, "Collective Bargaining in Universities and Colleges," Journal of the College and University Personnel Association XX (November 1968): 1-29.

4. Joseph W. Gabarino, "Creeping Unionism and the Faculty Labor Market," in Margaret Gordon (ed.), Higher Education and the Labor Market (New York: McGraw-Hill Book Co., 1973), pp. 8, 9.

5. Eugene C. Lee and Frank M. Bowen, The Multicampus University (New York: McGraw-Hill Book Co., 1971).

6. Gabarino, op. cit., p. 4.

7. Richard H. LeFrancois, "Bargaining in Higher Education: A Maze of State Legislation," NSP Forum IV (November-December 1970), pp. 14-16.

8. Seymour Martin Lipset and Everett C. Ladd, Jr., Varieties of Political Expression in Sociology (Chicago: The University of Chicago Press, 1972), pp. 197-235.

9. J. W. Goethe, Maximen und Reflexionen: Nach dem Handschriften des Goethe und Schiller-Archivs, hrsg.

von Max Hecker (Weimar: Schriften der Goethe-
Gesellschaft, 1907), v. 21, p. 125, no. 575. My
translation.

10. Benjamin Aaron, Some Painful Realities (Los Angeles:
     UCLA Institute of Labor and Industrial Relations,
     1971), pp. 14-15.

11. Bureau of National Affairs, Labor Relations Yearbook
     (Washington, D. C.: Bureau of National Affairs,
     1969), p. 825.

12. Labor Management Relations Act, as Amended by Public
     Law 86-257, 1959. Section 1(b).

13. 97 NLRB No. 424.

14. Ibid. at 425.

15. House Report No. 510, 80th Cong., 1st Sess., p. 32.

16. See discussion in Columbia University, supra at 426-27.

17. Ibid. at 427.

18. 183 NLRB No. 41.

19. Ibid. at 44.

20. Ibid. at 45.

21. 189 NLRB No. 109.

22. 189 NLRB No. 110.

23. 189 NLRB No. 109 at 16; 77 LRRM 1005-6.

24. 193 NLRB No. 23. Related cases are Catholic Univer-
     sity 201 NLRB No. 145; Syracuse University 204
     NLRB No. 85.

25. Ibid. at 22.

26. 195 NLRB No. 107.

27. Ibid. at 644.

28.   205 NLRB No. 16; 83 LRRM 1549.

29.   Ibid. at 12-14.

30.   For some bibliographical assistance, I wish to acknowl-
      edge Mr. Stanley Irvine of the University of Chicago
      Law School Library.

31.   For a side discussion of "quasi-unions" vide Gail
      Schlacter, "Quasi Unions and Organizational Hegem-
      ony within the Library Field," Library Quarterly
      XLIII (July 1973): 185-198.

32.   National Labor Relations Board. Division of Judges.
      Cases No. 13-RC-12404; 13-RC-12619; 13-RM-1012;
      13-CA-11447.

33.   R. E. Michener, "The University of Chicago Library
      Union: Rise and Decline." Unpublished manuscript,
      University of Chicago Graduate School of Business,
      1971. The interpretations of these events vary. For
      other accounts vide Library Journal August 1973,
      pp. 2223-4, 2235; American Libraries September
      1973, p. 460 and November 1973, p. 592. In-house
      publications include the "Librarian Jackdaw" and
      "Newsletter--U.C. Library Staff Organizing Com-
      mittee" for the union; the library administration
      prints "Staff Information Bulletin." Transcripts of
      hearings may be had from the Chicago Regional
      Office, National Labor Relations Board, Sylvia Pat-
      terson, Hearing Officer.

34.   Helmut Schelsky, "Die Strategie der Systemüberwindung:
      Der lange Marsch durch die Institutionen," Frank-
      furter Allgemeine Zeitung, December 10, 1971. No.
      286, p. 12. My translation.

35.   "Household Data," Employment and Earnings XVIII
      (September 1971): 42.

36.   Robert B. Cooney, "Loosening the White Collar,"
      American Federationist LXXII (July 1967): 19-23;
      Bureau of National Affairs, op. cit., p. 737.

BUSINESS LIBRARIES: ROLE AND FUNCTION IN INDUSTRIAL AMERICA*

Mildred S. Myers & William C. Frederick

Harry Brown's You Can Profit from a Monetary Crisis, Studs Terkel's Working, Peter F. Drucker's Management--all best sellers in the same week and all to be found in the business library![1, 2] Adam Smith's Supermoney, John Kenneth Galbraith's The New Industrial State, Charles Reich's The Greening of America--all best sellers in recent years and all to be found in the business library!

A business librarian who is aware that today's business literature is often represented on the best-seller lists can reasonably wonder why this exciting body of writing has sometimes been treated like a stepchild or a skeleton in the library family closet. Treated this way it has been and still is, as a study of the standard social science resource texts will quickly illustrate. B. F. Hoselitz's A Reader's Guide to the Social Sciences, even in its newest edition, gives cursory one-paragraph mention--in a chapter on "Economics"--to business periodicals.[3] The new edition (1973) of C. M. White's Sources of Information in the Social Sciences devotes most of its "Economics and Business Administration" chapter to economics.[4] The business sources it mentions are traditional, covering banking, business history, accounting, and the like. There is only a perfunctory bow to "management," even though management, or administration, is essential to every institution in our society, be it government, education, health care, or industry. Even the texts on business literature ignore its excitement, variety, applicability, and importance. H. W. Johnson's How to Use the Business Library identifies more materials and covers a broader range of topics than did its earlier editions and is the most-up-to-date source text of its kind.[5] But here, too, the emphasis is on

*Reprinted by permission of the authors and publisher from Journal of Education for Librarianship, Summer 1974, pp. 41-52.

traditional, standard, accepted sources. There is nothing wrong with noting these standard items; they continue to be vital parts of any business collection. But why does none of these texts describe the whole picture? Why have we not recognized the breadth, diversity, and importance of the literature of business and management? And why is it looked upon, by so many scholars and librarians, as merely a branch of economics, with no life of its own, an applied, practical sub-part of the more respectable mass of economic theory?

There is no single answer to these questions, but there are some possible explanations. It is sometimes impossible to draw clear dividing lines between "economic" literature and "business" literature.

> When one comes to examine the 'whole' of this general sort of literature, and not merely its 'parts, ' he finds no clearly marked dividing lines. All items must be regarded as falling in a spectrum, extending perhaps from a mathematical formulation of international trade to a 'come-on' flyer in Canadian uranium stocks. The differences are notable at the extremes, but there are no sharp breaks in the succession of types. Of course, the boundaries of ... 'economico-business literature' are also shadowy-- boundaries between economic and sociological, between business and technological, between 'political economic' and political, etc. [6]

The Development of Business Literature

In addition to being almost impossible to delineate business literature in any circumscribed form, as it exists today it is relatively new, in large part a 20th century development, although its roots go back nearly to Gutenberg's day. In The Historical Development of Economic and Business Literature, Arthur Cole notes that while agriculture was the main topic until the late 17th century, this early period also saw the forerunner to today's "how to get rich" best sellers, with the publication, in 1684, of The Pleasant Art of Money-Making. [7] The first public relations pieces also appeared in the 17th century, in the form of in-house defensive tracts, written in behalf of individual merchant companies and their activities.

Some important antecedents to modern economic-
business literature appeared during the 18th century, which
saw the first journals of price quotations for commodities
and other current-awareness literature, such as newsletters
of ship movements. Measurement, particularly in the form
of government statistical reports, also became important in
this period, especially in England. The first attempts to
synthesize information took the form of dictionaries or collections of information on various topics, the forerunners of
our business encyclopedias. Finally, and perhaps most importantly, this period saw the first attempts to describe or
analyze economic systems, with Adam Smith the best-known,
but not the only, actor in this scene.

By the late 18th century, increased trade, world-
wide, had made it impossible to depend on word-of-mouth or
letter as means of information exchange. The 19th century
brought increased government publication (in the U. S., notably
the censuses, of manufactures as well as of population) and
regular journals (such as Commercial and Financial Chronicle, still an important bi-weekly newspaper). Professional
society publications became important in this period, too,
with the advent of professional journals such as the Eco-
nomist and the London Statistical Society Journal. There
were publications from trade associations--the railroad group,
labor unions, chambers of commerce--and also from many
international congresses, such as the International Commercial Convention of 1868 and the International Statistics
Congresses, which ran from 1853 to 1874.

From "Business" to "Management"

From about 1885 on, the growth of technology resulting from the industrial revolution encouraged written
communication. Several major publishing houses, including
McGraw-Hill and Simmons Boardman, were begun by entre-
preneurs who saw an opportunity to make money in specialized business publications. During this period, too, government publication increased, as the regulatory agencies were
formed and began to issue instructions and reports. Many
more trade and professional associations were formed, e.g.,
the American Economic Association in 1885, as well as research agencies such as the National Bureau of Economic
Research (1920) and foundations such as the Carnegie Corporation (1911).

In the early 20th century, the idea of administration, or management, was linked to industry for the first time, most notably by Frederick Taylor, who introduced his theories of scientific management in a paper presented to the American Society of Mechanical Engineers in 1903. [8] Scholars still argue about the validity of Taylor's theories, but there is no argument about their importance to business literature. Taylor's writings signalled the emergence of the full-blown industrial order from its earlier beginnings in handicraft and small-scale entrepreneurial ventures. He glimpsed, as had Thorstein Veblen, the immense complexity of this industrial process and saw the need to explain and rationalize it for those whose responsibility it was to manage the system. [9, 10]

Cole points out three major themes in the period following 1885:

1) the realization that "principles" were possible with respect to business structures and performance;
2) abstractions of business functions--such as marketing, production, and finance--which tended to make all business institutions into an "extended kinship group";
3) the emergence of the college and university business schools which encouraged research and published research results. [11]

The literature of the period since Cole's book was written, from the mid-1950's until today, reflects each of these themes and illustrates their importance.

Business, business schools, and consequently, business literature have undergone, are still undergoing, a series of revolutions. By the beginning of this century, the industrial corporation had become an established feature of the economic and business scene, and the modern corporation is an organization in which corporate managers are in control of the institution's policies and operating procedures. The shift of corporate power from owners to managers has been referred to as "the managerial revolution," and this revolution spread through our society, becoming an "organizational revolution. "[12, 13, 14]

In the federal government, religious organizations, trade unions, colleges and universities, hospitals, and other aspects of American life, the manager, the bureaucrat, the administrator has emerged as the central focus of organiza-

tional life and seemingly the key element in the
successful life of the enterprise.... [15]

The "Theory vs. Practice" Dilemma

Responding to the managerial and organizational revolutions, as well as to other cultural factors, this country's
business schools underwent a revolution of their own in the
middle and late 1950's. The essence of it was to move from
specialized to generalized curricula, from short-run vocational preparation to long-run career preparation for managerial responsibilities, from an essentially trade-school outlook to one based on and drawing from the social, behavioral,
and quantitative sciences. These changes occurred partly in
response to demands from practicing businessmen for a curriculum more attuned to the rapidly evolving and highly complex world of management. However, one result of the
changes was that the gap between the immediate needs of
practicing managers and the scholarly disciplines of management academicians appeared to become larger. This gap
creates tensions which have implications for business literature.

The second-class citizenship often accorded to business literature, its place as a "poor relation" of economics
in the standard texts, reflects a more basic attitude among
some scholars toward business itself, its practitioners, its
teachers. It is not unusual, on a university campus, to find
the economics and political science departments looking down
their scholarly noses at the business school. Within the
business school itself, there may be friction between those
faculty members who teach in the behavioral science or business and society areas and those who teach the more "strictly
business" courses in accounting, finance, and production. In
truth, the faculty of a modern school of management is a
very heterogeneous group. Feelings and beliefs about business span a wide ideological spectrum, from those who support traditional business values to those who would change
the whole system, from those who are themselves in business
to those who consider themselves purely psychologists or political scientists or economists.

To carry this just one step further, business academicians themselves may tend to feel that they are scholars and
theoreticians, and they may be critical of the values of practicing managers, the very people who run the corporations

and financial institutions, the very people, in fact, who often have been graduated from business schools! There are a few academics who seem to have the impression that once their students get out into the corporation world, they will become heartless production machines reacting only to profit and loss figures. As a result, corporation executives may become defensive and sneer at the academics for being impractical dreamers. Neither group is entirely right, and neither is wholly wrong; it is not a simple question with a single answer. The attitudinal difficulties remain, but both groups now agree that the post-revolution business school has a far better chance of preparing future managers for an understanding of their world than did the older school. The tensions between the university and the practitioner's world (often seen between graduate library schools and working library managers as well) will remain and probably should, since they frequently take the form of dialog that is constructive to both participants.

Attitudes Affect Information Service

What has all this to do with business librarianship?

> There is one vital section of the community which has been left out and which is in fact always undervalued. We pay tribute to the importance of trade, but we despise the man who buys and sells. The food we eat, the clothes we wear, would be unobtainable without him: however vast our productivity, however efficient our industry, all would be useless without the skills of the entrepreneur. Without him we would starve. This is not a defense of capitalism: every state, however organized, must have experts in supply and demand, and ... this vital sector of the community is the least well-served with information services. [16]

Business librarianship has been affected by attitudes toward and debates about business as a profession. As a result, business literature is relegated to one paragraph of a chapter devoted to economics, and is unfamiliar to those who are at home with most material in the social sciences. If those whose specialty is information are not prepared to work with business information, their clientele will not be well-served. And yet, is it not possible that information

might be precisely what businesspeople need to tackle some
of the problems they face and some of the problems for which
society criticizes them?

> The problems that face the businessman are
> vast: they include languages, controls, the
> chauvinism of some governments, trade barriers,
> and many others--but the greatest problem is a
> lack of information. What makes it worse is
> the infuriating fact that the vast amount of this
> information is already published. It is our fault
> that the businessman doesn't get it, and our job
> is to see that he does. [17]

What Information Is Needed?

What are the types of information the businessperson
needs today? Anyone can quickly cite a few examples, such
as Statistics Sources, the Commerce Department's Business
Statistics and the Census of Business, Moody's Industrials,
and Standard and Poor's Standard Corporation Records. However, the enormous increase in the complexity and scale of
business operations today requires a more thorough answer.

Business people need directories--directories of companies, of services, of products, of professions, not only for
North America but for the whole world. Multinational corporations and international business are not merely catchword
phrases; they are reality. A directory showing the relationships between companies in different countries is a "must"
item today.

A businessperson needs periodicals, not only in his or
her own field of business, with which he or she is already
familiar, but in other fields, in order to find up-to-the-min-
ute information about new products, new markets, new
methods and procedures, new opportunities. He or she also
needs to be cognizant of on-going business research, and
periodicals are the forum in which much of this research is
reported. Many of these periodicals are issued by trade
publishers and are not difficult to identify, but many more
are issued by banks, professional and trade associations,
chambers of commerce, university business schools and research bureaus, and a host of other organizations. Although
often of great value to the businessperson, and sometimes
available free of charge or for nominal subscription rates,

those without access to business libraries frequently have no knowledge of their existence and no one to inform them.

Business people need newspapers, particularly the financial newspapers from all over the world. They need extracts and abstracts of the world's press reports on companies, trade, and products, and more and more of these, such as the Funk and Scott indexes, are becoming available with world-wide coverage. Many of them take the form of looseleaf services or indexes, and some are computer-produced and very current.

They need information on companies--who owns them, what their subsidiaries are and where, where their plants are, what they produce, their financial standing, what their sales volumes are, and on and on. They may be dealing with these companies, or they may be in competition with them.

They need statistics covering everything imaginable and some items one would not imagine. Getting these data is an enormous task, far bigger than any one library can handle, but we can get a great deal of help from governmental and quasi-governmental publications, ranging from the municipal to the international level. Without these statistics, people can neither understand the past nor forecast the uncertain future.

They need maps, commercial atlases, and other geographical information, primarily to help with marketing and distribution decisions. They need airline, train, bus, and shipping schedules, regulations and rates. They need to know about insurance rates, banking facilities, credit availability, interest rates, and much, much more. A great deal of this information can be found in business services, looseleaf compendia which are regularly updated (usually weekly). There are services providing company information, services explaining and interpreting government regulations (nationally and internationally), services specializing in international business, services covering specialized topics such as the environment and occupational safety and health.

In addition to all of this, there is available, if business people can find out about it, a vast amount of information about new techniques and trends in accounting, automation, cybernetics, data processing, distribution, human behavior, management, pricing, production, scheduling, and so on. In academic institutions and government agencies, research projects are undertaken regularly, projects that frequently finish up with a report to be filed somewhere. It is of no real value if the person who could really benefit from the information never gets to know about it.

Types of Business Libraries

The subject fields through which one must range to find the types of information business needs are many. Some business libraries try to provide a broad range of subject coverage, while others specialize in one informational area. The Directory of Special Libraries and Information Centers lists libraries specializing in business and business administration, and also in business history, accounting, advertising and marketing, banking and finance, industrial management, industrial relations, insurance, labor, management, personnel administration, and there are other specialties as well.[18]

In addition to subject specialties, business libraries may be divided by type of affiliation, and their functions and operations will differ somewhat from one organization to another, although they all have elements in common.

The library of a private concern, such as the corporation or bank library, is a very "special" library. It exists to serve the goals of the organization to which it is attached as a service function, and its collection will reflect the orientation of that organization. Its clientele are, for the most part, people engaged in the practical, day-to-day operations of the organization. They may not be scholars or researchers, but their need for information is as valid and perhaps more urgent than the researcher's needs. The nature of their work demands that they get information as quickly and as efficiently as possible.

The librarian in such an organization must live by the credo of service. It is not enough to have the information in the library; it must be made accessible, spoon-fed if necessary, to the person who needs it. The librarian does not point inquirers to Business Periodicals Index and expect them to do their own literature searches. Frequently, the search is done for an inquirer, who is presented with a list of articles or even with abstracts or photocopies of the articles themselves.

It is most likely that the concept of Selective Dissem-

ination of Information (SDI as it is frequently referred to)
was born in libraries attached to industrial corporations.
Many corporation librarians were using an SDI system long
before the phrase was coined.   Reduced to its simplest form,
it means seeing that the information is efficiently routed to
the person who can most benefit from it--a familiar practice
to most special librarians.   This means, obviously, that the
librarian must know the organization and the staff very well,
know the goals, plans, and interests of key departments and
people, and generally dedicate the library to the working
needs of the organization.

The business department or branch of a public library
has no such clearly-defined clientele, and so it must attempt,
in its coverage, to provide a wide range of information on
many business-related topics.   This may mean, depending on
budgetary considerations, that it cannot collect in great
depth in narrow or specialized subject areas, but must leave
those to the libraries attached to various business concerns.

The aim of the public business collection is breadth,
variety, and for the staff, versatility.   These qualities are
necessary for obvious reasons: one question may deal with
trade with China and the next with unemployment percentages
in Appalachia.   The rewards for the librarian here are different than those of the corporation librarian.   The public
business librarian may not be an integral member of a corporate team, but he or she is exposed to a huge and everchanging variety of people, questions, and information.

Public business libraries serve anyone who needs
them, from large corporations and universities with their
own libraries to the lone small businessman who has nowhere to turn but to the public library.   Therefore, it is
incumbent upon them to provide material that may not be
available anywhere else.   An expensive stock service which
would be used too infrequently in a university business library to justify its cost belongs in the public business library
located in the center of a city's financial and business district, where it can be consulted by anyone who needs it, including librarians from other concerns.   At the same time
the public library can serve as the nucleus of a business information network, referring questions to or borrowing materials from more specialized libraries in the area.

University business libraries in some ways must try
to cover the universe.   The librarian is part of the faculty,

sees the students daily and gets to know them, and practices
his or her own SDI system for the faculty members, because
he or she knows (or should know) their research and teaching
interests.

        The university business library's first responsibility
is to support the educational programs and faculty research
of the school, a charge which may cover a lot of ground.
The school may offer undergraduate, masters- and doctoral-
level courses in accounting, analytic methods, behavioral
science, organizational analysis, managerial economics,
marketing, finance, management of human resources, business and society, operations research, industrial relations,
international business, and other areas as well. Every
faculty member wants material for his or her area in the library. Obviously the library will be stronger in some areas
than in others, and it can draw on other libraries within the
university for material in peripheral areas. But the librarian does try to collect the basics in each area in which the
school offers a course.

        In addition, the library is the business library for the
university as a whole, which may mean supporting undergraduate courses taught in other departments and frequently
means serving as the university administration's own special
library for research and reference purposes. Along with the
business branch of the public library, the university business
library will be used heavily by individuals and corporations,
particularly by corporations which have established relationships with the school, so the university business library is
in contact with the world outside the university, too, and
therefore feels a very broad collection responsibility.

The Management Library in the '70s

        No one article can do full justice to a business library
or to business literature by simple description. But the
person who understands business libraries and their many
functions, who visualizes a collection which reflects the interests and research needs of accountants, economists, political scientists, psychologists, sociologists, lawyers, and
other such professionals, and which responds to the information needs of management practitioners, will see quickly that
business literature and business librarianship no longer de-
serve to be treated--if they ever deserved such treatment--
as stepchildren or poor relations of economics or any other

of the social sciences. A good management collection today
will include materials from all of the social sciences that
undergird the study of modern management practice.

Government "affirmative action" requirements, Ralph
Nader and the consumer movement, the women's movement,
the Black movement are societal developments which increase
and broaden a manager's need for an enormous range of information. One would not necessarily expect to find the
works of Charles Reich or Lewis Mumford in a business library, nor might one look for the Journal of Social Issues,
and 20 (or even 15) years ago, these types of books and
journals would not have been there. Until the last decade,
analyses of the relationship between corporations and the society within which they operate were few and far between,
and criticism of the corporation was even harder to find in
the business library. Today there is a constant stream of
such books as William Rodgers' abrasive critique, Corporate
Country, and the Committee for Economic Development's more
moderate policy statement, Social Responsibilities of Business
Corporations. Business and Society Review is only a few
years old, but has become a prestigious and highly respected
journal, and Harvard Business Review and California Management Review regularly feature articles on business's social role.

Management educators and management practitioners
are aware of the issues about which everyone is concerned--
pollution, energy shortages, discrimination, and the need for
meaningful work are only a few examples--and cognizant of
their relationship to management. Business literature reflects their awareness that any organization or system is
made up of people who must interact with each other and with
the institutions--local, national, and international--that form
our world. As a result, management collections are alive,
exciting, and fascinating in their diversity and breadth.

Notes

1. Publishers Weekly, Vol. 205, No. 18, May 6, 1974,
     p. 108.

2. The New York Times Book Review, May 12, 1974, p. 45.

3. Hoselitz, B. F., ed. A Reader's Guide to the Social
     Sciences. Rev. ed. New York, The Free Press, 1970.

4. White, C. M., and Associates. Sources of Information
    in the Social Sciences: a Guide to the Literature.
    2nd ed. Chicago, American Library Association,
    1973.

5. Johnson, H. W. How to Use the Business Library, with
    Sources of Business Information. 4th ed. Cincin-
    nati, South-western Publishing Co., 1972.

6. Cole, A. H. The Historical Development of Economic
    and Business Literature. Boston, Harvard Univer-
    sity, Graduate School of Business Administration,
    1957, p. 3.

7. Ibid., p. 7.

8. Hunt, E. E., Jr. Scientific Management Since Taylor.
    Easton, Pa., Hive Publishing Co., 1972, pp. 8-9.

9. Morison, E. E. Men, Machines, and Modern Times.
    Cambridge, Massachusetts Institute of Technology
    Press, 1966.

10. Veblen, T. B. The Instinct of Workmanship and the
    State of the Industrial Arts. New York, Macmillan,
    1914.

11. Cole, op. cit., p. 51.

12. See Berle, A. A., and Means, C. M. The Modern
    Corporation and Private Property. New York, Mac-
    millan, 1932.

13. See Burnham, James. The Managerial Revolution.
    New York, John Day, 1941.

14. See Boulding, K. E. The Organizational Revolution.
    New York, Harper, 1953.

15. Frederick, W. C. "The Cultural Matrix of Business
    Education," in: Clark, J. J., and Opulente, B. J.,
    eds. Professional Education for Business. Jamaica,
    New York, St. John's University Press, 1964, p. 1.

16. Thompson, Godfrey. "The Library's Economic Contri-
    bution." Unpublished address. London, July 1972,
    pp. 2-3.

17. Ibid., p. 4.

18. Kruzas, A. T., ed. Directory of Special Libraries and
     Information Centers. 2nd ed. Detroit, Gale Re-
     search Co., 1968.

Part II

TECHNICAL SERVICES / READERS' SERVICES

CATALOGING PHILOSOPHY*

Sanford Berman

I'm supposed to rap briefly on "Cataloging Philosophy. "
Which sounds kind of high-falutin', maybe also a little dry &
    ponderous.
But I don't think it is.
Because what's really crucial here are ATTITUDES:
How we catalogers view what we do & why we do it.

To venture into history for less than 30 seconds:
Too much of cataloging attitudes & practice in the past
has been frankly self-serving.
Cataloging has too often been performed for the exclusive
    satisfaction of catalogers themselves,
who seemed to conceive of themselves as members of a
    special mystery cult.
Only the properly initiated could really decipher or
    comprehend
what they were into.
Well, we don't dig that approach.
And there's growing evidence of what amounts to a
    "cataloging revolution" elsewhere in the country.

Our basic attitude--
however imperfect it may be in application
(after all, we're human, hallelujah!)--
is that we catalog for the people who use the library
and for our colleagues who help people to use the library.
Stated another way:
We DON'T catalog just for us.

*Reprinted by permission of the author from the Hennepin
County Library Cataloging Bulletin, April 5, 1974, pp. 9-13.
This was also reprinted in Library Journal, Sept. 1, 1974, pp.
2033-35.

What that attitude means in practice is, first:
trying to move stuff out as fast as we can.
Second: Trying to tag materials, especially non-fiction,
with a classification number
that best expresses what the items are all about.
(And when Dewey or LC doesn't give us the best number,
we either change it
or make a new one.
For instance, within the past few weeks we innovated
     specific numbers
for "War games, " "Landsailing, " & "Abortion. "
Earlier, we'd done the same thing for "Workers control" &
     "Counter-culture. "
And for whatever it's worth,
the people at the Decimal Classification Office in Washington
have indicated a definite interest in our number-making.
Even now we've got in the works an expanded breakdown for
     "Popular Music, "
which at the moment DDC limits to a single notation: 780.42.)

Third: In assigning added-entries & subject tracings
we try to consider as a top priority
how to make the particular work most accessible to users
who might want it.
For instance, reports by governmental commissions are
     typically entered
under "Commission..., " "Great Britain, " or "United States."
But very often they're better known by the chairperson's
     name or catch-title--
like the Wolfenden or Kerner Reports.
So, besides the "straight" main entry,
we give them extra tracings for, say,
"Wolfenden Report" or "Kerner Report. "
If LC--as it frequently happens--
hasn't chosen to accent particular subject aspects of a
     fictional or other work,
we add more tracings to do so.
Two recent & horrendously classic examples of this sort of
     "under-cataloging"
are Alternatives in print and the Somewhere else living-
     learning catalog.
The first title complements Books in print,
providing bibliographic & ordering data for publications
     issued by over 850 Movement,
counter-culture, Feminist, & radical groups.
The one tracing LC gave it was: STUDENT MOVEMENT--
     BIBLIOGRAPHY.

Which didn't exactly do the trick.
That's one I hope we made more accessible through
    additional tracings
for RADICALISM, COUNTER-CULTURE, and SOCIAL
    CHANGE.
The Somewhere else title is a directory of things
like free schools & universities, women's networks,
and alternative vocational guidance centers.
Unbelievably (or maybe not so unbelievably),
the only LC tracing it got was:
ASSOCIATIONS, INSTITUTIONS, ETC.
That, too, we corrected slightly.

Related to all this
is the recognition that a library catalog--
whether we personally like it or not--
is also an instructional tool,
even an attitude-moulder.
Employing a particular term or form in a catalog can have
    definite social effects.
Not all by itself, of course,
but certainly in tandem with terminology in literature, daily
    speech, & the mass media.
"As" constructions, for instance,
clearly imply that the persons or group denoted as doing a
    specific job or thing
maybe shouldn't be doing it
Or only do it on an exceptional basis.
That's surely the implication of JEWS AS SCIENTISTS,
    WOMEN AS LIBRARIANS,
or GURKHAS AS SOLDIERS.
In other words,
these forms make a judgment about the group or persons in
    question.
And almost invariably, that judgment is negative.
So what we've more-or-less systematically done
is to truncate those constructions, dropping the "as"
so they become simply (and inoffensively)
JEWISH SCIENTISTS, WOMEN LIBRARIANS, and GURKHA
    SOLDIERS.

Much the same criticism can be levied
at obviously sexist terminology,
which still flourishes in most subject heading schemes,
like LUMBERMEN, FIREMEN, SALESMEN, AND
    SALESMANSHIP.
Again, the implication is that

these work or occupational categories are strictly <u>male</u>.
Well, the U. S. Government itself
has lately changed such stereotyped nomenclature.
And so--to a large extent--have we.
Thus, you'll shortly find LUMBER WORKERS instead of
     LUMBERMEN,
FIRE FIGHTERS rather than FIREMEN,
etc.

Another objective here
has been to strive
for both authenticity & fairness.
Granted, most of the world knows about the "Bushmen" of
     South Africa.
But there are no people in South Africa who ever called
     <u>themselves</u>
by that name.
It's a monicker that Europeans laid on them.
Without asking.
Their <u>real</u> name is SAN: S-A-N.
And that's the one we use,
of course cross-referencing
from the wrong form,
printed in quotation-marks.
The same is true of NEGROES,
now AFRO-AMERICANS,
and several other peoples.

One more wrong-headed LC tendency we've tried to overcome
is that of either too slowly recognizing--
or altogether failing to recognize--
that many peoples of a distinct ethnic or national origin
at some point have become bona fide <u>Americans.</u>
Thus, we continue to find headings
for JEWS IN THE UNITED STATES, CHINESE IN THE
     UNITED STATES,
and UKRAINIANS IN THE UNITED STATES,
even though the works assigned these headings may deal
     largely,
if not wholly,
with 2d, 3d, or later generations
of Jews, Chinese, & Ukrainians "in America. "
In such cases,
we recognize their Americanness--
together with their ethnicity--
through headings like JEWISH-AMERICANS, CHINESE-
     AMERICANS,
and UKRAINIAN-AMERICANS.

And then there's the unabating problem of new
(sometimes even old)
concepts & topics
that unmistakably appear in books & other media,
but which LC hasn't yet got around to formally noticing.
As examples:
BERMUDA TRIANGLE, LAMAZE TECHNIQUE, RACISM,
    WOMEN STUDIES, SEXISM, NATIONAL LIBERATION
    MOVEMENTS, NATURAL FOODS, POLICE MALPRAC-
    TICE, RAPE CRISIS CENTERS, SONGWRITERS, STEEL-
    BAND MUSIC, ROSEMALING, WOMEN'S PUBLISHERS
    AND PUBLISHING, and the TRANS-ALASKA PIPELINE.
To illustrate quickly:
The LC tracings for a volume we lately received titled
    Sexism in education and society
were   1) EDUCATION OF WOMEN
and   2) SEX DIFFERENCES IN EDUCATION.
Not alone nor together do those two headings satisfactorily
    disclose
what the book deals with.

To enhance searching & finding,
a lot can also be done--
and we're trying to do it--
through cross-referencing.
Key here is that there's often more than one way
to say the same thing,
but only one of those ways will enjoy primary-head status.
To get specific,
someone searching for material on "babies" very well might
    not realize
that it's all listed under INFANTS.
But the searcher won't go away disappointed
if we've been clever enough to make a cross-reference
from BABIES to INFANTS.

What I've described as our "attitude"
ramifies into other areas, as well.
For one thing, we WANT feedback & suggestions from the
    people we serve:
you & the public.
We've begun to get it.
For instance, the BERMUDA TRIANGLE and LAMAZE
    TECHNIQUE heads just mentioned
were suggested by community librarians.
And another colleague has contributed a well thought-out
    recommendation

for expanding the Popular Music schedule in Dewey.
So if there are any new subjects or numbers you want,
let us know.
And also feel absolutely free to respond to what we print
in the Cataloging bulletin,
regardless of whether you approve or disagree.
It's intended as a free-for-all forum.
No holds barred.

Further along this line,
some of us have started to "agitate"
against imposition of the International Standard Bibliographic
    Description
--or ISBD--by LC.
This was discussed in recent bulletins.
And boils down to a change in cataloging format
that at best will mean nothing to our public
and at worst will toss in more garbage--
like Latin abbreviations and mind-blowing punctuation--
that COULD turn people off,
making them feel pointlessly stupid
and frustrated.
And it's worth underscoring that the "ISBD issue"
is not exclusively technical.
In fact,
it's a public service issue.

All of this may not constitute
a perfectly cogent statement of
"cataloging philosophy."
But maybe it conveys something
about where our heads are at.
And
our hearts,
too.

FIFTY YEARS OF YOUNG ADULT
READING, 1921-1971*

Margaret Hutchinson

        The purpose of this paper is to survey the field of
young adult reading for the last fifty years by examining
articles indexed in Library Literature from its inception in
1921 to the present. The articles selected were under the
headings Young People's Reading, Youth's Literature, Youth's
Reading, Young Adult's Reading, or Young Adult Literature.
Material on the techniques of working with young people, devices for motivating reading, how to give book talks, and so
on, have purposely been omitted.

        In an article published in 1968, Katherine P. Jef-
fery, [1] a young adult librarian, precedes a survey of book
selection policies with a little history. According to Jeffery,
"The earliest systematized attempts at specialized service to
adolescents were directed to the out-of-school youth, in particular, to those fourteen-to-sixteen-year-olds who left school
for economic reasons and went to work in factories, stores
and offices.... The book selection for these young people of
forty to forty-five years ago emphasized further education,
vocational training, the classics as part of an educated person's reading, how-to-do-it books, and popular fiction. "

        Most of the articles of that period, however, are
concerned, not with the out-of-school youth, but those young
people who were increasingly remaining in school through
high school. [2] Teachers faced with an expanding and increasingly diverse clientele were forced to abandon the notion that
every young person should read the same books. But with
the era of individualized reading, the need for reading guidance became apparent. In an early article on this subject,
Hannah Logasa, [3] then librarian of the University High School,

---

*Reprinted by permission of the author and the American
Library Association from Top of the News, November 1973,
pp. 240-253.

Chicago, concluded that, "The aim of reading guidance should
be to inspire pupils with an intellectual interest so strong
that it is a driving force. Technique for this type of guidance is
yet in its infancy." She listed the psychological and social considerations that enter into the reading guidance of high school
pupils. In 1927, Martha Pritchard[4] classified readers into five
types, and made suggestions for dealing with each type. Her
typology is not without interest nearly half a century later:

Type A.   The young person who absorbs everything available
          in print.
Type B.   Boy or girl who reads only fiction.
Type C.   The youth who spurns reading as a 'high brow' occu-
          pation which his manly mind (or her womanly activi-
          ties) has no time for unless the reading is a school
          assignment, hated and done as slightingly as possible.
Type D.   The practical minded person who reads for informa-
          tion or study but lacks appreciation of the imaginative
          in literature.
Type E.   The type wanting magazines, short stories or news-
          papers. Lacking sustained interest in a whole book.

      The interest in classifying readers into groups, in
order to be able to help them select books they will like, extended to groups that would nowadays be called "exceptional
children." Margaret Drew Archibald[5] described attempts to
make readers of girls with low IQs, many of them poor.
This is an unusual work for the time, because it simply describes the girls and their tastes as they are. Perhaps the
author knew there was no hope of ever leading these girls to
the classics. But this seems to have been the secret hope
of most who wrote about reading guidance in the 1920s, and
there was a good deal of discussion about developing "taste."
Mary S. Wilkerson,[6] a children's librarian, for example, de-
cried the low level of taste among older boys and girls:

          It seems unfortunately to be true that much of
          the fiction read by older boys and girls belongs
          to this group of unsuitable or mediocre books.
          The reason for it is two-fold: first, their taste
          is not sufficiently trained to discriminate be-

...books that are apparently discovered for oneself, not stiffened and chilled by having
been long set aside in the educational refrigerator for required consumption, possess almost always a lure of individual adventure for the young mind that makes their influence
deeper and more lasting and gives a richer savor to their quality. Required formalized
reading of the classics has forever deprived much great and beautiful literature of the influence it should have had in the later intellectual life of intelligent men and women.[9]
      I was and am convinced that the demise of those classics, so far as the average
boy or girl en route to college was concerned, is traceable directly to the college boards.[10]

tween the good and the cheap; and second their
craving for 'lots of excitement' leads them chiefly
to second-rate authors whose breathless activity
satisfies even the restless adolescent.   The
western and the mystery story are for this reason
the prime favorites.

Such books, the author argued, stunt mental growth, and
misrepresent life.   But the young people, then as now, seem
to have been sturdily resistant to the suggestions of their elders. [7] Secondary enrollments rose from 4,800,000 in 1929-1930
to 7,100,000 in 1939-1940, [8] and the experiment with "extensive
reading" continued.   Adherents of the classics did not yield to
the new methods without a struggle, however, for the literature
of the period includes a number of bitter attacks upon those who
taught them.

As a minority report, there is an amusing piece in
the New Statesman and Nation of January 1, 1938, which de-
fends the classics, and suggests, tongue-in-cheek, that the
popular modern literature be made unpopular by using the
same methods that had previously caused the young to be
bored with the classics: "Give the children lumps of it [The
Scarlet Pimpernel] to translate into French and make them
write out their favourite passage fifty times as an imposition."[13]
Nevertheless, the suspicion of "extensive reading," and of the
library, must have remained quite strong, for in 1932 we find
Azile Wofford[14] saying that "so far as we can determine there
is no direct connection between the use of the library and school
failures."

While some workers were busy discussing what young
people should choose to read, others were busy finding out
what they actually did choose.   These studies took three
forms.   The first grew out of the study of adolescent psychology and individual differences.   W. T. B. Mitchell, [15] a
medical doctor and student of mental hygiene at McGill University, for example, suggested that "Many adolescents read
voraciously.   There is a tremendous urge in the face of this
new-found concept of self to broaden their experiences
through reading," and Helen L. Bell, [16] after psychological

Well-meaning English teachers once dissected them for us, poked around for the
intangible in them, tried to unscrew the inscrutable for us, and fixed us, for the most
part, so we shall never open those books again. [11]
   Schools have so often been stupid in this respect.   In what is often well-meaning
zeal to educate taste--the admirable and real goal--they press too hard.   Instead of tact-
fully shaping their students' taste by a gradual process, they too often force certain established books and accepted standards upon them.   What very often results is that students become trained seals doing tricks nicely. [12]

study, suggested adolescents be given "(1) stories of adventure, (2) biographies of persons of significant achievements; (3) plays; (4) poems; (5) books of science, nature, hobbies, sports; (6) certain books labeled classics whose appeal is universal."

A second approach was more direct: some librarians and editors began to make surveys among the young people. In 1931 May Lamberton Becker, [17] who had been associated with the Saturday Review of Literature, St. Nicholas, and The Scholastic, summarized the contents of 774 letters from young people telling about their favorite books. "From these letters I found, of course, that romance and adventure topped the list. It is impossible to separate these two terms because so many of their favorite romances are also adventures and so many of their adventure stories are romantic." Lorna Doone, Ramona, and Ben Hur were favorites. Becker also noted: "There is an extraordinary continuance in popularity of such tepid, sentimental, and old-fashioned romances as Janice Meredith, When Knighthood Was in Flower, and Little Shepherd of Kingdom Come. Their popularity is much greater in the smaller, outlying districts, and the reasons for this probably are that the libraries are not so good as in the cities--" The young people wanted lots of action in their books, and they disliked introspective discussion. Another demand of the age group was for "stories about its own particular kind of life--stories about the young people of today, family stories, and school stories. There are very few good ones, because a good book for boys and girls must be written because the writer can't help writing it."

Not all librarians who made surveys had as large a sample as Becker, nor as much insight into the results. P. G. Chancellor, [18] librarian at a preparatory school, noted a high proportion of modern publications among the books the boys polled enjoyed. Their favorite authors (1938) were Kenneth Roberts, Nordhoff and Hall, Sinclair Lewis, Edgar Allan Poe, Somerset Maugham, Rafael Sabatini, R. L. Stevenson, Conrad, Steinbeck, O. Henry, and Charles Dickens. L. Toomey, [19] of the St. Louis Public Library, analyzing book reports, noted a dislike for slow-moving books and long descriptions. Louis E. Hill, [20] surveying a group of 1,500 junior high school students in California, found a tendency to read author series. "As was expected, the greater part of the books named were fiction. Animal stories, of course, took top honors, with mysteries a close second...." Howard Pease was the favorite author, and Silver Chief the favorite book.

Yet a third approach to understanding what young people like to read was made by experienced librarians contemplating their own libraries. Irene Smith, [21] describing a library in a predominantly Jewish slum, commented, "They want books that seem to the librarian years in advance of their age [Of Human Bondage, Lady Chatterley's Lover]--We have a sophisticated public. These boys and girls have grown up under post-war conditions, nurtured by the tabloid and the movie. They ask in perfectly casual manner for all the modern fiction that public libraries usually restrict or charge to gray-haired patrons with misgivings." Ethelwyn Wickson, [22] of the Toronto Public Library, noted, "When I look at our intermediate fiction shelves I feel that we have too much 'pretty stuff'--What we need are more books that are realistic, grim even, and yet not cynical--books which will give the average boy or girl the satisfaction of that contact with actual living which they seem to want most of all."

It was apparent by the mid-thirties that the selection of reading material for young adults was a key factor in what was coming to be known as the "reading problem." As one student put it, someone had to "pick out the ones [books] I picked out for myself."[23] Jean C. Roos, [24] of the Cleveland Public Library, pointed out that the responsibilities of those who select books for adolescents are particularly heavy, because the "standards, tastes, and judgments" of the young people are in process of change, and because they accept books as true pictures of life. She suggested that the most important problem was to select books with values, "values in the creation of real characters set in the midst of real issues." Mabel Williams, [25] of the New York Public Library, thought certain adult books should be added to the young adult collection: "some so-called mediocre adult books because they have the simplicity of style, language and plot that these boys and girls still require." These, she felt, could be used to bridge the gap between children's and adult's fiction. Alice Cowles Morris, [26] a high school librarian, suggested that the library must provide the kind of book which will prove popular, but because of the high school obligation to improve taste, only the best of each type.

But given access to well-selected books, would young people read? Librarians were apparently not sure that they would, for the decade of the thirties witnessed a proliferation of devices for motivating reading and advertising books that it is not within the scope of this paper to discuss. These devices went under the name of reading guidance, but the only

real advance in the technique of advising young people about
their reading, which Hannah Logasa and others had begun to
explore so hopefully in the previous decade, came with the
invention of "reading ladders." Ruby Ethel Cundiff, [27] of the
library school at Peabody College, strongly recommended
using such lists: "These are not just subject lists, but lists
of books which try to meet the interest which makes the
reader like the original book. Following that interest, the
next book broadens it...."

        In spite of everything, many young people were reluc-
tant to read, and in the 1930s there developed a gradually increasing awareness of the reasons for this reluctance. Margaret Scoggin, [28] of the New York Public Library, suggested
in 1936 that "By reluctant we too often mean reluctant to read
what we think they should read." She thought young people
might be discouraged by required reading, defeated by the
adult collection, limited in reading ability, or put off by library regulations. Homer P. Rainey[29] pointed out that many
young people had never mastered the mechanics of reading.
One author spoke of the value of books with no reading matter
but a few captions. [30] But it was Amelia Munson[31] of the
New York Public Library who, in 1939, tabulated all the
types of nonreaders.

> There are a few for whom the mechanics of read-
> ing set up almost insurmountable obstacles.
> Then there is the original thinker who distrusts
> books.
> One reason why some folks won't read is that
> they have not learned to find their way among
> books.   Put beside them another group that, far
> from not having been trained to read, has been
> overtrained.   Not only have ways been studied out
> and cleared for them through the jungle of read-
> ing, but jungles have been made to grow where
> none existed, solely for the discipline and mastery
> attained in hacking one's way out. I refer, of
> course, to the old-time presentation of literature
> in the schools.
> Non-readers who want entertainment from books.
> The manual-minded.
> A small group who deliberately turn their backs
> upon reading as unessential in their scheme of
> things--They have tried it and found it wanting.

Munson offered hope for each group but the last.   These find

their aesthetic satisfactions elsewhere than in books, and
Munson was content that they should do so.   Meanwhile, Dora
V. Smith[32] was asking that librarians "see the reading program whole, " with its facets of reading skill, reading guidance, appreciation and taste, recreational reading, individual-
ization, and sharing books.

At the same time, in the late 1930s, a reevaluation
of the reasons for reading was taking place.   If a knowledge
of certain classics was no longer to be considered the mark
of an educated man, why read at all?   The idea began to
evolve that the reason for reading was to broaden the reader's horizons.   As the author, Rachel Field,[33] who abhorred
book lists, put it, "No life is long enough, or full enough, to
hold all that we could wish of experience or accomplish-
ment, and so since we were all born with a hunger for experience we must reach out to supplement our own through
the experience and thought of others.   There is not time
enough for all we would see and hear and know. "   Reading
should not be overclassified and over-regulated; young people
should read about everything--even love. [34]   The hope was
that teenagers would be so enthusiastic about books that
widened their experience of life, that this type of fiction
would seem "as valid and imminent as any other reality, "[35]
and that the taste for hair-raising adventure stories and love
stories far from the truth would disappear. [36]   Walter
Prichard Eaton, [37] professor of drama at Yale University,
urged the need for realistic fiction with familiar settings:
"Their budding imaginations must be exercised on problems
of their own lives, on the problems which they see in the
lives around them.... As the power to recognize familiar
problems and experiences in the stories of life close at hand
develops, this same power of the imagination will broaden
and deepen so that the boy will find in the really great stories of other days and other times those common elements
that belong to human nature and human relationships and that
make every story of the sort we call 'classic' essentially
modern.... "

It is evident from what was being written in the 1930s
about young people and their reading, that a number of able
people were concerned with the matter and that a great deal
of intelligent speculation was taking place.   Mitchell's idea
of the self-concept as a motivating factor in reading; Becker's insight that young people need stories about themselves,
and the reason why there were so few good ones; Smith's
observation of the maturity of the reading done by the teen-

agers; Wickson's feeling that there was too much "pretty
stuff" on her library shelves; the realization of the importance of selection of books with values; the glimmering that
reading is not for everyone; the reexamination of the "why?"
of reading: all have a modern ring. It is possible to add
other examples. In 1934 Douglas Waples[38] lamented the lack
of basic research. In 1935 Dorothy Hopkins[39] began to explore the social significance of reading. In 1936 Cam[40]
spoke of providing library services in a neighborhood where
"There are few scholars. Life is certainly not cloistered.
It is lived principally on the street." In 1936 Constance
Rourke[41] noted that the barriers between reading for adults
and reading for children were breaking down. And by 1939
Waples[42] was suggesting that the development of a discerning
taste might be only for a lonely few. It must have been a
lively and interesting time to be involved with young adult literature. One gets the feeling that anything might happen.

The War and Post-War Years

What happened was the second world war. Energies
which might have been devoted to a new literature for the
young adult were expended elsewhere, and things went on
much the same as before. "Extensive reading" was a success, at least according to some writers:

> The general conclusions drawn from such investi-
> gations show that under such programs, if pro-
> perly guided, young people grow in their power of
> discrimination in choice of books and develop
> familiarity with various forms of literature.[43]

And the same author states: "Strange as it may seem, some
young people today are reading the 'classics' even when not
required to do so." The crux of the matter remained individual guidance, and a few articles continued to appear discussing problems and techniques in this area.[44]

There was some interest in the effect of the war upon
young people's reading. A survey by Ethel L. Cornell[45] in
1941 (before Pearl Harbor) contains little new except that, of
the fiction titles read, 55 percent were from the adult lists,
and that adult fiction was the most popular reading category,
followed by biography, young adult fiction, and drama, in
that order. By 1943 Marie Nelson Taylor,[46] a public librarian, was saying that young people could not be sheltered

from "the realities of the present conflict" and was publishing
a list of war-related books.   Margaret C. Scoggin[47] claimed
in the same year that the reading interests of young people
had not been materially changed by the war:

> Inevitably the war has had its effect upon young
> people's reading.   Since their courses, vocational
> guidance and training in jobs are all geared to
> 'total conflict, ' some of their reading reflects
> wartime uses and needs.   The comforting fact is
> that, despite special wartime applications, the
> reading interests of young people show amazing
> continuity.

Technical books and aviation books were, of course, popular,
but then they always had been.

> Of wide general interest to all boys and many
> girls are the accounts of the men in the thick of
> the fighting.   Here are hero tales; interest in
> them is as old as the history of mankind.

War had influenced the girls' reading more subtly:

> One gets the conviction that girls feel much less
> at ease in the world than boys, and are concerned
> mainly with carrying on until the war is over and
> the men come back.

But the basic lines of reading remained unchanged, and this,
Scoggin felt, was a hopeful sign.

        Other writers disagreed, and felt that the war had
caused a change in reading patterns.   For one thing, the
amount of reading done had declined sharply while young
people were reading war books, often "beyond their grade
level."[48] Journalist accounts and novels were the most popular types:[49]

> The adventure story, once western in flavor, is
> now military.   The vocational account must deal
> with WAACS and WAVES, servicemen and spies.[50]

        By the end of the war in 1945, Kathryn A. Haebich,[51]
a librarian and girls' counsellor, found teen-agers "somewhat bewildered by the world situation and what it is doing to
their normal dream of home and family life. " They wanted

books "which help them achieve their major tasks of adolescent development. They want to learn to get along with age-mates of both sexes, to achieve independence of adults, to accept social responsibility, and to develop a philosophy of life adapted to the world in which they live." Girls wanted love stories. Boys wanted books about adventure, sports, the sea, and war, "probably because the primary aim of every teen-age boy is to achieve mastery of body and adopt a masculine sex role."

This emphasis upon "developmental tasks" was not a new idea; it was a part of the discipline of psychology as it had evolved up to that time. In 1943 Gladys B. Johnson[52] had published a booklist for each of the five developmental tasks of adolescence as defined by the psychologist, Havighurst: adjustment to age mates (Huckleberry Finn), independence of family (Forsyte Saga), occupational orientation (Microbe Hunters), social participation (Barren Ground), and development of the self (Of Human Bondage). In the same year, Lucile Vickers,[53] a high school librarian, had published a list of nonfiction books on "problems of living." Books were also thought of as tools for teaching tolerance,[54] and good citizenship.[55] As early as 1940 Willard A. Heaps[56] was claiming that "books do aid in adjustment," although he admitted that "many adolescents resent any intrusion upon their privacy. If they feel that a book is being chosen in order to make a contribution to their welfare, they are bitterly indignant.... The individual appeal must be more subtle and ingenious."

Clearly, by the end of the second world war many people were thinking of books as a means to an end (adjustment), not as an introduction to the adult world, given to youth made intellectually and emotionally mature by the world crisis and by exposure to the media of radio, newspaper, and motion pictures.[57]

> The years of World War II marked a change in
> the status of the thirteen-to-nineteen-year-old person, both within the family and within the community. Because his labor was needed as older
> men and women went off to war and his financial
> status made him one of a commercially exploitable group, he had, as never before, money to
> spend on himself--money not needed, as during
> the depression years, for general family support.
> Intellectually, his increasing participation in

> affairs outside the home made him ripe for the
> development of the whole teen-age sub culture.
> Indications of this change appeared in the number
> of separate departments for teens, young adults,
> young people, and young moderns which developed
> in public libraries in the mid-forties and early
> fifties.... This is the period that marked the
> rise of the teen-age or junior novel, with its em-
> phasis on middle-class life, on the high school
> student, on popularity, on boy-girl relationship,
> on high school sports, and of the career story
> which was more story than career. [58]

It is obvious that the genre that came to be known as
the teen-age novel met the needs of the time. Not only did
the adolescent subculture develop following the second world
war, but it was a time of affluence, and money was available
for such luxury items as books for young people of a narrow
age range. Authors and publishers obliged with a spate of
books designed to please the young people: short, entertaining, easy to read, and about themselves. [59] At the same
time, they were designed to please parents and teachers by
dealing with teenage problems--always successfully resolved
--and thus hopefully giving the young people assistance with
"life adjustment. " It is neither surprising that books of this
type developed nor surprising that there were few good ones,
for most people seemed to have forgotten what Mary Lamberton Becker[60] had said in 1931: "a good book for boys and
girls must be written because the writer can't help writing
it. "

Criticism was a long time coming. It was not until
1955 that Richard S. Alm, [61] a professor of English and education, analyzed the group of junior novels. Many of them
he called "sugar puff" stories, lacking in insight and writing
ability. "Their stories, " he said, "are superficial, often
distorted, sometimes completely false representations of adolescence. " He also castigated them for stock characters,
too-easy solutions to problems, model heroes, saccharine
sentiment, oversimplification, single motivation, the notion
that nothing is impossible, the attainment of maturity without
development, and inconsistencies in characterization. In
spite of this list of sins, Alm did find some "better" junior
novels, including the extremely popular Seventeenth Summer
(Daly), and others by Cavanna, Felsen, and Stolz. Four he
categorized as "outstanding": The Yearling (Rawlings),
Johnny Tremain (Forbes), Goodbye My Lady (Street), and

Swiftwater (Annixter). Whatever their defects, it was recognized that these books were useful, for by "directing their
novels dead-center to adolescent interests and concerns, these
writers encourage younger adolescents to read."[62] Furthermore, they were popular (and profitable).[63] They were not
seriously attacked until the 1960s.[64]

     Young adults of the period were not confined in their
reading to the junior novel. A publisher of the time presented evidence that "the high school librarian thinks, buys,
and recommends primarily in terms of junior books, while
the attention of the young people's librarian in the public library is two-thirds devoted to adult books."[65] The selection
of adult books for young adults had become a matter of concern as early as 1948.[66] On May 15, 1948, Booklist published a "retrospective list of recent adult books for the more
mature young people of high school age," because there was
a "general demand" for such books.[67] While some books
were excluded from this list because their "appeal was judged
to be outside the range of even the most mature young person's interest," books were not excluded because of a certain
frankness that might be offensive to some. The Booklist
committee recommended "re-examination of standards in relation to the adult books for use with young people," and put
forward their own:

> Our questions were: Will it appeal to young
> people? Will it increase their insight into human
> motives and behavior, or does it distort and con-
> fuse?

     These committee members were obviously aware of
the problems of selection which were to come to a head a
year or so later with the publication of J. D. Salinger's
Catcher in the Rye. The history of this controversial book
was summarized by Katherine Jeffery[68] in 1968:

> first adopted by the then current crop of college
> students, then by their younger brothers and sis-
> ters, [it] is perhaps the archtypical problem book
> in the setting of standards of book selection for
> the young adult. Creating controversy by its use
> of vulgar language and its depiction of a young
> person in need of psychiatric help, it had violent
> partisans among young adult librarians and teach-
> ers, as well as equally violent vocal opponents.
> Meanwhile young people read the book and accepted

or rejected it as it answered their needs. It
finally arrived on the road to neglect by being
accepted for class study. In retrospect and in
the light of present day permissiveness the book
seems a small coal to have generated so much
heat.

Perhaps the furor over the Catcher in the Rye acted
as a warning. In any case, it seems that, with a few courageous exceptions such as Margaret Scoggin, who in 1952
was pleading with young adult librarians to accept the responsibility for "knowing and discussing with young people
themselves everything that they read,"[69] most young adult
librarians preferred to be conservative in what they chose
from the adult lists for the teenagers to read.[70]

The years following the second world war also produced an astonishing number of surveys of young people's
reading.[71] They tend to be repetitive, and may be briefly
summarized: Although the amount of reading done tended to
decline in high school, about two out of three young people
queried were reading some sort of book outside of school
assignments. The percentage of young people who really liked
reading apparently remained fairly constant. There was a
wide range of reading ability. Most young people read a mix-
ture of teen-age novels and adult works. They showed a
preference for recent works and best sellers. Several studies
noted the influence of movies and other media on book choices.
Sex was an important factor in reading interests. Boys preferred novels of adventure, girls those of romance. Some
claimed to notice "trends" towards sports (both fiction and
nonfiction), biography, science and science fiction, vocation-
ally oriented works, and personality development. There
were "shortages" in some areas, for example, hunting and
psychology. One author noted that "cowboys only create a
stir when their horses sell them to the readers" (Vroman).
Another noted that attempts to keep certain books from the
young usually failed: "No use not adding or banning Gentle-
man's Agreement, Deep Are the Roots, Citizen Tom Paine.
They will read them; you can be sure of that. " (De Angelo)

In addition to the surveys, there were a few commen-
taries on the reading of young adults. Lloyd W. Babb,[72] a
high school librarian, expressed dissatisfaction with the criteria which average high school students used in choosing
books for leisure reading, and attempted to classify their
reasons for reading. Virginia Tozier[73] commented upon the

effect of the peer group: "The majority of pupils in a secondary school are enslaved by the collective opinion of the group
which powerfully affects all personal activities including voluntary reading. " In 1955 Publishers' Weekly offered a pair
of articles on the reading motivations of young people. Lewis
Perry, [74] speaking of boys, stressed their desire for independent selection, which was, however, balanced by a fear
of being "different. " Esther Millett, [75] speaking of girls,
stressed their reliance upon fashion, even in reading, along
with their tendency to be in a hurry and to be lazy. This
made the need for easy access to books with "a minimum of
irrelevant description, honesty of purpose, simplicity and
clarity of style and construction" a necessity. Ruth Hill
Viguers[76] also spoke about reading motivation, suggesting
that young adults read in part because they are afraid: "they
want to learn how to talk and act acceptably today by the
practice they have while identifying themselves with the
characters in their stories. "

Moving into the Sixties: Content, Quality, Values

In contrast to these other writers, whose chief concern seems to have been with groups of readers, G. Robert
Carlsen[77] wrote about individuals:

> Each person must discover that reading is an ab-
> sorbing and fascinating activity. For most indi-
> viduals this discovery comes late in childhood or
> early adolescence. It comes when the individual
> has developed enough competence in reading skills
> so that these do not interfere with his interaction
> with the reading material. It usually comes when
> the individual has gained some maturity in his own
> living so that his interests have some stability.
> He finds a focal point for reading that meets a
> need he has.

This focal point may be the works of an author; a type of
book (e.g., animal stories); a historical period; a geographical area; "a particular tonality or quality"; or a topic on
which the young person seeks information. Carlsen suggested
that librarians know the reading interests of young adults, for
"Interests have remained fairly constant over the fifty-year
period that they have been studied and they show singularly
few geographical variations. " But the real challenge was to
find a good fit between a youngster and a book, and to build

bridges between one reading interest and another. He was
less concerned with the quality of reading than with keeping
the young person interested in some book, although he conceded that "when a child is in the middle of an all-consuming
reading interest, we do try to build ladders within it by suggesting to him books of increasing subtlety within the area."

Carlsen, a professor of English and education, continued his research into the reading of young adults. (He
seems to have been the first to do any such sustained research.) By 1966 he was beginning to publish his findings:
by studying the reading records of many young people, he
had been able to discover patterns in their reading.[78] Briefly
between twelve and fourteen "almost inevitably the child finds
that he likes a book of adventure in which an individual is
cast adrift somewhere and makes his way back to security,"
or a mystery, "the kind of stories that involve mistaken
identity, a lost will or stolen papers." The preferences of
boys and girls differ, within this framework, in predictable
ways. By fifteen or sixteen, girls like gothic romances and
historical novels, boys like stories of physical courage and
real-life adventure, while both like "stories of people like
themselves, living lives not far different from their own."
They may begin to read adult books. By seventeen, both
sexes ask for books in which the reader can continue his
search for personal values, books dealing with deprived or
persecuted peoples or social injustice, "books that skirt the
psychological fringes of the human soul," and, most appealing of all, books that show others maturing into early adult
life. Dr. Carlsen summarized by saying:

> the adolescent reader is generally in the process
> of discovering the really unconscious delight that
> reading can offer him in terms of escape to a
> world of intensified action and emotion. He is
> often in search of a world that will assure him of
> his own importance and gratify his ego, a world
> in which the adolescent is idyllically free of adult
> supervision. ... At about fourteen or fifteen a
> youngster finds the book a safe way of seeking out
> some of the answers to his own inner problems
> and fears. It will not invade his privacy as a
> counselor would. Finally, in late adolescence the
> reader begins to discover that literature has much
> to say about the basic dilemmas of mankind. The
> aesthetic delight in perfection of form and literary
> technique comes late in the reading scale.

Carlsen[79] suggested that many adolescents fail to develop in their reading because their teachers concern themselves with books of the right type or difficulty, rather than
with books of the right content: "the evidence is reasonably
good that they like or dislike a book or a poem or a biography or a play, pretty much on the basis of its subject
matter. Surprisingly, the so-called difficult books are not
difficult if the subject matter is appealing and books that are
called easy books are not easy for the adolescent if the subject matter does not fall within these established boundaries."
Nevertheless, he concluded that reading patterns could also
be determined by types of books, from the juvenile series
book, through the junior novel, to the popular adult book, to
the modern classic, and, at college age, the great classic.[80]

It was time that someone put the classic in some kind
of perspective, for the educational panic following the Russian
launching of Sputnik in 1957, combined with the pressure of
the war babies upon the colleges, had revived the debate
about their place in education. This debate had not been a
popular one since before the second world war, although a
Canadian, M. Fraser,[81] had wondered as early as 1951 "if
we are doing as much as we might for the very brightest."
By 1959 Sister M. Camillus,[82] a college librarian, was
classifying readers into three types: "going steady" readers,
who read to find answers to their social problems; "Peyton
Place" readers, who read to impress their peers with their
sophistication; and "Moby Dick" readers, who read for layers
of meaning. She added: "I think we, as librarians, must
make every effort to lift our readers step by step through the
'going steady' reading over the 'Peyton Place' reading and
into the Moby Dick reading as pleasantly as possible." In
the meantime the classic, or at least books that the whole
class read together, had returned to the classroom, in the
wake of the "New English" curriculum and the ready availability of the paperback.[83] In 1963 Florence Hascall[84] made
a strong plea that young people be made to read the classics
and be offered no special rewards for doing so: "Let us stop
shielding, babying, coddling their unformed minds in the
matter of books. Let us be realistic and expose them to as
wide and great a collection of writers as we can."

Clearly, the spirit of the times in the early 1960s
pushed young adult librarians into opening their shelves to a
wide variety of authors, old and new, writing on a wide variety of subjects. As early as 1958 Ruth Hill Viguers[85] had
pointed out that "teen age books are not enough. The young

people who became creative readers in the children's room
will not be satisfied with a steady diet of mediocre books;
and the good books, the books that will open new vistas to
them, should be available always." Even the high school libraries became less conservative. As one writer put it, "I
believe that high school librarians must take the responsibility for having the best literature on the shelves, both classic and modern."[86] And Margaret Edwards,[87] of Baltimore's Enoch Pratt Library, pushed vigorously for books
that would broaden adolescents' experience, both "the classics they can understand" and "the best of modern writing."

       Books for the young adult were to be selected not only
for literary excellence and maturity of content, but for the
values they contained. In 1957, the year of Sputnik, one librarian was claiming: "I have tried to untangle their childish
thinking by handing them the kind of books that will help them
formulate a basic philosophy."[88] The theme is repeated by
a number of authors in the next few years. Anne Emery[89]
spoke of the need for values in books for the young adult,
because youth is the time that standards and ethical convictions form. Madeline Irrig,[90] a college librarian, spoke of
developing character through reading. Dorothy M. Broderick,[91] a professor of library science, offered a bibliography of works treating such questions as:

> To what extent do books for children and youth
> reflect the values and ideals of our society? To
> what extent do they reflect national and world
> changes? Most important, to what extent and in
> what ways are children using books to form their
> values and to meet the social, psychological, and
> even economic problems that they face? How do
> books meet children's needs?

And somewhat later, Margaret Edwards[92] expressed her
opinion that "the present crisis in reference work with school
assignments is acute and must be faced but we must do more
than help the young barbarian pass his courses in school.
The awakening of his mind, the enlargement of his spirit, the
quickening of his understanding through books are still the
greatest contribution the library can make to him and his city
and his country."

The Sixties: Relevance, Realism, and Intellectual Freedom

       There was bound to be controversy. In 1958 Marie

Blanche MacDonald[93] published an article, "Shake Hands with
Mrs. Grundy, " in which she pointed out that adolescents live
under many restrictions and that their reading should be restricted, too. She felt that, "The average adolescent will
understand when we shall tell them that they are not quite
ready for the stories of adult experiences presented in serious fiction and will be content to wait. " Margaret Edwards[94]
disagreed. In "Mrs. Grundy Go Home, " published two months
later, she expressed the opinion that young people will not be
content to wait, but will find the books they want to read
someplace. She quoted Clifton Fadiman: "if a young person
cannot understand what he reads, it will not harm him, while
if he can understand, he is ready to read of life situations
truly presented. It is a disservice to the young, who mature
at different rates, to recall them to 'puerile interests and
simplified writing' when there is a desperate need for the
young to expand their experience of the world. "

        These were the opening guns of a battle over censor-
ship which raged in the first half of the 1960s. It centered
largely on sex, rough language, and sometimes the religious
or political content of a book. [95] Were these books damaging
to youth? Could youth be denied access to them in a democracy?

        There seems to have been pretty general agreement
that the activity of any group which tries to impose private
standards upon the general public is vicious, and that one
cannot "deny certain books to adults because they might possibly be read by the young also. "[96] The question of which
books to select for the young was more problematical--and it
came to be recognized that selection is a form of censorship. [97] As has been pointed out, standards of selection for
the young were being revised at this time in the direction of
admitting books that might formerly have been excluded, if
their intent was not to corrupt, [98] and of judging a book as
"a literary product, not a moral preachment. "[99] The crux
of the problem was whether youth should be permitted to read
anything, or whether certain material should be denied on the
grounds that it would be damaging at a period in the life of
an adolescent when character and values were being formed.

        Some writers favored completely free access, on the
grounds that salacious books were readily available anyway,
and that "Even sincere efforts at censorship raise uncomfortable questions: why do we want to censor? what areas of
human experience have we closed to discussion? ... Who is

to censor and on what grounds?"[100]   The important thing was
not access to books, but discussion of them with adults.   As
some of the advocates of free access pointed out, some of
the "classics" should make the censors' hair stand on end.[101]
This group won a victory when, in 1967, an ALA preconfer-
ence on intellectual freedom and the teenager took the position
that adolescents should have free access to adult literature.[102]

     But not everyone was convinced.   Max Rafferty,[103]
then superintendent of public instruction for the California
public schools, undertook to present "the other side." He
asked for careful censorship of books the young read, in the
sense of selection by teachers and librarians.   Questionable
modern books, such as the Catcher in the Rye, should be
assigned only to those who had read the classics, and thus
had a background for evaluating them properly.   Some books
should be banned altogether: "No one in a responsible position wants to barge in and start censoring books intended for
adults only.   But faced with the torrent of printed filth currently being poured into our society like sewage into a stream,
if librarians or anyone else think the American public is going
to sit passively while this kind of corruption is made available to children at the taxpayers' expense, they have another
think coming."   Books, Mr. Rafferty believed, influence behavior: "Logic, it appears, would compel librarians to concede that, if bad books don't do any harm, then good books
certainly don't do anybody any good."

     Mr. Rafferty was an angry man, and his speech was
in places lacking in good taste, as apparently were some
other speeches at the time.   His "Other Side" speech called
forth a number of letters, both praising and attacking him,[104]
but after that the controversy seems to have quieted.   Perhaps both sides were too embarrassed to continue.   It is also
possible that it closed prematurely, for a number of interesting points had been raised in its course.   The fact is that no
one knows the effect of reading upon the young adult.[105] It
had been suggested that youth did a good deal of censoring on
their own,[106] and that they did not really understand the
censorship issue.[107]   It was even suggested the pertinent
question was not intellectual freedom but the role of the emotions in reading and understanding.[108]

     Meanwhile, the emphasis on challenging reading had
brought teenage novels under attack,[109] not because they were
badly written (for, as Frank Jennings pointed out, "Most current teen-age fiction, whatever its other many shortcomings,

has a familiarity, an easy control over the mechanics, at
least, of our language that was hard to come by a generation
ago. "[110]) but because they were written to a pattern. Speaking of girls' books, Vivian J. MacQuown[111] said:

> A teen-age romance is a book written to fairly
> rigid specifications for girls between the ages of
> twelve and eighteen. The heroine should be a
> person of the upper middle class and she must
> have a problem to solve. The problem must be
> solved in approximately 200 attractively bound
> pages, in reasonably good English, with virtue
> triumphant.
>
> One of the serious failings of writing to such a
> pattern is that the characters are cardboard and
> the plots contrived. Stereotyped characters and
> unconvincing plots may emerge as the result of
> unskillful writing but I suspect that, in the case
> of the teenage novel, they arise from the strict
> and narrow form....   In fact, I submit that it is
> almost impossible to write a true work of art
> under the ground rules of this genre.

Worse, these books were attacked as lacking thought-provoking content. Kenneth R. Shaffer, [112] of the school of library
science at Simmons College, attacked not only the teen-age
books but the whole movement which isolated the young adult
in special rooms in the library, with a special literature advertised by all manner of devices. "In the end, " he said,
"we produced of course, a vacuum. Publishers eagerly and
profitably obliged by commissioning ... a literature ... with
a maximum intellectual impact of pablum...." The teen-age
novel, Shaffer[113] claimed, gives a false picture of life, even
of teen-age life. Furthermore, the genre was found on examination to be didactic. Arthur Daigon, [114] an editor, in-
vestigated the themes and values in books selected by sixty
girls and sixty boys in junior high school, with a range of
reading ability. He found that:

> In Freudian terms, these are 'super-ego' novels.
> They work on the assumption that males are ag-
> gressive and potentially dangerous to society,
> while females are passive, tending to jeopardize
> their individuality. These novels are society's
> means of redressing the imbalances, of curbing
> excessive groupiness in girls, and excessive indi-
> vidualism and aggressiveness in boys.

Such attacks did not go unquestioned, although it is noticeable
that the defense of the teenage novel took the form of mentioning its usefulness with "less sophisticated or less preco-
cious young persons"[115] or with slow readers. [116] Publishers, in any case, were ready to respond with more realistic
and more thought-provoking books.   Dorothy Broderick called
1965 "a banner year for thought-provoking books, and those
who would bury juvenile publishing had better take another
look at the corpse. "[117]

     Before examining these newer junior novels, it might
be well to take a look at the young readers of the 1960s.
Some surveys of the period[118] seem to indicate that little had
changed since the previous decade.   Others show some change
in reading interests toward books more mature and more
oriented toward special problems.   A report in 1960 lists
Animal Farm, Crime and Punishment, and The Ugly American among the favorites. [119]   Young adult librarians the following year reported that All Quiet on the Western Front,
Diary of a Young Girl, The Night They Burned the Mountain,
and To Kill a Mockingbird were popular in their libraries,[120]
while young people were nominating War and Peace and Of
Human Bondage as "good books. "[121] In 1963 Esther Millett[122] reported a group of ninth and tenth graders who were
slow readers being enthusiastic about such books as To Kill
a Mockingbird, A Separate Peace, Hawaii, and The King
Must Die.   And so the story goes through 1965 (Black Like
Me, 1984, Brave New World), [123] and 1966 (Lord of the Flies,
Up the Down Staircase)[124] and 1967 (Jazz Country, North to
Freedom). [125]

     The young adult of the 1960s seemed to be primarily
concerned with three areas:

     1. The individual--his growth, personality, and
         philosophy ...
     2. ... social problems and social responsibility,
         whether it be the great national concern of
         Civil Rights or the problem of the mentally
         retarded, the alcoholic, or the juvenile delin-
         quent.
     3. He is concerned for the world he lives in on
         both the national and the international levels
         ... [126]

These concerns were also noted by experienced librarians,
authors and other lay people.

The concern with the self was noticed first: as early as 1952 Elizabeth Ritts Goebel[127] was saying that all teens are much alike in their awareness of themselves, their unsureness, their hero worship, their clannishness, and their feeling of invincibility. In 1954 Dora V. Smith[128] noted that adolescents ask for a sense of reality in their stories. Increasingly, writers spoke of young people being confused, left-out, frustrated, in conflict with society.[129] Some writers bemoaned the organization child, his lack of family life, and the deadening of his curiosity by "how to" education.[130] By 1965 Jane Manthorne,[131] a public librarian, noted that young people were interested in people but not in heroes. And they wanted to do something about their world. Something was apparently happening to young people. The population explosion, urbanization, changing values, and, perhaps most important, the influence of the media, especially television, were changing them.[132] While the general development and major problems of adolescents had not changed drastically with the years,[133] their environment had made them a new breed.[134]

What this new breed was looking for in books was, according to various observers, first, people: "Unable to find them in our civilization of machines and statistics, they turn to books. For in the end books are but the voices of people...."[135] Second, they wanted the voices of these people to be honest, to give them a clear picture of the real world with all its shadings of good and evil.[136] As Kenneth Shaffer[137] put it in 1965, "The image of adolescence as happy-go-lucky, baton-twirling, automobile-driving, money-in-the-pocket, twisting, coke-drinking, boy-and-girl-hand-in-hand Elysium" had begun to look pretty thin. Third, they were looking for books about their real problems in the present-day world, books "reflecting the cool and cruel climb for status, the risks of daredevil dragging, the bewilderment of the young facing the mixed-up adult world, and youthful violence, presented without sensationalism."[138] They were looking for relevance.

The search by the young for books of relevance took them to school and public libraries and to paperback bookstores. Young adults were demanding the right to read anything, so that there came to be "no such thing as a young adult book."[139] At the same time, publishers were attempting to meet the demand in new books which they designated as for young adults in their lists.

Among the earliest were books about Negroes, a publishing venture which had grown to prominence with the Civil
Rights movement combined with the availability of federal
funds to buy books for schools in disadvantaged areas.   It
was hoped that, if young Negroes could find a picture of
themselves and of their way of life in books, it would help
them to overcome their reading difficulties and bolster their
self-image.   The fact that many of these children did have
reading problems had been recognized for many years, [140]
but special reading materials for them did not exist in any
quantity. [141]   There was a gradual increase in the number of
biographies, poetry books, and books of fiction between 1941
and 1959, and at the same time stereotyping diminished gradually. [142]   Then, in the 1960s, came an outpouring of books,
many of them second-rate. [143]   Such books presented certain
difficulties in addition to the normal problems of authorship.
In 1965 Gloria Johnson, [144] a school librarian, made a plea
for editing that "encourages the presentation of well-rounded
characters, not 'angels' or caricatures; ... encourages the
use of regional vernacular where suitable, not overdrawn and
inconsistent dialect, and ... discourages the use of deroga-
tory names and epithets except when needed for historical
accuracy or forceful action. " She also asked that authors
present Negro characters in all walks of life.   A number of
the books of this period, however, dealt with life in the
ghetto, and their authors made an attempt to "tell it like it
is. "[145]   Such books served the double purpose of stimulating
"understanding and empathy toward the problems of the underprivileged on the part of the relatively privileged majority
of youngsters, " and of giving youngsters living in inner cities
books that would interest them. [146]   The experiment was
sufficiently successful to stimulate the production of books
about minorities other than the Negro. [147]

Books about minority youth with problems were the
forerunners of books about all sorts of youth with problems.
Publishers queried in 1968 felt that teenage fiction was becoming more sophisticated because of changing tastes among
young people and because editors were allowing writers to
break many old taboos. [148]   Novels depicting teenage preg-
nancy (Sherburne's Too Bad About the Haines Girl) and imperfect parents (Neville's It's Like This, Cat) began to appear, [149] and in 1969 one writer noted that:

> During 1968 and 1969, an unusual number of juve-
> nile novels aimed at an audience of young teens

and attempting realism have allowed pot to be
puffed and sex to rear a timid head. [150]

A number of people felt that more intensified efforts along
the same lines were needed. Nat Hentoff, [151] for instance,
admitted that his Jazz Country was "deliberately diluted. "
Among school kids, he said, "criticisms were sharp and
frequent, both of me and of other writers of books for 12+.
There were many more hang-ups in being young, I was told
repeatedly, than were even intimated in most of the books
they'd seen. " Nevertheless, he felt that a writer could make
contact with these "children of McLuhan":

> because their primary concerns are only partially
> explored in the messages they get from their
> music and are diverted rather than probed on tel-
> evision. If a book is relevant to these concerns,
> not didactically, but in creating textures of ex-
> perience which teen-agers can recognize as ger-
> mane to their own, it can merit their attention.

Among other things, violence was to be admitted to books for
the young, at least under certain conditions. [152] And sex was
coming to be thought of as something that should play its part
naturally in the juvenile novel. [153] In short, young people
were thought to be "better able to dig sex, drugs, out-of-
wedlock pregnancies, and bumbling parents" than their "es-
capist parents. "[154] Faced with these demands for more and
more relevance and realism on the part of writers and young
people, however, editors and librarians have been accused of
timidity. [155]

Questions for the Seventies

At the present time, the issue of censorship seems to
be rising once more, but without the sound and fury that
characterized it a few years ago. In 1968 Eli M. Oboler[156]
broached the subject, suggesting that perhaps librarians are
not "truly interested in complete freedom for the young. " A
rebuttal was shortly forthcoming, stating the position that librarians can make their greatest contribution to the young by
guiding their search for values. [157] But the fact is, as
Oboler[158] pointed out, "At this point, we really don't know
for sure what the actual cause-and-effect relationship is between reading and behavior, " although one or two tentative
studies have been made. [159] In fact, we know very little

about young people and their reading, and there is need for
a great deal more research. [160]   Meanwhile,

> an assumption seems to be made almost univer-
> sally by the adult society that certain types of
> reading can have undesirable effects upon mind
> and character, and therefore necessarily upon
> conduct.   Therefore, the argument follows, that
> it is the duty of society to place restrictions upon
> the availability of such reading matter....
>
> The library profession itself, which owes its ex-
> istence in a sense to the (unproven) premise that
> books can have beneficial effects upon behavior,
> tacitly accepts the complementary premise that
> some books can have adverse effects upon the be-
> havior of some people. [161]

The question is a complex one, especially in the case of
schools, because of the "apparent incompatibility of two ideas:
(1) adolescents must gradually be led to the appreciation of
mature, adult literature, and to the development of their
critical faculties by exposure to controversy and (2) the
school's curriculum and the reading provided under the
school's auspices must reflect in some way the values of the
adult society. "[162]   Certainly some critics have found the
new, "relevant" junior novels to be didactic, moralizing, and
not entirely free from the traditions of wholesomeness and
the pontifications of wise adults. [163]

     The settings of some of these novels are realistic,
even grim, but none of the scenes depicted belong to an exclusively adult world; young people have long since entered a
realistic and grim world through the medium of television
and/or through the reality of their personal experiences.
"The programs our children watch are largely the ones
planned for adults and packed with violence.   In adult newspapers and photo magazines children follow the pictures as
eagerly as their parents. "[164]   Children nowadays know just
about everything their elders know. [165]   In view of this it is
necessary to look at books from a different perspective, and
it is not surprising to find The Diary of Ann Frank and Death
Be Not Proud are favorites in the sixth and seventh grades,[166]
or to find an 11-year-old commenting favorably on The Good
Earth. [167]   These are simple books, given a knowledge of
birth and death and the inhumanity of man.   But it may be
that we need to examine books and young people more care-

fully, and that if we do we shall discover criteria by which
to identify books for children, books that make a transition
between childhood and adult, young adult books, and books
for more mature adults.   Only a small start has been made
in this direction.   Both Virginia Heffernan and Dorothy M.
Broderick agree that there is a difference between the level
of factual material a young person can read, and the level of
fiction they can digest.   But level in fiction is a matter of
emotional rather than intellectual maturity, and is to be
judged by the ability to see behind the facts of a story, rather
than by the content of the story itself. [168]   (The demand for
"relevance, " for the here and now, may turn out to be a sign
of immaturity in reading, not of sophistication.)

        Another matter that deserves more careful study than
it has been given hitherto is the matter of access to books.
Becker[169] noted differences in the reading of young people in
centers with large libraries and of those in outlying districts
forty years ago, and there is evidence that such differences
are still with us.   Linda F. Lapides[170] recently published
the results of two surveys made at Baltimore's Enoch Pratt
Library in 1960 and in 1970.   This article documents a shift
in the interests of young people to such books as Joy in the
Morning and Mr. and Mrs. Bo Jo Jones, and to books about
the experiences and conditions of black people today.   Their
reading was revealed to be neither "light, recreational, or
diversional. "   While some of the titles in the Pratt survey
can undoubtedly be accounted for by the large number of Negroes in the population of Baltimore, the list as a whole
presents a startling contrast to another recent list of favorites in a small, midwestern high school, where senior boys
included Incredible Journey and Red Car among their favorites. [171] The only book on both lists was Black Like Me.
Without raising the question of which list is "better, " it does
seem pertinent to inquire into the effects of access to good
books in all its ramifications.

        But what is a good book?   There seems to be a trend
in recent years to judge books on their own merits instead of
whether they are good for some purpose.   Authors are being
asked to forget that they are writing for teen-agers, [172] and
the literary quality of a work is to be considered first in its
assessment. [173]   This means both the quality of the writing
and the author's honesty in speaking of the world as he sees
it.   As Newbery winner Emily Neville put it, "The real
world with its shadings of light and dark is so much more
beautiful than a rigid world of good and bad.   It is also more

confusing. I think the teenage reader is ready for both. "[174]
It is hoped that if authors are free to write as they think and
feel, certain stereotypes that are still with us will tend to
disappear. [175] Some controversial materials which have literary merit and honesty appear on the library shelves for,
as John Igo pointed out, most of the world's greatest literature is controversial or, as he put it, are "immoral books,
morally written. "[176] Contact with such books may do less
harm than contact with second-rate books, for "second-rate
books come from second-rate minds, and it is better to leave
people to make their own spontaneous approach to life than
clutter their thinking with cliché responses. "[177] On the other
hand, contact with a variety of original, first-rate minds
might make a "bastion against pressures toward conformity
which in large part are overwhelming motion pictures, radio,
television, and the press. "[178]

        While there is a new emphasis on book selection,
there are also stirrings of interest in a new approach to
reading guidance.   Authors must be allowed to speak for
themselves:

> ... we must remember to step aside and not in-
> trude ourselves between the author and the reader
> by sermonizing and pointing out lessons.   We
> must let the author tell the reader.   Our function
> is to interest the young person in taking the book
> and, after he has read it, enjoying it with him.[179]

The important thing is to bring individuals to books which
will provide them with "moments of being, " or at least the
impending sense of one. [180]   It is also coming to be recognized that such "moments of being" are available in other
media, and that "... much energy and time would be con-
served if we conceded that to many young people, reading is
a drag, and concentrated our efforts on the audiovisual epiphanies (moments of being) that might be triggered. " This
emphasis on the individual, if it is carried out with honesty
and with the support of intelligent investigation, is what gives
promise that media (including books) can be made the agents
for building autonomous personality in many of our young
people. [181]   They might even lead us back to a sense of
humor, "rooted and grounded in perspective on human experience, in a sense of proportion, of the relative value of
things. "[182]

Notes

1. Katherine P. Jeffery, "Selecting Books for the Young
    Adult Collection in the Public Library, " Library
    Trends 17:166-75 (Oct. 1968).

2. "American education grew phenomenally during the quarter
    century following World War One: each year more
    students studied in larger schools for longer periods
    of time.... " Lawrence Cremin, The Transformation
    of the School (Vintage Books, 1961), p. 274.

3. Hannah Logasa, "Elements in Reading Guidance, " Public
    Libraries 27:147-51 (1922).

4. Martha Pritchard, "Reading Guidance for High School
    Pupils, " New York Libraries 10:206-8 (May 1927).

5. Margaret Drew Archibald, "Teen Age Girls as Book
    Lovers, " Library Journal 52:856-57 (1927).

6. Mary S. Wilkerson, "Fiction Reading for Older Boys and
    Girls, " ALA Bulletin 16:266-67 (1922).

7. H. B. Preston, "Capitalizing the Pupils' Judgment of
    Books, " Library Journal 50:210 (1925).

8. Cremin, The Transformation of the School, p. 274.

9. Helen E. Haines, "Adventures in Reading for Young
    People, " ALA Bulletin 24:513-15 (1930).

10. Oscar H. McPherson, "Reading Hobbies, " Library
    Journal 56:733-38 (1931).

11. Lloyd Shaw, "Touching the Intangible, " Wilson Library
    Bulletin 10:110-13 (Oct. 1935).

12. P. G. Chancellor, "What School Boys Read, " Publishers'
    Weekly 134:2212-15 (31 Dec. 1938).

13. "Boring the Young, " New Statesman and Nation 15:8-9
    (1 Jan. 1938).

14. Azile M. Wofford, "Bridging the Gap, " Library Journal
    57:813 (1932).

15.   W. T. B. Mitchell, "Adolescent Interests and Their
      Reading, " ALA Bulletin 28:732-35 (Sept. 1934).

16.   Helen L. Bell, "Reading Guidance and the Adolescent, "
      Wilson Library Bulletin 9:235-38 (Jan. 1935).

17.   May Lamberton Becker, "The Tastes of the Teens, "
      ALA Bulletin 25:634-35 (1931).

18.   Chancellor, "What School Boys Read. "

19.   L. Toomey, "Reading Interests of the Teenage, " Wilson
      Library Bulletin 13:188-89 (Nov. 1938).

20.   Louise E. Hill, "High School Students Like Fiction, "
      Publishers' Weekly 135:1585-87 (29 April 1939).

21.   Irene Smith, "Adolescent Reading, " Library Journal
      57:837-41 (1932).

22.   Ethelwyn Wickson, "Reading Interests of Average Inter-
      mediates, " Wilson Library Bulletin 9:25-26 (Sept.
      1934).

23.   Shaw, "Touching the Intangible. "

24.   Jean C. Roos, "Book Selection and the 'Good' Reader,"
      ALA Bulletin 28:735-38 (Sept. 1934).

25.   Mabel Williams, "'Seventeen' and the Public Library, "
      Library Journal 59:821-23 (1 Nov. 1934).

26.   Alice Cowles Morris, "Book Selection as a Trust, "
      Library Journal 64:887-89 (15 Nov. 1939).

27.   Ruby Ethel Cundiff, "Will It Hold My Interest?" Pea-
      body Journal of Education 14:83-85 (Sept. 1936).

28.   Margaret C. Scoggin, "Do Young People Want Books?"
      Wilson Library Bulletin 11:17-20 (Sept. 1936).

29.   Homer P. Rainey, "How Can Libraries Help to Meet
      the Needs of Youth?" ALA Bulletin 31:406-14 (July
      1937).

30.   Rose McGlennon, "Aid to the Ailing: The Active School
      Library, " Wilson Library Bulletin 12:367-70 (Feb.
      1938).

31. Amelia H. Munson, "Some Folks Won't Read," Educa-
     tional Method 19:142-47 (Dec. 1939).

32. Dora V. Smith, "Reading--A Moot Question," ALA
     Bulletin 32:1031-40 (Dec. 1938).

33. Rachel Field, "Reading and Writing," ALA Bulletin
     33:677-80 (1 Oct. 1939).

34. Eva Schars, "What! No Love Stories?" Nation's
     Schools 19:31-32 (Jan. 1937).

35. Emma Gelders Stone, "A Parent's View of Young
     People's Reading," Library Journal 62:827-29
     (1 Nov. 1937).

36. Schars, "What! No Love Stories?"

37. Walter Prichard Eaton, "Imagination Needs Exercise,"
     Library Journal 63:667-68 (15 Sept. 1938).

38. Douglas Waples, "A Look Ahead at Adolescent Read-
     ing," ALA Bulletin 28:397-400 (July 1934).

39. Dorothy Hopkins, "Young Peoples' Reading and the Chang-
     ing Times," Wilson Library Bulletin 9:291-96 (Feb.
     1935).

40. Hester H. Cam, "A Social Approach to Adolescence,"
     Wilson Library Bulletin 10:379-81 (Feb. 1936).

41. Constance Rourke, "American Traditions for Young
     People," ALA Bulletin 31:934-38 (Dec. 1937).

42. Douglas Waples, "On Developing Taste in Reading,"
     Harvard Educational Review 9:413-23 (Oct. 1939).

43. Frieda M. Heller, "New Designs in Teen-age Reading,"
     ALA Bulletin 34:192-93 (Aug. 1940).

44. See Mabel Zimmerman, "The Library Goes to the Eng-
     lish Class," Wilson Library Bulletin 15:38-9+
     (Sept. 1940); Virginia Teitge, "Follow the Romany
     Pattern," English Journal 29:206-11 (March 1940);
     Ethel L. Cornell, "Can Librarians Help Unusual
     Readers?" ALA Bulletin 35:160-65 (March 1941).

45. Ethel L. Cornell, "The Voluntary Reading of High
     School Pupils, " ALA Bulletin 35:295-300 (May 1941).

46. Marie Nelson Taylor, "Facing the War with Our Young
     People, " Wilson Library Bulletin 17:656-58 (April
     1943).

47. Margaret C. Scoggin, "Young People's Reading Inter-
     ests Not Materially Changed in Wartime, " Library
     Journal 68:703-6 (15 Sept. 1943).

48. Helen L. Butler, "Motivating Reading in Wartime, "
     Library Journal 68:460-63 (1 June 1943).

49. C. R. P. Sievens, "Survey of Wartime Reading of
     Students at Brookline, Massachusetts, " Library
     Journal 69:752-53 (15 Sept. 1944).

50. Butler, "Motivating Reading. "

51. Kathryn A. Haebich, "What Are Adolescents Reading?"
     Wilson Library Bulletin 20:289+ (Dec. 1945).

52. Gladys B. Johnson, "Books and the Five Adolescent
     Tasks, " Library Journal 68:350-52 (1 May 1943).
     The books mentioned are merely examples.

53. Lucile Vickers, "Education for Living, " Wilson Li-
     brary Bulletin 17:654-5+ (April 1943).

54. Margaret Kessler Walraven, "Reading: The Librar-
     ian's View, " English Journal 32:198-203 (April
     1943).

55. Lillian M. Enlow, "Teaching Good Citizenship, " Wil-
     son Library Bulletin 15:392-93 (Jan. 1941).

56. Willard A. Heaps, "Bibliotherapy and the School Li-
     brarian, " Library Journal 65:957-59 (15 Nov.
     1940).

57. Louise Dinwiddie, "Best Sellers and Modern Youth, "
     Library Journal 65:957-59 (15 Nov. 1940).

58. Jeffery, "Selecting Books. "

59. Alice Cowles Morris, "A Good Short Book, Please, "

184

Wilson Library Bulletin 17:712-13 (May 1943).

60. Becker, "The Tastes of the Teens."

61. Richard S. Alm, "The Glitter and the Gold," English Journal 44:315-22+ (Sept. 1955).

62. Stephen Dunning, "The Most Popular Junior Novels," Library Journal 84:3885-87 (15 Dec. 1959).

63. Virginia Westphal, "The Teenage Novel, A Defense," Library Journal 89:1832-33+ (15 April 1964).

64. One cannot leave a discussion of the junior novel in the late 1940s and 1950s without mentioning the concurrent rise of "science fiction." For an analysis of this genre, see Robert A. Heinlein, "Ray Guns and Rocket Ships," Library Journal 78:1188-91 (July 1953).

65. Vernon Ives, "Teen-age Reading," ALA Bulletin 47: 400-4 (Oct. 1953).

66. A. C. Kennedy, "Serving the Young and Their Reading Interests," Library Journal 73:1794-95 (15 Dec. 1948).

67. D. Winifred Jackson, "Selecting Adult Books for Young People," Top of the News 5:5-6+ (Dec. 1948).

68. Jeffrey, "Selecting Books."

69. Margaret C. Scoggin, "Fables They Shall Not Read," ALA Bulletin 46:323+ (Nov. 1952).

70. In 1957, for instance, the "Interesting Adult Books of 1957 for Young People," chosen by the ALA, included seven nonfiction books; three biographies, one of them fictionalized; five books of memoirs, or "true stories"; and five works of fiction, two of them war stories. Selections for 1958, 1959 and 1960 are similar. I have read a number of these books, and find them, for the most part, wordy and dull.

71. Martha Huddleston, "Teen Age Reading Habits," Wilson Library Bulletin 22:53+ (Sept. 1947); "Teen

Agers Do Read, " Wilson Library Bulletin 23:178-
79 (Oct. 1948); Laura E. Vroman, "Trends in
Reading in Junior High School, " Wilson Library
Bulletin 23:678-80 (May 1949); Rachel W. DeAnge-
lo, "Trends in Reading in Senior High School, "
Wilson Library Bulletin 23:675-78 (May 1949);
Florence Powell, "Students' Choice, " Library Jour-
nal 76:488-91 (15 March 1951); Virginia Tozier,
"What Motivates Secondary School Voluntary Read-
ing?" Wilson Library Bulletin 30:166-69 (Oct.
1955); Aimee K. Kulp, "Teen-agers Won't Read!"
Wilson Library Bulletin 29:614-15 (April 1955);
Dorothy Pierman, "But Johnny Is Reading!" Wilson
Library Bulletin 30:623 (April 1956); and others for
the 1950s quoted in the sections "Ages Twelve to
Fifteen" and "Ages Twelve to Nineteen" of Jean
Spealman Kujoth, Reading Interests of Children and
Young Adults (Scarecrow, 1970).

72. Lloyd W. Babb, "Guidance in Recreational Reading, "
English Journal 41:201-4 (April 1952).

73. Virginia Tozier, "What Motivates. "

74. Lewis Perry, "What Makes Sammy Read?" Publishers' Weekly 167:1024-26 (12 Feb. 1955).

75. Esther Millett, "What Makes Sally Read?" Publishers'
Weekly 167:1022-24 (12 Feb. 1955).

76. Ruth Hill Viguers, "Invitation to the Feast, " Horn
Book 34:449-58 (Dec. 1958).

77. G. Robert Carlsen, "The Magic of Bringing Young
Adults to Books, " Wilson Library Bulletin 33:134-
37+ (Oct. 1958).

78. "Patterns in Reading, " Publishers' Weekly 190:29-39
(8 Aug. 1966). Report of a speech by Carlsen to
YASD of ALA at their 85th convention.

79. G. Robert Carlsen, "The Right Size, " Top of the
News 23:55-62 (Nov. 1966).

80. These findings formed the basis of Carlsen's Books and
the Teen Age Reader (Rev. ed. Harper, 1972) which
remains a significant contribution.

81. M. Fraser, "Youth and the Classics," Canadian Library Association Bulletin 7:175-78 (March 1951).

82. "Adult Books for the Young Adults," Top of the News 16:12-20+ (Dec. 1959).

83. Francis X. Cleary, "Why Johnnie Is Reading," Education 82:305-8 (Jan. 1962).

84. Florence Hascall, "No Lollipops," Horn Book 39:86-91 (Feb. 1963).

85. Viguers, "Invitation."

86. Lois Blau, "The Novel in the High School Library," Wisconsin Library Journal 60:178-81 (May 1964). Reprinted in Dennis Thomison, Readings About Adolescent Literature (Scarecrow, 1970).

87. Margaret A. Edwards, "A Time When It's Best to Read and Let Read," Wilson Library Bulletin 35:43-45 (Sept. 1960).

88. Frances Lombard, "Rid the 100s of Deadwood," Library Journal 82:1339-40 (15 May 1957).

89. Ann Emery, "Values in Adolescent Fiction," Library Journal 83:1565-67 (15 May 1958).

90. Madeline Irrig, "Developing Character Through Reading," Wilson Library Bulletin 33:571-73 (April 1959).

91. Dorothy M. Broderick, "The Opportunities That Books Offer," Library Journal 84:3891-3901 (15 Dec. 1959).

92. Margaret Edwards, "Taming the Young Barbarian," Library Journal 89:1819-21 (15 April 1964).

93. Marie Blanche MacDonald, "Shake Hands with Mrs. Grundy," Wilson Library Bulletin 33:148-49 (Oct. 1958).

94. Margaret A. Edwards, "Mrs. Grundy Go Home," Wilson Library Bulletin 33:304-5 (Dec. 1958).

95. John A. Myers, "The Realistic Novel and the Gold
      Ring, " Catholic Library World 38:167-71 (Nov.
      1966).

96. Frederic R. Hartz, "Obscenity, Censorship and
      Youth, " Clearing House 36:99-101 (Oct. 1961).

97. Hoke Norris, "Two Kinds of Censorship, " PTA Mag-
      azine 59:11-12 (March 1965).

98. "What Books for the Young Adult?" Library Journal
      89:4103-6 (15 Oct. 1964).

99. Norris, "Two Kinds. "

100. James R. Squire and Robert F. Hogan, "Where Is
       the Danger?" PTA Magazine 59:12 (March 1965).

101. John A. Myers, "The Realistic Novel. "

102. E. Geller, "Two Cheers for Liberty, " Library Jour-
       nal 92:3109-13 (15 Sept. 1967).

103. Max Rafferty, "The Other Side: Hardest of All Things
       to Come By, " Wilson Library Bulletin 42:181-86
       (Oct. 1967).

104. See Wilson Library Bulletin, 42:368-69 (Dec. 1967).
       Also Jean Smith, "A Public Library Trustee Looks
       at the 'Other Side', " ALA Bulletin 62:111-12
       (Feb. 1968).

105. David K. Berninghausen, "An Exploratory Study of
       Juvenile Delinquency and the Reading of Sensational
       Books, " Journal of Experimental Education 33:
       161-68 is an example of research on the subject.

106. Helen Gothberg, "Young Adult Censorship: Adult or
       Adolescent Problem?" Top of the News 22:275-78
       (April 1966).

107. Audrey Sabadosh, "Teenagers View Censorship, "
       Top of the News 22:278-80 (April 1966).

108. Esther Helfand, "Love and Humanity--Not Intellectual
       Freedom, " Top of the News 24:47-54 (Nov. 1967).

109. Jean E. Crabtree, "The Challenge of Quality Reading for Young Adults, " ALA Bulletin 55:419-20 (May 1961).

110. Frank G. Jennings, "Literature for Adolescents--Pap or Protein?" English Journal 45:526-31 (Dec. 1956).

111. Vivian J. MacQuown, "The Teenage Novel: A Critique, " Library Journal 89:1832-35 (15 April 1964). See also Catherine Robertson, "Young People and Spoon-Fed Reading, " Ontario Library Review 44:248-49 (Nov. 1960).

112. Kenneth R. Shaffer, "What Makes Sammy Read?" Top of the News 19:9-12 (March 1963).

113. _____, "Teenage Elysium: Our Own Delusion, " Library Journal 89:4976-78 (15 Dec. 1964).

114. Arthur Daigan, "Novel of Adolescent Romance, " Library Journal 91:2152-56 (15 April 1966).

115. Sarah L. Siebert, "Taking Shaffer to Task, " Top of the News 20:67-69 (Oct. 1963).

116. MacQuown, "The Teenage Novel. "

117. Dorothy M. Broderick, "Carping Critics, Instant Experts, " Library Journal 90:3690-92 (15 Sept. 1965).

118. For example, see Ruth G. Rausen, "The Junior High Reader, " Top of the News (Nov. 1966); Anthony J. Soares, "Salient Elements of Recreational Reading of Junior High School Students, " Elementary English 40:843-45 (Dec. 1963); Ruth Strang, "Teen-age Readers, " PTA Magazine 55:10-12 (June 1961); and articles by Charles E. Johnson, Beryl I. Vaughan, Jo M. Stanchfield, Paul Witty, and J. Harlan Shores reprinted in Kujoth, Reading Interests of Children and Young Adults.

119. Margaret W. Dudley, "What Young Americans Are Reading, " Library Journal 85:3170-71 (15 Sept. 1960).

120. "What Young Americans Are Reading," Library Journal
     86:1955 (15 May 1961).

121. Nick Aaron Ford, "What High School Students Say
     About Good Books," English Journal 50:539-40+
     (Nov. 1961).

122. Esther Millett, "We Don't Even Call Them Books!"
     Top of the News 20:45-47 (Oct. 1963).

123. Helen Wilmott, "YASD Asks the Young Adult," Top of
     the News 21:143-47 (Jan. 1965).

124. "Young Adults Disclose Favorite Reading, Library
     Uses, in Westchester Survey," Library Journal
     91:2184 (15 April 1966).

125. "Publishers Hear Young Adult Panel Talk about Read-
     ing Tastes," Library Journal 92:284-85 (15 Jan.
     1967).

126. Wilmott, "YASD Asks."

127. Elizabeth Ritts Goebel, "Teen-age Reading," Library
     Journal 77:941-43 (1 June 1952).

128. Dora V. Smith, "Books--A Source of Strength for
     Youth in a Free Land," Top of the News 11:9-17
     (Oct. 1954).

129. Jerome Cushman, "Today's Bewildered Youth," Li-
     brary Journal 84:611-14 (15 Feb. 1959).

130. Harriette Arnow, "Reading Without a Purpose," ALA
     Bulletin 53:837-39 (Nov. 1959).

131. Jane Manthorne, "The Age of the Acronym," Wilson
     Library Bulletin 40:84-86 (Sept. 1965).

132. H. B. Maloney, "Humanities Today," Clearing House
     38:380 (Feb. 1964). See also Cushman, "Today's
     Bewildered."

133. Compare, for example, two analyses of the adolescent
     by child-study experts: Marynia F. Farnham,
     "Who Is the Young Adult?" Top of the News 14:46-
     50 (Oct. 1957) and Armin Grams, "Understanding

the Adolescent Reader, " Library Trends 17:121-
31 (Oct. 1968).

134. Marjorie Sullivan, "Reading for Relevance," Library
      Journal 93:4693-95 (15 Dec. 1968).

135. Harriette Arnow, "Reading Without. "

136. Ursula Nordstrom, "Honesty in Teenage Novels, "
      Top of the News 21:35-38 (Nov. 1964).

137. Kenneth R. Shaffer, "Teenage Elysium, " Library
      Journal.

138. Susan Hinton, quoted in Sullivan, "Reading for Rele-
      vance. "

139. Mary Mace Spradling, "There Is No Such Book, " Top
      of the News 21:346-48 (June 1965).

140. Benjamin F. Smith, "The School Librarian and the
      Reading Process, " Journal of Negro Education
      17:114-119 (April 1948).

141. Dorothy Sterling, "Soul of Learning, " English Journal
      57:167-80 (Feb. 1968).

142. Charlemae Rollins, "Books about Negroes for Child-
      ren, " ALA Bulletin 53:306-8 (April 1959).

143. Ann Durrell, "Goodies and Baddies, " Wilson Library
      Bulletin 44:456-57 (Dec. 1969).

144. Gloria Johnson, "The Fifth Freedom: Presenting the
      Negro in Books, " Top of the News 22:62-63 (Nov.
      1965).

145. Sterling, "Soul of Learning. "

146. Frank Bonham, "Return to Durango Street, " Library
      Journal 91:4188-99 (15 Sept. 1966).

147. Frank Bonham and James Duggings, "Are We for Real
      with Kids?" Top of the News 23:245-52 (April
      1967).

148. "Change in the Teens and in the Publishers, " Pub-

lishers' Weekly 193:91-92 (26 Feb. 1968).

149. Phyllis Zucker, "The Junior Novel Revisited, " Top of the News 25:388-91 (June 1969).

150. Diane Gersoni Stavn, "Watching Fiction for Today's Teens, " Library Journal 94:4305-6 (15 Nov. 1969). But it is worth noting that novels of this type were not a completely new invention. Several earlier efforts are mentioned in Margaret Walraven, "Trends in Children's Books: Young People," Texas Library Journal 26:112-15 (Sept. 1950).

151. Nat Hentoff, "Fiction for Teen-agers, " Wilson Library Bulletin 43:261-65 (Nov. 1968).

152. James C. Giblin, "Violence: Factors Considered by a Children's Book Editor, " Elementary English 49: 64-67 (Jan. 1972).

153. John Neufeld, "The Thought, Not Necessarily the Deed, " Wilson Library Bulletin 46:147-52 (Oct. 1971).

154. Joan Bodger Mercer, "Innocence Is a Cop-out, " Wilson Library Bulletin 46:144-46 (Oct. 1971).

155. Lyle Wilson Warrick, "Where Hentoff Left Off, " Wilson Library Bulletin 43:266-68 (Nov. 1968); Mary Kingsbury, "Ostriches and Adolescents, " Journal of Education for Librarianship 11:325-31 (Spring 1971); and Linda Lapides, "Question of Relevance," Top of the News 24:55-61 (Nov. 1967).

156. Eli M. Oboler, "The Grand Illusion, " Library Journal 93:1277-79 (15 March 1968).

157. Vincent M. Inghilterra, "A Note of Dissent, " Library Journal 93:3183 (15 Sept. 1968).

158. Oboler, "The Grand Illusion"; also Beverly Sigler Edwards, "The Therapeutic Value of Reading, " Elementary English 49:213-17 (Feb. 1972).

159. Shirley Fehl, "The Influence of Reading on Adolescents, " Wilson Library Bulletin 43:256-60 (Nov. 1968); also Sister Mary Corde Lorang, Burning Ice:

The Moral and Emotional Effects of Reading (Scribner's, 1968).

160. Alexander Beinlich, "On the Literary Development of Children and Adolescents, " Bookbird v. 6, no. 1 (1968), p. 17-22.

161. John J. Farley, "The Reading of Young People, " Library Trends 19:81-88 (July 1970).

162. Farley, "The Reading of Young People. "

163. John S. Simmons, "Lipsyte's Contender: Another Look at the Junior Novel, " Elementary English 49:116-19 (Jan. 1972). Also Natalie Babbitt, "Between Innocence and Maturity, " Horn Book 48:33-37 (Feb. 1972).

164. Nancy Larrick, "Baby Dolls Are Gone, " Library Journal 92:3815-17 (15 Oct. 1967).

165. Margaret Mead, the anthropologist, speaks to this point in a number of her writings. The situation is, of course, a return to an older order of things rather than something new. See Philippe Ariès Centuries of Childhood (Vintage, 1965).

166. Larrick, "Baby Dolls. "

167. American Girl (April 1972), p. 17.

168. Virginia Heffernan, "The Blurred Boundary, " Top of the News (Nov. 1964) and Dorothy M. Broderick, "The Twelve-Year-Old Adult Reader, " Library Journal 90:2321-27 (15 May 1965).

169. Becker, "The Tastes of the Teens. "

170. Linda F. Lapides, "A Decade of Teen-age Reading in Baltimore, " Top of the News (April 1971).

171. Mary DesJardins, "Reading and Viewing, " School Libraries v. 21, no. 3 (Spring 1972).

172. Natalie Babbitt, "Between Innocence. "

173. John Rowe Townsend, "Standards of Criticism for

Children's Literature, " <u>Top of the News</u> 27:4
(Spring 1971).

174. Quoted in Ursula Nordstrom, "Honesty. "

175. See, for example, recent discussions of women in
      books for the young: Diane Gersoni Stavn, "The
      Skirts in Fiction about Boys: A Maxi Mess, " <u>Li-
      brary Journal</u> 96:282-86 (15 Jan. 1971); Mary
      Ritchie Key, "The Role of Male and Female in
      Children's Books--Dispelling All Doubt, " <u>Wilson
      Library Bulletin</u> 46:167-76 (Oct. 1971); Diane Ger-
      soni Stavn, "Reducing the 'Miss Muffett' Syn-
      drome, " <u>Library Journal</u> 97:256-59 (15 Jan. 1972).

176. John Igo, "Books for the New Breed, " <u>Library
      Journal</u> 92:1704-5 (15 April 1967).

177. Peggy Heeks, "Books for Adolescents, " <u>School Li-
      brarian</u> 14:133-39 (July 1966).

178. David Morris, "TV Selects Public Library Books, "
      <u>ALA Bulletin</u> 62:460 (May 1968); also Marjorie
      Sullivan, "Books, Readers, and Individuals, " <u>Top
      of the News</u> 27:292-98 (April 1971).

179. Margaret Edwards, "A Book Is to Read, " <u>Southeast-
      ern Librarian</u> 19:198-203 (Winter 1969).

180. Laura M. Jones, "Epiphanies or Plastic Bags?"
      <u>Canadian Library Journal</u> 28:373-77 (Sept. 1971).

181. Sullivan, "Books, Readers. "

182. Dora V. Smith, "Books--A Source. "

FOUR MISCONCEPTIONS OF MACHINE FANATICS
IN JUDGING DIRECT HUMAN-COMPUTER INTERACTION*

Janice M. Ladendorf

Librarians today are being haunted by a pernicious fantasy. The electronic gadgeteers keep reproducing the same impractical vision of library services in tomorrow's utopia. In their imaginary world, each individual user will be hooked into a computerized network. While comfortably sitting at his desk, a user will be able to locate relevant citations by deploying the appropriate machine search strategies. He will then be able to obtain copies of desired documents simply by pressing a button.

Such a pipe dream could arise only from the fevered imaginations of machine fanatics. Today many people do worship technological marvels; however, machines must be designed and used by fallible human beings. The most elaborate retrieval system is utterly useless unless someone is both willing and able to use it. In their enchantment with machines, the gadgeteers have overlooked certain inhibiting user characteristics. Machines can be programmed to act logically; humans cannot. It takes a skilled librarian to deal with most users. The machine fanatics have excluded this human factor from their dreams of the future. By doing so, they have insured the failure of their visionary systems.

False Prophets

This impractical pipe dream has been plaguing librarians more than twenty years. The computer prophets of the 1950s foresaw a great potential field for machine applications in libraries. Fortunately their predictions have failed to materialize. The reason for their failure is quite simple:

*Reprinted by permission of the author and publisher from the Wilson Library Bulletin, March 1974, pp. 561-564.

they were so overawed by the capabilities of the computer
that they overlooked the complexity of the library-user problem. [1] Computers can do fairly well at juggling citations,
but they are not very well equipped to deal with people. Electronic data-processing equipment has crept slowly into the
library's routine record-keeping procedures. As library organizations continue to grow in size, this infiltration will
probably continue. But handling bibliographic records is one
thing; handling people is another. Despite all the predictions
to the contrary, direct user-computer interaction will probably remain an illusion. Anyone who argues otherwise is
designing retrieval systems for mythical users with atypical
questions.

Misconception 1: Users Need It

The machine fanatics have based their fallacious predictions on four basic misconceptions about library work.
Misconception number one is a misapprehension about the
nature of the typical user query. In comparison to human
searchers, computers do have two important talents: they
can conduct comprehensive searches at high speed, and they
can handle very complex questions. Unfortunately, these
talents are rarely needed. In normal library operations, a
user who actually wants a comprehensive search is about as
rare as a blue whale. To quote M. Line, a researcher usually "wants his references in drips rather than clumps."
Drips fit into his normal work pattern: large clumps of references impede it. [2] After all, by the time a searcher has
looked at the first "drip," he may change his mind as to
what he really wants. Such redefinitions may then turn most
of the references in a "clump" into wasted effort. At present we know very little about the process of information
seeking. However, what we do know indicates that most
searches involve a dynamic interaction with the available information. In this process, the user continues to redefine
his problem as he becomes more familiar with what is
known. Printed indexes are usually more than adequate for
this purpose and demand much less sophistication from the
user.

In the normal process of literature searching, a computer is rarely able to help the typical user. For him, a
computer search usually results more in blunders than benefits. Once programmed, a computer must pull from its files
all the citations fitting the search pattern. Many of these

citations may represent noise; that is, they fit the search
pattern but not the subject of the actual query. The ones
which do fit the query may greatly exceed the user's real
requirements. Finding too many citations may be almost as
bad as finding none. Most users seem to have a very low
saturation point for irrelevant or unneeded citations. An excessively long list of citations may simply irritate the user
into not using the search results at all. Someone who wants
three good articles may be infuriated if he gets instead three
hundred useless citations. If we want people to use our libraries, we must give them what they want, not what some
impractical expert says they need.

Complex questions are almost as rare in library work
as comprehensive ones. According to Vavrek, complexity in
the context of reference work takes on a special meaning. It
refers to the number of cognitive or conceptual elements
contained in a user's query, not to the amount of difficulty
encountered in solving the user's information problem. A
complex question may turn out to be very easy to answer,
while a simple one may occasionally pose insurmountable
problems. Vavrek discovered that the typical reference
question rarely contained more than six conceptual elements,[3]
well within the range of human capabilities. People can
normally handle about seven such cognitive relationships.[4]
Given proper programming, a computer can correlate an almost infinite number of concepts. However, since normal
human beings formulate reference questions, they will rarely
exceed the human limits of seven. Of course, there are
times when answering a user's query may call for the coord-
ination of an unusual number of concepts. In such cases, a
good librarian does need to be able to recommend the appropriate computerized search service. But ordinary users with
ordinary questions rarely have any need for the computer's
ability to handle complex or comprehensive questions.

Misconception 2: Users Understand It

If the typical user query fails to suit computer capabilities, even less does the knowledge of the typical user.
The machine fanatics have greatly overestimated user willingness to learn the rules governing retrieval systems, which
points to a second misconception about the real nature of library work. Librarians have been attempting to teach people
how to use libraries for years and with very little success.
A user who is baffled by the card catalog is not going to be

willing to confront a computer. From the user's point of
view, a machine system simply represents one more frustrating barrier between him and the information he needs.
All the gadgeteers have succeeded in doing so far is building
more and more sophisticated systems to serve fewer and
fewer people, [5] mainly because most people tend to avoid unnecessary effort, or in terms of library usage, the more
learning effort a retrieval system requires, the less it will
be used. User studies have consistently shown that the more
applications-oriented a user is, the less likely he is to exert
himself in information seeking. In practically all fields,
practitioners and students far outnumber the researchers.
Therefore, sophisticated systems demanding a great deal of
effort from the user are bound to be used by very few.

Misconception 3: Users Are Understood

        Along with overestimating user willingness to acquire
knowledge, the machine fanatics have also managed to ignore
one of the most fundamental characteristics of language. They
have failed to grasp the major difference between machine
and human communication--a third basic misconception.
Machine languages may have grammars, but they lack semantic variability. Before a computer will accept a programmed request, all the life must be drained out of it.
Machines are able to successfully obey only orders which
are so precise that they leave no room for misunderstanding.
In contrast, communication between humans is usually vivid,
sloppy, and wide open to misinterpretation. To communicate
clearly, humans must use social context and non-verbal clues
as aids to understanding. Until machines can be reared in
human societies, they will be unable to handle this kind of
communication. [6] In the information field, the gadgeteers
have been attempting to make users over so that their requests will fit into the capabilities of their machines. The
result, of course, has been the development of retrieval systems which suit machines, not people. [7] This means that
people who refuse to be made over will get no service. Even
those who do accept redesign usually get limited results. No
computer could possibly deal with confused and inarticulate
people as another human can. For the foreseeable future,
humans will still be needed to help other humans deal with
complex retrieval systems.

Misconception 4: Users Are Alike

The fourth and final misconception of the machine
fanatics is to greatly underestimate the importance and complexity of the question-negotiation process. As any experienced librarian knows, five people can ask the same question
and actually want five different kinds of information. It is
almost impossible to have too much background information
about the inquirer and why he needs help. As a librarian is
skillfully drawing a user out about his problem, he is also
making judgments about this person's depth of knowledge in
the subject about which he is inquiring. Since people are
usually unwilling to openly admit ignorance, these judgments
must generally be made on the basis of social or nonverbal
clues, such as appearance and speaking style. Determining
the subject of the query is important, but it is just as important to determine the amount and level of the needed information. This is just the kind of thing a computer cannot
do. For example, four people--a nine-year-old schoolgirl,
a member of a citizen's action group, a sanitary engineer,
and an analytical chemist--might ask for information on mer-
cury pollution. To a librarian, it ought to be obvious that
each wanted something different; to a non-human machine, it
would not now be apparent.

There is a reprehensible tendency, both among gadgeteers and library administrators, to lump all users together into one amorphous mass. Users are individual
people, each with unique needs and educational experiences.
They cannot all be forced into one limited, arbitrary, ma-
chine-made mold. As yet, dealing skillfully and flexibly with
varied individuals is beyond machine capabilities. [8] Successfully helping people demands too much sensitivity, especially
in responding to what is left unsaid. As a librarian gropes
toward an understanding of his client's problem, he is also
conveying something to the inquirer. People usually do need
to feel that someone is really listening to them. No machine
could possibly convey the sense of helpfulness that another
human can. Most people resent being reduced to an imper-
sonal level by a mere machine. Even if they accept this
role, they may be unwilling to undertake the exertion of
learning to communicate with the machine in the limited
language it can understand. Overcoming human resistance
to their gadgets is one problem that the machine fanatics
have not yet managed to solve.

By now it should be clear why the nature of library

users and their needs make direct computer-user interaction
into a myth. Normal users with normal problems simply do
not fit into machine capabilities. The gadgeteers are going
to have to come out of their fantasy world and face some of
the hard facts of library life. For them the machine is a
hero and the villains are those people who refuse to utilize
their marvelous machine. To most librarians, the computer
is a villain, who is threatening to steal their jobs. The
truth, as might be expected, lies somewhere between these
two viewpoints.

Electronic data-processing equipment has helped get
the information explosion under bibliographic control; but by
doing so, it has added one more level of complexity to the
library-user problem. This means that librarians, who can
help the user get the most out of the available resources,
are more needed than ever. In this task, a human can do a
job that no machine can equal. The most elaborate programming and expensive equipment is no substitute for years of
living in human society.

Notes

1. Doyle, L. B., "I think, therefore i. r. " Sci-Tech News
    (Spring 1972), p. 5-7.

2. Line, M. B., "On the design of information systems
    for human beings, " Aslib Proceedings, 22:7 (July
    1970), p. 325.

3. Vavrek, B. F., "Communications and the reference in-
    terface, " Ph. D. thesis, Univ. of Pittsburgh, 1971,
    p. 76-78.

4. Miller, George A., "The magical number seven plus or
    minus two, " Psychological Review (1956), p. 81-97.

5. Havelock, R. G., Planning for Innovation, Ann Arbor,
    Mich., Institute for Social Research, Univ. of Michi-
    gan, 1970, p. 11-39.

6. Pierce, J. R., "Men, machines, and languages, "
    IEEE Spectrum, 5:7 (July 1968), p. 44-49.

7. Doyle, L. B., "Semantic road maps for literature
    searchers, " Journal of the Association for Computing

Machinery, 8:4 (Oct. 1961).

8. Meadows, C. T. , Man-Machine Communication, N. Y. ,
    Wiley, 1970, p. 396-401.

THE LIBRARY RESOURCES, INC.,
LIBRARY OF AMERICAN CIVILIZATION
DEMONSTRATION AT THE GEORGE
WASHINGTON UNIVERSITY LIBRARY*

Paul A. Napier, Annette D. Steiner
and Rupert C. Woodward

Introduction

Readers of Microform Review will be no strangers to Encyclopaedia Britannica's venture, through its subsidiary, Library Resources, Inc., into the field of micropublishing. The Library of American Civilization, its first project in ultrafiche format, is discussed both pro and con, along with NCR's PCMI collection, in the April 1972 issue. In addition, in the same issue will be found a review of the LAC by staff members of the Pennsylvania State University Library.

LRI deserves credit for its efforts to provide a total system package containing complete bibliographic support in the form of both catalogs and the optional sets of catalog cards. Regardless of specific criticisms that may be directed at the publication, the fact remains that LAC is a well-indexed, easily stored, readily retrievable, and--with the table model reader--a highly usable resource that should be of considerable value in many libraries. The present article, based on a one-year investigation conducted in The George Washington University Library (Washington, D.C.) under a grant from the National Home Library Foundation of Washington, D.C., sets forth the results of that study. It is being published in keeping with the prime purpose of the investigation, which was to develop information of assistance to other libraries (and perhaps micropublishers as well) in achieving maximum use of book resources in ultramicrofiche format.

As to the report itself, some explanation may be in

---

*Reprinted by permission of the authors and publisher from Microform Review, July 1974, pp. 158-176.

order regarding its apparent preoccupation with the specially
designed readers, a portable and a table model. It is axiomatic that the availability of a low cost, reliable, easy-to-
use, high quality reader, and access to a good service outlet, are crucial to the success of any micropublishing venture.
Hence the need for a critical examination of the hardware,
particularly when, as in the present instance, it is being introduced to the market for the first time. It was also observed from a review of the literature available at the time
the study began--January 1972--that little or no attention was
devoted to this part of the LAC package. And, finally, as
our users began to have problems, particularly with the portable reader, an effort was made to solve those problems by
first determining their causes. So numerous and varied were
the difficulties that developed with the portable reader that
considerable staff time was expended in the effort to correct
them.

          Some up-date of the GWU figures of usage of the LAC
may be of interest. As mentioned in the report, there were
recorded 511 instances of both on- and off-site use during
the grant year 1972. In 1973, this increased to 568 instances
of on-site use. One contributing factor is undoubtedly the
meagerness of the resources in American studies in the
George Washington University Library's holdings, which in
toto comprise some 470, 000 volumes and pieces of microtext.
As the report states, a check of 500 randomly chosen LAC
titles against the GW public catalog disclosed that only 56, or
11. 2 percent, were duplicated. It is believed, and the usage
tends to confirm this, that the library's holdings have been
considerably enriched by the acquisition of the LAC ultrafiche
collection.

Background and Purpose of Study

          In August 1971, The National Home Library Foundation
of Washington, D. C. , awarded to The George Washington
University a grant of $40, 000 to install a set of the ultra-
fiche Library of American Civilization (produced by Encyclopaedia Britannica's subsidiary, Library Resources, Inc.), together with all available associated equipment and bibliographic support. The GW library was to publicize the resource to a wide local audience and to permit its use both
on- and off-site during the calendar year beginning January 1,
1972. From its evaluation of the demonstration, the library
hoped to develop information of help to other libraries in

gaining maximum utilization of book resources in ultrafiche
(highly reduced) form. At the end of the one-year demonstration, George Washington University was to take title to
all materials and equipment used in the demonstration.

The Library of American Civilization (LAC) is the
first of a number of series planned in ultrafiche by Library
Resources, Inc. (LRI). According to the prepublication brochure, The Microbook Library Series, and information supplied at the time, it consists of approximately 13, 500 3" x 5"
microfiche containing over 6, 000, 000 pages and about 20, 000
volumes and covering all aspects of America's culture from
the beginnings to the outbreak of World War I. The installation at GW was to be accompanied both by printed (book) catalogs of the collection and by a regular set of catalog cards
for each of the more than 12, 000 titles in the collection, as
well as by table readers, a number of portable, "take-home"
type readers, and a reader-printer for those users desiring
paper copy.

It was believed that GW's acquisition of LAC would be
desirable because its American studies program is receiving
heavy emphasis at both the undergraduate and graduate levels.
The program currently has about 130 students enrolled each
semester in Introduction to American Civilization, about 45
students in the Proseminar in American Civilization, and
about 60 graduate students in one or more American studies
reading courses and seminars--totaling approximately 1, 400
semester credit hours per year. There are three full-time
and two part-time faculty members. There is substantial on-
going student and faculty research; because of limited library
resources in book form in the GW library, researchers at
present must make wide use of other library resources in
the metropolitan area. Hence, the potential for use of the
LAC collection. Before that potential could be realized, it
would be necessary for the pertinent students, faculty and
others to be made aware of the availability of the collection
in the GW library.

Publicity

It was evident at the outset that a multipronged publicity campaign would be required to acquaint all interested
persons with the nature and existence of the LAC collection
in the library. This took the following forms:

1.   Holding orientation conferences with LRI guest
speakers for faculty, graduate students, and library staff
members, both from GW and from the other Washington Consortium libraries--American, Catholic, Georgetown, and
Howard--and for interested librarians from nearby U.S.
government libraries, as well as for some non-librarians.

2.   Subsequent scheduling of demonstrations and orientation meetings of selected classes of students, along with
their professors.

3.   Furnishing to the department chairmen deemed to
have the largest number of potential student users--American
studies, history, and English (American literature)--complete
sets of the various author, title, and subject book catalogs,
as well as the Biblioguide Index volume.

4.   Distributing flyer describing the collection and
giving its location to thirty-two faculty members teaching in
fields touched by the LAC with the request that it be placed
on any bulletin boards within their control.

5.   Posting in appropriate places within the library
copies of the flyer, as well as wall posters and self-standing
placards furnished with the collection.

6.   Displaying in museum cases in the room in which
the collection was housed an exhibit depicting the history of
microfilm with emphasis on the evolution of the high-reduc-
tion ultrafiche concept.

7.   Filing the long-delayed catalog cards in the main
public catalog, an action which was completed in early June
1972, too late to be of use during the first semester of the
demonstration year.

8.   Publishing announcements in the D.C. Library
Association organ, Intercom, and in other more widely distributed journals to effect maximum public exposure to the
local and national library community.

The LAC Package

This consists of the following items, each of which
will be discussed in detail subsequently: the ultrafiche collection; the author, title, and subject book catalogs (five copies

of each); the Biblioguide Index (five copies); and two copies
of a soft-cover booklet, the Shelf List. In addition, ten
copies of the four hardbound volumes--author, subject, title,
and Biblioguide Index--were provided in ultrafiche. Included
was one table reader, with additional ones available at $450
each. The total cost of the basic package was $19,500.
Optional portable readers were available at $165 each.
Optional also was the set of catalog cards, estimated by LRI
to number 75,000 at a cost of $4,000 for the set.

Because the figures supplied in the pre- and post-pub-
lication brochures regarding the number of fiches, and of
titles, volumes, and pages photographed for the collection
exhibited some variation, it was decided to ascertain the
actual count of each. The results follow.

Fiches count: 12,474. This was determined by actually counting the fiches in the file. This figure agrees with
the latest LRI count as given in the introduction to the Biblioguide Index volume, which was published in June 1972.

Title count: 9,620. This was obtained by counting
all the titles, excluding alternative titles, in the Title Catalog, as well as those new ones in the Addendum, a leaflet
published separately at a later date. The prepublication brochure, The Microbook Library Series, gives the figure as
"over 12,000 titles."

Volume count: 15,347. This was derived from a
count of the volumes given in the Shelf List. When in a few
instances the number of volumes in a multivolume set was
not given, the number shown in the Author Catalog was used.
This total of 15,347 is broken down into 6,777 "single-volume works," 5,192 "multivolume works," 1,774 "periodicals," and 1,604 "pamphlets and short works." In addition,
the 1,604 pamphlets and short works on 152 fiches, each of
which contains reproductions of from four to fifteen such
items, were counted as individual volumes, although the fiches
count--152--would seem to be more appropriately considered
as "volumes." With the latter method of counting, the total
volume count would therefore be reduced to 13,895.

The number of volumes given in the prepublication
brochure is "approximately 20,000 volumes," and in another
postpublication leaflet entitled The Microbook Library of
American Civilization it is shown as "19,000 bibliographic
volumes."

Page count. For obvious reasons, no attempt was
made to count the vast number of pages photographically reproduced on the fiches in the collection. This figure is estimated at 6, 000, 000 in the prepublication brochure and at
more than 6, 700, 000 in the later one.

The differences between the LRI figures and the actual
counts made at GW may be accounted for, in part at least,
by the following admission contained in the introduction to the
Biblioguide Index: "Not all of the titles nominated by the Ad-
visors and by the Final Board of Review could be found,
despite the fact that one of the [photographing] sites was the
Library of Congress; and some titles, though found, could
not be filmed for technical reasons. In addition, permission
to include in the Library certain copyrighted titles could not
be obtained from the proprietors. " Nothing is said about the
number of titles or volumes represented by these selected
but unphotographed items nor whether the search for them
continues or has ceased.

The Ultrafiches

So named because of the high reduction--55X to 90X--
employed to reduce photographically the pages of originals to
economic dimensions, these 3" x 5" (7. 2 x 12. 3 cm.) film
transparencies can accommodate as many as 1, 000 page
images each, arranged in fifty columns and twenty rows.
Because of this high reduction ratio, special reading equipment with suitable lenses to enlarge the page images to leg-
ible size is required. The images themselves are positive
reproductions of the pages photocopied. The large capacity
per fiche permits the desirable practice of reproducing only
one title on each, except for the multivolume works, the
periodicals, and the pamphlets included in the collection.

Each fiche has an eye-legible heading containing the
main entry, the title and volume number, etc., as needed to
identify the contents. In addition, in the upper right-hand
corner is the distinctive LAC serial number assigned to each
fiche for use in filing and retrieval. The fiche physically is
composed of three layers of material: two outer Mylar plastic
laminated sheets fused onto a sheet of cellulose acetate in the
center to form a stiff cardlike unit. Although quite tough in
some ways, the Mylar covering sheets exhibited a high degree of susceptibility to image-disfiguring and image-obliter-
ating scratches produced in normal use in the reading ma-

chines. They also have a low melting point, as was ascertained during the demonstration project when excessive heat
was focused on them in the portable readers, causing the
Mylar to blister or pucker and thereby to sustain permanent
damage.

Some of the fiches (see below) contain images of texts
which, when viewed on the screen of the table (912) reader,
are just above the threshold of legibility and could hardly be
read extensively without eye discomfort. On the portable
(710) reader with its lower magnification--75X--the level of
legibility becomes unacceptable. Falling in this category are
thirteen volumes of Niles' Weekly Register and twenty-two
volumes of Niles' National Register that are reproduced on
fiches LAC 31256-62 and 31263-31273 respectively. By way
of contrast, the reproductions of these same volumes on roll
microfilm published by Xerox/University Microfilms in the
American Periodical Series II are quite readable.

The photography of the fiches varies in quality, with
uneven densities and occasional bits of dirt or dust blotting
out a word or part of one here and there.

Each fiche comes in a filing envelope on the front of
which is printed pertinent bibliographic data as found in the
Author Catalog.

The method of arranging the photographic images of
the pages on the fiche is rather inefficient when used with the
two types of readers provided. After going through the first
fifty pages from left to right, the user, instead of dropping
to the page in the row immediately beneath, is required to
"knurl-knob" his way back to the beginning of the next row
and proceed again from left to right. Pursuing the analogy
of the book for which the fiche is supposed to be a substitute,
this is tantamount to going from the fiftieth page in a book
to the hundredth and then backing up to the fifty-first before
resuming reading. This backtracking puts an unnecessary
burden on that part of the fiche transport mechanism in both
readers which, already, because of its function--page chang-
ing--is subject to the most wear. In addition, it was determined experimentally that such reversal of direction required about sixteen normal twists of the horizontal scan
knob on the 912 table reader and about thirty-five such turns
on the 710, consuming about fifteen to thirty-five seconds
each, respectively. Therefore, not only is the researcher's
thought interrupted when passing from the fiftieth to the fifty-

208

Library Lit. -74

first page by this procedure, but he is also lengthening his use of the machine.

These difficulties could have been avoided had the page images been placed on the fiche in the boustrophedon method (alternately in rows from left to right, then right to left, and so on, so that the fifty-first page would be found immediately below the fiftieth, etc.).

The present method of arranging the pages on the fiche, therefore, seems to be at odds with LRI's avowed intent "to develop a technology that offers comfort, convenience, and ease of use for extended book reading on microforms."

Replacement fiches, at a cost of $2.50 each, plus handling costs, are available from stock at LRI in Chicago. Discounting on large orders is also available. Should items wanted be out of stock in Chicago, according to information furnished by LRI, it may take up to ninety days to have them supplied by the manufacturer, UMF, Inc., in Los Angeles.

The Author Catalog

This consists of one, 998-page well-printed and well-bound volume, with entries printed two columns to the page and arranged in a manner similar to those in the National Union Catalog. Examination of this LAC catalog, which gives complete bibliographical data for each entry, including tracings, disclosed the following shortcomings:

a. Maiden names have been omitted from entries for married women.
b. Political jurisdictions have been omitted from some entries, as, for example (state) was omitted from the main entries on p. 643 (LAC 16227 and 14941) which read: "New York. Chamber of Commerce of the State of New York." In another case (p. 605), the "see reference" reading "Metropolitan Museum of Art" should read "Metropolitan Museum of Art, New York."
c. Also noted was incorrect punctuation in the main entries, which affects filing, as "Massachusetts, Constitutional Convention, 1853" (p. 591), which should read: "Massachusetts. Constitutional Convention. 1853." On page 391 the see reference

"H. H. " should read "H. , H. "

d. Some errors in spelling names were also noted,
    as "Madison, Dolly" which should read "Madison,
    Dolley"; and "Brandeis, Louis Demblitz, " which
    should read "Dembitz. "

The Subject Catalog

This volume of 854 pages with two columns per page
contains in alphabetical arrangement by Library of Congress
(LC) subject headings entries for all titles in the collection.
The entries are shortened so that they extend only through
the imprint line, and each contains the identifying LAC filing
control number. In some cases, as with the LC practice,
some titles will be entered under more than one subject as
appropriate. The authority for the subject headings and
cross-references is Subject Headings Used in the Dictionary
Catalogs of the Library of Congress (7th ed.).

The Title Catalog

This volume, well-printed and well-bound as are the
other two in the set of three, contains 480 pages of titles
and alternative titles, arranged two columns to the page. As
with the subject catalog, entries are abbreviated to extend
only through the imprint line. The main entry is printed below that line to facilitate reference where needed to the
Author Catalog where the complete bibliographic data will be
found. The LAC number is also given here as in the other
two volumes to permit direct access to and retrieval from
the collection file of the title in question. A check of the
titles listed disclosed that fifty-seven were of works in
French, German, Italian, Latin, and Spanish.

The Biblioguide Index

This is a 952-page, well-bound and well-printed volume that was designed as a topical index to permit the locating of information on themes or topics more specific than,
or that cut across, conventional subject classifications.
Numbering 565, these topics are indexed regardless of whether
found in whole works, parts of works, or the periodicals included in the collection. The 565 topics are in turn grouped
into 29 subject areas or chapters; under each appear topics

or headings leading to the source citations to be found in the
collection.

As the introduction explains: "Of the 565 topics or
headings in the Biblioguide Index, 176 are major headings,
the rest sub-headings or sub-sub-headings. "

This volume--not received until mid-July 1972--has
seen very little use, according to questionnaire returns and
LAC user interviews.   This disuse is not surprising in view
of the fact that the indexing scheme used is rather complicated and therefore difficult and cumbersome to use and explain to others.   The introduction is not much help, for it
fails to give a clear, explicit, step-by-step account of the
method of use.   LRI, somewhat belatedly recognizing this
deficiency, issued some five months after the original volume was published a four-page leaflet detailing the seven-
step procedure required for optimum usage.   This information should have been included in the introduction to the original bound volume.

As a randomly chosen example of the complexity mentioned, suppose that a student from Louisville, Kentucky,
without knowing whether he has selected one of the "565
themes, " wishes to do a research paper on the construction
of the canal around the falls of the Ohio River there and its
effect on the growth of the city.   As a starting point, the
student sets out to ascertain if there are any histories of the
city in the collection that might yield information on the topic
chosen.   Following directions in the leaflet, How to Use the
Biblioguide Index, he turns to the list of chapters and reads
through sixteen such subject area headings before coming on
one that looks likely: "17. The City. "   A subordinate entry
beneath that is "17.3 Histories and studies of particular
cities. "   The student then goes to chapter 17, which is located on page 501, and finds that "17.3" is located on page
512.   On that page, he is required to read the headnote,
which informs that "under this heading references are organized alphabetically according to the subject, which appears
in boldface at the head of each group of references. "   Further
on, he learns that there is another category, "other cities
and towns, " the references to which "are ordered alphabetically by city, the name of which is enclosed in parentheses if
it does not appear in the title. "   Confronted with this dichotomy and not knowing in which of the two categories will be
found the references, the student turns first to the boldface
headings on page 513 and goes through Baltimore, Boston,

Chicago, Cincinnati, then New Orleans without finding Louisville. Going next to the second category, "Other cities and
towns, " on page 522, the student is required to search not
through boldface headings as before but through both titles
and bracketed (not parenthetical) city names, until on page
525 are found five references to the name of the city sought.

As a consequence of this complexity, the Biblioguide
Index requires interpretation of its use to students and others
seeking references there. Interpretation, in turn, is clearly
a reference function, but skilled reference staff may not always be available in the microform reading area where the
collection is located.

Some of these problems might have been avoided had
the simple, direct, and familiar indexing technique used in
the Readers' Guide to Periodical Literature, modified to include whole works and parts of works, been employed here.
The result would have been a more comprehensive and more
usable key to the contents of the collection than that afforded
by the Biblioguide Index.

It might be observed somewhat parenthetically at this
point that the student, although he would be unaware of it,
has for all his labor been shortchanged. Two relevant references in the LAC collection were not listed with the five
that were found. In DeBow's Review, v. 14, n. s. , no. 1,
for January 1853 is found a historical sketch entitled "The
City of Louisville" (LAC 31377). On fiche LAC 13546 is reproduced Gabriel Collins' Louisville and New Albany Directory and Annual Advertiser for 1848, which contains on page
258 the 23rd Annual Report of the President and Directors of
the Louisville and Portland Canal Company wherein will be
found, among other information, statistics for the years 1831-
1847 of the number of boats passed through the canal, their
tonnages, and the tolls collected.

The Shelf List

This is a reproduction of a computer-type printout
which contains the LAC numbers of the abbreviated titles of
the fiches in a serial arrangement. The number, of course,
appears in the headings on the fiche in the upper right-hand
corner and also on the envelope in which it is stored. The
LAC numbers are subdivided into four groups: 10, 000 series,
single-volume works; 20, 000 series, multivolume works;

30,000 series, periodicals; and 40,000 series, pamphlets and
short works.

    Unfortunately, not all numbers are used in each ser-
ies, as a study of the shelflist discloses. Consequently, it
is difficult to maintain the file integrity of the collection of
12,474 fiches. Misfiles are certain to occur, and unless
such items are located by frequent searches of the entire
file, they are unavailable for use. Had all the numbers been
assigned to the fiches in a continuous sequence, this check
could be made very quickly without even resorting to the
shelflist, except to identify any missing number in the sequence. As it is, the shelflist numbers must be compared
laboriously one by one against the fiches, especially in those
areas of the number sequence where the breaks occur.

The Catalog Cards

    In order to maximize the use of the LAC collection
and also to permit the evaluation of all the items of bibliographic support available for use with it, a set of the optional catalog cards was purchased and filed. According to
the estimate furnished by the GW library catalog department,
which was based on a linear measurement of the cards when
received, the set consists of approximately 42,350 cards.
The cost for the set was $4,000. While not LC cards, they
follow that format with the main entry printed in boldface
type, the body of the card through the imprint line in large
readable type, and the collation, notes, tracings, etc., in
much smaller print, which, however, as with the LC cards,
is readable. No LC call numbers or order numbers are
shown. Headings are printed at the tops of the cards, with
the subjects being printed in black, upper-case letters. Full
sets of cards are supplied for each title in the collection,
except for the shelflist, which is furnished in book form as
mentioned above. The cards were received arranged in sets
for each title and in alphabetical order by main entry. Approximately 150 cards were found to be duplicates, and only
twelve were so badly printed that substitutes had to be typed
for them. No cross-reference cards are included in the
package, although approximately 495 such entries are found
in the book Author Catalog.

    Prior to filing the cards in the GWU library catalog,
which is divided into three separate sections--author, title,
and subject--all cards were stamped with the identifying

symbol "Microfiche A7." Thereafter, they had to be sorted, of course, into the three categories for final filing. As of possible interest, the following data on the prefiling prepara- tion and filing costs in terms of man hours and materials are given:

> Clerical: stamping cards, 80 hours (5 people)
> Supervisory: 240 hours (2 people)
> Clerical: filing, 950 hours (17 people)
> Clerical: identifying and typing 495 cross-reference
>   cards, 70 hours
> Materials: 4,000 filing flags, $14.00; 12 alphabe-
>   tizers, $37.80; 12 stamps and pads, $39.60

After the cards were filed in the public catalog in early June 1972, a rather serious problem developed with respect to their use in the GW library. The distinctive LAC number, which is used for storage and retrieval of the fiches, is printed in the extreme upper right-hand corner of the cards. However, following GW library practice, we have stamped our designator, "Microfiche A7," in the upper left-hand corner of each card where a book call number is normally placed. This designator serves only to identify the LAC as a set and not the individual titles within the set. Users, because they are accustomed to copying book call numbers or other retrieval information from the left-hand side of the card, do not come to the microfilm reading area with the LAC number that is necessary for retrieval of the title sought. Had this number been printed in the left-hand margin of the cards, about 1-1/2 inches from the top or about where the notation "Microbook Film Card" is now printed, this problem would have been avoided. Dropping the number down that distance from the top of the card would allow room for the insertion above of locator symbols in li- braries using the latter for materials in microtext.

Installation and Operation

The materials and equipment obtained for use in the GW demonstration consisted of the following items:

1. One set of the LAC collection, totaling 12,474 fiches.

2. Sixteen sets of the three book catalogs--author, title and subject, with Addendum and Errata--and the Biblio-

guide Index. These were distributed as follows: two sets
with LAC collection; one set to GW cataloging department;
one set to GW acquisitions department; one set to GW reference department; one set to GW history department; one
set to GW English department; five sets to American studies
program department; one set to American University library
reference department; one set to Catholic University library
reference department; one set to Georgetown University library reference department; and one set to Howard University library reference department.

        3.   Ten sets each of the above book catalogs and Bib-
lioguide Index on ultrafiche.

        4.   Two copies of the Shelf List.

        5.   One set of catalog cards, totaling about 42, 350
single cards.

        6.   Three Microbook 912 table readers (two originally
received and one added later in December 1972).

        7.   Twelve Microbook 710 portable readers.

       The fiche collection, together with five author catalogs
in book form and two Microbook 912 table readers, arrived
in late October 1971. The fiche came in thirty 3" x 5" file
boxes packed six to a large carton, for a total of five shipping cartons. Checking to insure receipt of all fiches was
difficult because there were numerous gaps in the numerical
sequence, as already noted, and some fiches were not received in numerical order. The publisher, however, provided lists of the unassigned numbers to assist in the inventory.

       The check revealed that seventeen fiches were missing,
twenty-three lacked the catalog imprint data on envelopes,
sixteen were duplicates, and ten were listed as having unassigned numbers. Most of these problems were later solved
by phone calls, correspondence, and form letters from LRI.
Two copies of the Shelf List were forwarded by LRI in February 1972, with the suggestion that a final check be made
against it to insure that all material listed had been received.
Some of the incorrectly imprinted or blank envelopes were
replaced in February 1972.

       After putting the fiche collection into a complete and

usable state, it was then made available to the public in
space set aside in the Special Collections Reading Room where
the library's other microforms are housed. Controlled lighting is also available in this area, and it is open for use
eighty-three hours per week.

Two table readers were placed on 3' x 5' (later 4' x
5') tables close to wall electrical outlets which had been
modified by an electrician to accept the three-prong power
plugs on the readers. This latter modification was made
after the arrival of the table readers, as the requirement
was not noted in the advertising nor mentioned in our negotiations with the publisher.

The fiches were stored in a standard wooden upright
card catalog-type cabinet containing 3" x 5" file drawers.
The entire collection occupies fifty-four such drawers half-
filled and with the rods removed.

On tables nearby are placed the various book-type
catalogs, along with the Biblioguide Index volume. At the
outset, before the catalog cards became available (early June
1972), it was necessary for the prospective user to consult
the separate book catalogs for author, title, or subject to
ascertain the fiche number and then turn to the file cabinet
to obtain the desired fiche. After use, the student drops the
fiche in a tray to be refiled by the staff.

For off-site use with the Microbook 710 portable readers (Portareaders), which arrived on February 4, 1972, the
fiches were issued in 8" x 10" clasp-type manila envelopes,
along with a copy of the necessary operating instructions reproduced from the instruction booklet. On the outside of the
envelope was placed the impression of the library's property
stamp, along with a date due slip. The fiches so circulated
were identified on the retained charge-out card by the LAC
serial number and as a cross-check by the first word or sur-
name in the main entry. The Portareaders were identified
by recording their serial numbers on the charge-out cards.

All first-time users of the collection were asked to
complete a questionnaire designed to elicit information that
might be helpful in determining reader reaction to the demonstration and assessment of the usefulness of the collection.
(The analysis of the responses to the questionnaires will be
given later in this report.)

Reading Equipment

The Microbook 710 Portareader. Approximately five
pounds in weight, this reader has a glossy screen 7-1/8" x
10" and has a 75X lens. It was designed as a portable lap
reader and has been characterized as "the key that will free
the Microbook materials for circulation" ("Microbooks, a
New Library Medium?" Publishers Weekly, November 9,
1970, p. 50). The machine, an optional item, is manufactured by Technicolor, Inc., of Costa Mesa, California; it
sells for $165 and comes equipped with a three-wire electric
power cord terminating in a three-pole plug. Although important for off-site use, this fact is not mentioned in the
(brown) advertising leaflet issued to prospective customers.

The lamp used in this reader is, according to the
operating instructions booklet, "a specially designed Sylvania
projection lamp (DZP-type)" and is rated for 150 hours of
life. It sells now for about an average of $7.50 each, if
ordered in quantity. However, despite the statement in the
booklet that "replacement lamps are available through Sylvania
lamp dealers, " this did not prove to be so in the Washington, D.C., metropolitan area. Such lamps must be purchased directly from the manufacturer of the reading machine
in California.

Problems with these readers began to appear as early
as the day of their receipt (February 4, 1972). At this time,
when the twelve readers ordered were checked, it was found
that in one the lamp would not light at all; in another, the
lamp blew out as soon as the machine was plugged into the
wall outlet and was turned on. In a third machine undergoing
testing, the lamp burned for five minutes, blinked, and then
went out completely, with the fan still operating. Thus, on
25 percent of the machines, lamp replacement problems arose
immediately. The manufacturer, Technicolor, replaced them
free of charge, even though they are specifically exempt
under the guarantee. Meanwhile, of course, the three
machines were unusable.

Except for these free replacements for damaged lamps,
attempts to stockpile a supply for replacement purposes from
local sources ran into difficulties. The local Sylvania dis-
tributors had none in stock, nor did the two area authorized
service agencies. So an order for twenty-four lamps was
placed in February with Technicolor. The shipment arrived
six months later, with no explanation for the long delay. The

inspection of the lamps, each of which was packed individually in shock-insulating, plastic air-bubble envelopes, disclosed that three out of the twenty-four (12.5 percent) were
defective. In the case of one lamp, only half of the glass/
quartz capsule that encloses the filament was present. In
the case of the other two, the lamps, when inserted in a
properly functioning reader for testing, lit up when the power
was turned on; then after it was turned off and then on again,
it refused to relight. Examination of these latter two lamps
disclosed that the pigtail filaments that produce the illumination had broken loose from their moorings between the two
current-conducting antennae, this being the same defect noted
in the faulty lamps received in the shipment of readers mentioned above.

At the time of arrival of this long-delayed shipment
of lamps, the decision had already been reached to return
all the portable readers to LRI in Chicago as unsatisfactory.
Consequently, the lamps were no longer needed and were returned in September to Technicolor with an explanation and a
request for a refund. The refund was received five months
later.

Apart from the lamp problems, difficulties began to
develop early in this reader in the off-site use. The first
student borrower complained about having to refocus from
page to page and found it so uncomfortable to use that she
could read on it only for one hour at a time. In another
instance, the horizontal scan knob pulled loose on its shaft
and would not allow the fiche to move out of the case. Another user returned a reader with the complaint that it would
no longer focus properly. Another comment recorded in the
user log states, "Machine 1235B returned defective--hori-
zontal knob not advancing film. LAC 40089 caught inside."
This was another instance of the horizontal scan knob coming
loose on the shaft. Again from the log: "Machine 1228B
returned--defective--no power." "Machine 1226B returned--
horizontal knob not working--fiche LAC 13291 stuck inside."
"Machine 1231B returned--defective--overheats."

At this point when additional complaints of overheating
and buckling or puckering of the Mylar laminates encasing
the fiches began to filter in, all fiches previously circulated
for use in this portable reader were examined, and most
were found to exhibit signs of some damage. All twelve
portable readers were recalled and withdrawn from further
circulation when tests showed that the overheating problem

was common to all. After discussion with LRI headquarters
in Chicago about this problem, GW learned that the manu-
facturer--Technicolor--would shortly supply a new lens adapter,
which was expected to take care of the problem. The other
problems--failure of the focusing mechanism and the loose
horizontal scan knobs--were discussed at the same time, and
it was agreed that they should be handled by the local authorized service agency under the warranty. This was done,
but meanwhile the affected machines were unavailable for use.

On April 24, 1972, approximately two weeks before
the close of spring semester, the LRI engineer came to
Washington to install the new lens adapters, to check all the
readers, and to correct the focus malfunction problems in
two of the readers and the power failure in another. He rejected four of the machines as defective for a variety of
reasons (uneven illumination, a noisy fan with a bad bearing,
and fiche holder broken) and suggested they be returned to
the factory as unsatisfactory. Upon his return to Chicago,
he promptly shipped six replacements.

Thereafter, even though the installation of the new
lens adapter seemed to remedy the fiche puckering problem,
the focusing mechanism breakdowns continued to occur, along
with the loosening of the horizontal and also occasionally of
the vertical scan knobs, and other problems. At this stage,
the conclusion was reluctantly reached that the 710 portable
readers were completely unsatisfactory for library use, primarily for the following reasons, and would have to be returned:

1. Lack of sharpness of image on screen and frequent refocusing from page to page required. (It is suggested
that the frequent refocusing required, which is more than that
of the 912 table reader, may be due in part to the use of the
rubber roller fiche transport mechanism in the 710 portable
reader instead of the usual glass flats found in the 912. As
a relatively cool frame of film moves into the hot spotlight
in the 710 where it is in suspension between the two pairs
of rollers, it has sufficient play to allow the normal amount
of expansion produced by the heat to move it toward or away
from the lens slightly but sufficiently to fuzz the focus; in
the 912, the fiche being clamped between two glass plates,
which themselves may dissipate some of the heat, has less
freedom of movement in and out of the focal plane and thus
tends more or less to stay in focus under such conditions.)

2.   Glossy screen surface produces eye-straining ambient light reflections and exhibits distortions in areas where pressure clips hold the screen in the frame inside the case. (It is suggested that reversing the screen so that the non-glossy or matte side is turned outside, instead of inside the case as now, might eliminate or reduce the reflections, although admittedly this might result in some degradation of an already none-too-sharp picture.   Also, the use of a stiff wire retaining ring instead of the clips to hold the screen in its frame inside the case might, by more evenly distributing the stress, eliminate the distortions.)

3.   As issued, the reader came without a carrying case to protect the soft screen surface from scratches and the entire device against damage from rain or other inclement weather incurred in take-home use.

4.   Frequent breakdown of the focusing mechanism.

5.   Frequent malfunction of vertical scan knob.   (In one case, both horizontal and vertical knobs became inoperative simultaneously.)

6.   Frequent loosening of horizontal scan knobs preventing them from moving the fiche.

7.   Frequent trapping of fiches inside case, making it impossible to retrieve them until the reader cools off. This happens even in those machines equipped with the new heat-dissipating lens adapter.

8.   Vertical smudge marks (possibly from overheated rubber transport rollers) are deposited on fiche which remain stationary in machine for short periods of time.

It is suggested that 6, 7, and 8 are all problems which may be caused by the accumulation of excess heat in the case.   As the heat builds up to the point where the fan and small vent can no longer cope with it, the excess causes the close-fitting rubber fiche transport rollers to expand and in the process to become too tight to allow the fiche between them to advance or retreat.   This in turn causes the user to put unusual strain on the horizontal scan knob to attempt to retrieve the locked-in fiche and thereby to break loose the set-screw on the drive shaft.   In addition, this excess heat is apparently causing a decomposition of the rubber/plastic transport rollers, and the decomposed particles are being deposited on the fiche as vertical black smudge marks. Apart from the undesirability of having these removable but disfiguring smudges on the fiche, the undue acceleration of the roller decomposition caused by the excess heat will tend to unnecessarily shorten the useful life of the transport rollers.

It was suggested to the LRI engineer and other LRI officials that these apparent heat-related problems could probably be solved by cutting with an electric sabre saw a number of slots in the bottom and top of the back of the case to permit normal air convection currents to assist the overworked fan in evacuating the excess heat now trapped inside the case.

9.   Uneven illumination of screen.   (Perhaps a lamp-adjustment procedure similar to that used in the table reader is needed.)

10.   Horizontal shallow scratches are imparted to the fiche as it moves back and forth between the transport rollers.   (Tests and observations in usage indicate that these scratches, which will in time tend to reduce the readability of the microscopic page images on the fiche, are caused by grit and dirt, which is transferred from the fingers of the fiche user, or others handling it, via the fiche surface to the rubber transport rollers where it becomes imbedded and thus forms an abrasive surface over which the fiche travels. No instructions are given in the operating instructions booklet about the need for and the method of cleaning these rollers periodically.   The abandonment of the easy-to-inspect and easy-to-clean conventional glass plates fiche carrier mechanism in favor of this roller concept seems to have introduced unanticipated problems.)

11.   The machines do not bear the Underwriters' Laboratories seal, so their electrical safety as determined by the tests performed by that agency is unknown.

12.   The readers come equipped, as stated earlier, with three-pole power plugs, whereas none of our users had corresponding three-hole outlets in their quarters. The operating instructions booklet offers no help on this problem, merely cautioning, "Be sure to use a three-hole receptable to insure proper electrical grounding." When this matter was called to LRI's attention, their engineer suggested that the readily obtainable "pigtail" grounding adapters be em-

ployed to permit the use of the three-pole plugs in two-hole
outlets.   But proper use of these requires that the green
"pigtail" be attached to the screw holding the wall plate onto
the wall outlet box.   Thus, the library staff is put in the
position of trying to instruct the would-be user in the technique of grounding the pigtail and issuing a warning to be
careful not to let the screwdriver blade slip inadvertently into
the activated slot in the wall receptacle, etc.   Obviously,
such people cannot and should not be expected to assume this
responsibility.   Moreover, effective grounding of the pigtail
results only if the metal conduit for the circuit is properly
grounded.   This is obviously something that only an electrician should determine.

The countersuggestion was then made by the LRI engineer that the green pigtail safety ground wire be clipped
from the adapter.   Doing this, of course, defeats the very
purpose for which the third pole was put on the plug in the
first place--grounding the machine in the event it becomes
inadvertently energized, to reduce the shock hazard to the
user.

By way of contrast, the following notice came on the
cards accompanying the 912 table readers: "For your protection this product is equipped with a 3-wire power cord that
grounds the unit when the plug is installed in the power receptable.   If by necessity an adapter must be used, the green
grounding wire of the adapter must be connected to a good
ground in order to maintain the protective function."   The
notice fails to inform how to ascertain if the "good ground"
exists, however.

In this connection, the National Association of Home
Appliance Manufacturers estimates that 80 percent of the fif-
teen- and twenty-ampere outlets in use in homes today are
not properly grounded, and discourages the use of pigtail
adapters.

Under the circumstances, it would appear that for
safety's sake in the off-site library situation, the use of a
low voltage self-contained lightweight rechargeable battery
kit would have to be explored as a source of power for this
reader.

13.   The machine comes equipped with a "silent"
lamp-cooling fan.   The user is instructed: "Do not operate
reader if fan does not start."   Presumably this injunction

also applies in the event of fan failure during operation, but the possible consequences in either case are not detailed. However, certainly overheating and a possible fire hazard may exist. It is unrealistic to expect a student reading the text on the screen to be constantly alert to the operation of a silent fan. Moreover, in off-site use, as in a dormitory, for instance, it is not clear what might happen when the student walks out without turning off the power and leaves a lighted reader surrounded by paper, notes, match folders, and other flammable materials and during this period of absence the fan burns out a bearing or for other reasons ceases to function. Or, to give another illustration, a tired student falls asleep while reading in bed and leaves the power turned on and the fan fails. The use of the reader in such cases is not without some risks--both to the individual and legally to the issuing institution. (To prevent such accidents from occurring, it is suggested that readers for off-site use be so wired that a fan failure would interrupt the flow of current to the machine and thus nullify the hazard.)

14. The brown, one-page advertising leaflet states that the machine has a "mechanically detented two direction fiche transport mechanism with fine tune override." using phrasing identical to that used to describe the 912 table reader in a similar brown leaflet. On the 710 portable reader no such detent mechanism could be found.

15. The 710 reader came advertised as a "lap" reader. As a matter of fact, because of the heat inside the case, its use in such a position for more than five or ten minutes at most would become uncomfortable. This is not surprising: the exhaust ports designed to remove the heat emitted by the lamp have been placed on the back of the machine exactly where it will rest on a knee or thigh in a lap-reading position. In addition, persons wearing shorts and sitting with bare feet on the ground floor of a basement apartment might find not only that the reader in their lap was uncomfortable but also hazardous as well should they inadvertently spill liquid on an active machine in such manner that they themselves become part of the electric circuit.

16. The lamp bulbs furnished in the machine, as well as those received separately, are too delicate and fragile for use in a portable reader. Witness, for example, the three defective lamps received in the eighteen machines shipped by LRI from Chicago and three such in the separate shipment of twenty-four bulbs from Technicolor. Thus, six out of forty-

two, or one out of seven bulbs was defective on receipt. Obviously, if they cannot withstand the minor jars of handling and shipment in the well-packed, shock-insulating materials and cartons used in both instances, their successful library use in portable, take-home readers, where they are subject to much rougher treatment, is dubious at best. Moreover, the factory warranty indicates that the lamps are not guaranteed.

17. The manufacturer's warranty on this reader states in part, "This Microfiche Reader is warranted to be free from defects in materials and workmanship for a period of ninety days from the date of delivery." Further along, however, it continues, "This Warranty does not extend to (i) damages to a Microfiche damaged by this Microfiche Reader, (ii) lamps, and (iii) shipping charges." The most important part which is emphasized by its capital letters, reads as follows: "THIS WARRANTY IS EXPRESSLY IN LIEU OF ANY FURTHER EXPRESS OR IMPLIED WARRANTIES BY ANY PARTY, INCLUDING ANY IMPLIED WARRANTY OF MERCHANTABILITY OR FITNESS FOR A PARTICULAR PURPOSE, AND OF ANY OTHER OBLIGATIONS TO THE PURCHASER."

So far as the manufacturer, Technicolor, Inc., is concerned, the reader is not guaranteed to do the job for which it is being sold by LRI. The purchaser is left largely unprotected by the terms of this manufacturer's "warranty." However, the LRI operating instructions booklet, which accompanies each reader, states: "The Microbook Model 710 Portareader is designed to project the pages of the Microbook film card, enlarged 75 times, on a 7-1/8 by 10-inch screen for easy, comfortable reading." In view of Technicolor's disclaimer, it would seem that LRI should offer their own written guarantee of satisfaction. But this is not the case, for LRI merely quotes the full text of Technicolor's "warranty" and affixes that firm's name to the end of the quotation. The closest LRI comes to accepting such responsibility is the statement: "If any unusual problems arise in connection with your Portareader--or if you have difficulty in obtaining satisfactory service--call Library Resources' Customer Service Manager, collect." This statement, however, can hardly be considered a suitable substitute for the specific terms of a written guarantee of satisfaction or money refunded by LRI. It should be emphasized again, however, that in the GW demonstration, when the entire lot of 710 Portareaders was returned as unsatisfactory, LRI refunded

224 Library Lit.-74

the full purchase price. LRI also replaced free of charge
all fiches damaged in the readers.

The withdrawal from use at the end of the spring
semester in early May 1972 and later return of these portable readers resulted, of course, in restricting the fiches
to on-site use with the only available remaining reading equip-
ment--the large model 912 table reader.

The Microbook 912 Table Reader. Weighing fifty-two
pounds, this machine has a nonglossy screen about 8-1/2" x
12" and a magnification ratio of 90X. It is manufactured by
the Dukane Corporation of St. Charles, Illinois, and sells for
$450. The lamps used in this reader are the standard FCR-
type, they cost around $9 and have, according to the LRI in-
struction booklet, a standard life of 250 hours, although the
Sylvania carton in which each lamp is shipped gives the figure
"50 hours." Generally speaking, users found this reader
fairly comfortable to work with, even for several hours at a
time. However, some difficulties did develop in its use, and
other faults were disclosed by experimentation.

1. Insertion and withdrawal of the fiche between the
glass plates (or "flats") resulted in vertical scratches appearing on the outer (front) plastic laminate cover of the
fiche. This operation, repeated five to twenty times, produced scratches first on the outer edges and then on the
areas between, all of which contain photographic images.
These abrasions eventually make it difficult or impossible to
read the words and textual fragments beneath them. A close
study of the steps followed in this loading-unloading operation
indicates that the abrading is brought about by a forward
flexing of the fiche, which causes the soft plastic cover to
rub against the inside upper beveled raw ground glass edge
of the front plate. Such flexing is necessary for loading and
unloading, despite the directions given in the instruction
booklet which illustrates an impossible way of vertically in-
serting the fiche. (The booklet substitutes an artist's sketch
for an actual photograph of the fiche carrier that would show
the overhanging superstructural frame member obstructing
free vertical access to the glass flats loading area.)

This abrasion problem was brought to the attention of
the LRI engineer during his visit to the George Washington
University Library in April 1972, and the suggestion was
made to him that these rough edges on the plates should be
rounded off and polished. He rejected the proposal because

of the supposed cost of $50, and later sent two additional
plates as replacements. Tests showed that the new plates
continued to scratch the fiche at almost the same rate as
their predecessors.

At this point, the two front plates from the two readers were taken to a local plate glass window replacement
firm for rounding off and polishing of the scratch-producing
edges in the center of the plates and to an optician for rounding off and polishing the two outside edges, since neither
could do the entire job. This was done at a total cost of
about $10 per plate. After testing, the improved plates are
believed to have reduced the scratching to an irreducible
minimum.

In addition, it is to be noted that inevitably a certain
amount of unnecessary scratching of the soft Mylar fiche cover
will come about by virtue of the fact that the user will, by
failing to put the proper pressure on the "Press to Load"
bar, not completely separate the glass flats, particularly in
the unloading step. Some of this abrasion might be reduced
by relabeling the bar "Press to Load and Unload," but the
trouble could have been avoided had the machine been equipped
with the automatic flat separation feature for loading and unloading that is found on many conventional microfiche readers.

2. Because the fiche carriage assembly comes out
of the machine at an upward angle, it necessarily has a locking mechanism to prevent it from sliding downward while
loading or unloading. It is difficult to return the loaded fiche
carrier into the machine unless it is first pulled toward the
user and then pushed away with a sharp jolt to disengage the
locking mechanism. No mention is made of this difficulty in
the instruction booklet. In addition, such jolting is not conducive to long lamp life, especially if the lamp is lighted at
the time, as it might well be in the case of changing from
one fiche to another. The carton in which the lamp is packed
has a note that cautions: "Avoid rough treatment to the pro-
jector while lamp is lighted. Do not bump or bounce pro-
jector."

3. The thumb cut ("insertion trough") in the glass
plates is rather shallow and causes people with short or no
fingernails to have some difficulty in extracting the fiche.

4. The detent mechanism is supposed to center the
pages and/or the rows automatically once they have been set

manually by the detent override; it seldom does that for more
than a few pages. The earlier (now superseded) instruction
booklet mentions this shortcoming in a passage deleted for
some reason in the later edition when it states, "Because of
variations in book page sizes, formats and margins, the de-
tenting mechanism may not always provide a properly centered image on the viewing screen. Adjustments in the cent-
ering of the image are easily made by pushing in on the
Scan knobs and turning them. "

        5. Concerning the use of the machine, this super-
seded instruction booklet warns the user, after turning on the
power, to "check that the fan is operating by feeling at the
top of the ventilation grille at the top of the cabinet. Do not
continue to operate the machine unless the fan is operating."
The newer current booklet (blue cover) merely warns,
"Screen should light; air should blow through air vent on top
of the reader. Do not operate reader if cooling fan fails to
start. " While the damage resulting from failure to follow
these latter instructions is left unmentioned, presumably it
could occur equally at the inception of, or during, reader
use. The earlier, superseded instructions which refer to
checking while continuing to operate the machine are therefore more apposite.

        Moreover, in a library situation, this attempt to im-
pose on the student the responsibility of remaining constantly
aware of the fan operation while he is trying to concentrate
and perhaps take notes about the text viewed on the screen,
is impractical. What is needed here, perhaps, is a safety
device, such as a ruby warning light or electric-power-in-
terrupting circuitry to alert the user in the event of a fan
failure during operation.

        6. Another problem that developed in the use of this
reader involved the "Press to Load" bar. One heavy-fingered
user pressed the bar too strongly in the center where instructed and bent the bar inward at that point. This action
in turn caused the two hanger strips to which the bar is attached to buckle forward and catch on the edge of the loading
window frame, thereby preventing the fiche carrier from
moving beyond that window into the carrier assembly in the
proper position for viewing. This damage was corrected by
removing the bar assembly and bending the "Press to Load"
bar back to its original flat state. However, if in the man-
ufacture of this item the lower edge of the bar were to be
bent inward at right angles to match the upper edge which is

already so bent, sufficient rigidity should have been imparted
to it to prevent such accidental damage, and perhaps in the
process to obviate the need for a costly service call.

7.   The students found that refocusing from page to
page was required, although not so often as on the 710 portable reader.

8.   The 912 readers come equipped with three-pole
power plugs, but in on-site use this did not prove to be a
great problem, although it did require the installation by an
electrician of matching three-hole grounded wall receptacles
to accommodate them.

9.   After considerable usage, the plastic horizontal
scan drive belts tend to jump off their toothed wheels, but
with readjustment of the tension on the belt drive mechanism,
the problem was corrected.

10.   Lamp replacement on the 912 is rather easy.
However, following the instructions in the operating booklet
for adjusting the screen illumination may be hazardous in
some cases.   The operator is told to "place the blade of a
metal screwdriver with a wood or plastic handle alongside
the (lighted) lamp near its top, " and "while observing the
screen gently move the lamp to one side then the other until
the screen is evenly illuminated. " Some screwdrivers, such
as those sold with interchangeable blades, have adjustable
metal chucks at the bottom of the plastic handle, and this
metal should not be touched while making such adjustments.
Other available screwdrivers have a metal one-piece blade
which extends upward completely through the wooden or plastic handle.   Such a tool would have the metal shaft exposed
in the palm of the hand during the adjustment operation.
Breakage of the lighted lamp while being moved by such tools
might result in electrical shock to the person making the adjustment.   Another potential for such shock and/or machine
damage exists in the area at the base of the lamp where the
current-conducting prongs fit into their exposed all-metal
socket strips.   Regardless of the type of screwdriver used,
the person making this adjustment runs the risk of inadvertently touching one of these strips with the metal blade, or
even bridging the narrow gap between the sockets, and creating a short circuit at that point.   The likelihood of this taking place is increased by the fact that the operator's left
hand must hold the tool to move the lamp, which is located
on the left-hand side of the case, while he tries at the same

time to check the evenness of the illumination on the screen.
These dangers in the use of the tool are even greater in a
library because students or other unskilled staff members
may be called upon to change lamps and make this adjustment.   Under the circumstances, it would seem to be desirable for the manufacturer to provide a suitable tool made of
heat-resistant and dielectric materials that could safely be
used for the purpose.   (Totally insulating screwdrivers (blade,
shaft, handle) are available from electronic supply houses--
Ed.)

The guarantee covers defects in material and workmanship for one year but exempts film which is damaged, as
well as the lamp.

The Reader-Printer.   Although promised and reprom-
ised for delivery on various dates, this machine for making
enlarged paper prints from the fiche had not materialized as
of the close of the demonstration project on December 31,
1972.   Several of our users expressed dissatisfaction with
the lack of such a device, and undoubtedly there is a need
for one.

Collection Usage

Comprising a collection that has been amassed since
early in the nineteenth century, the George Washington University Library's holdings number some 400, 000 volumes.
In an effort to ascertain the degree of duplication between
them and the 9, 620 titles in the LAC collection, a check was
made in the GW library public card catalog of 500 titles
selected at random from the LAC Author Catalog.   Fifty-six
duplicated titles were noted--or 11. 2 percent.

Thus, a good potential for use of the LAC collection
existed not only because of the paucity of books in the area
covered by it but also, as mentioned earlier, because of the
strong, ongoing American studies program.

To translate this potential into actuality, however, required, in addition to the steps taken to publicize the availability of the LAC collection in the library, close cooperation
from all to whom that publicity campaign was primarily ad-
dressed--faculty, students, and library staff.   It was necessary for the faculty to make assignments requiring the use of
the collection and then to refer the students to it for the ma-

terials needed to complete such assignments.   The library
staff, especially those concerned directly with assisting the
students in the use of the various book catalogs and the associated reading equipment, had the additional duty of exercising tact and patience in giving such guidance to overcome
any "reader resistance" that might arise.

That such cooperation did, in fact, take place was
confirmed by the actual use made of the LAC, in spite of
the slow deliveries of the subject catalogs (received on
March 8, 1972, six weeks after spring semester began), the
catalog cards (in April and May), the Biblioguide Index (in
mid-July), and the development of numerous difficulties with
the portable readers.   During the period from January 1 to
May 31, 1972, which included spring semester, seventy on-
site transactions were recorded by the staff attendants at the
duty station just across the aisle from the LAC reading area.
According to the circulation records of off-site use, which
was impeded throughout and finally halted at the end of the
semester by frequent portable reader breakdown, in twenty
separate transactions, eighty-one fiches were circulated to
ten different users.   During the summer months from June 1
to August 31, fifty-six on-site transactions were noted, with
no off-site use because of the withdrawal from use of the
portable readers.   From September 1 through December 31,
the usage, then also restricted completely to the on-site type,
leaped to 365 transactions.   Thus, counting the twenty separate off-site transactions as instances of use, the total for
the calendar year sums up to 511.

The upsurge in usage in the last quarter of the year
was determined by the questionnaire and interviews to be due
in large part to the fact that by that time the users, by consulting the cards in the public catalog, were becoming increasingly aware of the availability in the LAC of the titles
they sought.   Other factors indicated by the same sources
as contributing to this increase were the availability of the
various book catalogs to the students and faculty members in
the American studies, the history, and the English departments where copies had been deposited, and the advertising
resulting from the bulletin board flyers that had been similarly distributed to interested departments.   It is concluded
that the funds expended for the printing of the flyer, for the
purchase and filing of the catalog cards, and for the extra
copies of the book catalogs paid good dividends in terms of
increased usage.

Aspects of usage other than purely statistical were
explored by means of the questionnaires. These were administered to all first-time users of the collection. Two
slightly different forms were issued, one in the spring and
summer sessions and the other in the fall. Some thirteen
questions were listed requesting information about school affiliation; level of study; major field of research; means
whereby availability of LAC collection was ascertained; LAC
fiches used; course of study connected with such use; familiarity with microforms; problems, if any, with reading equipment; what, if any, items of bibliographic support were consulted; length of time spent at the viewer; purpose in consulting the collection; whether felt that having access to collection was of substantial help; and finally to give comments.

A total of 117 questionnaires was received--43 in the
spring and summer and 74 in the fall. There were 93 un-
dergraduates, 21 graduates, 2 faculty, and one nondegree
respondent in this total.

All except one respondent (a visitor from the University of Pennsylvania) reported GW affiliation. Although
copies of the book catalogs and the flyers were distributed
to the other four D. C. Consortium libraries--American,
Catholic, Georgetown, and Howard--no evidence of usage by
their students or faculty, who were limited to consulting the
LAC collection on-site at the GW library, was reflected in
the questionnaires. Telephone interviews with their reference
librarians, to whom the catalogs had been sent, confirmed
this lack of use by their patrons.

The major fields of study ranged over fifty-one areas,
with American studies and American civilization not unex-
pectedly showing the greatest response. Fifty-one different
courses of study were represented. These embraced, among
others, architecture, art, anthropology, education, journalism, American literature, black history, religion, and business administration.

Up to the end of the first semester, with only the
book catalogs available, the source of knowledge about the
existence of the collection was from library staff members
and faculty. However, after the catalog cards were placed
in the main public catalog in early June, this source altered
radically to show that 68 percent of the respondents were
learning about the collection by consulting those cards, and
to a lesser degree from their professors, from the library

staff members, etc. There is sufficient evidence in the responses, taken together with information elicited in the interviews, to permit the following conclusion to be drawn: The availability of the LAC cards in the public card catalog not only increased the usage of the collection but also extended that usage to fields of study not previously exploited by the other forms of publicity.

The respondents were about equally divided as to whether they had previously used microforms.

The printed book catalogs were consulted as follows: author, forty-five times; title, thirty times; subject, fifty-three times; and the Biblioguide Index, five times.

The length of time spent at one sitting at the table (912) reader averaged out to sixty-four minutes, whereas on the portable (710) viewer it was thirty minutes, according to responses and interviews concerning these matters.

Regarding the purpose for which the collection was used, the majority, 64 percent of the respondents, indicated that they did so to enable them to write a paper. Others--to a much lesser extent--used it to consult primary sources, to verify a reference, for collateral reading, for extensive reading of a complete work, or to answer a reference question.

Of the 113 responding to the question as to whether they felt that it was of substantial help to them to have access to the collection, 107 responded affirmatively and 6 negatively.

Twenty-four patrons out of the 117 submitting questionnaires exercised the option of commenting on the collection. Some of the more insightful and informative remarks appear below:

"Very helpful. Easy to use and much more accessible than most data. " (From a graduate student who had used microforms before.)

"Just to say that it has been very helpful. " (From an undergraduate who had used microforms before.)

"This microbook business is a godsend. " (From a graduate student who had not used microforms before.)

"Much more convenient than the Library of Congress and having a lot together in one place on American civilization makes working in two subjects--history and literature, for example--much easier and faster. I like having access to documents and periodicals which otherwise would be hard to obtain. " (From an undergraduate who had used microforms before.)

"I appreciated the helpful assistance ... a table by the machines to take notes on would be useful. " (From a graduate student who had used microforms before. Larger tables were subsequently provided to solve this problem.)

"A collection of this sort seems invaluable to a department like American studies that is new and has a very small collection of its own, and to supplement the library's frankly weak holdings in the American studies field. Especially since a new library will be opening soon, I think much greater emphasis should be placed on the microfilm type collections the library holds, and they should be built up in the other fields. " (From an undergraduate who had used microforms before.)

"I'd just like to say that the system seems most desirable for safe storage for vast amounts of books in limited space. The equipment [table reader] is easy to use. " (From an undergraduate using microforms for the first time.)

"... Vertical and horizontal scan [on the table reader] does not always advance the same distance causing readjustment in order to read the next page ... focusing is a constant problem. Eye strain is the worst setback of this system. I routinely read two hours at a sitting before a break, but fifteen minutes with a viewer is like an all-day reading exercise. " (From a graduate student who was a prior user of microforms.)

"I am doing a paper ... and could not find adequate information at the D. C. Public Library (Martin Luther King branch). Using this LAC collection has certainly helped me in completing this paper and I will undoubtedly use it again in the future. " (From an undergraduate using microforms for the first time.)

"It was simple to locate and use the materials involved. I think it is a really good addition to the library." (From an undergraduate using microforms for the first time.)

"It would be of great assistance to have a machine that would copy selected pages from microfiche. " (From an undergraduate who had used microforms before.)

"I found it easy to use and also fun. But more important, I was able to do reading out of books that would have normally been checked out. " (From an undergraduate who had not used microforms before.)

"The collection is very fine and should be expanded. " (From an undergraduate who had used microforms before.)

"Focus [on the table reader] has to be adjusted frequently; otherwise completely satisfied. " (From an undergraduate who had used microforms before.)

"Very convenient to have material available and set up like this, plus the room is pleasant to work in--important to me. No worrying about the book being out or in the wrong place. Great way to do research!" (From an undergraduate who had used microforms before.)

Under the circumstances, the usage during the demonstration period was very good, but it could have been better had an adequate supply of satisfactory and properly functioning portable readers been available for off-site use. After the rejection and return of the 710 portables, usage on the two table readers remaining increased to the point that a third had to be purchased to relieve the congestion.

Collection Evaluation

Although no attempt was made to evaluate the LAC collection as such, some steps were taken to develop information regarding it that might be helpful to libraries desirous of making such an assessment.

One of these involved the checking against a standard bibliography of the titles in the LAC collection. Chosen for this purpose because it covers the same area as the LAC-- all aspects of American civilization--was the following work:

U. S. Library of Congress. General Reference and Bibliography Division. A Guide to the study of the United States of America: representative books reflecting the development of American life and thought. Washington, GPO, 1960.

Although there are 6, 487 numbered entries in this annotated bibliography, 485 of these are individually numbered
author biographical items. Deducting these latter from the
total provides a list of 6, 002 title entries for comparison
with the LAC collection. The check of the titles listed in
the LAC Title Catalog disclosed that there were 350 (or 5. 8
percent) identical editions of LAC titles to be found in the
Guide. It must be observed, however, that the LAC is
largely, though not completely, confined in its selection of
photographed titles to those published up to the outbreak of
World War I (1914), whereas the Guide has a cutoff date of
1955 with some exceptions. A further check of the Guide
listing itself disclosed that only 912 titles, or about 15 percent, had imprints falling within the self-imposed time span
of the LAC, and therefore the bulk--85 percent--were from
1914 onward.

By way of contrast, despite its announced cutoff date,
the LAC collection does include imprints from 1914 onward.
It was determined that these number 1, 051 of the 9, 620 titles
(11 percent), with the remainder--(89 percent)--representing
the pre-1914 ones. These LAC figures of course, represent
the reverse of the chronological emphasis found in the Guide
listing. It was noted during the course of the title check of
the LAC against the Guide that, though some titles, particularly literary works, are found in both places, the Guide
prefers more recent editions that often contain prefatory and
critical remarks lacking in the older editions reproduced in
the LAC collection.

The selection of 1913 as the cutoff date was dictated
--one assumes--primarily by copyright considerations. Since
the maximum life of a U. S. copyright is fifty-six years
(twenty-eight initially and twenty-eight more if renewed) and
since work on amassing the LAC materials began in 1969-
1970, the choice of that date would permit the unfettered reproduction of all titles selected that bore imprints of 1913 or
earlier. Unfortunately, though, the effect of such a constraint was the omission of the works of virtually all modern
American literary figure, as well as of such important land-
mark books as Charles and Mary Beard's The Rise of American Civilization, Vernon Louis Parrington's Main Currents
in American Thought, The Cambridge History of American
Literature, Spiller, Thorp, Johnson, and Canby's Literary
History of the United States, and Van Wyck Brooks' The
Flowering of New England, to name only a few. As a consequence, the items in the LAC collection consist mostly of

the older materials: first editions of the collected works of
writers of the nineteenth century, as well as older historical
works, treatises, periodicals, pamphlets, and so on.

These findings should be borne in mind in any attempt
to determine whether the LAC has fulfilled its promise to become "a collection of materials that would be fully adequate
to support an undergraduate American studies program in
colleges and a masters program in American history in most
universities. "

Other steps taken to provide information useful in the
assessment were checking on the number of incomplete sets
of multivolume works and the number of reprints photocopied
in the LAC collection. It became obvious shortly after the
receipt in October 1971 of the original fiche collection that
efforts were then being made to fill in incomplete sets that
had been reproduced on the fiches, since new fiches containing the complete sets were being issued as replacements
from time to time, and later the Author Catalog Errata leaflet was published to show the new, corrected holdings. Still
incomplete, however, according to the revised entries in that
leaflet, are the Archives of Maryland (v. 3 wanting), the His-
toria general de los hechos of Antonio de Herrera y Torde-
sillas (v. 5-7 wanting), The Outlook (v. 59 and 71 wanting),
The Portfolio (v. 5 wanting), and The Southern Literary Messenger (v. 22 wanting). Other incomplete sets noted in the
Author Catalog are: The Works of Francis J. Grimke (v. 1
wanting) and The Writings of Henry David Thoreau (v. 2,
Walden, wanting). LRI informed by letter that fiche LAC
23863 for the missing Grimke volume and LAC 31109 for the
missing Southern Literary Messenger item have been deleted
from the LAC collection.

With regard to reprints, ninety-seven instances (or
about 1 percent of the titles) of the use of such in lieu of
originals were noted in the LAC fiche collection. Most of
the reprints used in the photographing are of recent issue
and are from well-known reprint publishers, such as Johnson
Reprint Corp. , Kennikat, Kraus, AMS, Arno, Gregg, Da
Capo, Peter Smith, Burt Franklin, Augustus M. Kelley,
Books for Libraries and others. Almost one-third (thirty)of
the cases noted involved fiche reproductions from reprints
issued by Negro Universities Press.

So far as the method of selection of titles for inclusion is concerned--a matter that is touched upon in the pre-

ceding reference as well as in the sales brochures--in the
final analysis it would seem that it is more important to
know what was finally chosen rather than how it was done.
Therefore, any attempt to evaluate the potential usefulness
of the LAC collection to any given library could, perhaps,
best be done by closely studying a borrowed copy of the
Author Catalog, since in that volume will be found all the
bibliographic data required to assist in arriving at some determination in that regard.

Bibliography

Aaron, Richard.   "An Encyclopedia in Your Waistcoat
        Pocket. "   Times (London), 28 April 1971, p. 14.

"Britannica to Publish Ultramicrofiche Library. "   Publishers
        Weekly 194 (January 6, 1969): 25.

Doebler, Paul.   "Libraries on Microfiche: LRI's Experience
        in the Field. "   Publishers Weekly 202 (December 18,
        1972): 27-30.

Evans, Charles W.   "High Reduction Microfiche for Librar-
        ies: An Evaluation of Collections from the National
        Cash Register Company and Library Resources, Inc."
        Library Resources and Technical Services 16 (Winter
        1972): 33-47.

Grieder, E. M.   "Ultrafiche Libraries: A Librarian's View."
        Microform Review 1 (April 1972): 85-100.

Hawken, William R.   "Systems instead of Standards. "   Li-
        brary Journal 98 (September 15, 1973): 2515-2525.

_____.   "The Application of Integrated Circuit Photography
        to Microphotographic Document Reproduction. "   Micro-
        fiche Foundation Newsletter 23 (October 1971): 6-9.

Hawken, William R.; Klessing, K. K.; Nelson, C. E.; and
        Kristy, N. F.   "Microbook Publication--A New Ap-
        proach for a New Decade. "   Journal of Micrographies
        3 (1970): 188-193.

Jackson, W. Carl; Brown, Helen M.; and Morroni, June R.
        Review of The Library of American Civilization.
        Microform Review 1 (April 1972): 143-148.

"Microbooks--A New Library Medium?" Publishers Weekly
    198 (November 9, 1970): 48-50.

Spaulding, Carl M.   "UMF Collections: Good for Libraries?"
    Micrographics News & Views 4 (March 31, 1972):
    1-2.

Spreitzer, Francis F.   "Developments in Copying Micro-
    graphics, and Graphic Communications, 1971." Li-
    brary Resources and Technical Services 16 (Spring
    1972): 138, 144.

Taylor, Robert S.   "Libraries and Micropublication. " Micro-
    form Review 1 (January 1972): 25-27.

Tebbel, John.   "Libraries in Miniature: A New Era Begins."
    Saturday Review 54 (January 9, 1971): 41-42.

"Ultrafiche Libraries: The Publishers Respond and a Re-
    joinder. " Microform Review 1 (April 1972): 101-111.

"Ultramicrofiche Library Series: Encyclopaedia Britannica."
    Library Journal 94 (March 1, 1969): 937-938.

"Ultramicrofiche Will Be the Medium for a New Resource
    and Research Library Series to Be Published by En-
    cyclopaedia Britannica. " Wilson Library Bulletin 43
    (February 1969): 499-500.

Van Doren, C.   "Library of American Civilization. " Cali-
    fornia School Libraries 40 (March 1969): 128-133.

Veaner, Allen B.   Letter to the Editor, June 9, 1971.
    Microdoc 10 (1971): 104-106.

_____.   "Micropublication. " In Advances in Librarian-
    ship 2 (1971): 179.

INTER-LIBRARY LOANS: THE EXPERIENCE
OF THE CENTER FOR RESEARCH LIBRARIES*

Gordon Williams

      In the centuries-long history of libraries, inter-library
lending is a very new innovation. Its history has not, to my
knowledge, been exhaustively studied, but regardless of when
the first inter-library loan may have occurred, the practice
did not become common until about 1917 when the American
Library Association adopted its first inter-library loan code
for the guidance of United States libraries. The somewhat
negative nature of the code (i.e. its emphasis on what it was
not appropriate for one library to request of another) makes
clear the commonly held attitude that each library was expected to acquire and have in its own collection the books
and other library materials needed to satisfy the needs of its
readers, if such materials were available for purchase at
moderate cost. Any budget limitations of the borrowing library were clearly not a sufficient excuse for it to borrow
an item from another library. A loan to another library was
regarded as an imposition on the lending library and justifiable only on the basis of quid pro quo. On the assumption
that there would in fact result a roughly equivalent balance
between lending and borrowing at each library, the imposition
on the lending library was the fact that while the item was
away on loan to another library it was not available for use
by the lending library's own readers. And although the
reader at the borrowing library clearly benefited from the
practice of being able to consult a title within a few weeks
instead of having to wait the usually much longer time it
might take his library to acquire a copy, he did not really
like the practice. It took him longer to consult the book than
if it had been in his own library's collection when he wanted
it, and in any case he could not depend on it for the reliable
satisfaction of his needs since there was no assurance that if
his library did not have a copy of the title another library

*Reprinted by permission of the author and Unesco from
Unesco Bulletin for Libraries, March-April 1974, pp. 73-78.

would have it, or would lend it on inter-library loan if it did.

The result, at least for major university and other research libraries, was continuing pressure for them to buy every title there seemed to be even the smallest probability that one of its readers might sometime need. The goal was self-sufficiency for every library, and for years librarians and scholars tended to act as if they thought this goal might be achieved, given just a few more thousand dollars for acquisitions and a few years of time. The idea, apparently, was that a somewhat larger budget would enable the library to buy all of the newly published materials of significance and leave enough over for the library to buy, within some years, copies of all the previously published works it had not yet acquired that its readers might sometime need. Probably no library seriously thought it could acquire all the publications in the world, but only that it might acquire at least all of those likely to be wanted. Unfortunately, though, three factors nullified this theory. One was the exponential increase in the amount of new publications under the stimuli of an increasing population, higher educational levels for a larger proportion of the population, and the growing contributions from developing nations and areas. Another was the expansion of research interests and educational programmes to include areas and fields previously ignored, requiring libraries to collect much already published material that they had previously regarded as out of their collecting scope (for example, newspapers, trade and technical journals, etc.). And finally, it is gradually becoming apparent that, in time, the readers in any research library are likely to want virtually everything published and real self-sufficiency is possible only if the library, in fact, has everything published.

With more materials needing to be acquired and annually increasing budgets with which to acquire them, libraries grew in size very rapidly. Statistical analysis of major university research libraries discovered that they showed an almost uniform growth rate: regardless of the difference in the size of their collections nearly all were doubling in size every sixteen to seventeen years. Their total expenditure (for acquisitions, personnel, supplies, etc.) were found to be doubling even faster--about every seven years.

But severe as the budgetary and space problems were becoming, librarians and scholars were realizing that the socially even more significant problem was that, despite their

accelerating rate of growth, the collections were becoming
less adequate to satisfy the needs of readers, rather than
more adequate. It was apparent that the goal of self-sufficiency for every library was impossible of achievement.
Scholars had reacted to the increasing accumulation of information and amount of publication by specializing more and
more, so that the amount they need cover remained manage-
able. But this reaction was not possible for the library, for
it still had to serve the informational needs of all the specialists. Clearly the solution lay in libraries finding some
effective way of co-operating to share the use of books,
journals and other library materials. Inter-library loan,
though undoubtedly helpful, was in practice too slow and uncertain, and too restrictive, to be a sufficient answer. Given
the common interests of readers served by all major research
libraries, and similar budget limitations, unco-ordinated developments offered no assurance to a library that if it did
not have a publication a reader needed one of its colleague
libraries would have it either, or would be willing to lend it
if it did.

At the same time librarians were becoming aware that
a firm basis for cooperation between libraries in sharing the
use of materials lay in the fact that many of them were infrequently used. This knowledge was based on general observation only, rather than on accurate measurement, and
while there was general agreement on the fact, there was no
agreement on whether "infrequent use" meant once a year,
or once in twenty years, or just what, or on what proportion
of a library's collection was infrequently used by whatever
definition was chosen. But equally important, both librarians
and scholars also knew from experience that many of the
books a reader needed, even though owned by the library,
were not available when required because they were already
in use by someone else. It was the reader's frustration
from this cause that made libraries unwilling to lend many
of their publications on inter-library loan, since they feared
that one of their own readers might need it while it was
away from the library. This fact of conflict in use indicated
that co-operation between libraries in the sharing of resources would have to be limited to a fairly small number of
libraries within the same region.

Recognizing the necessity to co-operate, and with these
views on the limitations to what might be practical, in 1949
ten major universities established what was then called the
Midwest Inter-Library Center through which they could co-

operate more effectively to increase the library materials
available for their readers' use.

First the centre was to be a library to which the
members could give the infrequently used materials now in
their own collections. In a building designed specifically for
the most economical storage of books, journals, and other
library materials, they could be housed more cheaply than in
the expensive space of university libraries. Moreover, since
what was deposited would become a common collection readily
available to all libraries in the group, and since what was
deposited would be selected for its infrequency of use, one
copy would be adequate to meet the need. Thus all duplicate
copies deposited could be weeded out, and the group would
be paying for the housing of only one copy in inexpensive
storage rather than, as they were then doing, each one paying to house its own copy in the expensive space of its own
stacks.

Second, the centre could buy, at the shared expense
of the members and for their common use, those books,
journals and other materials not already available in the
member libraries that could be anticipated to be infrequently
used, thus helping to increase the resources available to its
readers for research. Such materials could be either newly
published works, or older materials they had not been able
to buy in the past. This money, formerly spent by the group
on unnecessarily providing a copy for each library, when one
readily available copy could be adequate to satisfy the use in
all ten, could be used to buy nine other titles that none had
previously been able to afford. In essence, $100 contributed
by the members to the centre for joint acquisitions had the
effect of a $900 increase in their own individual acquisitions
budgets. At the same time it slowed the growth in size of
their own collections and thus slowed the demand for more
space for each library.

Third, since the centre was established solely for the
purpose of lending the materials in its collections to the
member libraries, and unlike the usual library it had no
local clientele that it was its first responsibility to serve, it
could be organized to respond more quickly to inter-library
loan requests than other libraries. Further, every item in
its collections was available by right to its member libraries,
not merely by courtesy, and was thus assuredly available.

On these principles, and with these assumptions about

use, the centre began its operations, with membership being
limited to major research libraries in the mid-west region of
the United States. In the beginning the members were naturally very cautious in the selection of materials from their
own collections to be deposited, and in the materials they
authorized the centre to acquire for their joint use. None
the less, its collections grew in size very rapidly, and at the
end of the first few years of operation amounted to more than
half-a-million volumes. But despite this large collection,
consisting almost exclusively of unique titles from the de-
positing library's collection (that is, with minor exceptions
the centre would not accept a title for deposit if it was
merely a duplicate of one still being retained in the deposit-
ing library's own collection), the number of titles borrowed
from the centre was astonishingly low and conflicts in use
were so seldom encountered as to be negligible. Also, the
centre's response time on requests (material is sent out the
same day the request is received) made it several times
faster than inter-library borrowing from another library had
been. With this came the recognition that distance from the
centre was not the significant factor that had been assumed.
It was the time required to get a borrowed item that was important, not the distance from which it came, and given
modern communications (telex and telephone) and transport
(including airmail for longer distances) the time differential
in delivery from the centre to a library 1, 000 miles away
and one only 25 miles away was very small. As indicated
above, the institutions establishing the Midwest Inter-Library
Center had feared that if its base was made too large and included too many libraries, too many conflicts in use might
develop. Consequently, membership in the centre was limited
to mid-western institutions. None the less, the decision was
made that, on an experimental basis, the centre would lend
anything in its collection to any library in the country, in
order to find out by experience what conflicts might develop.
This experimental policy proved very wise, for the anticipated
conflicts did not develop although the centre's collections of
several types of material fairly quickly became the largest
and most comprehensive in the United States and were widely
used. (As examples one can mention the centre's collection
of foreign doctoral dissertations, now amounting to over half
a million titles, and its collection of foreign language newspapers published in the United States by various immigrant
groups.) Further, it also became apparent that even a base
as large as that of the institutions in the mid-western United
States was not large enough to afford to acquire all of the li-
brary-research materials from time to time needed by readers
within the region.

Accordingly, in 1961, the centre changed its policy and dropped all geographic restrictions on membership, and a few years later it changed its name from the Midwest Inter-Library Center to the Center for Research Libraries to avoid any regional connotation. Membership in the Midwest Inter-Library Center had grown from the original ten founding institutions to twenty-one, including all but one major university in the mid-west region. When the geographic restriction on membership was dropped, institutions from outside the region quickly began to join, and have continued to do so steadily. Membership now includes seventy-eight institutions in both the United States and Canada--making the centre a truly international organization--and its membership spans the continent from Harvard to California, and beyond the continent to Hawaii. The centre's collections now include over 3 million volumes in their original printed format, plus several hundred thousand volumes in microform of scarce older printed works and manuscript archives.

In the meantime, and augmenting the experience of the centre, careful research was begun to measure more precisely the patterns of use of books and journals in library collections. One of the best and most comprehensive of many such studies is that by Herman H. Fussler and Julian L. Simon, Patterns in the Use of Books in Large Research Libraries (Chicago, University of Chicago Press, 1969). They found that as much as 25 per cent of the collections in some fields were used no more often than once in 100 years. A study by R. W. Trueswell, "A quantitative measure of user circulation requirements and its possible effect on stack thinning and multiple copy determination" (American Documentation, vol. 16, no. 1, January, 1965), found that in the Science and Technology Library at Northwestern University, over 99 per cent of the use was limited to only 25 per cent of the collection. In other words, 75 per cent of this library's collection was being maintained to satisfy less than 1 per cent of its readers' use. In the university's main library collection, serving the humanities and social sciences, over 99 per cent of the use was limited to 40 per cent of the collection, with 60 per cent of the books and journals being maintained in the library to satisfy less than 1 per cent of the use.

Another very significant study is William H. Kurth's Survey of the Interlibrary Loan Operation of the National Library of Medicine (Washington, United States Department of Health, Education, and Welfare, 1962). This study is particularly significant because the National Library of Medicine

(NLM) has the largest and most complete collection of medical literature in the United States, perhaps in the world, and it attempts to maintain a current subscription to every significant medical journal published, and because a few years before Kurth's study NLM had begun a policy of providing a free photocopy of any periodical article requested by any library in the United States. Since most libraries in the United States will not lend their journals on inter-library loan, and require the borrower to pay for a photocopy, this makes it a safe assumption that a major portion of all inter-library loan (photocopy) requests for medical-journal articles during the period of the survey were sent to NLM which had approximately 17, 000 titles in its serial collection, about 6, 000 of which were live titles being currently received. During the twelve-month period covered by the survey, 88 per cent of the serial titles in the collection were not used even once, and of the 12 per cent that were used, 28 per cent were used only once. In fact, only 500 titles accounted for over 99 per cent of all use.

Generally similar patterns have been found in all studies of use. To mention only one more, the National Lending Library for Science and Technology (NLL) in the United Kingdom, which has a collection of all currently published journals in these fields (and many older titles as well), freely lends journal issues, or provides photocopies, to any library in the United Kingdom and in addition extensively serves libraries in other countries, recently reported that during the last twelve months it received no request at all for any article from about half of the journal titles in its collection. (In 1970 NLL processed nearly 1 million requests.)

In summary, the evidence from many sources, both individual libraries serving primarily their local readers and central lending libraries, indicates clearly that a great many library materials, both books and journals, are so infrequently used that a single copy, if readily available for loan or photocopy when needed, can serve a great many libraries. Obviously there are gradations in frequency of use. Some titles are used so frequently that one copy can serve only a relatively small region such as a major metropolitan district, or a county, state, or province. For other titles, one copy in a nation or a continent is adequate. Finally, the evidence strongly suggests that there is a significant number of titles used so infrequently that one readily available loan copy is sufficient to serve internationally and intercontinentally.

The experience of the Center for Research Libraries indicates that most provincial government documents fall into this latter class, as do most provincial newspapers, most doctoral dissertations, many currently published journals, many archival materials and many older books and journals that are not too rare and precious to be lent. In many cases these titles are being collected comprehensively in the country of origin because they are an essential part of the country's historical record, and if international library agreements were made to lend these items freely, or photocopies of them, the necessity for duplicating similar collections elsewhere would be reduced and libraries could give far better service.

For example, the Center for Research Libraries is collecting comprehensively all official documents of all fifty states of the United States, many provincial newspapers on microfilm, foreign doctoral dissertations, United States (and many foreign) archival materials on microfilm, many infrequently used current journals, and has extensive collections of older books and journals, all of which are available for inter-library loan to United States libraries. The frequency of use of any one title from these collections is very low even by United States libraries, and presumably would be even lower by libraries in Europe, Asia, Africa, and Latin America, yet libraries in all of these areas have some need for some of the titles in this collection. It appears highly probable that the centre could make its collection of these titles available on inter-library loan to any library in the world with very little likelihood of any conflict developing. Such conflict as might develop would no doubt be limited to only a few titles that the centre could duplicate in its collection with only minor additional expense.

In view of the cost of acquiring, processing and housing a collection as extensive as the documents of the United States states, for example, few libraries in countries outside of the United States could justify the cost of building up a similarly comprehensive collection for the infrequent use it would receive. If the center were to make its collection of these documents and of similar infrequently used titles available on a world-wide basis, most other libraries would be freed from the expense of acquisition, processing and housing their own extensive collection of these simply in order to assure their availability when needed.

In total, the additional cost to the centre for processing

such international loans would not be insignificant, but this expense could readily be justified if there were similar collections of their own provincial documents, newspapers, little-used journals, etc., in other countries available for loan to United States libraries. The saving to the centre in not having to acquire and maintain its own collection of such titles would be far greater than its cost of processing foreign inter-library loan requests. Only such an arrangement seems likely to provide scholars with the access to all information they need and can profitably use.

Such an international arrangement probably is best made through national central collections of materials available by policy for inter-library loan, or photo-copy, such as those of the Center for Research Libraries in the United States and the National Lending Library for Science and Technology in the United Kingdom. Dependence upon collections in libraries with primary responsibility for serving a local clientele of patrons is likely to be unsatisfactory unless special funding is provided exclusively for a separate inter-library loan division. Without this, the operation is likely to be a stepchild with inadequate funding and too limited service because of the library's giving it a lower priority than service to its local readers. Unless there is assurance of access to all titles within a clearly defined and understandable class, and of fast response time, other libraries cannot take advantage of it to limit their own acquisitions with confidence, and it is in this ability to avoid acquiring what will be needed, but only infrequently, while retaining the assurance of ready access when wanted, that the great advantage lies for both libraries and scholars. For libraries are going to continue to be unable to acquire everything, and as long as present trends continue probably will be unable to acquire as much of the totality as in the past. To be able to concentrate their funds on what is frequently needed, to provide immediate access to these, and to improve other library services, they must know that what they do not acquire will be readily available to them. They have no responsible alternative but to continue to acquire diffusely, serving no one well.

Part III

COMMUNICATION AND EDUCATION

THE INFORMATION EXPLOSION*

Wilfred Ashworth

A fair illustration of the civilized world's fearful reaction to the growth of published information is to be found
at the end of St. John's Gospel: "If it were all to be recorded in detail I suppose the whole world would not hold the
books that would be written. " His plaint is paralleled by
many more modern outbursts, mostly from scientists, who,
illogically adding to the paper if not the information explosion, quantify and analyse the growth of publication and pro-
phecy the imminence of their world being buried under its
own literary products. Even if one ignores the wilder ex-
trapolations, the continuing appearance of such articles is
proof of serious concern. There is no doubt that many people,
in spite of being exposed to an incessant flow of data, still
feel insufficiently informed because they judge it impossible
to read all which might be of interest. Because of this concern, it seems appropriate that my professorial lecture
should be a review of the current information situation, followed by my solution, in terms of future research and academic library services, of the difficulties which so many
people fear have reached crisis proportions.

The Problem

We must first consider the size and nature of the
problem. Attention has been given to the total growth of
published knowledge, using as measures the number of books
issued or the increase of stocks in copyright libraries, but
most of the quantitative study has been focused on the dra-

*Reprinted by permission of the author and The Library As-
sociation from Library Association Record, April 1974, pp.
63-68, 71.

matic expansion in scientific publication which, in the last
hundred years, has dwarfed that in other disciplines. The
available criteria for measurement of growth, such as the
number of monographs, reports, journals, papers or abstracts published, are unfortunately only crude indicators and
can be interpreted in different ways. Nevertheless, all who
have attempted to analyse the growth impetuously chose the
exponential curve to describe its rate, in which they were
perhaps showing an understandably human preference for using an erudite-sounding word! However, whatever form of
measurement is chosen and whatever branch of science is
used, there is a sufficiently close empirical fit to make the
exponential model acceptable. According to the sub-section
of science chosen, and the particular indicator used, figures
of from 4-8 per cent annual growth and a consequent doubling
period of from 10-15 years are quoted in the literature. It
is now accepted that the present rate of growth falls somewhere within these ranges. Estimates suggest that there are
now about 80, 000 regular scientific and technical journals in
a world population of some 150, 000 journals with valid information content. The corresponding number of abstracting
periodicals in science is around 1, 500 in a world population
of perhaps 3, 500. When one comes to the world publication
of new books guesses are wilder, but a fair estimate is
300, 000 titles a year of which 90, 000 are in the English
language. At any given time it is said that 3, 000 million
titles are in print. If you like spectacular statistics then
consider the rate of production of abstracts by Chemical Abstracts. It took almost 32 years, from 1907 to 1938 before
the millionth abstract was reached. In contrast, however,
the second million came in 18 years, the third in 8, the
fourth in 4 years 8 months and the fifth million in only 3
years and 4 months.

There has been a threefold panic reaction to the explosive growth of publication. The first, naïve but predictable, was a call for voluntary limitation of publication,
tougher refereeing of papers, or restrictions on the languages
in which publication of serious scientific articles is made.
What is truly surprising is that in spite of the obvious vested
interests of authors and publishers, and of national pride, in
a world in which voluntary limitation is always for the other
man, such ostrich-like articles still continue to appear. The
second reaction was more constructive--the attempt to enable
coverage to be achieved by condensation in the form of reviews, digests and abstracts. The first scientific journals
did not attempt to carry original articles but were alerting

publications intended to draw attention to material appearing
elsewhere.   They quickly changed their character, however,
and thus greatly aggravated the problem they set out to solve.
There is no doubt that abstracts, reviews and other secondary publications are a necessary part of the modern dissemination of information process, but they have present and increasing limitations.   Because they are an essential adjunct
to primary original publications they add to the quantity of
material to be read.   In attempting to find all information in
a particular field, several appropriate abstracting journals
must be used together, but there is considerable overlap in
their coverage (up to 25 per cent in chemistry, for example)
so that each extra one consulted adds less to the return
achieved.   Worse still, at least a third of all published
papers escapes the abstracting net.

As the third panic reaction, salvation is seen to exist
in turning the whole problem over to computers.   J. C. R.
Licklider[1] in his Libraries of the Future is typical of the
people who believe in this approach.   Though admitting that
the printed page is superb for displaying information, that a
book contains enough material to occupy its reader for a convenient time and allows him to control the mode and rate of
inspection, he sees it as so unfavourable in its storage, organization and retrieval capabilities as to cause it to be rejected as the basis of future libraries of knowledge.   He
made a calculation of the total corpus of recorded knowledge
and its growth and concluded that computer systems technology is advancing even more rapidly.   We can therefore
look forward, he said, with reasonable confidence to a time
when, in spite of exponential increases, we will be technic-
ally capable of processing the entire body of knowledge in almost any way we can imagine.   Further, he predicted that
possibly in ten and probably in twenty years time we should
be able to command machines to "mull over" separate sub-
fields of the corpus and organize them for our use--if we
can define precisely what "mulling" should mean and specify
the kind of organization we require.   However, eight of those
ten years have already passed with negligible progress in
computer retrieval capability.   We have available only a few
rudimentary systems based on free-text searching or poor indexing and offering pathetically inadequate on-line interaction
with users.   Costs remain prohibitively high.   Nor has there
as yet been any real tendency to replace paper-based dissemination by any other system.   A weakness of the use of
computers in dissemination is that they do not convey meanings as readily as facts and therefore may operate more

successfully for science and technology than they do for the
humanities. If libraries were to subject themselves to such
a technological communication system it would tend to screen
out concepts which did not fit, thus impeding free interaction
of ideas.

The real fallacy with all proposals to replace current
methods of publication by a new communication system based
on the importance of dissemination of information is revealed
if one studies the reasons why monographs and research
articles are written. The primary purpose seems to be the
need, on the author's part, to establish a reputation, to stake
an innovative claim, or to earn a fee rather than to make his
ideas available to others. The dissemination stage often
occurs earlier on a limited and informal scale by prior circulation within a closed group of sympathetic colleagues and
co-workers in a field followed by wider circulation to local
colloquia and national conferences. This method is adopted
so that the new ideas may be tested and modified before ultimate publication. Thus the valuable dissemination characteristic of the final published paper may be no more than a
by-product in terms of the author's original intention and
dissemination cannot, therefore, be made the basis of a communication process. Typical of such failures was the idea of
replacing the writing of articles by the circulation of ideas
within Information Exchange Groups of which seven were set
up in the early 1960s, only to be abandoned because they
evaded bibliographical control and so prevented group members from attaining their desire to have a widely acknowledged
and accessible record of their achievements.

The Explosion Itself

But let us return to the explosion. If exponential
growth of publication is to be assumed to continue, then
clearly the expressed fears remain realistic because such
introductions as condensation and automation to the closed
system can only act as palliatives to delay final doom. We
may gain a few years, but that is all. A detailed consideration of the growth of science and its publications was made
by D. J. de Solla Price[2] in his Little Science, Big Science
(1962). Though now more than ten years old it remains the
definitive study. Those ten years have not altered the validity of its argument and one can assume that growth in other
disciplines, social science, for example, which is now catch-
ing up, is likely to follow a similar pattern. Price's tongue-

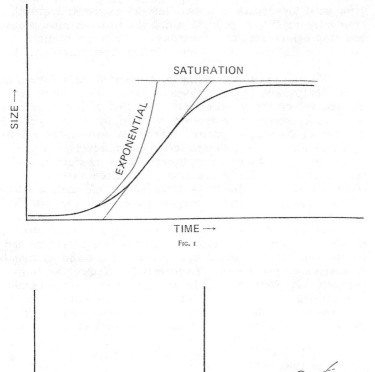

FIG. I

ESCALATION   CONVERGENT OSCILLATION

FIG. 2

in-the-cheek extrapolation based on the figures he quotes for American science predicted that absurdity would be reached in less than a century, when there would be two scientists for every man, woman, child and dog of the present population and twice as much money as would then be available would need to be spent on them. Of course, as Price points out, continued exponential growth would be a most abnormal state of events. In the real world things do not grow and

grow until they reach infinity. Instead exponential growth
eventually reaches a point at which the process must slacken
and stop before reaching absurdity. The more realistic function is the logistics curve which Price illustrates (Fig. 1).

In his discussion of the properties of such curves he
shows that where human influences are involved there is a
marked reluctance to accept any flattening of a growth curve.
As soon as restraint is applied, whether by shortage of resources or conscious control, there is a restorative reaction
which usually overshoots and then in turn receives over-
correction. In other words the cybernetic phenomenon of
hunting sets in. There are several possible variants of
which the two most likely to occur in the information situation are escalation and convergent oscillation (Fig. 2).

Price predicted a rapidly increasing concern about the
problems of adequate manpower, snowballing literature and
consequent inflated expenditure that would demand solution by
extensive reorganization. Such tentative changes as were
partially successful would, he said, lead to a fresh escalation of rapid growth with later more severe restraints.
Changes not efficient or radical enough would cause hunting,
producing violent fluctuations and consequent crisis.

Crisis Is Reached

There is already a good deal of evidence that the
point of inflexion has been reached with appropriate crisis
reactions against curve-flattening. Witness, for example,
the enormous growth of American university and other research libraries in the twenty years prior to 1965--a
"flourishing" of libraries as Dr. Robert Vosper described it
at a public lecture last year at the U. S. Embassy. Faced
with a sudden realization that libraries were losing ground
against the tide of available material, panic set in and un-
precedentedly high funds were voted from both local and federal resources. The Farmington Plan and other blanket
ordering procedures for nonselective worldwide acquisition
brought in a wealth of material and a corresponding load of
dross, but since nobody was bold enough to reject any--after
all who could predict what might be wanted in future?--it
was indexed, catalogued and housed in larger and larger
buildings. Such a halcyon boom was too wasteful to last.
The time taken to gain access to specific items of material
deteriorated from minutes to hours. Over-correction has

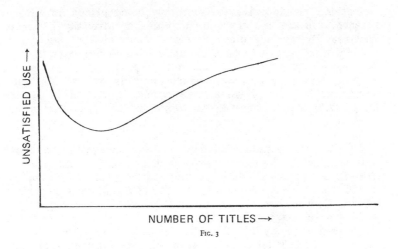

NUMBER OF TITLES →

Fig. 3

now set in and federal funds have dried up to the point of
creating redundancy in the U. S. library profession and chaos
in former show-place institutional libraries.   A parallel
boom-to-slump collapse has occurred in large-scale industrial
libraries not only in the U. S. but also in the U. K.   Started
by a sharp decline in U. S. government-sponsored research,
and fed by growing economic difficulties, industry reacted by
gross cutting back or even opting out of the expensive business of keeping abreast of information.   Of course it was the
stupidest possible action to take in the circumstances but it
is evidence of a growing feeling that the pursuit of information is as expensively elusive as perpetual motion.   Recovery
will undoubtedly follow but it is probable that academic libraries will never again be so generously funded and that industrial librarians will find great difficulty in regaining lost
ground.

       On a more direct level there are distinct signs of the
limiting effects of current shortages and inflationary tenden-
cies on publication itself.   While paperback and ephemeral
material is still on the upgrade it is very much at the expense of the conventional hardback trade.   Here costs have
risen so much that libraries have become the major buyers
and therefore the dominant customers.   Publishers have not
yet seen that their attempt to retain the status quo by ex-
pecting libraries and other institutional purchasers to subsidize publication is doomed to failure.   Inevitably there will
be a decline in the number of units purchased and forced

selection. Periodicals are similarly being priced out of existence. In the last three or four years university libraries
in Great Britain and other Western countries have been forced
carefully to survey their periodical subscription lists to de-
lete lesser-used titles. Since many highly-specialized periodicals exist only because libraries buy them it seems that
the mortality rate of serial publications is now likely to rise
in a Malthusian manner to counter a period of unusually high
birth rate.

A further indication that we have passed the point of
inflexion on the logistics curve is more subtle. As Bar-
Hillel[3] points out in 1962 the information explosion in science
could well have been ignored if specialization were acceptable. Does it matter, he asked if in 1961 a scientist's area
of research has half the extent it had in 1949, or that it will
be halved again by 1973? Oddly enough it does seem to
matter. Bar-Hillel blames the humanists for unsettling scientists with taunts that they knew more and more about less
and less, until they became emotionally convinced that specialization is evil and resented its apparent necessity. Thus
specialization has become a dirty word to an extent which
makes its avoidance a hidden panic reaction to the information explosion in science. Those of us who strive, perhaps
overhard, to make all education interdisciplinary need to consider whether doing so is to some extent an overcorrection.
Maybe the next generation will unsettle us with remarks about
degrees which are a little of everything and therefore good
for nothing and then cybernetic hunting will be well under
way! There are other signs of panic reaction such as the
present apparent world disillusion with higher education shown
by a falling-off of student numbers, especially in the sciences and engineering, when every forward calculation suggested a continued rise.

All these pointers suggest that we are probably at the
onset of a critical stage in the information explosion. If so
the time is ripe for a reassessment, the better to face the
fluctuating changes as saturation conditions are approached.
Though a more steady and contained state of growth will
eventually be reached there will remain the problem that the
total amount of knowledge available in the world keeps on increasing.

What academic librarians, in particular, should realize is that the period of storm through which we are passing
has already wrecked some of their hopes and ideals. Users

who expected library services to continue to meet the challenge of a growing body of information have been disappointed.
Reassessment will point the way to new strategies.

Classical Librarianship

In making the reassessment let us begin with classical,
conventional librarianship. It was born in an age of moderate
documentation and took as its proper functions the collection
of literature and its organization for convenient use. But
classical librarianship grew up in an age of increasing documentation while continuing to believe that control of the situation far into the future could be achieved by merely increasing the scale of its operations. The information explosion
has hastened the recognition of the fallacy of this belief. Unfortunately the classical library viewpoint has long been, and
still is, supported by the majority of users who take it as
axiomatic that the making of fully comprehensive collections
is a desirable and achievable objective. To the man-in-need
-of-information it appears obvious that his own library, or at
least some specialist collection, or at the very least his
nation's libraries taken all together, must collect everything.
How otherwise can he be certain that nothing important is
missed? The snag is that libraries which collect comprehensively inevitably become bogged down by the quantity of
noise (in the information sense of interfering extraneous matter): noise which is a concomitant of collecting for collecting's sake. This is all the more so when the material collected has been generated in a period of unusually rapid
growth. De Solla Price demonstrates that the effort to gain
more workers in any field increases the number at lower
levels faster than it does those at higher levels and therefore at the cost of lowering the average standard of both the
workers and their literary output. In fact, logistic decline
from a protracted period of exponential growth takes place
because of a scraping of the bottom of the barrel. There
comes a point at which the overall decline in standard becomes a significant feature and selection must then be practised to counteract it. If you think I have exaggerated the
danger of irresponsible comprehensive collection in libraries,
hear a disillusioned American research librarian[4] on the
subject:

> In an attempt to interpret and anticipate needs li-
> braries may collect in dormant fields or those in
> which there is really no interest; but one has to be

catholic, for who can tell where future research needs might lie? In many academic libraries the collecting habit has become established to the point where future needs become today's necessities and at this stage, ironically, the library graduates to the status of a research library, that is to say a library for everyone and for no one.

Perhaps you feel able safely to ignore what takes place on the other side of the Atlantic? Then consider a recent editorial in the Times Higher Education Supplements in which the commentator wrote:

> At present there is a kind of institutional autarchy where collections are often built up willy-nilly. The Librarian is blown along by academic furies and fashions and each library aspires to be another bibliographical 'centre of excellence.'

Now if librarians are indeed being blown along by furies and fashions it can only be because those forces are stronger than the librarians' power to put up adequate resistance to being expected to do the wrong job. The classical librarian has just begun to realize that there will never again be a time when adequate funds will be available to support his kind of library. In his terms he has become poor. Of course, poverty is a relative term. There will be sufficient money available only if libraries concentrate on improving their cost effectiveness. New ways must be found of getting better value for money out of libraries. This will involve consideration of a number of factors concerned with the nature of the literature to be handled, the pattern of its present and optimum use, and the part libraries should play in the innovative process of developing new ideas.

To begin with it would be well to tackle the major fear of users, that of missing vital information through lack of access to everything. This is one of the most commonly-expressed fears resulting from the information explosion, yet it is quite irrational because total access never has been achievable. The standard classical library reply to any problem posed was to produce a list of references which was as comprehensive as possible. The production of a fully comprehensive list is, however, impossible and the further one reaches on the way to comprehensiveness the higher the production costs rise. If subject indexes to abstracts are good, and in many fields they are not, a 65 per cent re-

covery of the papers actually abstracted is achievable. By
checking back from authors of relevant papers through the
author index, and by repeating the whole process in several
parallel sets of abstracts, recovery might, with a bit of luck
as well, be raised to 85 per cent, but the list of references
will now have risen in cost to five or six times as much and
the proportion of noise will certainly be higher. Remember,
too, that this search has still been almost entirely confined
to the journals covered by the sets of abstracts used. It
has not offered access to all available information on the
subject. To fill in even part of the gap would necessitate
use of citation indexes, consultation of the references in
papers found to be applicable, and page-by-page coverage of
recent copies of journals likely to contain relevant information. It will take a long time but in a well documented field
the return could well be about four-fifths of the total body of
knowledge on the subject. But most of the papers last found,
at greatest expense in time, will probably be in the lesser-
known languages and therefore costly to extract information
from. There is a high chance that they will also be of low
quality.

Yet in spite of the fact that access to everything known
is impossible, discoveries continue to be made. How, if it
is important not to miss anything, can this be so--and how
can one explain away the phenomenon that the same new discovery is often made simultaneously in several widely-sepa-
rated places where access to information varies a great deal?
It seems that the birth of discoveries is more dependent on
the readiness of the time for them, or on a social climate in
which they can successfully emerge as concepts, than on universal access to all knowledge. Good ideas (in the sense of
their timeliness) persistently grow, and then pervade univer-
sally with surprising rapidity. From an extensive magma of
knowledge there is constant coagulation of ideas. Thus there
is, at any given time, no real need to survey the entire body
of knowledge but rather to examine the coagulum which is an
accepted consensus of expert opinion. Because this is so,
wise selection of material can enable a library to offer its
users an excellent chance of finding what they need even in
a limited collection.

An interesting curiosity of the information explosion
was noted by Dr. Bradford of the Science Museum and, surprisingly, it offers some practical help towards achieving
optimum value from library expenditure. Dr. Bradford
evolved his Law of Scatter empirically while preparing bibli-

ographies for users of the Science Museum Library and his
first paper on the subject appeared as long ago as 1934. [6]
He found that if a large collection of scientific journals is
ranked in order of decreasing productivity of papers relevant
to a given topic, this rank may be divided into a nucleus of
periodicals particularly devoted to the subject and several
following groups containing the same number of articles as
the nucleus. Under these conditions the number of periodicals in the nucleus and succeeding groups rises as $1: a : a^2$
and so on for some constant a which Bradford found to be 5
for the cases he studied. For example, one of his cases
showed that in 248 journals there was a nucleus of 8 highly
productive ones; this then gave 5 x 8, that is 40, moderately
productive ones, and 5^2 x 8, that is 200, journals of low productivity. It is clear that had he wished to find a further
batch of relevant papers, consultation of no fewer than 1000
extra journals would have been necessary. Bradford himself
thought little of his discovery and commented wryly that "the
law deduced conforms to the mathematician's criterion of being no practical use whatever." It has amused a number of
people since to retest distributions and refine the mathematics
but, for a long time, scatter remained one more facet of the
information explosion to bewail as further proof, if any were
needed, that total coverage was becoming more and more
elusive. But Bradford's Law, if looked at in the opposite
way, can be seen as a mathematical expression of the rate
of diminishing returns in the use made of scientific periodicals. It can assist in the design of library and information
services by indicating which journals should be bought as the
best value for the money available and enabling one to calculate the expected coverage which would then result. Pointers
can also be obtained to the best disposition of journal collections between central and satellite libraries, and the best
division of a particular collection between primary and secondary stores.

Dr. D. J. Urquhart, also when at the Science Library,
studied the usage of scientific serials. His experiments have
been repeated elsewhere and it has been demonstrated that in
most libraries 80 per cent of the demand falls on only 10
per cent of the stock. Dr. Solla Price discusses the parallel
which can be drawn between these findings and the Pareto
law for distribution of incomes, according to which half the
wealth of a population is held by the square root of that number of people. In the case of our 80,000 known scientific
journals, half the total reading will be done in only 283 of
the journals.

Another relevant study is concerned with age which
again has been found to follow relatively simple laws with
surprisingly dramatic fall-off.

There is no need at present to go fully into the mathematics involved but by making use of the two factors of
scatter and obsolescence the Library Research Unit of Lancaster University[7] has been able to derive a formula for the
unsatisfied demands which would occur in a library of finite
size containing a given number of journals retained for a
specified number of years.   The function was found to have
the shape as in Fig. 3, the minimum point representing the
optimum stock pattern.   Such a library might well be expected to satisfy 75 per cent of requests from its own stocks.
It is clearly possible to derive similar formulae to establish
the best use of limited funds (some of which will be spent on
acquisitions and some on storage) instead of the best use of
limited space.   Other potential applications could be to determine the binding policies or, in the special case of setting
up a new library, to plan a purchasing policy which would
meet a specified percentage of demand at a minimum cost.
It is eminently sensible for us in Great Britain to make
severe cuts in the proportion of library budgets spent on the
acquisition and storage of material for which demand is
small and intermittent because we have already access to the
British Library Lending Division which is the envy of the
world.

Exploitation of Stocks

Having achieved better selection a second major way
in which the effects of the information explosion can profitably be parried is by improved exploitation of available stocks.
A relatively small percentage increase in usage in most of
our libraries would do more good than a considerable expansion of their size.   This improvement would oblige librarians
to play a much larger part in teaching users about sources
of information and in showing them how to tailor their own
handling of information, both current and retrospective, more
accurately to their special needs, because it is a highly individual process.   Experience in industrial libraries showed
me that very few people know the simple rules of current
awareness and I was led to formulate them in a paper[8] which
has since been constantly cited as a child's guide to information retrieval!   Every scientist will find he needs to read a
few periodicals thoroughly, not only for their articles but also

for news of personalities, new products, conferences and
meetings. A larger group of periodicals, about three times
as many, will be found to repay the time spent on quickly
scanning through them. Trial and error will soon show
which periodicals fall into which groups. It is good practice
also to dip from time to time into a few periodicals well outside the range of one's normal interests. Current awareness
services (abstracts, title lists of current papers and library
bulletins) make it possible to cover a wide range of material
otherwise inaccessible because of lack of time or of ready
availability. These publications are usually broadly grouped
under sub-topics or may be limited to a small subject area,
so that consultation need not take up too much time. Complete familiarity with a journal speeds scanning considerably
so it is advisable to shop around until one's own "best buy"
is found and then to stick to it. I pointed out that the mental
state of scanning is not at all conducive to remembering and
recommended that an immediate note should be made of anything which interests the scanner even though at the time he
may see no possible use for it. The mind which has been
intrigued by an idea is predisposed to be able to find an application if the right opportunity arises, but if no note is
made then the information may not be recoverable when
needed.

There are, however, some parts of the retrieval process and literature searching which can most economically
be handled by trained information workers. This remains a
field barely explored in academic and public libraries, but
acceptance of the principle could lead to further gains in exploitation potential. In industrial libraries, the only ones in
which cost-effectiveness has been given much attention, the
expenditure on staffing and exploitation has reached a figure
of three times the cost of acquiring material. Academic libraries have still a long way to go along this route to opti-
mization.

The Innovative Process

Lest you think I am too firmly casting librarians
amongst the demi-gods, I will admit freely that the classical
librarian exhibited almost criminal complacency. He has had
to learn from study of innovators and communicators that
reading does not directly play so overwhelming a part as he
was ready to believe. Non-literature sources of information,
or chance occurrences, have at least as much significance

and, at some stages of any given project, are more important. A particularly detailed survey made at the Centre
for Research in Scientific Communication at Johns Hopkins
University[9] found that in the initial stages leading to the publication of a research paper, journals supplied most information and local colleagues the next most. During the intermediate stage when ideas were being tested against the general conspectus of opinion, the situation switched, local colleagues becoming the major source. It is during the final
stage that we find the major use of formal sources (journals
and books) and this is the only stage during which books become a more useful source than the informal media. There
is thus no continuity of library use through all stages of the
work, though information supplied by colleagues can often be
traced to a literature source. This is especially so where
"gatekeepers" are involved. These are the useful individuals
noted by Professor T. J. Allen[10] of the Massachussetts Institute of Technology, who get a kick out of collecting information and being know-alls to their friends! Libraries play
a vital and irreplaceable part in the development of innovative
ideas in two distinct ways. Firstly, many new ideas are
sparked off by published information; secondly, it is to published sources that workers turn at key stages in their research for support, answers to problems and confirmation of
conclusions. The very recognition of these two distinct stages
goes part way towards finding an answer to the apparent un-
bridgeable gap between libraries which cannot continue to expand indefinitely and a corpus of knowledge which will keep
on growing even if not exponentially.

There is one other thing for which the classical librarian can be blamed--he has fed the fears engendered by
the information explosion by his firmly-held idea that there
is a perfect answer to every problem. If one believes this,
it is logical enough to imagine that the safest way to ensure
finding that answer is to have access to everything--hence
the massive collections. But whatever the user may think he
wants or says he wants (and these are by no means always
the same thing), the plain truth is that what he really seeks
in approaching a library is a lead, the better to develop his
ideas or project, and for this there will be not one perfect
answer but rather a plurality of valid, acceptable answers
from which a choice will have to be made. The effectiveness
of each will depend on the context in which it is to be used.
Whichever lead is chosen will turn the searcher in a different
direction and to this extent the choice is critical, but had he
made some other choice he could well have still arrived at a

satisfactory, though different, endpoint. It is here that the
modern librarian steps right into the centre of the picture.
He has recognized the mechanics of the innovative process
and knows how to optimize the finding of those leads most
appropriate to each worker and his circumstances. Operating with a limited but well-selected stock, he can devise systems to extract from it the most potentially profitable information without wastefully overloading his users with irrelevant
material. Under such conditions the information explosion
and the size of the total corpus of knowledge (though the librarian has to be concerned with them) become irrelevant to
each individual user. He has only limited time and resources
and needs only as much information as he can absorb and develop, and the librarian can give him this.

I have dealt with the process of innovation and the
part the librarian can play in providing information to make
it possible. There is one significant feature of the innovative process which needs to be given special consideration
when designing retrieval systems because it can elude the
net of classification which has long been the mainstay of librarianship. This feature is that innovation most often takes
place by the combination of previously unrelated ideas.
Arthur Koestler, speaking at the British Association Meeting
in 1965, quoted various authorities on the subject:

> 'Invention or discovery, ' wrote Jacques Hadamard,
> 'be it in mathematics or anywhere else, takes place
> by combining ideas.... The creative act does not
> create something out of nothing like the God of the
> Old Testament, it combines, coagitates, reshuffles
> already existing ideas, facts, frames of perception,
> cognitive structures....' According to Sir Frederick
> Bartlett, 'the most important feature of original ex-
> perimental thinking is the discovery of overlap ...
> where formerly only isolation and difference were
> recognized. ' Jerome Bruner considers all forms
> of creativity a result of 'combinatorial activity. '
> McKellar talks of the 'fusion of perceptions, ' Kubic
> of the 'discovery of unexpected connections between
> things, ' and so on back to Goethe's 'connect, al-
> ways connect. '

In a paper[11] which I presented to an Aslib meeting a
few years ago, I suggested that this need for combination is
so fundamental that library systems, at least those which
have as part of their function the support of research activity,

should be designed to encompass this requirement.   It cannot
be done merely by logical arrangement.   It has been shown
to be achievable in a situation where there is close rapport
between the library staff and users.   Amongst a group of research workers the librarian can occupy a unique position.
Much information passes through his hands and he alone,
since he is not confined by the narrow specialization of his
colleagues, can become aware of current problems on the
one hand and solutions which already exist on the other.
Classification as a technique has the by-product that it can
show where gaps in knowledge exist, just as it can show
where there is a gap in a library's holdings.   The librarian
handling information should also (if he is aware of his users'
interests) be able to perceive which items of knowledge might
profitably be combined even though they may exist in disciplines far apart from each other.   Though it is not his business to discover new knowledge, it would be possible for him
to deduce or infer consequences from stored knowledge provided that he can redesign his systems not only to allow
combinations of ideas to be made readily, but also to disclose automatically when there are statistical correlations
between them and therefore a matter possibly worth investigation.   It is this kind of activity which will most readily
beat the information explosion because it will make the maximum possible use of the information actually received by (or
noted in the secondary publications received by) each library,
and do so in the most constructive way possible.   Arising
out of such thoughts I postulated a new function for the librarian emerging out of the necessity created by changing
conditions, and a new direction for library research, namely
into systems which can both retrieve information when it is
requested and point to fields of potential interest, ahead of
requests.   I laid down the criteria for an ideal retrieval system as follows; it must be organized:

1.   To enable access by any level of enquirer, and
     whether generic or specific knowledge is sought.

2.   To demonstrate automatically when ideas are
     neighbours of each other, and therefore are re-
     lated.

3.   To uncover, automatically, valid statistical cor-
     relations between apparently unrelated matters.

4.   To enable methods found useful in one discipline
     to be retrieved if they are potentially useful for

totally different applications in any other.

> 5. To provide for evaluation of pertinency of infor-
>   mation, so that the requirements of each particu-
>   lar search can be accurately met.

These ideal criteria can only be met if several systems are used together and are only fully successful when
operated by experienced information workers. The choice of
systems at present available ranges over classification, co-
ordinate indexing, natural and controlled language indexing,
free text searching, Boolean search strategy, citation indexing and weighting. Always there will be need to monitor the
output, but where this is done with proper evaluation before
the information is passed on to the users, it is possible to
come somewhere near to the ideal situation. The evaluating
and sifting stage is important because innovation can be as
readily stifled by too much information as inhibited by too
little, but strangely, nobody expresses fears of an over-rich,
too plentiful diet--it is always fear of being unable to con-
sume everything! Far more often than not part of the information available on a topic is more useful than all of it
would be. In any case an enquirer need only persist until
he has found the answer to his problem or a promising lead.
Afterwards the whole of the remaining body of knowledge on
the subject is of no further consequence to him just then and
is ignored. This is the universal principle of intelligently
looking for what one wants by seeking it in the best available
market. The principle is used when buying a car, choosing
a birthday present for a favourite aunt who already has everything, or finding a wife! It applies equally well when looking
for a creative lead in original research.

The "Active Band" Concept

Classical librarianship has failed to find an answer to
the information explosion because it has attempted the impossible. It has assumed that all information, past and present, must be collected, stored permanently and organized
so that all has equal accessibility. The modern librarian
should see instead that in the continuum of knowledge there
is at any given time an active and changing band representing
the part which is at that time appropriate for development of
new ideas and creative progress. It is this relatively narrow band with which he must be concerned. It is true that
this active band is now of greater extent than in any previous

age, and that explosions of information in particular fields
can cause extensive local perturbations. Nevertheless, the
laws which prevent infinite expansion will inevitably limit the
active band according to the resources available to work upon
it.

An important new resource which will enable the size
of the active band to be maintained as great as possible is
the exploitation potential of active librarianship. Tested in
the industrial library field, it has just begun to enter the
area of academic librarianship. One of the very first papers
I wrote for my professional association's journal in 1939[12]
was a young man's spirited plea, crazily before its time, for
the use of information officers in university libraries. Thirty
years later the Office of Scientific and Technical Information
gave a grant to set up a pilot scheme for just such a service.
Perhaps it is not too late for me to see this answer to the
information explosion mature in my lifetime!

References

1. Licklider, J. C. R. Libraries of the Future. Massa-
    chusetts Institute of Technology Press, 1965, 219 pp.

2. De Solla Price, D. J. Little Science, Big Science.
    Columbia University Press, 1963. 118 pp.

3. Bar-Hillel, Y. "Is information retrieval approaching a
    crisis?" Amer. Doc., 14 April 1963, 95-98.

4. Horn, R. "Think big: the evolution of bureaucracy."
    Coll. and Res. Libr., 33 (1) January 1972, 13-17.

5. "Reorganizing libraries." Times Higher Educ. Suppl.
    (84) 25 May 1973.

6. Bradford, S. C. "Sources of information on specific
    subjects." Engineering, 137 (3550), 26 January 1934,
    85-86.

7. Buckland, M. K. and Woodburn, I. Some Implications
    for Library Management of Scattering and Obsolescence.
    University of Lancaster Library. Occasional Papers
    No. 1. Lancaster University, 1968, 25 pp.

8. Ashworth, W. "Information retrieval, and what to do

about it. " Phys. Bull., 19, August 1968, 262-264.

9. Garvey, W. D., Lin, N. and Tomita, K. "Research
   studies in patterns of scientific communication: III.
   Information exchange processes associated with the
   production of journal articles. " Inform. Stor. Retr.,
   8, 1972, 207-221.

10. Allen, T. J. "Organizational aspects of information
    flow in technology. " Aslib Proc., 20 (11) Novem-
    ber 1968, 433-453.

11. Ashworth, W. "Librarianship and other disciplines. "
    Aslib Proc., 18 (6) June 1966, 152-159.

12. Ashworth, W. "The information officer in the univer-
    sity library. " Libr. Ass. Rec., 41 (12) December
    1939, 583-584.

EDUCATION FOR CATALOGUING*

J. Balnaves

The "Annus Mirabilis" was nearly one hundred years ago, and we surely know what cataloguing is. Nevertheless, your indulgence is craved for a brief discussion of the nature and purpose of cataloguing, because it has a direct bearing on the kind of learning experience provided in programs of education for librarianship. Cutter defined a catalogue as "a list of books which is arranged on some definite plan." The objects of cataloguing he stated as:

> 1. To enable a person to find a book of which either (A) the author, (B) the title, (C) the subject is known.
> 2. To show what the library has (D) by a given author, (E) on a given subject, (F) in a given kind of literature.
> 3. To assist in the choice of a book (G) as to its edition (bibliographically), (H) as to its character (literary or topical).

The means to those ends he stated to be:

> 1. Author-entry with the necessary references (for A and D).
> 2. Title-entry or title-reference (for B).
> 3. Subject-entry, cross-references, and classed subject-table (for C and E).
> 4. Form-entry and language-entry (for F).
> 5. Giving edition and imprint, with notes when necessary (for G).
> 6. Notes (for H). [1]

In a footnote in the second edition of his <u>Rules,</u> Cutter

*Reprinted by permission of the author and the Australian Library Association from <u>Australian Library Journal,</u> April 1974, pp. 95-99.

says: "this statement of Objects and Means has been criti-
cized: but ... I suppose it has on the whole been approved."
And so it has been, and is. Ninety-eight years later, we
want not to criticize it but to open it up to make it more receptive of wider interpretations. The following notes are
offered rather as a gloss on Cutter's statement than as a
criticism of it.

Cataloguing is description of documents, identification
and labelling of document classes and creation of files. "Documents" means any kind of recorded communication, in any
form. Cataloguing is concerned with recorded communication
in any medium (through sight, hearing, touch, taste or
smell) in any form (codex, scroll, tape, film, whatever) and
of any kind (informative or imaginative, verbal or non-
verbal). Description of a document entails identification and
expression of all data elements needed to provide a document
surrogate such that, with the document in hand, the surrogate
can be recognized as being of that document and only that
document; and that, with the surrogate in hand, the document can be located and recognized.

Identification and labelling of document classes is indexing, whether author and title indexing ("descriptive cataloguing" in its broader sense) or subject indexing. Indexing
is pointing. It is not describing and it is not allotting documents to pre-determined categories. It is not (pace Cutter)
attempting to predict where the reader is likely to look. It
is, in principle, attempting to identify and label all the
classes, of whatever kind, to which a document belongs so
that no matter what characteristic or group of characteristics
is sought documents having the sought characteristics will be
retrieved.

A catalogue is a list or file. Document surrogates
are filed and access to the file is got by the labels assigned
to document classes.

The purpose of cataloguing is the retrieval of document surrogates from the file, so that the documents themselves may be retrieved. There are four inter-related aspects, which may be expressed as known item; literary unit;
retrospective search; and current awareness. A known item
is an item which a reader in some sense knows, no matter
what he knows about it or how he knows. A literary unit is
any group of documents which are bibliographically related.
A retrospective search is a search of the whole file. Current

awareness entails a search of current additions to the file.

Learning Problems

The nature and purpose of cataloguing are not easily understood. There seem to be five reasons:

1) Indexing is an activity which, in the last analysis, can be learned only by doing it. In that respect, it is like riding a bicycle. It is easy to make the right verbal responses in relation to what it means to ride a bicycle, but making the right verbal responses is no guarantee of ability to ride.

2) There is a reasonable human tendency to talk in vague and general terms rather than in precise and exact terms. It suffices, because natural language has much built-in redundancy and because most communication is interactive. Indeed, most discussion which is not purely social intercourse consists in large part in refinement of statements leading toward either agreement or definition of areas of disagreement. Indexing languages are artificial languages with little of the redundancy of natural language. In indexing it is essential to be precise and exact from the outset because what has not been explicitly identified and labelled at the point of input of data cannot be precisely retrieved.

3) Beginning indexers find it hard to unlearn preconceptions about indexing. They think of it as pigeon-holing rather than labelling.

4) Beginning students are confused by the wide variety of methods of indexing and find it hard to realise that exhaustivity and specificity can be achieved in many different ways and to recognize when indexing is exhaustive and specific in various systems.

5) Beginning students find the literature of cataloguing in general and indexing in particular confusing because "there is such confusion in the use of terms."[1] That was true in Cutter's day and he did much to remedy it. But there are still large areas of confusion today. The term "specificity," for example, has at least five different meanings and it is seldom clear in what sense an author is using it.

Education for cataloguing ought to fit the student, after
a period of professional experience, to solve the problems of
cataloguing in any environment. He should be able to apply
the principles in any situation in which he finds himself, now
or in the future. But students (and even experienced cataloguers) find it difficult to make the transfer from the nature
and purpose of cataloguing to its application in individual systems. It does not seem to be possible effectively to learn
cataloguing principles without some study of the embodiment
or exemplification of those principles.

How we attempt to overcome learning problems will
be influenced by the environment in which we envisage cataloguing being practised. It is relatively easy to train cataloguing technicians, because the environment of present libraries and cataloguing practices is known. It is harder to
develop programs of professional education because that involves an attempt to predict the cataloguing environment a
quarter of a century from now.

The need to look forward twenty-five years arises
from a combination of two factors. The first is that those
of today's students who are going to reach influential positions in the profession will do so within twenty years. It is
true that it was a young Cutter, a young Dewey and a young
Poole who revolutionized cataloguing in 1876, but if one of
the major objects of a profession is to institutionalize genius
we ought now to be able to predict our internal revolutions.
The second factor is that educational change at the tertiary
level is slow, governed by three-year cycles of triennial
planning and five-year cycles of accreditation, within which
major changes are difficult to effect. One need only reflect
upon the changes that have occurred in the cataloguing environment since 1950 to appreciate the extent of change that
may occur in a twenty-five year period.

The Cataloguing Environment

If we had to predict only internal revolutions there
would be little difficulty. But cataloguing is not done in a
vacuum. The cataloguing environment twenty-five years from
now will be largely governed by economic and social factors
beyond our individual control and only to a limited extent
within our professional control. We do not know whether the
future holds wealth or poverty, universal education or mass
ignorance. There seem to be two extremes of prognostica-

tion. The one extreme envisages a continued expansion of information services leading to increasing development of data bases and their exploitation through networks. In such an environment the whole information industry would undergo radical changes involving publishers and booksellers as well as librarians, and libraries as discrete collections of books would virtually cease to exist. The other extreme envisages a reversion to a condition the world has known for a much longer period of time, in which information services are of little account. In such an environment the primary function of libraries might again be preservation of documents and each library, struggling to exist at all, would be obliged jealously to guard its collections.

At this moment both extremes may seem equally probable. There are as many reasons to suppose that we shall overcome problems of population, pollution and plundering of the planet as to suppose that we shall not. And between the two extremes is a whole spectrum of possibilities. Clearly, though the essential nature and purpose of cataloguing would not change, cataloguing practices would be quite different in libraries which are the equivalent of monastic libraries in the sixth century from those of Licklider's library of the future. [2]

It is impossible, in a program of professional education, to give equal weight to the whole spectrum of future possibilities. Since the designer of a program is obliged to make a choice, it seems reasonable to make that choice in accordance with what he would like to see happen in the future, if only because in doing so he may succeed in influencing what happens. The environment of the future is what we make happen as well as what happens to us. Variety in programs of education for cataloguing seems not only inevitable but desirable. There is no reason why all library schools should attempt to provide the same kind of learning experience in cataloguing. There is plenty of room for different approaches and different emphases and for the offering of different kinds of cataloguing expertise.

Core, Elective and Higher Studies

Problems of curriculum design are most acute in the "core" of a program leading to basic professional qualification, to the extent that it is tempting to drop altogether the notion of a core. In the Australian situation, exigencies of

academic staff resource, student numbers and cost per
student place prevent that.   Dropping the core would result
in a system of "required electives" which in fact constitute
a core.

If one leans toward the first extreme outlined above,
the cataloguing content of the core will tend to deal with the
nature and purpose of cataloguing in the context of making a
data base, deriving various products from a data base and
exploiting data bases.   It will tend to concentrate upon the
use of the computer for those activities, in the environment
of local, national and international networks rather than of
individual libraries.   There will be an emphasis on various
methods of indexing (including mechanical methods) and file
organization, on search formulation, and on evaluation of
systems, rather than on conventional cataloguing.

Such an approach will be justified by the event if the
prognosis upon which it is based proves to be correct.   But
even should the prognosis prove false, there are certain advantages which do not appear to accrue if the content of the
core derives from predictions tending to the second extreme.
The first such advantage is that an understanding of the nature of bibliographic data elements and the importance of
their identification is facilitated by the discipline which input
of data in machine readable form imposes.   The second advantage is that the computer makes it possible for the student
to simulate a much wider range of systems (especially
methods of indexing and search formulation) than he could
without the computer.   Simulation of manual systems requires
so much time and effort of a purely clerical nature that it
offers little valuable educational experience.   Simulation of
computerized systems eliminates much of the clerical effort
and opens a wide range of choice of emphases or directions.
The third advantage is that experience of computerized systems throws light also on manual systems, not only because
the student can derive a conventional catalogue or bibliography
from the data base which he constructs, but also because the
analysis required for computer production of those catalogues
or bibliographies needs to be more exact than for their manual production.   It is possible that a student who has had
such an opportunity will be at least as well equipped to cope
with problems of cataloguing in the dark ages as his colleague who was offered a more traditional learning experience in cataloguing.   He will be aware of a wider range of
options and he may have a deeper understanding of the nature
and purpose of cataloguing and be better able to adapt to

changing circumstances. He will certainly be better equipped
to cope with problems of cataloguing in the age of enlighten-
ment.

   The last decade has seen a reduction of course requirements in cataloguing and classification in library schools
generally, as much because of the existing cataloguing environment as because of possible future environments. When
ready made cataloguing data are available for up to 90 per
cent of English language materials and up to 70 per cent of
foreign language materials acquired by research libraries,
there is a decline in original cataloguing activity in individual
libraries and a corresponding decline in emphasis on cataloguing in educational programs.   Another factor influencing
the conventional teaching of cataloguing has no doubt been the
score or so of catalogue use surveys, most of which indicate
that "from 70 to 80 per cent of patrons were successful in
their use of the catalog. "[3] Conventional educational programs have not even produced very good conventional catalogues.

   At the same time, there is a need in the work force
for a small number of excellent cataloguers, to provide cataloguing data of very high quality for national and international
consumption.   There is a growing awareness of the importance of audio-visual resources and of problems of their bibliographic control.   There is a continuing need for development and control of collections of rare and early printed
books.   These, and other requirements, call for elective
courses in programs of professional education.   Such elective
courses can also offer students an opportunity for historical
study of cataloguing, for comparative analysis of cataloguing
codes and classification schemes, for study of union listing
and co-operative cataloguing, for investigation of problems of
shelf arrangement and open access and for examination of
problems of administering the cataloguing department of a
library.

   The kind of cataloguing core suggested above lays a
sound foundation for a wide range of elective courses which
enable students to pursue areas of special interest to them
in a program of education for librarianship leading to basic
professional qualification.   And programs of that nature would
seem to offer a reasonable preparation for work at the
masters and doctoral levels, in which specialization is
appropriate.

Conclusion

          According to Osborn, "Margaret Mann used to give ...
a superb demonstration of how, in the Armour Institute ...,
a dignified bearded gentleman would demonstrate in front of
the class with a broom how library floors ought to be
swept. "[4] Teaching students how to apply cataloguing codes
and manipulate the schedules of classification schemes has
an important place in programs of training for library technicians. It may be an exaggeration to say that it has about
as much place in programs of education for librarianship as
teaching students how to sweep library floors, but it comes
close to the truth. Teaching codes and teaching from codes
was probably never very successful. Today we have a significant advantage in that we can offer students an opportunity
to simulate a range of systems and to produce a range of
products. Students need no longer do "practical cataloguing"
by cataloguing and classifying individual works discretely and
in a vacuum (about as impractical a process as could be
imagined). They can actually create files and manipulate
the records in them and the data in the records in various
ways, and appreciate the essentially synthetic nature of cataloguing. They can also experiment with much larger files
than they themselves create, not only in the form of the
many book catalogues and bibliographies which are now available, but also by working with machine readable data bases
(MARC, ERIC, MEDLARS) which offer many more modes of
file access. What matters is not so much what students
learn about the computer (though hopefully that too may prove
to be of benefit) but what the computer enables the student to
learn about cataloguing. There may not be any electronic
computers in the year 2001. Even if there are not, provided
that there are still libraries, what students learn now with
the aid of the computer will stand them in good stead.

          An educational experience ought to be like Abelard's
heaven, ubi non praevenit rem desiderium, nec desiderio
minus est praemium. In education for cataloguing, the student ought to be motivated to understand the nature and purpose of cataloguing and his desire ought not to fall short of
that goal as learning cataloguing rules falls short. The prize
we offer should be no less than an ability to apply the principles of cataloguing in any environment he may encounter in
his subsequent professional career.

Notes

1. Cutter, C. A. <u>Rules for a Dictionary Catalog.</u> (4th
    edition, Washington, Government Printing Office, 1904.
    Republished by the Library Association, 1948).

2. Licklider, J. C. R. <u>Libraries of the Future.</u> (MIT
    Press, 1965).

3. Palmer, R. P. <u>Computerizing the Card Catalog in the
    University Library: a Survey of User Requirements.</u>
    (Libraries Unlimited, 1972).

4. Osborn, A. D. "The Design of the Curriculum for the
    Third Era of Education for Librarianship. " In
    Goldhor, H., editor. <u>Education for Librarianship: the
    Design of the Curriculum of Library Schools.</u> Uni-
    versity of Illinois Graduate School of Library Science,
    1971).

TO EACH GENERATION
ITS OWN RABBITS*

Dennis Flanagan

Richard Adams's epic novel about rabbits, <u>Watership</u>
<u>Down,</u> has received a remarkable amount of critical attention
in Britain and in this country. On the whole the verdict has
been favorable, with almost universal admiration being expressed for the book's unexpected narrative power. In my
own view <u>Watership Down</u> is even more interesting for what
it represents than what it says. It is a significant expression of the current state of relations between the literary
culture and the scientific one.

"The two cultures" is now well-established as a figure
of speech. As a concept, however, it has had its vicissi-
tudes. When C. P. Snow gave his Rede Lecture titled <u>The</u>
<u>Two Cultures and the Scientific Revolution</u> in 1959, [1] the lit-
erary culture was, so to speak, laying for the scientific culture. It also seems as if it had been laying for Snow. He
was riding high as a popular novelist, on the strength of his
coping with "real" worlds of modern life: science, the government, academia and so on. He was nonetheless out of
literary style in a time when most serious novels were more
introspective. He was not much praised by literary critics,
and there even seemed to be a certain amount of resentment
that this somewhat old-fashioned approach was going over so
well with serious readers--even though it was fortified by inside knowledge and considerable storytelling skill.

In this critical environment Snow's metaphor of the
two cultures was assaulted with remarkable violence. The
best-known attack was delivered by the distinguished Cambridge critic F. R. Leavis. [2] At least some of these com-
mentaries were based on a curious misconception: that in

_____

*Reprinted by permission of the author and publisher from
<u>Wilson Library Bulletin,</u> October 1974, pp. 152-156. Copy-
right 1974 by the H. W. Wilson Company.

placing science on the same cultural footing as literature
Snow was trying to upgrade science and downgrade literature.
Others assumed that Snow was somehow advocating a division
of the two cultures. Even the redoubtable Aldous Huxley
wrote: "Snow or Leavis? The bland scientism of The Two
Cultures or, violent and ill-mannered, the one-track, mor-
alistic literarism of the Richard Lecture [by Leavis]? If
there were no other choice, we should indeed be badly off."[3]

        Actually, of course, Snow was simply calling attention
to the deepening fissure between the two cultures and fretting
over it. What was really happening, in my view, was that
many people in literary circles had become resentful of the
rising influence of science, particularly in the universities, and
Snow's fame as a novelist of the other culture and gave them an
uncommonly handy target. Such critics might have been doubtful of their ability to meet science head-on, since they knew so
little about it, but Snow, after all, wrote novels, and that was
something they did know about. Something had to be done to
stop the intellectual juggernaut of science from overwhelming
all the finer things of life: literature, painting, music, the
dance and so on.

        It is a pity that the idea of the two cultures should
have been the locus of such a volcanic eruption of intellectual
passions. It all came out as a scrimmage between the tribal
institutions of literature and science, whereas the original intent had been to take a step in the direction of reconciling
the two. Snow's original formulation is correct, and hardly
anyone really doubts it: there are people who have considerable knowledge of the arts and very little knowledge of the
sciences, and there are people for whom the reverse is true.
This bifurcation is one of the main weaknesses in modern
man's ability to improve his personal and social lot. The
proper recognition of that fact, and efforts to do something
about it, must surely rank high on the agenda of the perfect-
ibility of man.

Merging the Cultures with Rabbits

        What does all this have to do with Watership Down?
A good deal more than one might think. Watership Down is
a book about rabbits. It is soundly based on modern knowledge of the rabbit. Who gathered this knowledge? Biologists.
What is a biologist and what does he do? He is a scientist
and he does science. (Adams, who is not a member of the

scientific culture, generously acknowledges his debt to The
Private Life of the Rabbit, by the naturalist R. M. Lockley.)
In other words, Watership Down is a scientific novel, a work
that embraces the two cultures.

What happens in the creation of such a book, it seems
to me, is that a thoughtful and imaginative nonscientist masters a certain body of scientific knowledge and begins to
think on it. What would it be like, he might say to himself,
to be a rabbit? How might I convey in human terms what it
is like to be a rabbit? What could being a rabbit tell us
about what it is like to be human? We are all the beneficiaries of such efforts to inform our factual knowledge with its
potentialities. One can even argue that the main social function of art is to encompass factual knowledge and then to
imaginatively dilate on it, to consider not only what is but
also what might be.

Watership Down, of course, is about what it is like
to be a rabbit. It is a gripping tale, full of adventure,
deadly combat, blood, sadness and triumph (not much sex,
in spite of what most of us are led to expect of rabbits). It
is refreshing that the rabbits in the book are not cute little
humans; these rabbits are tough, brave and resourceful.
They are also ecological, that is, they are treated not simply
as individuals but as members of an animal population interacting with its environment. They are a far cry from Peter
Rabbit, a homunculus who would not pay the proper heed to
his mother. The difference is probably no accident; it may
be that each generation has to have its own rabbit legend.

One may be grateful for Watership Down, but if
Adams's main purpose is to tell us what it is like to be a
rabbit (in the light of modern knowledge about what a rabbit's
life is like), the book has some major flaws. For one thing,
the rabbit characters in Watership Down talk, which automatically introduces a feature of human life that rabbits do
not share. Adams even goes so far as to introduce a rabbit
vocabulary called Lapine; for example silflay, to browse,
tharn, paralyzed with fright, and hraka, fecal pellets. He
has a mouse character who speaks pidgin English with an
Italian accent, and a heroic seagull who speaks with what I
take to be a Norwegian accent. The choice here was clear:
either use the more descriptive third person or the more
dramatic first person.

The Odor Is the Message

There can be no doubt that human speech is the most highly developed form of communication in the biological world (at least on this planet). Speech, however, is only one of a great many different forms of communication. It is well known, for example, that many other mammals communicate intensively by means of odors. In Watership Down Adams refers to the fact that rabbits rub their chin on objects around their home burrow. He does not say, although he probably knows, that they do this because they have glands in their chin that secrete odorous substances. When a rabbit rubs its chin on a log near its burrow, it is leaving a message something like: "This is Joe's place. Keep out!"

Experiments conducted by Dr. Roman Mykytowycz in Australia indicate that for rabbits odors are a veritable symphony of messages. [4] Rabbits frequently urinate on each other for communication purposes. If a rabbit smelling of strange urine enters a warren other than its own, the other rabbits will attack it violently. The rabbit also has a well-developed set of glands around its anus that secrete odorous substances; these substances give each rabbit's fecal pellets a unique smell. When rabbits pass hraka, as Adams would say, they often park the pellets in a place where they will be encountered and sniffed at by other rabbits. Rabbits have a social hierarchy, or "peck order," and Dr. Mykytowycz has shown that the odor of the fecal pellets can convey a message rather like: "Joe, No. 1 rabbit in the warren, goes along here."

Adams may know these things too, but the point is that the social life of the rabbit may be even stranger, richer and more intriguing than his book makes out. If such notions as rabbits communicating with each other by the smell of urine and fecal pellets are offensive to us, that is not the fault of the rabbits. If we seek to understand another animal and its role in the same natural system to which we belong, we must allow it the dignity of its own way of life.

Whatever Became of Renaissance Man?

Of course, when nonscientists think of science, they do not usually think of biology. Everybody loves plants and animals, and it is easy to forget that most of what we know about these organisms is the result of the patient labor of

280 Library Lit. -74

recent generations of scientists. "Science" is usually taken
to mean hard science, the technical stuff that nobody can
understand. The fact is that there is no technical stuff;
there is only lack of knowledge and failure of communication.
None of the findings of modern science is inherently more
difficult to understand than the anal glands of the rabbit,
given a remarkably modest amount of background information.
Advances in scientific knowledge do not make nature more
complicated and more remote from common understanding;
they make it simpler and more accessible. For an intellectual to assume that an entire realm of knowledge is beyond
his comprehension is for him to cut himself off from a part
of his shared humanity.

For a person who has solved this problem there is a
descriptive figure of speech much older than "the two cultures." It is "Renaissance man." What ever became of the
Renaissance man, the Leonardoesque figure who was supposed to encompass all aspects of culture? He is not much
mentioned today as a model for personal striving. The exceptions, however, are instructive. One is Thomas Pynchon,
whose novels abound in flights into quantum mechanics and
relativity. Another is Vladimir Nabokov, who was once, to
be sure, almost as much a biologist as a writer.

Nabokov himself apparently has a rather stern view of
the two-cultures problem. Alan Friedman of the University
of California at Berkeley recently called my attention to some
remarks Nabokov had made about it to Alfred Appel:

    I would have compared myself to a Colossus of
    Rhodes bestriding the gulf between the thermody-
    namics of Snow and the Laurentomania [referring
    to D. H. Lawrence] of Leavis, had that gulf not
    been a mere dimple of a ditch that a small frog
    could straddle.... One of those 'two cultures' is
    really nothing but utilitarian technology; the other
    is B-grade novels, ideological fiction, popular art.
    Who cares if there exists a gap between such
    'physics' and such 'humanities'....

    Science means to me above all natural science.
    Not the ability to repair a radio set; quite stubby
    fingers can do that. Apart from this basic con-
    sideration I certainly welcome the free interchange
    of terminology between any branch of science and
    any raceme of art. There is no science without
    fancy, and no art without facts.

There is something admirable about this aristocratic
view, but the fact remains that many cultivated people are
unable or unwilling to straddle the ditch.   Let me tell you a
little story about an encounter I once had with Pauline Kael,
New Yorker's excellent film critic.   Miss Kael and I had not
met before, and she asked me what I did.   I said I was the
editor of Scientific American.   She remarked: "That's nice.
I know nothing about science. "   I said, perhaps a little too
aggressively, "Whatever became of the idea that an educated
person should know a little something about everything?"
Her eyes snapping a bit, she said: "Ah, a Renaissance
hack. "

My feelings were not hurt.   That, I think, is what it
is all about.   It is not enough for a few gifted Renaissance
men to write things we can enjoy (assuming we can follow
the fun).   We all have much to gain from a more unified culture, not only for intellectual reasons but also for reasons
of survival.   It is widely believed that science and technology
are somehow at the root of our trouble, and that if we could
only "get back to nature" the trouble would go away.   For
better or worse our entire culture has been based on technology since men first learned how to make stone tools, and
technology is always based on knowledge, that is, scientific
knowledge.   It is genuinely impossible to turn back.   There
is plenty of room for a more humane science and technology,
but if we are to have it, a much larger component of society
will have to understand and love the stuff.

To Reweave the Rainbow

How does the scientific culture get separated from the
literary one, anyway?   One reason is fear and loathing of
mathematics, and here many teachers of science willingly
help to dig their own grave.   It is widely believed that mathematics is the essence of science, whereas it is not the
essence at all.   It is a tool, a language, a way of expressing relations and laws.   Anyone who has taken the pains to
learn this language wants to speak it to others, even if it is
not essential to their general understanding of the subject.
To be sure, mathematics has its own fascination for many
people, and no one would suggest that it is not essential to
the work of science.   It may be, however, that the scientist
who is a teacher has to choose between teaching the student
what he has learned and teaching the student to do what he
does.

The trouble probably lies, however, at a deeper level. Fear and loathing of scientific knowledge has a long history. John Keats put it best:

> Do not all charms fly
> At the mere touch of cold philosophy?
> There was an awful rainbow once in heaven:
> We know her woof, her texture; She is given
> In the dull catalogue of common things.
> Philosophy will clip an Angel's wings,
> Conquer all mysteries with rule and line,
> Empty the haunted air, and gnomed mine--
> Unweave a rainbow.

Keats was keening over Newton's explanation of the rainbow, but he was of course expressing an even older split in human conceptions: the dualities of feelings and thoughts, emotion and reason, body and mind, heart and head. Such dualities are probably the best explanation we have of the dualism of the two cultures. The bifurcation of culture is established early in our lives by a pervasive pattern of myth-making in which schools, teachers, parents and literature benevolently and unwittingly participate. The role of children's literature is particularly interesting. We live in a golden age of children's literature. The great classics endure, but the sheer weight of first-class children's books being published today dwarfs anything that has gone before. The best children's books are written by members of the literary culture, and under present circumstances that is inevitable and even right. The imagination of a child is not going to be stretched by books that merely recite facts. The present state of affairs does, however, reinforce the duality of culture. Here is where the case of Watership Down is particularly instructive. Even though Adams has not escaped the bonds of anthropomorphism, his epic of the rabbit does more to encompass the facts than anything that has gone before it.

Animals bulk very large as characters in children's literature. For the most part they have not caught up with the splendor of real animals. When we see a leopard in the zoo, we admire its beauty and grace. That, of course, is only a small part of what a leopard is about. A leopard is the result of an evolutionary symphony, a counterpoint between predator and prey, animal and plant, and animate and inanimate nature. If we are to understand the leopard and allow him to live, we need to see him not as an object but as a part of a seamless web of life with a past, a present

and a future.   It is this symphonic view that is usually missing in the treatment of animals in children's literature.

Where Is Fancy Bred?

If Watership Down is the rabbit epic of our generation,
the next generation's animal epics will probably be informed
by the evolutionary view.   It is a remarkable fact that it has
only been about 150 years since men began to have some
real notion of the past and the future.   When it came to esti-
mating the age of the world, an educated Englishman in Vic-
toria's time had only Archbishop Ussher's calculation that it
had been created in 4004 B. C.   Today we know that the universe began between 20 billion and 10 billion years ago, that
the earth was formed five billion years ago, that terrestrial
life arose two billion years ago, that modern man (there
were earlier members of the genus Homo) appeared 40, 000
years ago.   Our modern knowledge of the past tends to put
things in perspective, and yet the evolutionary mode of
thought has not yet been much integrated into our daily philosophy.

To choose only one example, consider the prevailing
view of death.   Most people regard death as a tragedy, and
in a limited sense it is.   In the larger biological sense,
however, it is otherwise.   Death is a progressive evolutionary invention.   Every living species is a population; every
member of the population is a fleeting experiment in the
crucible of the environment.   The same is true of man, even
though much of his environment is created by himself.   More
primitive organisms were immortal and evolved slowly; more
advanced organisms incorporated the mechanism of death and
evolved rapidly.   Without death there is little change.   I
find it hard to believe that a wider acceptance of the evolutionary view of death would not have a benevolent effect on
life in our death-obsessed society.

If such views are to be encompassed by children's
literature, the writers and illustrators of children's books
will need to pay closer heed to Nabokov's "There is no art
without facts. "   The facts in this case are not nuts and bolts
but the larger view of man and nature that has been gained
by modern science.   The other part of Nabokov's dictum is
no less important: "There is no science without fancy. "
Here we are listening to an echo of Shakespeare's "Tell me
where is fancy bred, Or in the heart or in the head?"   As

Nabokov suggests, it is bred in both places.

Notes

1. The Two Cultures and the Scientific Revolution, by
    C. P. Snow. The Rede Lecture, 1959. Cambridge
    University Press, New York, 1959.

2. Two Cultures? The Significance of C. P. Snow, by
    F. R. Leavis. Chatto and Windus, 1962.

3. Literature and Science, by Aldous Huxley. Harper &
    Row, 1963.

4. "Territorial Marking by Rabbits," by Roman Mykytowycz.
    Scientific American, Vol. 218, No. 5; May, 1968.

LITERATURE BEDEVILED:
A SEARCHING LOOK AT FILMSTRIPS*

Ethel L. Heins

Seventeen years ago, I innocently embarked on a project to explore the maze of current storytelling and dramatic recordings for children. Searching for something of value, I was almost immediately appalled at what I found--an overabundance of commercial discs which lacked any respect for the literature reproduced as well as for the children who were to listen. "[W]ith sentimentality substituting for emotional depth, and dreary silliness for real humor.... diluted retellings [and dramatizations] of well-loved tales ... totally fail to keep the spirit of the originals."[1]

At that time, the multi-media approach to children's literature was still in its infancy; not until the next decade did Marshall McLuhan prophesy the doom of the printed word. In the sixties, educational technology became both an industry and a respected profession. Visual aids--in addition to aural --were hailed as an essential factor in motivating a new generation of children to learn to read and even to appreciate literature; and there was a great proliferation of the little rolls of transparencies known as filmstrips.

From the very beginning, Morton Schindel, founder of Weston Woods, wisely realized that much of the appeal of picture books lies in their illustrations and in the interdependence of artwork and text. The unique Weston Woods films and filmstrips, phenemonally successful in schools and libraries all over the world, have demonstrated the feasibility of producing book-based audio-visual materials scrupulously faithful to the originals. In this work, Morton Schindel clearly was the pioneer.

*Reprinted by permission of the author and publisher from The Horn Book Magazine, June 1974, pp. 307-313.

Other companies are now making filmstrips--usually
accompanied by cassettes or records--with pictures accurately reproduced from books. Teaching Resources Films,
for example, has issued filmstrips made from such favorites
as the Amelia Bedelia stories, the Curious George books,
and Virginia Lee Burton's Maybelle the Cable Car and Katy
and the Big Snow. Viking Press has prepared an excellent
group of filmstrips made from its own picture books; and
Macmillan has moved similarly into the audio-visual field
with Threshold Filmstrips, filmed from a dozen of their own
titles. At this writing, another forthcoming group of picture-
book filmstrips has just been announced as a joint venture of
Scribner/Miller-Brody. Spoken Arts' Treasury of Modern
Tales includes Edward Fenton's The Big Yellow Balloon and
Don Freeman's The Guard Mouse; and McGraw-Hill has
made filmstrips of eight Happy Lion stories.

Several sets of splendid filmstrips have been adapted
by Lyceum Productions from Ann Atwood's handsome photographic books. Teeka the Otter and Sammy the Crow, both
written by Elizabeth Baldwin Hazelton, are pleasing nature
stories. Much more important are the filmstrips solely
based on Ann Atwood's work. The Wild Young Desert--a
successful combination of geology, ecology, and aesthetics--
is straightforward yet poetic, factual yet lyrical. Haiku:
The Mood of Earth series consists of beautiful, experimental
filmstrips in which two pictures are used to express the
haiku: first the long view of a whole scene and then the
closeup of a fragment. Thus, "it might be said that the
words illustrate the photographs." Haiku: The Hidden Glimmering, based on Ann Atwood's recent book My Own Rhythm:
An Approach to Haiku, discusses imagination, emotion, and
insight in the work of three Japanese poets--Bashô, Issa,
and Buson. The author's aim is to sharpen awareness of
and to quicken responses to the natural world; authentic Japanese music is used sparingly and discreetly. Such filmstrips are really photographic essays combining visual and
verbal poetry; and in the melding of words and pictures,
they demonstrate the peculiar characteristics and limitations
of the medium used to the fullest advantage.

But popular McLuhanism, joyfully proclaiming the
new media, has frequently ignored the study of the message.
And the development, technology, and organization of the
media center have often been of more urgent concern to
some librarians than the significance of its materials. Not
surprisingly, scores of filmstrips have been reiterating and

compounding the sins of many of the old literature recordings
of the 1950's.

We need not discuss the role of the filmstrip in general instruction. It is obvious that for any subject which
can be clarified by photographs or diagrams, a good filmstrip can smooth the road to learning; indeed, a graphic representation of facts or abstractions is often essential to understanding.

But reading a literary work is not like studying science or history; nor is it the same as looking at a picture
book. There is nothing wrong with the idea of translating a
wholly verbal work into a pictorial composition; but the film-
strip--unlike the film, which has developed into a legitimate
art form--is severely limited. Reducing a story to a collection of indifferent drawings, a filmstrip can only be--like the
Emperor's nightingale--an impoverished imitation. Nowhere
is the inevitable failure more obvious than in the filmstrips
concocted from Newbery Medal books (Miller-Brody). Consider the Horn Book review of Mrs. Frisby and the Rats of
NIMH: "a talking-beast tale which blends scientific probability and fantasy. . . . an intriguing adventure made plausible
through vivid descriptive prose and meticulous selection of
detail. " And of The High King: "More than a series of exciting adventures, the book has the philosophical depth and
overtones of great fantasy. " Can the producer of these film-
strips--carefully researched and planned though they are--
claim that the essence of the books is captured in a series
of colored pictures? Where is the subtlety of characterization, the emotional power, the style? Where is true wit,
and the virtuosity of great writing?

The timeworn defense of mediocrity--that the filmstrip will inspire an unenthusiastic child to read the complete book--is unsupported. Not only do most filmstrips
present a warped idea of the story, they also remove some
of the excitement of discovery by leaving a vague, false impression of familiarity. But listening to the story read
aloud might well send the child to the book; no filmstrip can
whet the appetite like oral reading articulated with conviction
and zest by a teacher or a librarian. And the more reluctant or inept the reader, the more desperate is his need to
be read to.

For we must preserve language not dismiss it. "We
have the most inarticulate generation of college students in

history, " said the poet Karl Shapiro; and Richard Peck,
speaking of adolescent readers, wrote: "Many young people
... are patients in the remedial reading clinic. Some of
them appear to be terminal cases. The permissive home
and the watered-down school curriculum have betrayed them.
The basic skills were not imposed, and attention spans were
not stretched. "2

      As filmstrips, many books and stories long-treasured
in the public domain have been subjected to one indignity
after another; many of them are no more than classic comics
updated. Typical is a series called Favorite Children's
Books (Coronet), in which Peter Pan, Gulliver's Travels,
A Little Princess, Robinson Crusoe, A Wizard of Oz, The
Happy Prince, and A Dog of Flanders are all reduced by an
anonymous artist to their lowest common denominators.

      One of the most ambitious productions consists of the
thirty-six filmstrips in the McGraw-Hill Films Children's
Literature Series. "In all cases our primary concern was
to capture the flavor and nuances of the book, while creating
an entertaining and exciting filmstrip. In some instances,
there was not enough original artwork in the book or the
pictures would not have adapted well to the filmstrip format,
so new artwork was created. Color was added to drawings
where appropriate. "   Hence, Peter's Long Walk, deprived
of Barbara Cooney's crisp, fresh illustrations, moves into
the tawdry filmstrip world where cats and rabbits so often
look like greeting card kittens and bunnies. The Limerick
Trick, drastically abridged, loses the individuality of its
characters; while the flat, bare pictures fail even to approx-
imate the lively fun of the book. A Pair of Red Clogs fortunately retains Kazue Mizumura's illustrations; but why
should Many Moons, a Caldecott Medal winner, have been
chosen for re-illustration? Evan's Corner, too, has been
tossed into the blender; and now, without the sympathetic,
warmly effective drawings, it has been reincarnated with
garish pictures of expressionless children. As artistic units,
the books have been destroyed. And surely, Mr. Magoo's
Literature Series (also McGraw-Hill)--an incredible collection of classics such as William Tell, King Arthur, Treasure
Island, and The Three Musketeers filtered through the mind-
less interpretations of the cartoon character "to join learning
and laughter"--is a total travesty.

      A flagrant example of contempt for both children and
books in the pursuit of crass commercialism is the filmstrip

world of the folk tale.   Largely a universal plastic kingdom,
it is populated with comic-book characters wearing regulation masks for horror, anger, innocence, or joy.   One is
reminded of the Mock Turtle's branches of arithmetic--"Ambition, Distraction, Uglification, and Derision. "   But just as
folk tales can be made into beautiful picture books, so they
could, conceivably, provide the texts for acceptable film-
strips--if first-rate illustrators were employed.   However,
after years of critical attention to picture books and to the
art of illustration, a dismaying double standard still permits
an audio-visual reviewer to criticize a filmstrip set of
legends for having flat and lifeless pictures, and then to observe that the series would be useful for school curricula
and story hours.   Yet the American Library Association's
1969 Standards for School Media Programs specifically ad-
monishes the professional staff to guide "students to develop
desirable reading, viewing, and listening patterns, attitudes,
and appreciations. "

One experienced producer of many acceptable recordings (Spoken Arts) issues filmstrips abounding in coyness
and sheer ugliness.   Mother Goose, wearing sun glasses,
resembles a senior citizen on a holiday.   The Happy Prince,
in a dreadful, watered-down version, only widens the gap
between literature and its audio-visual transformations.   In
"Rapunzel" (Troll), the princess' tower room--like an illustration in a domestic magazine--is furnished with blue wall-
to-wall carpeting and a tip-top table; the princess' father
wears a stiff Victorian collar while the prince's costume is
pure seventeenth-century baroque.   Recalling Adrienne
Adams' charming books, one shudders at the same producer's renderings of "Jorinda and Joringel" and "The Elves
and the Shoemaker. "

Other producers are even further from the mark.   In
a mockery of "The Three Billy Goats Gruff, " the troll wears
red breeches and a blue jacket; and in the simplified text
printed directly on the film, the gamboling goats gently say:
"I hope this bridge is safe.... I hope the old troll is fast
asleep. "   Many traditional stories are distorted with didacti-
cism.   One "Little Red Riding Hood, " hitting hard at filial
obedience, ends with: "Now she was always going to remember to mind her mother"; while "Cinderella" turns into
a moral tale as her sisters beg for forgiveness.   In "The
Boy Who Could Do Anything, " gaudy coloring masquerades
as Mexican atmosphere, while the sound-effects technicians,
as meticulous as ever, imitate every twanging arrow, every

chirping bird. African Legends and Folktales (CCM Films),
a set of six filmstrips, conscientiously researched, is to be
praised for its authentic folklore and for its effective storytelling by Moses Gunn. But the filmstrips are often commonplace and inelegant, and do not bear comparison with the
brilliant Anansi interpretations of Gerald McDermott or Gail
Haley.

        American tall tales and legends--especially those about
Paul Bunyan, Pecos Bill, John Henry, and Johnny Appleseed
--have been thoroughly exploited. Paul is often pictured
as a fat, rather voluptuous infant; Babe as excessively blue,
with curly hair and long eyelashes. Undignified, sentimental,
grossly unattractive, and inaccurately costumed, the figures,
lacking the cleverness of true cartooning, show only the
vapid, familiar faces of cheap comics. And on the recorded
texts, sounding like television at its worst, are convention-
alized folksy voices, speaking incongruous, tasteless, present-day slang and jargon. Perhaps no character has been
so bowdlerized as Johnny Appleseed--piously bearing his
Bible; wearing the inevitable saucepan on his head; surrounded by smiling rattlesnakes, bears looking like benign stuffed
toys, and Indian stereotypes; and at the end of his life, walking away into the setting sun.

        Classical mythology fares no better than other tradi-
tional literature. The few attempts at filmstrip presentation
are oversimplified or ludicrously popularized. A set entitled Mythology Is Alive and Well (Guidance Associates) is
a barbarous attempt to justify and prove the relevance of
mythology to older young people. Pictures of mythological
subjects alternate with photographs of present-day adoles-
cents--all synchronized with a fatuous, yet pompous, text in
dialogue form. To heighten audience appeal, a rock group
intermittently sings popular music. A discussion of Pluto,
for example, is followed by several photographs of a ceme-
tery, highlighting a flower-bedecked coffin; and a sequence
on Apollo includes a picture of the rocket--"which has at
last soared to the moon, bringing Apollo to Artemis"--pre-
ceding a photograph of a modern bathing beach crowded with
young sun-worshippers. At one point, one hears: "You can
still see Hermes doing his thing for the flowers-by-wire
services"; and from Aphrodite, we are told, comes the cry
"that what the world needs now is 'love, sweet love.'"

        Hans Christian Andersen, Kipling, and Washington
Irving are all dealt cruel blows by producers eager to cap-

italize on well-loved stories. With grotesqueness and maud-
lin sentimentality replacing humor and subtlety, and with
texts diluted almost beyond recognition, the Andersen tales
look like outrageous caricatures of the originals. In "Five
Peas in a Pod," the green peas have round, dimpled faces;
the mother duck in "The Ugly Duckling" wears a kerchief
around her head. "The Nightingale" appears again and again
in many versions, all of them full of pseudo-Chinese clichés,
the Emperor a figure of offensive vulgarity. The Jungle
Book also has been abridged and debilitated. An elaborate
offering (Spoken Arts) includes the usual added attractions:
a collection of activity sheets for student participation and
a guide for teachers. Unfortunately, whatever dramatic
quality is preserved in the abbreviated story is wasted on
the pallid, insipid pictures. In a Just So Stories series
(Coronet), the Elephant's Child, thoroughly emasculated,
looks like a blood brother of Dumbo; and there is no evidence of any attempt to preserve the tokens of Kipling's
genius. Thus one looks in vain for the Bi-Coloured-Python-
Rock-Snake, the Kolokolo Bird with his mournful cry, or the
slushy-squshy mud-cap--as well as for the author's efferves-
cent diction.

Not even poetry has been immune. Certainly, visual
images can reinforce verbal ones, and pictorial analogy can
be important in the study of poetry. One need only look at
the photographs on the handsomely-designed pages of Reflections on a Gift of Watermelon Pickle and Other Modern
Verse to perceive how a poem can be illuminated and its
emotion intensified by parallel images. But mundane, literal
interpretations stifle, rather than stimulate, the imagination.
Two filmstrips, Favorite Poems about Children's Adventures
and Favorite Poems of Fun and Laughter (Troll), offer dull,
flat drawings, easily surpassed in creativity and spontaneity
by the pictures which school children themselves often make
in response to oral poetry.

Two other productions, both frankly educational tools
aimed at the classroom, present an interesting contrast. A
program called What Is Poetry? (Caedmon) consists of ten
recordings, beautifully read by Claire Bloom and featuring
also the voices of Carl Sandburg and Ogden Nash. The
readings are matched by imaginative filmstrips, in which
the pictures, speaking a visual language of their own, merely
suggest and intimate, but never mimic. On the other hand,
Lee Bennett Hopkins has made a set of six sound filmstrips,
Pick a Peck o' Poems (Miller-Brody), to provide "a unique

conceptual approach to learning through poetry. " But while
the texts are carefully selected and prepared, and the reading, for the most part, is acceptable, the filmstrips are
weak and undistinguished. Once again, literal, commonplace
pictures utterly fail as analogies to the figurative language of
poetry; and the drab, realistic drawings merely show the objects mentioned in the poems rather than convey an idea of
the moods and images created by them.

    "Where are the enduring classics of the filmstrip?
Who quotes them? Who remembers them?" So asked,
somewhat plaintively, William R. Eshelman in The New York
Times Book Review. 3 Teachers, librarians, parents are
all eager to inspire creativity in children; but literature in
filmstrip form is too often a nonproductive short-cut, blandly
entertaining, or at its worst, rendering only custodial service. For such filmstrips--with their predetermined, super-
imposed pictures--make no demands on the imagination; and
literature, in this form, is shorn of its power to humanize,
to stir, or to enliven the wasteland of indifference in which
so many children are wandering. "It's not the book that
suffers, " says Lloyd Alexander. "Great literature is eminently durable; it survives all sorts of bedevilments. " But
the children "come out a little poorer, a little smaller than
[they] might have been. "

                        Notes

1.   Ethel L. Heins, "For Listening Children, " Horn Book
     XXXIII (December 1957), p. 514.

2.   Richard Peck, "In the Country of Teenage Fiction, "
     American Libraries IV (April 1973), p. 205.

3.   William R. Eshelman, "Audio-Visual Aids: Fallout from
     the McLuhan Galaxy, " The New York Times Book
     Review (May 6, 1973), p. 32.

JOHNNY STILL CAN'T READ*

Daniel Melcher

Once upon a time, the slow readers in our schools just dropped out. Nowadays they aren't allowed to, and there isn't a school that isn't acutely embarrassed by the number of its reading failures, rarely below 20 percent of the pupils. According to the U. S. Office of Education, some seven million elementary and secondary school pupils have reading problems severe enough to make them potentially unable to compete in society. This is not to say that the children whom the schools count as "reading failures" could not pass a literacy test. Our nation is, according to the census figures, almost 100 percent "literate." Just about everyone can do more than just read and write his name. Far too many, however, do not read for pleasure and do not look upon print as a practical means of self-enlightenment. Print is nearly as impenetrable to them as musical notation is to most of the rest of us. Call them slow readers, call them nonreaders, call them dyslexics--whatever word you use, for them reading is a skill they never quite master. For them speech is speech, but reading is deciphering a code.

Early reading is sometimes discussed as if the issue was whether to let a pushy mother gain an unfair advantage for her child. The question is asked whether early reading should be encouraged, unless a way can be found to make it effectively available to all children, not just some.

Instinctively, many educators respond to this problem by proposing to lower the age for starting school. California school officials are currently seeking to lower it to age four; New York State school officials are thinking of recommending that children begin school at age three. The assumption is that only in this way can children from de-

*Reprinted by permission of the author and publisher from School Library Journal, October 1973, pp. 79-87.

prived homes be prevented from falling behind children from more privileged homes; that the child in the classroom must inevitably be learning more than the child in the home--at least the average home.

Unless and until all or most children routinely learn to read early, the schools will still have the thankless task of trying to start the nonreaders on material geared to their reading level, such as, "Look, Jane, see the dog." Out on the playground the same youngsters have been debating about space satellites and using a speaking vocabulary in excess of 5000 words, yet they are expected to go back into the classroom and get interested in word-counted "baby stuff" geared to an assumed reading vocabulary of 50 words.

Assumptions about Nonreaders

Many of us clung briefly to the hope that Rudolf Flesch had the answer (phonics) to this reading problem in his best-selling book Why Johnny Can't Read and What You Can Do About It (Harper, 1955). Unfortunately, those schools that had been using phonics right along sadly admitted that even with a strong phonics program, an unacceptably high percentage of children had to be counted as reading failures.

The temptation has been to assume that it is children who come from deprived home environments who become the nonreaders. Perhaps more nonreaders come from the less privileged homes, but highly privileged homes also produce their share of nonreaders, and not infrequently a nonreader will have brothers and sisters who read very well indeed.

At first glance, that seems to leave "intelligence" as the significant variable, a theory supported by examination scores unless the exams are oral so that the student's ability to answer the question isn't limited by his ability to read it. On oral exams, many nonreaders do quite well.

Though the incidence of nonreaders, even in privileged school populations, rarely goes below 20 to 25 percent, there is reason to suspect that the incidence of true nonreaders may not go much higher either, even among children from grossly underprivileged homes, once you allow for those whose "nonreading" is more a protest against assignments they can't relate to than a true disability. In his Hooked on

Books (Berkeley, 1968), Daniel Fader tells of a reform
school in which some of the nonreaders of Dick and Jane
suddenly became avid readers when allowed to read books
such as Black Like Me or The Autobiography of Malcolm X.

Among themselves, educators tend to blame themselves (i. e., their methods) for their reading failures and
have been desperately seeking better methods. They have
tried phonics and they have tried the "look and say" method.
They have tried reading aloud and reading silently. They
have tried beginning reading instruction earlier, in kindergarten, and starting it later, in second grade. They have
tried placing the slow starters in special classes, so they
can be given extra drill.

There is really only one thing they haven't explored--
the possibility that the age for starting school is far too late
to start learning to read, just as it would be far too late to
begin learning to talk. They haven't really explored the
possibilities of encouraging youngsters to learn to read at
home, as early as they learn to talk, and by the same unstructured methods. This is hardly surprising. After all,
teachers don't get a child until he is of "school age. " What
happens between a mother and a two year old is not only
outside their experience, it is presumed to be outside their
assignment and beyond their reach.

Reading Readiness

Famous early readers include John Stuart Mill,
George Bernard Shaw, and Norbert Wiener. It was easy to
assume, however, that such early readers as these either
had exceptional intelligence or had exceptional help from exceptional parents--or most likely both. It was easy to assume that early reading could not, in any case, provide a
solution to the schools' problems, since few children could
be expected to have parents with the necessary time, dedi-
cation, or skill to teach them to read. Once this basic assumption had been made--namely that it was superior intelligence that led to early reading, rather than early reading
that might have helped release the superior intelligence--
many a study was made that seemed to buttress the assumption.

For example, the concept of "reading readiness" was
developed, and tests for measuring reading readiness were

devised. It was observed that the child who can already
read his name before he starts school generally makes
quicker progress with the school's reading lessons: accordingly, such a child was assumed to have reached a state of
"reading readiness" by age five or six and was placed in a
"fast class. " Other children who brought no such "prereading"
skills from home were assumed to need more time for
reading development and were often put in a "slow class. "
(If, however, a mother proposed to help develop earlier
reading readiness in her preschooler, she would be warned
against it. If she asked what harm it could do, she was
frequently offered the improbably unscientific observation
that caveats developed out of experiments in toilet training
could be assumed to apply to the teaching of reading as
well.)

Physiological Development and Reading

        Careful studies were made as to the age at which the
average child walks, talks, and reads--from which the inference was drawn that since the average child did wait until
age six to begin reading, then this must be the age at which
he should begin reading. (The very same "logic" applied in
Great Britain, where reading instruction starts in kindergarten, would, of course, "prove" that reading instruction
should start at age five.)

        One investigator thought that reading readiness might
hinge to some extent on the simple development of the capacity to see fine detail, and demonstrated that at age five
only one child in ten could distinguish a b from a d. (Of
course, it could equally well have been that only children
who could already read would see any reason to distinguish
a b from a d.)

        Another investigator, noting that the average child's
brain is not even fully developed until age seven or eight,
theorized that the cells involved in reading might not be
fully developed by the time a child reaches the age for entering school. (Of course, in this case, it could also be
that brain development, like muscle development, is a result, not a prerequisite, of brain use.)

        Many investigators are now beginning to suspect that
any child can learn to read as early as he learns to talk,
and will do so far more easily at that age than at a later

age, just as he can learn a second language far more easily
at the age when he is just starting to talk. They are beginning to believe that reading is in no way a higher skill than
speech, and can in fact be learned along with speech by employing much the same informal and unstructured methods.
John Holt has said, "If we taught them to talk the way we
teach them to read--they'd never learn," and Professor
Dolores Durkin, in her book Teaching Them to Read (Allyn
& Bacon, 1970), says, "So far as is now known, nothing
about six-year-old children makes this age level the very
best time for beginning reading."

     When some of these assumptions were questioned--as
in books such as Glenn Doman's How to Teach Your Baby to
Read (Random, 1964), Siegfried and Therese Engelmann's
Give Your Child a Superior Mind (S & S, 1966), David Eng-
ler's How to Raise Your Child's IQ (Criterion, 1958), and
Joan Beck's How to Raise a Brighter Child (Trident, 1967)
--the reaction from many educators was that mothers (often
described as "too emotionally involved") should keep hands
off, should not "push" the child, should not "spoil his precious childhood," and should not risk teaching him reading
habits that he would only have to unlearn later. Nothing
would be gained from early reading it was said, since any
seeming initial advantage would even itself out by the sixth
grade in any case.

     Happily, evidence is piling up that these assumptions
aren't valid and never were. (I say "happily" because the
research that was being done within the context of these
rather negative assumptions had pretty much come to a dead
end. Some new breakthrough was badly needed.)

The Work of Doman, Delacato, and Fay

     Some of the most impressive evidence that a child
(any child) can learn to read as early as he learns to talk
is to be found in the work being done by Glenn Doman and
Carl Delacato at the Institutes for the Achievement of Human
Potential in Philadelphia. They got into reading almost by
accident. Their primary work is with children who often
cannot walk or talk, let alone read, the kind of children who
sometimes have to be taught to breathe, and who might have
to be institutionalized if they cannot be successfully treated.
Their goal is to develop normal functions in children with
mental or motor handicaps originating from brain injury,

children diagnosed as cerebral palsied, autistic, athetoid, spastic, epileptic, hyperactive, mentally retarded, or emotionally disturbed.

Thus the children they see would not by the wildest stretch of the imagination be expected to assay very high in "reading readiness." (Doman's own story of this work will be published by Doubleday in the spring of 1974 under the title The Brain Injured Child.) Nevertheless, these children are routinely learning to read within eight months after joining the program, often before they learn to talk. In fact, out of 399 children under age four, sequentially accepted for treatment, some 385 learned to read before their fifth birthday. Furthermore, they learned at home, since the treatments were all carried out at home, and it was Mother who did it, usually with a few minutes of instruction each day. (The child of two who learns even one word a day will have learned 365 words before he's three!)

One might suppose that such consistent success would have to be based on some broad-scale breakthrough in teaching methods. Doman's view, however, is that there are really only two "secrets." First, you should start by age two if you can. Later is harder. Second, for at least the first few words, it pays to use VERY LARGE TYPE. Beyond that, almost any method works, provided you make a game out of it and stop before the child wants to stop.

Doman and Delacato's techniques for helping the brain-injured vary greatly with the diagnosis (age, symptoms, probable nature, and location of the brain injury), but one overriding policy is to try to compensate for any reduced capacity to see, hear, or feel by radically increasing opportunities for the child to see, hear, or feel. In fact, a double increase is indicated--first just to get through to the child, then to help him catch up. It isn't easy, however, to think up ways to keep a handicapped child interested and active throughout every waking hour, seeing, hearing, feeling, moving, experimenting, correlating. You have to use every resource you can find. Reading has proved to be one of the most valuable resources.

In the beginning, simply learning to read was a better game than pattycake; and as soon as the children got the general idea--namely that printed words have spoken equivalents--they'd start on their own to decipher package labels, newspaper headlines, advertisements, and books. These

were not, remember, children who had been selected for
their promise. In fact, to begin with, Doman's typical four-
year-old brain-injured patient might be performing at no
higher a level than that of a normal two year old.

Nevertheless, these hurt children almost invariably
learned to read and had fun doing it. Take, for example,
two-year-old Mary R. Her mother, who had been instructed
not to "push"--not to teach her more than one word a day--
reported that Mary had taken to the game so enthusiastically
that the first thing she would say when taken from her crib
in the morning was, "Let's get the new word!"

Or take bilingual two and one-half-year-old Susan, who,
on the fourth day of the word game, was holding the card
for her fourth word, table, and just beginning to sense the
potentials of reading. In great excitement, she held up the
card for the Puerto Rican maid to see and said in Spanish,
"Look, look, I can read it, it says mesa."

In point of fact, the home may be a far better place
than the classroom for doing a number of things. (It is
often charged that mothers are "too emotionally involved,"
but "emotionally involved" is nearly synonymous with "highly
motivated," and, besides, this tiresome label seems generally to come from educators themselves who regard mothers
with all the emotional detachment with which a trade unionist
regards a scab.)

Glenn Doman faced a "moment of truth" early in his
career that resulted in his acquiring a deep and abiding respect for mothers. He was then a young man working with
Temple Fay, the famous neurosurgeon. Comparing brain
injured children treated in a hospital with those left untreated
at home, Fay and Doman had to face an uncomfortable moment of truth: the children remaining at home, with nothing
but their mother's care, were not only doing as well as the
ones being brought to the hospital for professional care--they
were doing unmistakably better! In that instance, taking
children out of the home turned out to be a very poor alternative to leaving them in the home, even in underprivileged
homes.

In fact, the Doman case histories indicate that again
and again massive "enrichment of the environment" of
severely retarded children has increased not only their skills,
but their head size! With these children, brain capacity

seems to increase in proportion to the demands made upon
it, not in anticipation of them.

If you examine Doman's evidence, based on thousands
of case histories, you have to believe that neither high IQ
nor special aptitude is needed to enable children to learn to
read as early as they learn to talk. Reading readiness may
come with reading, not with age.

The Home Environment and Reading

The home is, after all, the place where children
learn their native language--and learn it far, far better than
any school will ever teach them a language.

If the best and most efficient learning we ever did
was when we learned our own language--before we got to
school--the methods we used warrant study. Perhaps it isn't
the untrained mother who uses the wrong methods--perhaps
it is the trained teacher who uses the wrong methods, mis-
guidedly trying to improve on the methods that mothers (and
Mother Nature) have been instinctively applying and perfect-
ing for a million years.

Take the spoken word milk. In the classroom, the
teacher would say something like, "Now children, what do
we call this white liquid I have in this glass?" And every
child would shrivel in his seat and pray, "I hope she doesn't
call on me, I hope she doesn't call on me." Mother, on the
other hand, just says, "Drink your milk."

Or take the printed word milk. A teacher would spell
it out on the blackboard, m-i-l-k, and then verbalize the
letters. Mother would just let the carton sit on the kitchen
table day after day, quietly proclaiming its contents. The
child might easily get to the point where he could, without
even thinking about it, "read" well enough to distinguish between cartons of whole milk, skimmed milk, buttermilk, or
chocolate milk in the same unconscious way he could distinguish his Aunt Mary from his Aunt Margaret. If, however, you took note of this reading and set out to "help" him
by saying, "Well, if you want to read, let me explain about
the alphabet," the child might well back off, thinking, "I
thought I was reading, but if it is that complicated, forget
it."

Perhaps three questions need to be answered. First, can two year olds learn to read? Second, if they can, should they? Third, if they can and should, how can this privilege be made available to all two year olds, not just those whose parents have the time and inclination to encourage early reading and can be told how to go about it?

Reading and Motivation

It may well be that not more than ten percent of five year olds can perceive the difference between a b and a d. Considering that some 96 percent of Doman's brain-injured children under five could, nevertheless, read words, this may be like observing that very few children (or adults, for that matter) can tell the difference between a bee and a wasp unless at some point they have had some reason to take note of the distinction. It is not a matter of visual acuity; in fact, babies very early learn to tell Mommy from Auntie even though any two human faces differ far more subtly than a b and a d. This may explain, however, Doman's observation that if you want a child to take note of the difference between the words mummy and daddy, you would do well to start with lettering four or five inches high. The same would probably apply if your goal was to help an adult take notice of the differences between two Japanese characters. The problem is not whether the child can see detail. The problem is whether he takes notice of it.

A while ago, my then 15-month-old son Fred gave me a dramatic demonstration that the ability to see is primarily the ability to recognize and that seeing is not just an optical function, it is also a brain function.

We were leafing through Life magazine and had come to a full-page advertisement for golf clubs. Fred said excitedly, "Airplane, airplane."

I said, "I don't see any airplane. I see a golfer. He has a golf club. He's about to swing at the ball."

"No, no," Fred insisted, pointing, "airplane, airplane."

"Fred," I said, mystified, "that's not an airplane, that's a golfball."

"No! Airplane!" Fred persisted.   Then I saw it.   On
one of the dimples of the golfball was the manufacturer's
trademark, not more than 1/16 of an inch across, in the
shape of an airplane.   I don't know if Fred had ever seen a
golfball, but he had long been greatly interested in airplanes.

Fred gave me another demonstration that indicated
motivation may have more to do with reading ability than
does visual acuity.   Just after his second birthday, a dozen
relatives and friends were gathered for a Christmas Eve
party.   Presents for everyone were stacked under the tree,
and we decided to let them be opened in random sequence by
having Fred bring them to his mother, one at a time, so
that she could read the card and pass the package to the intended recipient.   To our growing astonishment, the first 20
presents selected by Fred were all for him!   At age two, he
could infallibly recognize his own name, in any handwriting,
large or small, whether spelled Fred, Red, or Frederic.   I
am only sorry we did not draw the obvious conclusion and
provide incentives for extending his reading skills.

Even granting that children can learn to read as early
as they learn to talk, however, the question remains: "Would
this be wise?"   Early reading could be both possible and
safe without necessarily being significant.   Considering, however, that the common condition of most children, most of
the time, is boredom ("Do stop bothering Mother and go play
with your toys or look at television!"), the resource of early
reading cannot help but seem a potentially important means
of enriching a child's environment.   If a two year old seems
to enjoy the process of learning to read (and at that age it is
pretty hard to make him do anything he doesn't want to do)
and if he enjoys reading itself, it seems too bad not to let
him have that added resource.

Effects of Early Reading

You can say, "All right, suppose kids can learn to
read as early as they learn to talk, but should they?   Why
take the risk of making them into misfits at school?"   Fortunately, this fear has been laid to rest in a study of Professor Dolores Durkin entitled Children Who Read Early
(Teachers' College Pr., Columbia Univ., 1966).   Professor
Durkin identified those children who could already read when
they first entered the Oakland, California schools, and she
noted their progress through six years.   Her findings were

unequivocal. Early readers were not harmed--they got on
well both scholastically and socially. Furthermore (contrary
to widely held assumptions), the early readers were by no
means those with well-educated or pushy mothers; many
seemed to have taught themselves to read. Nor did early
reading necessarily correlate with other measures of high IQ.

When Professor Durkin began her study, only about
one child in a hundred could read upon first entering school.
Six years later the ratio was one in thirty. Resourceful
first grade teachers would let such children read on their
own or coach other children. The incidence of early readers
could mount, however, from three percent to ten percent or
even 20 percent without solving the schools' problems with
the nonreaders.

Some reading specialists concede that early reading
may do no harm but insist that it is not important either because by grade six everything will have evened out anyway.
Not so, says Professor Durkin. Early reading is not only
without adverse side effects, it also conveys positive and
lasting benefits. She says, "The average achievement of
early readers was significantly higher than that of compar-
ably bright non-early readers, and this lead was maintained."
She adds, "The value of an early start might be especially
great for children with the lower IQ's."

Early Reading and Brain Patterning

Granted that universal early reading may be unattain-
able. On the other hand, given a high enough priority, maybe it isn't. And consider the advantages! For instance,
imagine the relief to a first grade teacher if she could start
the children on books keyed to their interests instead of their
reading limitations! Imagine the child's relief! Imagine the
extra ground that could be covered if the time now spent on
the teaching of reading could be allocated to other subjects!
What a happy solution to the current problem of whether to
place an early reader with his academic peers in the third
grade, or with his chronological peers in the first grade!

And let's consider the possibilities that early reading
might solve the problem of late reading and that those 20
percent who are reading failures might not be so if the
schools got them earlier. For this 20 percent, perhaps the
very delay between learning to talk at age two and learning

to read at age six provides an opportunity for the brain to
delay in organizing its language centers. No one has yet
claimed to know for sure just how the mental processes of
a good reader differ from those of a poor reader. It could,
however (to borrow the terminology of the computer sciences), be far more a matter of programming than of hardware. It could be that we are all born with a brain (the
hardware) fully adequate to handle both speech and print. It
could be that our slow readers somehow got started on the
wrong foot in their method of use of their mental equipment.
Not even the best computer can perform properly if poorly
programmed.

In most people, surely, the brain not only sets up a
two-way filing system to equate the sound of a word with its
meaning, but goes on to make this a three-way filing system that equates sound, sight, and meaning. Consider, however, the possibility that in the slow reader this efficient
three-way system never got set up. Consider the possibility
that the slow reader is slow precisely because he somehow
got started storing his reading vocabulary separate from his
speaking vocabulary.

Perhaps slow readers are a bit like hunt-and-peck
typists. Their efficiency is low, but it would be even lower
during any changeover, and the longer they stay with the
wrong systems, the harder any changeover becomes. If this
is in fact what happens, it explains a lot. It explains, for
example, why the slow reader often wants to sound out a
word. He is, in effect, converting the print into speech, as
a means of letting his reading centers ask his speech centers whether that word is in his speaking vocabulary.

This may also explain why some children tend to
write some words backwards, was for saw, for example.
Let's suppose that in a normal person the information on
spelling is in the dominant hemisphere, as is also the control of the hand that does the writing. In an individual with
mixed dominance, however, print (i. e., spelling) might have
to be drawn from the subdominant hemisphere and then be
reflected through the dominant hemisphere, mirrorlike, on
its way to the writing hand. There have been numerous
cases where reading and writing and spelling difficulties have
cleared up after a change was made from writing right-
handed to writing left-handed, and one thing that slow readers do tend to have in common is a tendency toward so-
called mixed dominance. (One of the simple tests for mixed

dominance is to hand the subject a rolled tube of paper and ask him to look through it. If, for example, he takes it with his right hand but puts it to his left eye, the examiner begins to suspect the existence of mixed dominance.)

As I mentioned this possiblity one day, a friend broke in and said, "Listen, an experience my sister had in first grade may just support your theory. She was left-handed, but they insisted that she use her right hand for writing. One day she wrote a paper in which the first, third, and fifth lines went from left to right in the ordinary way, but the lines in between went from right to left. She herself saw nothing odd about it, but the rest of us could not decipher the second, fourth, and sixth lines without holding them up to a mirror. She had written the first line with her right hand, the second with her left hand, and so forth."

Something prompted me to go to the <u>Librarian's Glossary of Terms Used in Librarianship and the Book Crafts</u> and open to the word <u>boustrophedon.</u> Sure enough, this was defined as a style of writing practiced in ancient Greece for several centuries in which the odd-numbered lines were written from left to right and the even-numbered lines were written from right to left. In the latter, each letter and word were reversed, mirrorlike.

On impulse, I looked up the Greek alphabet, and, sure enough, no letter in it could be mistaken for any other merely by mirror reversal. In fact, further research revealed that the Greek scribes, like the Phoenician scribes before them, thought nothing of making mirror reversals of their letters. To them an ∃ was an E , just as a → was a ← , and a ℧ was a ℧ . Further research revealed that equivocal letter forms like our present day b̲, d̲, p̲, and q̲, did not come into use in any alphabet or language until more than a thousand years later.

Is this significant in the context of an article on dyslexia? I think it is. Man was a speaking animal for a million years before he was a writing animal. During all that time, and even longer, there must have been great survival value in being able to imagine how a thing would look if, the next time you saw it, it was facing the other way or you were looking at it from the other side. <u>Of course,</u> ⅁ would be seen as identical to ϒ . How else? So why wouldn't ∃ be seen as identical to E ?

I was startled to get what seemed like a confirmation
of this during a holiday in the Galápagos Islands.   As I
walked among the sea lions sunning on the beach, one would
occasionally open a sleepy eye and look me over.   Usually
he'd just shut it again--human visitors are neither a threat
nor a novelty to these sea lions--but sometimes he would
rear up and really inspect me.   When this happened, he
would not only do what we call a double take, cocking his
head right, then left, but he would end by revolving that rubber neck of his to the point where he could look at me upside down.   And this wasn't just happenstance, this seemed
to be policy.   Sea lion after sea lion really seemed to want
to know what I'd look like if seen upside down.

Once I got into the water with the sea lions, I thought
I saw the rationale for this.   Under water, sea lions spend
a great deal of their time upside down, cork-screwing or
barrel rolling through the water.   Functionally, I daresay it
broadens their field of view.   But it also means that a good
part of the time they are seeing their world upside down.   In
all probability the ability to recognize things whether seen
right side up or upside down--food, foe, or refuge--has un-
mistakable survival value.

Land-based humans don't have the same need to record an upside-down impression of things normally seen right
side up, but have you noticed how often very young children
do experiment with looking at their world upside down?

A sea lion would have no problem recognizing that a
b was a p upside down and a q was a d upside down, just as
an untutored preschooler would have no trouble recognizing
that a p was just a q seen from behind and a b was a d seen
from behind.

In the whole evolutionary history of the animal kingdom, even including man's first million years on earth, there
was every reason to see a b as identical with a d, and no
reason not to.   Even after picture writing was invented, there
was no reason to see a ᗉ as different from a ᗡ .

For a long, long time after the invention of the alphabet, the letters could go either way also.   However, words
couldn't go either way.   The word was, seen from behind,
becomes the word saw.   As man became a reading animal
and then graduated from pictographs to the use of an alphabet, suddenly, for the first time in the history of life on

earth, it became counterproductive to take note of how something would look if seen from the other side.

I realize I am presenting not one but two hypotheses, which may or may not be related. Let me try to recap them.

1) Perhaps the slow reader has set up two sets of two-way files (sound/meaning and sight/meaning), whereas the fast reader has developed an integrated three-way file relating meaning, sound, and sight.

2) Where word reversals are part of the reading difficulties, perhaps print/meaning data are not being restricted to the hemisphere that controls the writing hand.

Let me leap, then, to another intriguing hypothesis. Doesn't it sound plausible that good readers have learned to suppress their brain's capacity to equate a word to its mirrored equivalent, whereas poor readers (at least those who tend to reversals like was for saw and nip for pin) have somehow not stumbled upon the value (for this sole purpose) of suppressing this otherwise useful and highly sophisticated brain capacity?

A high correlation between reading difficulty and mixed dominance has been fairly well established. This leaves unsettled, however, the question as to whether it was some inborn tendency toward mixed dominance that led to the failure to read properly, or perhaps the failure to read properly that left the brain without any pressing reason to resolve the mixed dominance. (Forms of life other than man are not known to show dominance or "handedness.")

A good, sobering question to ask of anyone who is letting himself get too absorbed in this kind of speculation is, "So what?" What if it could be shown that poor reading originates from inefficient neural organization of the reading function? Is that any different from saying that poor reading originates from poor reading habits, known all along?

Well, by this time, it won't surprise you to know that I think a way exists to forestall later reading difficulties. It is to get the brain off on the right foot by starting it on three-way correlations (meaning, sound, and sight) early enough to prevent it from inadvertently getting too far committed to two-way correlations of just meaning and sound.

In point of fact, a very good start has been made with such educational television shows as Sesame Street and, especially, Electric Company. (The planned target of the latter was the second grader who was having reading difficulties, but pre-schoolers form its most enthusiastic audience.)

TV's commercials have also (accidentally) given pre-schoolers some pretty good opportunities to take in meaning /sound/sight correlations in the form of brand names and trademarks, opportunities often supplemented by visits to the supermarket, exposure to signs, etc. Given just this es-sentially accidental exposure to opportunities for meaning/ sound/sight correlations, many preschoolers are figuring out reading for themselves, or, if you like, expediting their own "reading readiness."

If children are getting this far on their own without any planned help from us, think how much further and faster they might go if we gave them just a bit of conscious help! I don't suggest putting them in any classroom. I don't pro-pose to "spoil their precious childhood" by drills or testing. I just propose we move more consciously and deliberately to enlarge their opportunities for subconscious absorption of sound/sight/meaning correlations.

The Montclair Reading Project

The town of Montclair, New Jersey has a voluntary project going whose goal is to have at least half of the town's children reading on their own by the time they enter first grade in the fall of 1976. The program was started in the spring of 1973. Within about four months, close to 400 mothers of two year olds had been contacted, and more than half of them had obtained the special materials provided and were swapping progress reports through a project newsletter.

The schools are not directly involved, but they will, of course, be judge and jury of the results when these children enter first grade. The superintendent of schools has said that the schools must know how to take full advan-tage of the results if the project succeeds.

There have, of course, been doubters. One man, a candidate for a degree in education at Montclair State Col-lege, wrote a letter to the Montclair Times charging that early reading might overstrain immature eyes. But a local

eye doctor, responding, saw no danger whatever for the
child with normal vision, and an actual advantage to the
child with subnormal vision, insofar as this might be noticed
earlier and thus get attention sooner.

Even if a dedicated group of volunteers can get half
of Montclair's children reading before they enter kindergarten
or first grade, the big question is, What good will it do?
The schools would, presumably, still have to deal with the
other children--and for all that can be argued to the contrary,
it is certainly possible that the first grade of 1976 (estimated at 500 children) will contain the same 20 percent of
dyslexics as would have been there without the program.

Suppose, however, the Montclair program succeeds.
What have we learned? Well, if we get five out of ten of
Montclair's two year olds reading before they get to school,
this certainly will lay to rest the theory that only one child
in ten is up to early reading.

Perhaps we shall also have demonstrated that what is
called "reading readiness" is no more and no less than evidence that the child has started reading, i. e. , that "reading
readiness" comes with reading.

What I hope we shall also demonstrate is that none of
the early readers develop reading problems, and that only
the usual percentage of the other children do so. Should
this be the case, it would seem safe to argue that early
reading might well be the way to prevent late reading.

Suppose Montclair gets half its preschoolers reading
through a volunteer effort of the mothers. What next? Won't
this just create new problems, such as a gap between the
readers (privileged) and the nonreaders (underprivileged)?

Preschoolers Are Ready to Read!

First, let it be said that other mothers than just those
in Montclair are encouraging their preschoolers to read
early, thus putting them in line for the consequent advantages over their fellows noted by Professor Durkin.   Hundreds of thousands of mothers have purchased Doman's book
How to Teach Your Baby to Read, and over 50, 000 wrote in
to the Ladies Home Journal for a special Early Reading Kit.
(This was back in 1965.   When these mothers were queried

eight years later as to how they made out, half of those responding had successfully taught their preschoolers to read and were glad they had, about 40 percent had been talked out of trying it, and about ten percent had tried and failed or had not followed through.)

If early readers start ahead and stay ahead, as Professor Durkin tells us, the answer to any ensuing inequality of opportunity may not lie in discouraging early reading, but in extending it to all children either by means that don't depend entirely on Mother, or by means closer to those so demonstrably effective in teaching the child to talk.

Preschoolers are learning to read despite our assumption that they are not ready for it. If you doubt it, test any two year old on words like stop, ice cream, milk, and, of course, his own name. Some will continue on their own toward reading at a far more sophisticated level.

After one skeptical mother had surprised and convinced herself by this simple test that her boy of two and a half was actually reading, she began to realize that this had been going on for some time, quite without her notice. For example, she remembered how he had puzzled her by asking at the ice cream parlor, "Mother, what's Italian ice?" No one had spoken those words. She now realized that he had simply been reading them from a sign.

In another home, a three year old asked to have Campbell's chicken noodle soup for lunch, then brought the correct can from the shelf. Considering that there is no way to tell one kind of Campbell's soup from another except by words printed on the label and considering that the pantry shelf had contained other kinds, this mother was stunned to realize that her daughter was probably able to read the words chicken noodle, which proved to be true.

This kind of evidence that very young children are reading is sometimes dismissed on the ground that what they are doing isn't really reading, it is just pattern recognition. The premise seems to be that you aren't really reading it unless and until you can spell it. Isn't this pretty much like contending that no child is really speaking unless and until he can dissect his sentences into subject, verb, and predicate? The fact is, the only language we ever learn really fluently is the one we learn to speak long before knowing anything about its "rules" of grammar.

   Phonics may be a far more useful tool than grammar
(and Rudolf Flesch makes a strong case for giving every first
grader a solid grounding in this technique for sounding out
unfamiliar words), but first grade phonics does not preclude
a preschool whole-word approach.   In fact, the only weakness in the arguments of the "look-and-say" people may lie
in their timing.   Perhaps the "look-and-say" (impressionis-
tic) approach is "right" for ages two, three, and four,
whereas the phonics (analytical) approach should come along
about the time the child is beginning to observe on his own
that the construction of words seems to have a sometimes
predictable logic.

   During the teaching of reading in school, we concede,
early on, that one must get past the stage of reading letter
by letter and read word by word, if not phrase by phrase,
but we continue to suppose that we simplify things by starting with the letters.   Do we?

   In this connection, let me report on some work being
done in Japan.   There, in the factory day care centers of
the Sony Corporation, two year olds are routinely learning to
read.   Japan, however, has two ways of writing, the scholarly one using the ancient Chinese characters, of which there
are thousands, one character to a word, and the "simplified" one in which an unlimited number of words can be built
from a limited number of letters, somewhat as in English.
It was assumed, of course, that two year olds would best
begin with the simplified approach used in elementary and
high school.   To the great surprise of the investigators, two
year olds seemed able to read in the scholarly mode as
easily as in the simplified mode.   They could tell two Chinese
characters apart as easily as two human faces.

   Incidentally, in these day care centers, operated
under the supervision of the Early Development Association
of Japan, two year olds are not only learning to read Japanese, but even learning to speak and read English, to play
the violin, to do mathematics, and much more.   A book about
this work, entitled Kindergarten Is Too Late, has been a recent best seller in Japan.   It was written by Masaru Ibuka,
board chairman of Sony, who became acquainted with the
Doman work on early reading when he was seeking help for
his own brain-injured child.

The Role of Librarians and Publishers

     Well, to keep this close to home, let's consider how
public libraries could help. Let's say a mother comes in
ready and anxious to surround her preschooler with materials to increase his opportunities to discover meaning/sound
/sight correlations. She wants, basically, pictures of familiar things, each with the name underneath in large type.

     If you will take a serious look at what you have to
offer, seen in this perspective, you will be shocked to realize how little you have to offer.

     One possibility is the Pyramid Primary Dictionary
No 1 (75 cents in paperback, Pyramid, 1971). Although the
type size is smaller than Doman would recommend and the
type is seldom under the object described, as I personally
feel it should be, at least you find 171 pictures of familiar
things, each with its identifying word, and what's more, the
word-picture relationship is usually fairly unequivocal.

     Another possibility is Richard Scarry's Best Word
Book Ever (Golden Pr., 1963), with 1400 objects illustrated.
However, once again the type is disappointingly small.

     It seemed such a modest request--pictures of familiar
things, each with its name beneath it, in large type, but try
to find these. You will probably find yourself proffering
either things that don't meet the specifications at all (like
alphabet books or read-aloud books with type much smaller
than you remembered), or else you might dig up a disposable
copy of an old Sears, Roebuck catalog and suggest that
mother and child cut it up to make their own words-under-
picture book.

     I am, however, no little intrigued by the fact that
children seem to be learning to read from TV commercials.
Perhaps I will lay myself open to having my lifetime ALA
membership rescinded if I suggest that some of those children who became our good readers may have gotten their
very first meaning/sound/sight correlations from words like
Exxon, A&P, Sugar Krispies, and the like. In the last
analysis, reading is reading, and I guess I believe that any
reading is better than no reading. I have no fear that the
child who can read easily and well will spend his entire time
reading junk. I have great and well-justified fear that the
child who cannot read may have to spend all his school
years on junk--the junk in the remedial readers.

We must all be concerned that at present each intens-
ification of the schools' efforts to reach the reluctant reader
seems to build reading resistance faster than reading competence.   Too often the most conspicuous consequence of
trying to "help" the slow reader by giving him extra drill is
to make him hate books.

Before I close, let me return to the problem of finding books appropriate for use with two and three year olds
who are beginning to read on their own.   Libraries have no
dearth of good books for Mother to read to them, and no
dearth of materials to offer them once they are really reading, but, as mentioned before, practically nothing really
suitable for helping them graduate from listeners to readers.
(This is hardly surprising, inasmuch as we have been assuming they would not make that transition until age six.)

In all our picture books, the type is clearly for
Mother.   In our preschool story hours we read the type and
show the pictures, under circumstances where even the readers can seldom read the small print.   I hope that publishers
will think about this and move to fill the gap.   Let's have
new editions of transitional books in which the type is handled as if it might be of as much interest to the child as the
pictures.   It will be.

I can hear someone saying, "But surely we do now
have plenty of lovely books in which the type is handled as
if it might be of as much interest to the child as the pictures.   They are called alphabet books. "   I would agree up
to a point.   Some alphabet books contain lovely pictures and
large type, but, unhappily, they are by their very nature
phonics oriented.   If, as I am certainly persuaded, it is
counter-productive to start telling two and three year olds
about the alphabet before they have even fully grasped that
there is such a thing as print, then true alphabet books
would be most appropriately prepared for older children, or
else divested of their pseudophonics content and offered just
as word-and-picture books.

I say their "pseudophonics" content because some of
them are very strange indeed if taken seriously.   For example, let's say a mother comes in and asks for an alphabet book.   Let's assume her child can read his name, he
can read the names of everything advertised on TV, he has
been watching Electric Company, and he is beginning to ask
about the letters.   Shall we give her perhaps Elizabeth Mac-
Kinstry's ABC book?   If we do, her child is going to learn
that G is for Gnomes!

Imagine the confusion of a child who is just on the
verge of one of the greatest discoveries he will ever make,
namely that there is a logic to the way words are constructed
out of letters. He may not be very sure of himself yet, he
may be just testing a hypothesis, he may be thinking that if
A is for Acorn, and B is for Bee, and I is for Ice cream,
then maybe G is for, well, maybe Gee whiz? But no. The
book Mama is reading says that G is for Gnome, and that
other ABC book by Bruno Munari says that K is for Knife or
Knothole. Wouldn't you have thought that N would be for
Gnome, or Knothole, or Knife? Well, you can just hear the
child saying to himself, "Another good theory shot down. "

I submit that this is serious. We can say if we like
that an alphabet book is not a textbook, was never so intended, and is just a book to enjoy for its rhymes and pictures, and we can say if we like that it would be a shame
to inhibit the author and illustrator with a lot of strictures
about logic in spelling. But what if the mother is saying to
us in effect, "Please give me an alphabet book because my
child is getting interested in the sounds of the letters.

At this point many of us, taking our cue from the
reading experts, have just begged off, saying, "How old is
he? Oh, well, he isn't ready for reading yet. Time enough
for that when he gets to school. But if you want an alphabet book, we have some lovely ones. " But have we? We
have the Petersham's ABC, but in it K is for Knickerbocker,
and T hasn't the T sound at all, it is for Thanksgiving. In
Munari again, E is for Eye--and isn't that confusing!

Suppose Munari's editor had said, "Please, not E for
Eye, perhaps E for Ear, or Eagle, or Evening?" Would
such a stricture have reduced a work of the imagination to
a pale imitation of a textbook?

Librarians and others working with preschoolers have
thus far seldom been urged to encourage early reading and
have often been advised to "leave it to the schools. " The
schools, however, have been failing that assignment. The
schools' only chance for success may lie in new kinds of
help from those people currently working in, or preparing
to specialize in, the preschool area.

DUMPED FROM A WHARF INTO CASCO BAY: THE HISTORICAL RECORDS SURVEY REVISITED*

Leonard Rapport

A few years ago when the International Council on Archives met in Washington, one of the French representatives, trained in the Ecole des Chartes, asked Lyman Butterfield why was it that the United States, in the midst of a great depression, was able to carry out an unprecedented survey of its historical records, publish many excellent volumes of guides, calendars, and inventories, and then, in its more affluent years, abandoned the great task and left it unfinished? It is a good thing he picked Butterfield to ask this question of. Many--most--persons wouldn't have known what he was referring to. Also, it was fortunate that he didn't ask what had happened to the products of that unprecedented survey. To have had to answer would have been embarrassing to Butterfield, and the answer would have shocked the visitor from France.

I don't know what response Butterfield gave, but it could have been this: the primary purpose of that unprecedented survey--the WPA Historical Records Survey--was not to survey records but to give work to the unemployed. With the coming of World War II the need for make-work ceased, and the Historical Records Survey ended. The participants, particularly those who had been on relief and who for survival had been dependent on the survey's monthly wage, sometimes as little as $50 or $60, were willing to put behind them that part of their experience. For three decades there was no serious effort to revive the Historical Records Survey. Only recently have there been the stirrings of another such effort, the National Historical Records Program, which is being proposed for somewhat the same reason, the glut of historians and others who can't find jobs for which they have

*Reprinted by permission of the author and publisher from The American Archivist, April 1974, pp. 201-210.

been trained. Meanwhile, for three decades the products of
the Historical Records Survey--unpublished and published--
have remained unused, for the most part forgotten, and
sometimes discarded.

The movements during the nineteenth century and the
first thirty years of the twentieth to survey the records of
this nation have been described more than once. So here we
will start with a happening in the first year of the depression. It was an event that was shortly to prove significant.

In 1930 the American Council of Learned Societies
and the Social Science Research Council established a Joint
Committee on Materials for Research, with Robert C. Binkley as chairman and T. R. Schellenberg as secretary. This
action laid the groundwork for a national survey of local
records.

In the next several years there were, under the Civil
Works Administration and the Federal Emergency Relief Administration (FERA), a few surveys of state and local records. Then, in January 1934, in answer to a call of the
joint committee, a conference met in Washington to consider
the possibility of a nationwide survey of archives. In February the joint committee directed Schellenberg to draft a
proposal for a survey, and it formed a subcommittee (the
Commission on National Archives Survey) to promote such a
program.

The commission proposed a survey of state, county,
and local archives to be carried out by 2, 775 workers during an eight-week period, and alternate projects of two and
twelve months' duration. However, a provision of the Emergency Relief Act of February 1934 prohibiting federal projects squelched these proposals. But there was a loophole.
Though the FERA could not initiate projects it could encourage state and local governments to start them on their own.
By October 1934 the FERA was circulating among the state
ERA offices a set of working procedures for surveys of historical records. Some states apparently got survey projects
started under the FERA's grant-in-aid program.

We turn now to the Princeton campus, spring 1935.
Princeton, more conservative then than now, let go what
seemed to the university to be a radical young Texan, an
assistant professor of political science. Outraged at the
university's action, one of the young Texan's students invited

him to spend a weekend with his family. As a result the
student's father, Herbert Bayard Swope, asked Raymond
Moley about the possibility of a job in Washington for the
dismissed professor. Moley called Harry Hopkins. This
led to the young political scientist's traveling to Washington
and talking with Hopkins. Few actions in the history of what
was to become the Historical Records Survey were to be as
significant, for it brought onto the scene the dominant personality of the survey, the one who, more than any other,
was to be responsible for making the survey the success it
was. And it was successful, even though it is now mostly
forgotten and overshadowed by projects such as the Federal
Writers' Project with which it is constantly confused but which
can scarcely hold a candle to it in terms of achievement.
The young political scientist was, of course, Luther Evans.

     We return to Washington, June 1935. Harry Hopkins
had noticed in the basement of the Capitol a jumble of old
records. Doing something about them would be, he thought,
a good project. Evans diplomatically explained that the recently established National Archives could best take care of
these records. However, said Evans, since they were on
the subject of records a useful project would be a survey of
federal records outside of Washington--the records that were
in the customs houses, federal courts, and federal offices
throughout the country. Hopkins, interested, suggested that
Evans explore the idea and return.

     Evans talked with officials at the National Archives
and in July returned with the proposal that was to become
the Survey of Federal Archives. In a second interview Hopkins raised the question of doing something similar for state
and local records. Evans asked about federal jurisdiction
and, assured that there was no problem, began drafting plans.
Schellenberg at the National Archives made available the
plans of the 1934 commission. Evans submitted to Hopkins
a statement of purpose, an administrative plan, an estimate
of the cost of such a program, and a proposal for an advisory committee to assist in working out detailed plans.

     In July 1935 the Archivist of the United States, R. D.
W. Connor, meeting with the chief of the National Park Service Historical Division and with Works Progress Administration officials, entered into a tentative arrangement under
which the National Archives would cosponsor a survey of federal records in U.S. depositories outside the District of Columbia. This became the Survey of Federal Archives. The

conferees also agreed on a survey of state and local records, to be sponsored by the National Park Service. Evans spent August and September drafting plans for this survey. Assistant Historian of the Park Service Herman Kahn provided office space, a typewriter, and advice.

By October, Evans, now WPA "Supervisor of Historical Projects," had completed his plans. In November $1,195,000 became available. This appropriation was broken down into separate allotments by state, which meant that there was to be a series of state projects, coordinated by Washington but initiated and controlled by the states. The allotments were made and rescinded on the same day. The money was then given in a single allotment, and the Historical Records Survey became a WPA-sponsored federal project under the Federal Writers' Project. The National Park Service dropped out as cosponsor. This assignment to the Writers' Project seems to have been for administrative convenience. As might be expected, it led to trouble; and in October 1936 the HRS became a separate project within the Women's and Professional Division of the WPA. Meanwhile, state HRS projects were organized, and by May 1936 there was one for each state.

Although its public image was considerably better than those of the other arts projects, the HRS eventually became a victim of increasing congressional hostility toward the arts projects, hostility that culminated in a provision that such federal projects end by August 31, 1939. Thereafter the states set up their own projects and the federal government shared the expenses. This wasn't as drastic a change for the HRS as for the other arts projects, most states having agencies or bodies with archival jurisdiction. In November 1939 Librarian of Congress Archibald MacLeish persuaded Evans to become director of the library's Legislative Services Division. Though officially off the HRS payroll as of December 1, 1939, Evans unofficially directed the headquarters office until March 1940, when his long-time assistant, Sargent Child, became HRS national director.

The 1939 Appropriation Act wiped out the national headquarters office of the HRS. But the Library of Congress sponsored a District of Columbia project (the WPA treated the district as a state) and hired most or all of the HRS headquarters office personnel and some of the Writers' Project headquarters staff. The HRS part of the LC project provided technical guidance and assistance to the state HRS

projects. The LC project lasted until August 1940. Thereafter the WPA carried a few HRS technical personnel on its
administrative payroll. By June 1941 twelve were left; by
year's end, four. By February 1942 any remaining HRS
activities had to be war-related. And by February 1943, the
HRS, federal and state, was dead.

Program of the Historical Records Survey

In December 1935 Luther Evans's advisory committee,
which included Binkley, Waldo Leland, A. R. Newsome,
Solon Buck, and Schellenberg, held an organizational policy
meeting. A majority favored a program limited in concept,
time, and money; a minority favored projects of varying
kinds but limited geographically. (That is, instead of in-
ventorying the records of all counties in a state, inventory-
ing intensively in a single county all documents of significance. Other counties would, presumably, follow the lead
and procedures of this pilot project.) The majority view
prevailed until 1938 when it was reversed, the number of
relief workers was trebled, and the HRS began (and left un-
completed) a variety of projects, "few of which" (to quote a
scholar familiar with the survey) "achieved the technical excellence of the original project," the survey of county records.

Public records. Although the HRS surveyed records
of all jurisdictions within the states, the category for which
it is most remembered--and its major achievement--was the
survey of county records (in New England, of town records).
By the time it ended, the project had, according to the estimate of its last director, completed the fieldwork for the
inventories of 90 percent of the 3,066 counties in the United
States. Of these completed inventories perhaps 20 percent
were published. The rest, on stencils (which were never to
see a mimeograph machine), in typescript, or hand-written,
were caught by the war and stored in the states.

Manuscripts. Surveys of manuscripts in public repositories such as historical societies and libraries, and,
occasionally, in private possession, resulted in statewide
guides summarizing what was in each repository; in guides
to the holdings of particular repositories; and in calendars
and inventories of individual collections.

Church records. Though sometimes taking other

forms, descriptions of church records were generally inventories of records of a single denomination within a state.

Inventory of early American imprints. This bibliographical listing of all copies of all imprints through 1876
or later was the project furthest removed from the original
program of the HRS and the least significant.

Other. Some states compiled union lists of their
newspapers, indexed certain newspapers, inventoried portraits, transcribed or microfilmed old records, and did
other similar projects. Individual projects included a bibliography of American literature, an index of U.S. musicians,
an atlas of congressional rollcalls, a continuation of Richardson's Messages and Papers of the Presidents, and an index
of presidential executive orders. Many of these followed
the 1938 policy reversal.

Survey of Federal Archives. Finally, there was the
project mentioned and about which a little more should be
said. The Survey of Federal Archives was not originally
part of the Historical Records Survey. Backed by a provision of the Records Act that empowered the Archivist "To
inspect personally or by deputy the records of any agency of
the United States Government whatsoever and wheresoever
located, " R. D. W. Connor in the fall of 1935 filed with the
WPA an application for a "Survey of Archives of the Federal
Government Outside of the District of Columbia. " He received an authorization of more than a million dollars and
appointed Philip M. Hamer as national director. In 1937
Hamer and his staff were transferred to the HRS, but they
continued as a separate unit with offices in the National
Archives. The fieldworkers were transferred to the state
HRS projects. By the time the Survey of Federal Archives
finally closed, it had published 506 volumes; only 81 remained unpublished. The Survey of Federal Archives essentially finished what it set out to do. [1]

The Unpublished Inventories

And now let us turn to the products of the survey,
what became of them, and to the question of what their value
is. I discuss these matters subjectively and hope my experience will supply or suggest answers.

Fifteen years ago I knew as much about the HRS as

the average person, which was approximately nothing. Then
I began a job that involved locating public records and private documents of the late eighteenth century.   In seeking
these out I gradually came to know and to value the inventories, guides, calendars, and other finding aids prepared
by the survey.

        In the course of this search there came a time when
it looked as if I might have to locate and examine certain
New England town records, particularly the 1787-91 town
meeting minutes.   In New England, unlike the rest of the
United States, the important local records-keeping body is
the town, not the county.

        I knew then that only a small fraction of the HRS in-
ventories of town records had been published--probably a
smaller fraction than of the county records.   I knew that
these unpublished inventories of the hundreds of New England
towns had been deposited, in 1942, in the various states
wherever space could be found.   And I knew the locations of
these depositories as of 1942.

        I had also determined that if you visited a town clerk
the chances were about fifty-fifty of his knowing whether or
not he had his town's minutes for 1787-91.   The odds were
about one in four that he didn't know but was willing to make
a search, and about one in four that he was certain he didn't
have them and that they didn't exist (and this in towns where
there was good reason to believe they did exist).

        Why good reason to believe they existed?   In about
1908 the records of certain Maine towns were surveyed and
the results published.   Thus, there were available the names
of some towns whose 1787-91 minutes had survived into the
twentieth century and, presumably, were still in existence.
I visited a number of these towns between Kittery and Portland, Maine.   It is on the basis of my experiences with
clerks of towns I knew to have the records I wanted that I
make my estimates.

        But the pursuit of these records in the hundreds of
old New England towns would be endless.   And I wouldn't
have, as I had in Maine, evidence enabling me to insist politely that a clerk conduct a search for something he was
positive didn't exist.   So the HRS inventories--the few published, the many unpublished--provided the needed key. They
revealed which towns had their 1787-91 minutes and which

didn't. (Here let me say that when a series description
showed gaps it gave whatever information could be discovered to explain these gaps--fire, flood, or whatever.) Thus
these inventories provided a list of towns that had, as late
as the 1930's, their 1787-91 town meeting minutes. The inventories would provide the location of the minute books
down to room, shelf, or cabinet drawer; they would provide
probably an exact description of the volumes. This evidence
could be persuasive with clerks who might contend that such
records didn't exist.

I used the set of published HRS volumes in the National Archives (which has the most nearly complete set--
nobody has all of them). Then I started out to find and examine the unpublished HRS inventories.

Connecticut's unpublished inventories were deposited
in 1942 in the Sterling Library at Yale, a good, safe depos-
itory. I went there. The Sterling's records showed that on
a certain day in October 1950 a truck from the Connecticut
State Library had picked up these records, 108 cases of
them. Since these were state records, that was a proper
transfer. Eventually I got to the State Library. I spent a
month there, examining the official and unofficial documents
of late eighteenth-century Connecticut. I found no trace of
the HRS materials. Sylvie Turner, who was then state
archivist, did an extensive search in her own administrative
records and in the administrative records of the library.
She talked with people still there who had been with the library at the time and with people who had since retired.
Neither on paper nor in anyone's memory could she or could
I find any clues as to what had happened to the 108 cases.
And to this day there has been, so far as I know, no clue.

And that, as it turned out, was to be the story of the
New England Historical Records Survey. Over a period of
time I learned that with the exception of one state, or possibly two, all of New England's records had disappeared.

The one certain exception was Massachusetts. The
records survived in Massachusetts because they had been
stored in the Forbes Library in Northampton, because the
Forbes is one of the best libraries in this country, because
the successive chief librarians of the Forbes had an appreciation of the value of the material entrusted to them, and
because the material itself was stored out of the way in the
library's high attic. One reached that attic by going up a

tall stepladder to the top of a cabinet, then from the top of
the cabinet up iron rungs on the wall, then through a push-
up trap door in the ceiling.   There, in a surrealist circus-
tent setting--with beams and rafters and steel cables and a
high peaked roof (everything but a trapeze, and underfoot,
instead of tanbark, itchy rockwool insulation)--were the unpublished records of the Massachusetts Historical Records
Survey.   They were in 132 bundles, wrapped like laundry but
feeling like short-weight sacks of portland cement, about a
ton and a half of them, resting on a specially built platform
and extending almost across the attic, and covered against
leaks with heavy plastic.   We are all indebted to the Forbes
Library.

    With about an eight-foot dropcord plugged into the
socket in the hall below, I spent a Saturday afternoon samp-
ling these bundles.   There, for Massachusetts, was the information I wanted.   And there was much, much else: forty-
five bundles of town inventories; ten bundles of county inventories; fourteen bundles relating to church records; four
bundles of material gathered for a "Guide to Manuscripts Relating to the Negro in Massachusetts"; ten bundles relating
to portraits, engravings, silhouettes; and more besides.

    Several years later the Ford Foundation made avail-
able enough money for me to make a hasty survey, by long
distance telephone and form letter, of what survives of unpublished Historical Records Survey inventories throughout
the United States.   I wasn't able to locate the material for
all the states, but I was able to get the general picture. The
greatest loss was in New England.   There were other states
that didn't answer or whose answers were too vague to determine whether or not they had their unpublished materials.

    I reported these findings to the Ford Foundation and
sent summaries to the American Historical Association, the
Organization of American Historians, and the Society of
American Archivists.   The only one of these organizations
that did much about it was the OAH, which in 1972 submitted
by way of the American Council of Learned Societies to the
National Endowment for the Humanities a proposal for a
grant to locate, preserve, and publicize the unpublished inventories.   The National Archives volunteered to conduct, if
asked to, this search.   The National Archives would seem
to be the logical agency because it has, scattered throughout
the country, its regional archives, each with a historian-
archivist who could if necessary investigate collections that

might or might not be HRS materials (for custodians sometimes have trouble distinguishing between HRS and Federal
Writers' Project materials).

Recently the executive secretary of the OAH reported
that the HRS proposal is not included in the 1974 fiscal year
budget of the National Endowment for the Humanities. And
that's where the matter now stands. Whatever is being done
to locate and preserve and publicize these unpublished inventories is now being done on an informal, ad hoc basis.
In 1973 we learned by chance that a state university library,
custodian of its state's unpublished HRS inventories, was
moving to a new building and wanted to get rid of the material. We passed the word on to the state archives, which
has since accessioned the records.

Historical Records Survey material deposited in other
state universities didn't always fare as well. One librarian
reported that the material survived there for some years
until the file cabinets and space were needed; then the records were thrown out. Another state university librarian
wrote: "We know where the files were in 1958, and approximately where they were in 1963 or thereabouts. I have
seen corners of the building I have never been in before,
and sampled transfer files and boxes I had not previously
known were in the building. Former librarians have been
queried by long distance.... We do not know how it can be
so, but we can only conclude that, somehow, the files no
longer exist. "

Finally, we will return one last time to the state of
Maine. In August 1942 the WPA official in charge of the
records of the by then defunct Maine Historical Records
Survey wrote to WPA headquarters in Washington, "We have
made several attempts to have the material stored at the
University, and other college libraries, and the State library.
The librarians at these various places state that they do not
have room available, and are not interested in the manuscripts which are stored in our warehouse. " On September
2, Washington replied: "This will acknowledge a letter of
August 27, 1942, from Miss Twombly, concerning a deposi-
tory for the files of the Historical Records Survey. The
Library of Congress will pay shipment of that material to
the Library for the duration. " That is the last document in
the file.

I had high hopes that we would find this material in

the Library of Congress. Many interested members of the staff aided in the search, first in the Manuscript Division, then in the other divisions, then in the library's various warehouses. There was no trace of the Maine material. Finally, I wrote to Elizabeth Ring of the Maine Historical Society, who had been with the Survey. She did some detective work, located Miss Twombly, who had since married, and then wrote me that the former Miss Twombly recalled that "failing to find a Maine Library who would accept the HRS and Writers' Project materials they were dumped from a wharf into Casco Bay--. "

Note

1. This, in brief, is the history of the Historical Records Survey. For anyone who wants more details William F. McDonald's book, Federal Relief Administration and the Arts (Columbus: Ohio State University Press), which Professor McDonald completed close to the event, in 1945, but which was not published until 1969, is an excellent account to which this one is indebted.

THE EFFECT OF LITERARY AWARDS
ON CHILDREN'S BOOK RECOMMENDATIONS*

Dorothy J. Schmidt & Jeanne Osborn

Although library budgets are more adequate than in years past, problems of effective book selection remain as troublesome as ever. Expanding publication lists carry titles many of which must surely be minor, if not inferior in quality. Librarians, no longer able to read each new book before or after purchase, rely heavily on reviews and selective bibliographies. Yet most annotations, even reviews, are merely descriptive, and frequently copied verbatim from bookjacket, title-page, or preface. Book Review Digest formerly tagged citations as favorable, unfavorable, or mixed, but no longer does so, partly because modern reviewing fashions often render the attempt meaningless.

One way to cope with the need for reliable evaluation might be notice of various book awards as evidence of quality. Do the review media report such prizes? Even a superficial survey shows that they seldom mention any except two influential awards. But are those the only literary honors worthy of note? If periodical reviews usually appear at the time of the book's publication, before most prizes are given, retrospective bibliographies have not that excuse. Are book list selectors careless, lazy, indifferent, or are the less well-known awards of little significance as indicators of value?

Seven Children's Literature Awards, 1960-1968

This study attempts to evaluate the literary impact over the past decade of seven awards established in the United States to stimulate children's books and reading. Narrow re-

*Reprinted by permission of the authors and the American Library Association from Top of the News, April 1974, pp. 257-266.

gional prizes, those sponsored by publishing companies, and
the highly visible Caldecott and Newbery Awards are excluded. Basic data were found in Bowker's Literary and Library Prizes, 6th ed. (1967) and in Children's Books: Awards
and Prizes, published by the Children's Book Council in 1969.
The awards are there fully described, together with title
lists. The seven chosen for this survey were:

    1. The Jane Addams Children's Book Award, founded
in 1953 by the U. S. Section of the Women's International
League for Peace and Freedom.

    2. The Aurianne Award, granted from 1958 through
1966 by the American Library Association with funds from a
private bequest.

    3. The Boys' Clubs of America Junior Book Awards,
given from 1948 to 1968.

    4. The Child Study Association of America Child-
ren's Book Awards, first granted in 1943.

    5. The Thomas Alva Edison Foundation National
Mass Media Awards, given from 1955 through 1967.

    6. The Dorothy Canfield Fisher Children's Book
Award, established in 1957 by the Vermont Congress of
Parents and Teachers together with the Vermont Free Public
Library Commission.

    7. The Children's Spring Book Festival Awards,
sponsored from 1937 to 1967 by the New York Herald-Tri-
bune, taken over in 1968 by Book World, published jointly
by the Chicago Tribune and the Washington Post. This
award is available only to books published between January
and May of the award year.

    The time span of the study is that during which the
awards were granted, not that during which the titles were
published. Analysis of publication dates shows between
twelve and eighteen of the 134 award titles published each
year from 1959 through 1966. Two titles appeared in 1958,
eight in 1967, and three in 1968. These findings reflect
customary stipulations that titles published in the two years
immediately preceding the grants be favored.

    Only seven Aurianne Awards were granted during the

period studied, one each year from 1960 through 1966. The
highest number of awards (forty-eight) came from the Boys'
Clubs. The Edison Awards numbered thirty-two (second-
high) although they were discontinued in 1967. The Addams
and Fisher Awards were given nine times each, the Child
Study Association Award eleven times, and the Spring Book
Festival Award twenty-seven times (see Table I).

Eight books were multiply awarded, an average of one
per year. Seven books received two of the seven awards;
the eighth, three. Thus the total unique titles involved were
reduced to 134 for the 143 prizes given. Table IV shows
that all seven programs were involved in the overlap, although there was no duplication with Caldecott or Newbery
titles. Six of the eight books (75 percent) were fiction, the
other two non-fiction. Five (62.5 percent) appealed to intermediate grade levels; the other three to junior and senior
high school readers. Table II shows, however, that the full
list of award titles covered a wider range of 8 percent easy
or picture books, 45 percent fiction, and 47 percent non-
fiction. Age-wise, 12.7 percent were for primary children,
50 percent for the intermediate grades, and 37.3 percent for
junior and senior high school readers.

Subject analysis of the non-fiction titles, as indicated
by broad Dewey classes, shows nearly all to be in the natural and social sciences, with biography and history especially prominent. Certain themes stressed by some award
programs were no doubt responsible. The two non-fiction
Addams titles were collective biographies. The two non-
fiction Aurianne titles were classed in 599 (animal stories),
as was the one non-fiction Fisher book. The one non-fiction
title on the Child Study Association list was a social history.
By contrast the Edison Awards showed little fiction, but
much natural and social science emphasis. Boys' Club and
Spring Festival Awards were more eclectic, though the
former tended slightly to non-fiction, the latter to fiction.

Not shown in the tables are data on publishers. Twelve
of the books were published by Harper, ten by Harcourt,
eight by Viking, seven each by Doubleday and Little, six
each by Houghton and Criterion, five each by Dutton, Mor-
row, and Pantheon, four each by Atheneum, Crowell, and
World, and three each by Follett, Lippincott, and Scott.
Thus 92 of the 134 award titles came from sixteen publishers. The remaining 42 came from thirty-two more houses,
ranging from American Heritage, Columbia University,

and the University of Michigan to Golden Books, Grosset, and Parents Magazine.

Were the Award Books Reviewed?

One hundred nineteen (89 percent) of the 134 titles, including all of the eight multiply awarded books, were found in Book Review Digest. Reviews for all the Aurianne and Spring Book Festival titles, 97 percent of the Edison, 91 percent of the Addams and the Fisher, 90 percent of the Child Study Association, and 77 percent of the Boys' Clubs titles were there (see Table I).

Some 824 reviews for the nine easy, fifty-two fiction, and fifty-eight non-fiction titles were cited, an average of nearly seven reviews per title. These figures indicate a broader coverage of good children's books by BRD than is commonly assumed. On the other hand, thirty reviews were readily found covering thirteen of the fifteen titles not cited there. These included ten of the Boys' Clubs books, and one each for the Child Study Association, the Edison, and the Fisher Awards. No reviews were found for one of the Addams books nor for one Boys' Club prize winner.

Are the Award Books "Recommended"?

The award titles were checked in the seven widely used annotated recommendation lists named below, with the results shown in Tables I and III.

1. Best Books for Children (BBC), a Bowker publication revised annually. The 1969 edition included some 4,000 of the over 20,000 in-print juvenile titles.

2. Books for Children (BC), a compilation of notices from the ALA's Booklist. Originally issued in 1965, supplemented annually through 1968-69. The first edition included 3,068 of the approximately 12,000 juvenile titles published from 1960 to 1965. Supplements add some 500 to 1,000 titles.

3. Children's Catalog (CC), 11th edition, 1966, supplemented annually. An H. W. Wilson publication covering some 4,500 to 5,000 titles.

TABLE I

Seven Juvenile Literary Awards

Award	Themes and Conditions	Recognition	Titles Awarded 1960-1968	Titles in the Book Review Digest	Titles in Seven Bibliographies
Addams	Brotherhood. Creative solutions to life problems through sympathy and understanding. Literary merit.	Book jacket seal to publisher. Certificate to author	E 1 F 6 N-F 2 — 9	E 0 F 6 N-F 2 — 8	E 0 F 6 N-F 2 — 8
Aurianne	Develop humane attitudes toward animal life. For ages 8-14.	$200 to author.	(1960-66) F 5 N-F 2 — 7	F 5 N-F 2 — 7	F 5 N-F 2 — 7
Boys' Clubs	Preliminary selections by mail vote of Boys' Clubs members.	Medals to authors and/or illustrators.	E 5 F 19 N-F 24 — 48	E 4 F 13 N-F 20 — 37	E 5 F 16 N-F 18 — 39

Award	Description	Terms	Col 1	Col 2	Col 3
Child Study Association	Today's world honestly reflected. Realistic approaches to vital problems.	Scroll to author.	F 10 N-F 1 11	F 9 N-F 1 10	F 10 N-F 1 11
Edison	(1960-67) Four award categories: Science bks. for ages 9-13. Science bks. for ages 13-17. Character develop., 8-12. America's past, ages 13-16.	Scroll to publisher $250 and scroll to author.	F 5 N-F 27 32	F 5 N-F 26 31	F 4 N-F 25 29
Fisher	Picture books excluded. Book by a living American for grades 4-8.	Scroll to author.	F 8 N-F 1 9	F 7 N-F 1 8	F 6 N-F 1 7
Spring Book Festival	Titles published Jan.-May. Three award categories: Picture-book, ages 4-8. "Middle" ages, 8-12. Over-12 readers.	$200 to author.	E 5 F 14 N-F 8 27	E 5 F 14 N-F 8 27	E 5 F 14 N-F 8 27

Note: E--easy or picture books; F--fiction; N-F--non-fiction.

TABLE II

SUBJECT AND AGE EMPHASIS

Dewey Class	Titles	Age Appeal	Titles
E (Easy/Picture books)	11		
F (Fiction)	60	Primary	17
N-F (Non-fiction)	63		
300's	11	Intermediate	67
500's	23		
600's	4	Junior high school	45
700's	1		
800's	1		
900's (excl. biog.)	13	Senior high school	5
92's (indiv. biog.)	6		
920's (coll. biog.)	4		
Total books awarded	134	Total books awarded	134

4. Elementary School Library Collection (ESLC), 1967
edition, published by the Bro-Dart Foundation, covering 6,558
titles.

5. Illinois Reading Service publications (IRS) including
the Basic List for Elementary School Libraries supplemented
by the 1969-70 Complete List of School Library Books, offering well over 4,000 titles.

6. The Junior High School Library Catalog (JHSC),
1965, supplemented annually. A Wilson publication covering
some 3,500 to 4,000 titles.

7. The Senior High School Library Catalog (SHSC),
9th edition, 1967, supplemented annually. A Wilson publication covering some 4,500 to 5,000 titles.

Later supplements or editions of one or two of these
bibliographies may have included an occasional title not listed
at the time of this study. Since only 11 of the 134 award
titles were published after 1966, it is not likely, however,
that many were missed. The eight multiple award titles were
all included in more than one bibliography, though no title was
found in all seven. It was therefore necessary to adjust gross

totals in Table III to avoid misrepresentation of the number
of the titles found in each bibliography. Table IV analyzes
the multiple award books in greater detail. Only Best Books
for Children and the Elementary School Library Collection
contained them all.

Perhaps the percentages in Table III tell more about
bibliographic coverage of worthy books for children than about
the literary impact of the various awards. Only three of the
seven lists included more than half of the award titles. Bowker's Best Books for Children had the highest number of
titles, followed at some distance by ALA's Books for Children and by Bro-Dart's Elementary School Library Collection.
The three Wilson publications fell well below 50 percent, as
did the Illinois Reading Service list. Titles not on any list
included nine of the Boys' Clubs, two of the Fisher, and
three Edison titles (see Table I). The Addams book for which
no reviews were found was also not on any list.

If "Recommended," Is the Award Citation Noted?

As previously noted, retrospective bibliographies would
seem better situated to report award citations than periodical
reviews or annotations appearing when the book was published.
In fairness to Books for Children we must remember that its
annotations are reprinted verbatim from the review periodical
Booklist. Even Caldecott and Newbery winners go unidenti-
fied there. The other six bibliographies did regularly identify titles winning those two prizes, though seldom other
prizes. Only 3 of the 143 awards studied here were mentioned, none for the eight multiple award titles. ESLC noted
that Branley's Experiments in Sky Watching and Haber's
Stars, Men and Atoms received the Edison Award. CC and
JHSC did the same for DeGering's Seeing Fingers: The Story
of Louis Braille.

Five other titles were credited with awards not surveyed here:

1. Chauncey's Devil's Hill (Boys' Clubs 1961). BRD
(excerpting from Library Journal) noted its 1959 Australian
Children's Book of the Year Award.

2. Holm's North to Freedom (Boys' Clubs 1966). CC
observed its 1963 Gyldendal Prize for the best Scandinavian
children's book.

TABLE III

AWARD TITLES IN SELECTIVE BIBLIOGRAPHIES

Bibliographies	Addams	Aurianne	Boys' Clubs	Child Study Assn.	Edison	Fisher	Spring Book Festival	Adjusted Totals	Ratio
Titles awarded	7	7	48	11	32	9	27	134	100%
Best Books (BBC)	7	5	26	7	22	6	22	84	63%
Bks. for Child. (BC)	6	4	23	9	20	5	17	75	56%
Children's Cat. (CC)	5	3	21	3	12	2	15	56	42%
Elem.Sch.Libr. Cat. (ESLC)	7	3	28	4	18	6	16	72	54%
Ill.Read.Serv. (IRS)	4	4	11	3	10	5	12	36	27%
Jr.High Sch. Cat. (JHSC)	5	4	13	6	16	4	7	48	36%
Sr. High Sch. Cat. (SHSC)	1	2	1	0	7	2	2	12	9%

TABLE IV

MULTIPLE AWARD TITLES, 1960–1968

Author	Title	Awards	Book Review Digest (BRD) and bibliography listing*
Burch	Queenie Peavy	Addams 1967 CSA 1967	1) BRD 2) BBC 3) BC 4) CC 5) ESLC 6) IRS
Burnford	Incredible Journey	Aurianne 1963 Fisher 1963	1) BRD 2) BBC 3) BC 4) ESLC 5) IRS 6) JHSC 7) SHSC
Haugaard	Little Fishes	Addams 1968 Sp. Bk. Fest. 1967	1) BRD 2) BBC 3) ESLC 4) IRS 5) JHSC
North	Rascal	Aurianne 1965 Fisher 1965	1) BRD 2) BBC 3) BC 4) ESLC 5) IRS 6) JHSC 7) SHSC
Ottley	Boy Alone	Edison 1967 Sp. Bk. Fest. 1966	1) BRD 2) BBC 3) BC 4) CC 5) ESLC 6) IRS
Sommerfelt	Peaceable Revolution	CSA 1964 Edison 1964	1) BRD 2) BBC 3) BC 4) ESLC 5) JHSC
Schechter	Road to Agra	Addams 1962 Boys' Clubs 1962 CSA 1962	1) BRD 2) BBC 3) BC 4) CC 5) ESLC
Viereck	Summer I Was Lost	Edison 1966 Fisher 1967	1) BRD 2) BBC 3) ESLC 4) IRS 5) JHSC

*See Table III for bibliography coding.

3.   Kennedy's Profiles in Courage (Addams Award
1964 for the Young Reader's Edition).   CC recorded the 1957
Pulitzer Prize for the original 1956 edition.

4.   Lindgren's Rasmus and the Vagabond (Boys' Clubs
1961).   Both BRD (quoting Library Journal again) and ESLC
said it had won the 1958 Andersen International Award.

5.   North's Rascal (Aurianne 1965; Fisher 1965).
JHSC reported that it received the 1963 Dutton Animal Book
Award.

There is evidently little chance that most awards will
be noted in selection aids as evidence of a book's quality.
While the 134 titles were generally well received by reviewers, their prizes were profoundly ignored.   The oversight
may not be so much intentional as a result of routine modes
of information gathering within the trade.   Yet Caldecott and
Newbery Awards are consistently reported.   They seem to
have become the favored offspring of a kind of state marriage between the book trade and the library profession.
Their sanctions and prerogatives include respectful acclaim
by all students of children's literature.   Not all of their
winning titles are still to be found in selective bibliographies,
but those which are always are identified.

As for reinforcement between a book's career in the
reviewing media and its status as an award winner, there
was, by and large, high correlation.   The forty-eight Boys'
Clubs titles, for which preliminary selection came from
mail polls of youthful readers, received the lowest percentage (77 percent) of listings in BRD, as well as in the seven
bibliographies (81 percent; see Table I).   Could these figures
indicate an incipient generation gap between young readers
and mature reviewers?   This straw in the wind cannot be
studied further because the Boys' Clubs National Program
Service told the writers that their letter was the first asking
"why?"   He then explained that the relatively few young
readers which Boys' Clubs had been able to involve made
the distribution and processing costs of the program unduly
high.   An inquiry to the Edison Foundation, which halted its
awards program in 1967, was returned unopened for forward-
ing information.   Presumably a similar combination of expense and lack of response led to its demise.

There is some further evidence of a pecking order in
book prizes.   While lesser award choices substantially over-

lapped, none during the nine years studied ever received a
Caldecott or Newbery medal. The diversity may have been
pure accident. At least five of the seven awards in the survey originated outside familiar bibliographic circles. No
doubt there was some tendency on both sides to remain self-
engrossed and aloof. Yet it is remarkable that no Caldecott
or Newbery award duplicated, say, the early and fairly numerous selections for Book Week's Spring Book Festival. Did
the prestigious selection committees avoid titles already
awarded? Even within library circles there is a tendency
toward favoritism. The brief career of the Aurianne Awards,
under sponsorship of the ALA Children's Services Division,
shows what appears to have been a more or less perfunctory
handling with comparatively little publicity. Perhaps because
the project was thematically and financially limited there was
little incentive to do more than name and announce the stipulated winners, avoiding encroachment on, or competition
with, the big two. The current Batchelder and Wilder
Awards, administered by the same division, likewise receive
considerably less publicity than Caldecott and Newbery selections.

    Objectively considered, discrete nonduplication could
be a healthy sign. Wide diversity of themes and selection
techniques, and a broad range of award titles, should be advantageous to all. Children's literature is not so small a
field as to prohibit successful maintenance of more than two
literary award programs which are widely respected. With
annual publication of about 1,400 new juvenile titles in the
United States, there would seem to be ample incentive for at
least one or two influential prizes originating outside the li-
brary-oriented in-group. They could foster that spirit of
healthy pluralism by which variety and dissent challenge our
comfortable presuppositions.

    The results of this study leave the impression that
worthy new books, in their progress through review media
into retrospective bibliographies, seldom get freshly written
evaluations. Selection committees no doubt work conscientiously at compiling lists of outstanding titles, but neglect to
review original assessments in the light of later information.
Bestsellerdom is not always reliable evidence of a book's
public stature, but recognition and use does contribute to its
effective life-span. Perhaps annotative revision is thought
to be too costly and time-consuming, particularly if it includes poll-type research into popularity. Or perhaps there
are other, unspoken reasons why none but the "establishment" awards are deemed worthy of bibliographic notice.

THE FIRST AND LAST FRONTIER OF COMMUNICATION: THE MAP AS MYSTERY*

Wilbur Zelinsky

The map as mystery? The question sounds frivolous or even mischievous. Surely we geographers and map librarians, who are so helplessly smitten with map-love, know and understand the objects we cherish, those beautiful, fascinating things that are so much a part of our working lives and inmost thoughts and feelings. After all, a map is a map, isn't it?--something even the dullest school child can recognize and describe. Unfortunately, as is the case with many another simple-seeming phenomenon, the real nature of the geographic map is still far beyond our grasp. (If you find this disconcerting, so do I; but the history of science is one long series of embarrassing revelations.) The problem is similar to that of the terrible complexity of verbal language. Anyone can recognize a piece of written language or identify certain noises as being linguistic in character; but how many can define precisely the ways in which I am transmitting information to you by means of words? Even though we learn the rules and syntax almost subconsciously in early childhood, there are still exceedingly few scholars who have begun to master the real grammar of the English language, something, by the way, that is not taught in grammar school.

In the case of maps, another major mode of communication, our knowledge is still more rudimentary. To put things as bluntly as possible, we have as yet no truly adequate definition of the map; and we have scarcely begun the serious study of its grammar. Thus we do not really know the fundamental nature of the things we are so intimately

*Reprinted by permission of the author and publisher from Special Libraries Association, Geography & Map Division Bulletin, December 1973, pp. 2-8.

enmeshed with, nor do we know what it is we really see or
think when maps are being looked at.   This may sound like
empty, gratuitous mystification, or like disturbing the public
peace by playing at academic sadism.   But I would argue
that, quite to the contrary, it is only by rejecting the com-
monsensical perception of maps and by subjecting them to
deep scrutiny that we can register any truly major scientific
and practical advances, just as happened when some busy-
bodies became restless and curious about the real nature of
physical matter, the motion of falling bodies, the color of
garden peas, or the scenarios of our dreams.

        Let us begin this excursion in intellectual discomfort
by tackling the definitional question.   It is truly astonishing,
but, to the best of my knowledge, in none of the standard
texts or treatises on cartography or surveying, the monographs on map design or reproduction, the histories of maps
and map-making, or the treatment of any other specialized
topic within cartography does the author attempt to provide
the reader with a rigorous definition of the map.   Usually
he plunges immediately into the discussion without offering
any definition at all, on the unspoken assumption that any
idiot can distinguish maps from other classes of objects. If
we turn to lexical definitions--and Webster III is as good as
any--we find a literally superficial entry in our dictionary,
one that quite clearly reflects the casual impressions of the
man-on-the-street:

        ... a drawing or other representation that is usu.
        made on a flat surface and that shows the whole
        or part of an area (as of the surface of the earth
        or some other planet or of the moon) and indicates
        the nature and relative position and size according
        to a chosen scale or projection of selected fea-
        tures or details...

This statement is roughly equivalent to describing the map
as a kind of modified, stripped-down vertical air photo. If
we turn to the mathematical literature, we find a quite different, but equally unsatisfying approach, as in this recent
text on topology:[1]

        A map is a network, together with a surface
        which contains the network.

Such definitions are rather like meals in a Chinese restau-
rant, as one of my departmental colleagues has noted; you

are hungry almost as soon as you have finished devouring
them.

I would suggest that neither approach--the iconic, or
the highly abstract mathematical concept of the map as a
network of points on an n-dimensional surface--is very productive. To consider the map as just a physical object, a
self-contained, free-standing totality of some sort, a thing-
in-itself, that is usually a rectangular sheet of paper or
cloth containing linear and point symbols, edges, and perhaps colors, numbers, and words, one which is a sort of
severely touched-up, blurred snapshot of some part of the
earth's surface, does not allow us to penetrate very far into
the real meaning of maps. Neither does the austere vision
of the topologist. How, then, can we begin to understand
the basic essence of the geographic map? (For the sake of
simplicity and brevity, as well as simple ignorance, let me
avoid discussing other species of maps, even though their
exploration would probably take us down equally interesting
routes.)

The document we denote as a map can only be understood as one of several elements in a complex series of
transactions, in a constant state of flux, involving 1) an objective reality of some sort, 2) explorers or observers,
3) the mapmaker, 4) the document, and 5) the mapreader or,
more realistically, a community of mapreaders, and that indeed the map exists and has meaning only as it connects
with other aspects of an interlocking communicative structure.
Incidentally, the same observation would apply to any other
physical artifact, be it painting, photograph, architectural
drawing, perfume, jewelry, or whatever, that is concerned
with the flow of information.

Perhaps the best way to drive home this point is by
means of an analogy, one which at first blush may appear
highly superficial, but is, in actuality, uncannily close to
our cartographic dilemma, and deeply illuminating. Suppose
we ask the question: "What sorts of objects, or merchandise,
do music-dealers and music librarians handle?" The obvious answer is: Mainly musical scores, recordings, and
perhaps books about music. It is equally evident that although these items are intimately concerned with music-
making or, to use a rather more inclusive term, musical
behavior, they certainly do not encompass the entire range
of such activity. If we take the musical score, the item
most closely analogous to the geographic map, then a great

deal, indeed very likely the overwhelming preponderance, of
all music ever performed is played or sung without benefit
of score or is never reduced to notational form.   My point
is that, in precisely parallel fashion, the geographic map is
just one element in that assemblage of things which, for
want of a better term, we can designate collectively as
"mapping behavior, " and indeed it may not even be a necessary ingredient in that assemblage.

        The overt differences between the map and the musical
score are interesting, but do not vitiate the basic claim.
Thus almost any adult or child of more or less normal intelligence and vision can read or interpret at least the simpler types of geographic maps with only the most minimal
sort of training, or perhaps none at all, so that we find
maps appearing with great regularity in automobile glove
compartments, subway stations, newspapers, postage stamps,
telephone directories, television screens, and doodles. This
universal skill is a matter of some significance to which we
shall return in a moment.   On the other hand, even though
almost anyone, except perhaps the deaf or tone-deaf, can
make or enjoy music of some sort, the proper reading of
even a simple musical score requires some difficult, rigorous training, and thus skills confined to a small, élite fraction of the total population.   (The only instance of which I
am aware when the cultivated layman was expected to read
and perform from a musical score was Elizabethan England,
a land and an epoch when, by a probably meaningful coincidence, the art and science of cartography happened to be
making important strides.)   Furthermore, to consummate
the analogy, it must be admitted that the musical counter-
part of map-reading, which is the transformation of a set of
conventional symbols into some sort of mental image or
construct, would include not only the ability of a trained
musician, or conductor, to scan a score, while hearing
sounds in his mind's ear, but also the act of transforming
the notations into audible sounds, often by means of an elaborate, expensive aggregation of instruments, performers,
vocalists, auditorium, and audience.   Thus, in general, the
full reading and expression of a musical score is a much
more ambitious undertaking than the parallel activity involving maps; but with the advent of sophisticated optical devices
and computer routines for the analytic scanning of maps, the
gap begins to close.

        Another interesting difference is that the map object
is frequently an aesthetically pleasing thing.   In fact, unless

maps or globes are wretchedly executed or reproduced, they
tend to be naturally handsome or at least visually arresting.
Thus they have become a standard element in the interior
decorator's craft; and many of us hang maps on walls or
mount globes on elaborate pedestals as sources of visual
gratification rather than for their scientific or informational
merits. Only the unusually fine musical holograph is suitable for framing, and not even the most abandoned musical
fanatic is likely to experience much rapture upon contemplating a phonograph disc or magnetic tape.

        The point, then, is that the map is only an incidental,
or even expendable, portion of the total mapping experience,
just as its close analogue, the musical score, is but a single
element, if that, in musical experience. A loose definition
of the concept of mapping experience, or mapping behavior,
is that it is one of several modes of communication practiced by human beings, specifically that concerned with selectively sensed data about objects and events in their
spatial-temporal context, the storage and manipulation of
such data as cognitive maps (and only potentially as documents), and the thoughts, movements, and other behavior
consequent upon the sensing, sorting, arrangement, and symbolic transformation of such data. In short, we are speaking of one of the variety of ways, conscious or otherwise,
whereby the human mind strives to make sense of a perceived universe by ordering things into some abstracted
spatial framework.

        It needs to be added that, just as in the case of
musical behavior, mapping behavior is normally a socially
shared entity, involving transactions among people, as well
as between individuals and those animate and inanimate objects that envelop them. In its most elementary, or ancient,
aspects, mapping behavior is a continually ongoing set of in-
teractions concerned with spatial concepts, namely the constantly modulating impact of sensory and ideational input upon
the individual or collective cognitive map, along with the un-
ceasing impact of such patterned concepts upon the things
being cognized. It is most significant that even in the absence of documentary materials, the cognitive map may be
fleshed out in the form of bodily gestures or games involving position and movement. There may well be the tightest,
most profound structural connections between the essence of
the graphic map and various kinds of dance, sports, sculpture, and playing with toys, all of which somehow involve
the abstraction and modeling of spatial experience. Formal

cartography seems to be a relatively late, though well-nigh universal, human achievement. To quote Blaut, McCleary, and Blaut:[2]

> Cognitive mapping is phylogenetically the primordial mode of mapping behavior; ontogenetically, it is at least as primitive as the earliest detour strategy of the crawling infant. Cartography, by contrast, is in general the most complex mode, the one concrete mode which is most peculiarly specialized for the storage of spatial information, and the one which is most nearly ubiquitous in human cultures.

But elaborate and sophisticated though the modern map may have become, it still retains much of its primaeval tactility and choreographic quality. One has only to recall Charles Chaplin's exquisite pas de deux with a globe in "The Great Dictator" to understand the point. And it is brought home for me almost every day by the behavior of both adult and child visitors in the corridor outside my office. Along some 25 feet of the wall surface, we have mounted a raised-relief map of the entire Appalachian highland region from Quebec to Alabama; and I have become accustomed to the sight of strangers dreamily oozing along that wall tracing and fondling the ridges and valleys with their fingertips, as they grope and gesture in an exploratory ballet--and apparently with much pleasure.

It might be profitable to digress and wonder why the exuberant communicative talents of young children--many of whom show indications of sheer, unadulterated genius in mapping behavior, as well as drawing, singing, dance, and game-playing--is not channeled and developed more productively as they grow older, why indeed there appears to be almost a silent conspiracy to bring about the atrophy of those natural aesthetic and kinetic impulses that are so great a part of our joie de vivre. The experiments of Blaut and Stea and their students, which had young school children in Massachusetts and Puerto Rico in intensive, joyous floor contact with large air photos and maps of their localities point to some exciting possibilities.[3] But I lack the knowledge or skill to pursue the point any further.

But, to return to the main argument, if we perceive the mapping experience as an interacting system, a structured, but elastic, set of relationships among sensory data,

cognitive maps, and spatial behavior, then the invention and
adoption of the formal graphic device known as the map--that
frozen bodily and mental gesture, a written dispatch from
our inner storehouse of cognitive patterns--greatly complicates that set of relationships. The making of maps involves
the collection of information through the shared perceptions
of a community or the observations of groups of explorers,
surveyors, census enumerators, interviewers, and the like,
the invention and application of special conventions in symbolization, and, finally, their perusal. Fully as important
as the mechanical busy work going into map-making is the
fact that the map in its documentary form can be a most
powerful shaper of cognitive maps, in effect instructing us
how to think about the arrangement of things out there; and
such knowledge or faith, in turn, persuades us to behave in
ways that are much different from what our actions would be
in lieu of maps, and thus in ways that actively impinge upon
and reshape all manner of things falling within the domain
of the cartographer. If the history of geographic ideas is so
densely crammed with instances of such interplay among
maps, human minds, and landscapes that I need not pause
for examples, let me note nonetheless that there have been
precious few efforts to study such cases in depth. In the
same way, incidentally, the preservation of musical thoughts
in the form of scores, in essence messages collected by
listeners with unusually acute hearing from that mysterious
everchanging ocean of musical ideas that surges through our
collective mind, has had a reflexive impact upon that great
source as subsequent composers (the cartographers of musical ideas) and listeners read, listen, interpret, and reinterpret. Even more to the point is the way the invention of
writing and, subsequently, the reduction of spoken language
to durable form, the large-scale fabrication of literature
conceived in a visual rather than an oral mode, and that indefinite embalmment of ideas in texts, has had a major impact on linguistic behavior, that is, upon the further evolution of language, our verbal thinking, and the entire universe
of human ideas.

Thus the map, painting, written narrative, or musical composition graduates from the passivity of a mere reflection or image to a lively potency as generative factor.
Just as certain sequences of tones devised by Bach, Mozart,
Beethoven, or Brahms convey a tremendous emotional wal-
lop even when heard out of context, and probably will so
long as men can hear and feel, or it is impossible for me
to see sunflowers, a certain style of chair, or an orchard

in bloom except through the eyes of Vincent Van Gogh, or to
glimpse a certain muted shade of brown without stepping
through a door into the world of Peter Breughel, so too the
art of the cartographer has, among other things, conferred
a vividly animate life, a kind of totemic significance, upon
certain shapes arbitrarily oriented in a certain direction,
very much in effect a flag. Strange, for instance, how the
outline of Great Britain sheds its singular grace when it is
inverted, or how acutely uncomfortable one can become when
the map of the United States is seen in mirror image. In
fact, certain kinds of maps, perceived as a threat to our
cultural integrity, may be a sufficient condition for warfare.
Consider, then, as a first stage in defining the map truly
the statement that it is a dialectical proposition, understandable only as it takes and gives, as it mediates between
an outer world and our cognitive world within, in accordance
with a yet to be defined set of rules.

The claim that the map may be the oldest form of
communication is largely speculative. My reasoning is that
one can postulate a rather smooth transition from the mapping behavior observed among the lower animals, e. g. , the
dance of the honeybee or the territorial signals sung by
birds, and their presumptive cognitive maps to those of human beings, culminating in the most sophisticated forms of
cartography. In other words, our ancestral species may
have been engaged in rather elaborate mapping behavior well
before achieving truly human status, although it was only
then that mimetic mapping, i. e. , simply plotting things as
observed, camera-fashion, was supplanted by symbolic, and
thus highly abstract, imaginative mapping, including, among
other things, cognitive maps of an afterworld, and the more
embryonic modes of map transformations. The momentous
passage from an exclusive use of signs to a heavy reliance
on symbols may not have been readily observable outwardly
in mapping behavior. In contrast, there must have been a
rather sudden shift, a sharp discontinuity from pre-linguistic
sounds to the use of genuine language, from animal play (or
human horseplay) to full-fledged games with their elaborate
sets of abstract rules, or from instinctual twitchings and
cries to genuine dance and song, and ultimately drama.

In speaking of the map as alpha and omega, as the
last, as well as the earliest, frontier of communication, I
wish to convey the notion that the grammar peculiar to that
language known as maps has yet to be deciphered, and that
when this feat has been accomplished there may be some

quantum leaps upward in the communicative skills of the
mapmaker. This is not to deny the impressive technical
progress in map design, symbolization, and reproduction of
recent decades. The definitive treatises on map projections
and the more recent work on map transformations must be
characterized as elegant. We are learning a great deal
about the perception and thus the correct use of various
kinds of point and linear symbols, of color and texture, and
the more effective means for delivering statistical information via maps. But, as David Harvey has pointed out quite
rightly, "this substantial technical literature ... contrasts
markedly with the almost total lack of consideration for the
logical properties of the map as a form of communication....
It is a complex language ... whose properties we know very
little about."4 Yet until we can answer the basic question
of what kinds of visual thinking the human eye and brain
perform when scanning the map as a total entity--and not
just how we apprehend isolated elements and aspects of a
drawing under laboratory conditions--until then, the ultimate
potential of the map cannot be realized. Only then can we
represent in usable graphic form various kinds of information
that are now stored only in cognitive maps or in statistical
tables. For example, as a population geographer, I hope to
survive long enough to witness a methodology for plotting
complex assemblages of human migration streams in intel-
ligible form. Currently, neither word, table, graph, nor
map does the trick at all adequately.

       This task of mapping the grammar of maps will not
be an easy one. It has proved difficult enough to unravel
the basic logic of linguistic meaning or of musical meaning,
despite the fact that these are essentially one-dimensional,
linear modes of communication, with any additional dimensions being at most implied rather than explicit. The intrinsic multidimensionality of the map greatly complicates
the agenda of its grammarian. Even the simplest drawing
invokes the special mysteries of two-dimensional space, with
all the unsolved psychological questions of shapes, sizes,
edges, orientation, position, and relations of different masses.
To these initial dimensions, we often add the third, either
in actual physical fact on raised-relief models or by means
of contours and other symbols, or even the fourth, temporal
dimension through a variety of devices. Then, in a very
real sense, color, brightness, and texture constitute three
other dimensions. The problems of how all these dimensions and entities are perceived in visual congress are rather
similar to those encountered in the field of painting, where

there are also complexly patterned ways for communicating
both aesthetic and semantic information; and in that sector
despite a great deal of careful research and thinking, many
of the essential riddles are far from being resolved.   To
make things even more frustrating, the map may contain, in
addition to all the dimensions already enumerated and a large
vocabulary of conventional symbols, some purely pictorial
representations, most notoriously in the teeming fauna so
rampant in the cartouches and ocean wastes of Renaissance
maps, but in other ways as well and, of course, a goodly
complement of words and numbers.   The map, then, is an
example of "multi media" with a vengeance.   The only other
modes of communication of equal complexity to come to mind
are grand opera and the motion picture.   The latter, by the
way, with its peculiar warping, slicing, splicing, and re-
ordering of space and time offers large problems of psychological interpretation no less exasperating than does the map.

        I close, then, with a sense of bafflement in being un-
able to offer any clear prescription as to how to get on
quickly with the chore of learning the hidden language of
maps.   It is scarcely necessary to note that a convergent
set of analytic techniques is called for.   But it is important
to dwell upon the probability that some quite deep, subter-
ranean strata of the human psyche will have to be explored
before the mission is accomplished and that some shame-
lessly subjective, intuitive, introspective strategies may be
profitable, along with the conventional objective and analytic
approaches.   I can do no better here than to cite the revelations issuing from the insights of the French philosopher
Gaston Bachelard in coping with house architecture in his
"Poetics of Space. "[5]

        I will know the problem is solved if I ever under-
stand what it was that I saw, or was looking for, in a map
encountered some years ago.   It was one sheet out of many
in a series of large-scale topographic maps.   This particular quadrangle was especially striking because it contained
nothing but a solid expanse of blue ink depicting the ocean
surface.   Evidently this was the corner cell in a rectangular block of sheets, and the designers of the series simply
included the superfluous item out of some compulsive sense
of order and symmetry.   Much time was spent scanning this
sheet and trying to interpret it, to pluck out its covert message, dreaming over unseen lines and patterns; and, in fact,
I came back to it several times.   What did I see?   What
was I looking for?   I do not know.   The map is a mystery.

Notes

1. B. H. Arnold, Intuitive Concepts in Elementary Top-
    ology (Englewood Cliffs: Prentice-Hall, 1962), p. 43.

2. James M. Blaut, George S. McCleary, Jr., and
    America S. Blaut, "Environmental Mapping in Young
    Children," Environment and Behavior, Vol. 2, No. 3
    (Dec. 1970), p. 338.

3. J. M. Blaut and David Stea, "Studies of Geographic
    Learning," Annals of the Association of American
    Geographers, Vol. 61, No. 2 (June 1971), pp. 387-
    393.

4. David Harvey, Explanation in Geography (New York: St.
    Martin's Press, 1969), p. 370.

5. Gaston Bachelard, The Poetics of Space (New York:
    Orion Press, 1964).

DISESTABLISHING THE SCHOOL
AND THE PUBLIC LIBRARY:
The Ideas of Ivan Illich
Applied to Libraries*

Leo N. Flanagan

> Scholastic machinery is as estranged from social
> life as if this and all its problems were outside
> its compass. The world of education is like an
> island where people, cut off from the world, are
> prepared for life by exclusion from it.

> --Maria Montessori, The Absorbent Mind

Maria Montessori's observation is certainly not a new
one. Twenty-five hundred years ago Socrates noted the
same failure, and died trying to correct it. Five hundred
years ago Roger Ascham in his Scholemaster lamented the
thorough failure of the schools to cope with reality. One
hundred years ago Charles Dickens pointed out that English
schools were ruining youth by assumptions unfounded in
reality. In this country, in addition to Maria Montessori,
Jean Piaget, John Dewey, Charles Silberman, Jerome Brun-
ner, Jonathan Kozol and a host of others have attacked the
very foundations of educational philosophy. In fact, so many
good and intelligent people have attacked the repeated blunders of the schools for the past several thousand years that,
in even the lightest reading of a handful of their works, one
can almost be led to despair of reform amongst school
masters and school mistresses.

It has hardly been surprising to see the schools falter
in the past decade. While the old burden of two and a half
millenia of pedagogical abuses was still bearable, new bur-
dens proved to be the proverbial "straw." With exposure

*Reprinted by permission of the author and the California
Library Association from the California Librarian, July 1974.

after exposure of secret service to the military-industrial complex, many of the nation's most reputable universities began to lose friends on all sides. [1] In disgust, students took to burning down the colleges, or blowing them up. In embarrassment, government and industry took their bags of gold and went home. Then, with the report of a special presidential commission, we learned what most children know too well, that primary and secondary school is no less than a dreary experience for them. And with the publication of Christopher Jenkes' now famous study we heard what three generations of American poor had discovered long ago, that education is not a significant factor in a youngster's way of life. And that is because Maria Montessori was correct, because education has been divided from life.

What can be done? The state of schools in general today is so pitiful intellectually, pedagogically, administratively, economically, that drastic solutions and drastic actions are necessary. And it is to be expected that Ivan Illich, often the proponent of a drastic solution, would have one to offer for the problems of the schools.

In his recent book, Deschooling Society, Illich advocates, even predicts, the disestablishment of the schools in the near future. [2] This volume of essays, a synthesis of discussions at Illich's Center for Intercultural Documentation at Cuernavaca, of many articles he has previously written and of his experiences in Latin America and Europe and New York, is, I would think, of vital concern to all librarians. Not only is it a pointed attack on the schools with which librarians have long been allied, but it is an indictment of the society of which the schools are a product, the whole white middle-class industrial culture with its social structures that separate men from each other and from themselves. It is a plea for open educational institutions, ones anyone can use, almost anytime, such as libraries. It is an outcry against western institutions that have blocked communication between men, and so it is of consequence to librarians, who are especially responsible for one agency of communication. Most importantly, it is a mine of ideas for all learning institutions, models for reaching out to all people at the most minimum cost. Such ideas should not be ignored by libraries in their attempt to gain more local support by providing more service despite minimal budgets.

In a Saturday Review article, "The Alternative to Schooling, " in which Illich has condensed his book, he states his indictment of the schools:

> 1. the schools force "all children to climb an open-ended education ladder" which must "favor the individual who starts out earler, healthier, or better prepared";
>
> 2. the enforced education deadens "for most people the will for independent learning";
>
> 3. the schools package knowledge as a scarce and private commodity;
>
> 4. most insidiously of all, however, the schools by the very structure of their assumptions, a hidden structure, promulgate a course of instruction or "hidden curriculum. "[3] In other words, the medium of schooling is itself a message.

The "hidden curriculum" had become a rite de passage for the young, says Illich, a ritual with its own doctrines or values:

> 1. only education acquired in a school through a graded process of consumption is valuable;
>
> 2. the degree of success an individual will enjoy in society depends on the amount of learning he consumes;
>
> 3. and learning about the world is more important, more valuable, than learning from it.

The first doctrine or value allows the schools a monopoly on education. Doctrine two legitimatizes existing social and economic distinctions by creating a new class structure, a "meritocracy, " specious in essence because schooling in no way guarantees occupational competence. And the third doctrine allows the schools to discredit most men's most important teacher, experience. In sum, what the schools teach, says Peter Schrag, in speaking in Saturday Review of Illich's observations, "is the importance of schooling itself, not worthwhile trades or literacy or any humanly important attitude or skill. "[4] And all recent educational improvements and theories fail to some degree or another, concludes Illich, because they leave this "hidden curriculum" of the school unexamined and intact.

The "hidden curriculum" is essentially a product of
the medieval heritage of the schools, a myth, a set of assumptions, what Illich calls the "occult foundations. " These
assumptions spring from a time when men believed that one
substance could be changed into another through rather mechanically graded steps, from a time when a single ecclesi-
astical institution governed all education and was the single
infallible source of authority on all matters. This set of
assumptions, this myth, has been weakened obviously, because alchemy is no longer the ultimate explanation of physical reality, and because most people no longer believe in
human infallibility. However, the myth has not totally collapsed because many people still believe in learning by
stages and because they still believe rigid authority is necessary to educate the young. The myth not only still has
some of its original life, but as the force behind the ritual
of schooling it has found new strength from its harmony with
the modern myth of the middle-class competitive free-enter-
prise industrial society. The old myth, and its consequent
ritual, fills the needs of the propagators of the new myth by
furnishing the industrial system with graduates who have a
high level of tolerance for elder authorities, who possess
peculiar respect for order and conformity, who willingly and
docilely submit to disciplined work even when its relevance
is not apparent, who obey orders and refuse individual responsibility, who see all elements of life, and death, as
packaged commodities. These are Herbert Marcuse's "one-
dimensional men" and worse, certified robots, creatures
who at thirty years of age are not interested in (and can not
quote) Shakespeare because they "had that" ten years ago,
they used it then and they have put the battered remains of
the commodity away in the attic lumber rooms of their heads
forever more. These are computers who can tolerate only
their own kind, machines with "paper" souls composed of
birth-citizenship-high school-college certificates and marri-
age-driving-retail licenses and housing-stock-auto titles and
bank-credit-identification cards. These are the ultimate
products of schools, unchallenged until now. But Illich
claims that true education is soon to be divorced from
"schooling, " and the divorce will be speeded up by three
forces.

The first force is the Third World which can not use
"schooling. " "Given their limitations in resources, " observes Peter Schrag, "Latin American schools can never
take the majority of children through more than the fifth
grade (nor will there ever be room for that majority in the

affluent middle class). "[5] The second force catalyzing the
separation of schools and education is the university students
of the world, the experts who have had all of the "schooling"
and know first-hand exactly how badly it has failed. And
the third force fighting the schools' brand of education are
the poor of the United States, that fifteen per cent of the
population which earns less than $3,000 a year, and which
knows they can never employ the few techniques of democracy or free enterprise which they might have been taught by
"schooling." And they haven't been taught anything else,
such as courses on birth control, the draft, the law and
their civil rights, and the economics of daily living.

It just costs too much for the schools to teach much
to many. And the poor are the first to be hurt in a budget
crisis, even when they are given as much as everyone else.
For their needs are much more severe. The greater needs of the
poor, not radical conflicts, are the real nitty gritty of the
school busing problem. Were thorough busing done on a
wide scale, every school would feel the want of money to
cope with those severe needs. Without the money every
school, not just the few, would become dismally ineffective
in teaching a fair part of its students, and would begin to
demand more money to do its job. And American taxpayers,
now spending eight per cent of the gross national product for
schools, would balk at the demand. They're balking right
now at current costs, so it is impossible to imagine that
they might want to provide for all a better type of schooling, say, the kind of schooling now available to the most
favored twenty percent of American students. That kind, including a mediocre college education, could cost 250 to 300
billion dollars a year, or 1/4 to nearly 1/3 of the annual
gross national product. This is just too much for "schooling." And even the United States, the richest country in the
world, can not afford it. It can not afford to educate all
children, let alone adults in need, as it educates the top 20
per cent, if it uses schools to do the job. Schooling is
simply not an efficient way to get education to the people.
The impossible problem of the costs of schooling everyone
commands Americans, rich as they are, to examine alternatives to find other avenues to education than the schools
alone. Even the United States, with 210 million people, six
per cent of the world's population, with the power to annually gobble up 50 per cent of the world's resources, even
the United States does not have the intellectual, the human,
the monetary, and the material resources to give every one
of its citizens a college education. [6] The poor, and the poor

education they receive, are a constant reminder of that
failure.

The schools may be crumbling, but genuine learning
is coming. Illich is quite convinced of this. He feels that
a decent society would guarantee <u>real</u> education by supporting an educational system with three purposes:

> 1. to provide all who want to learn with all of the
> available resources at any time in their lives;
>
> 2. to put those who want to share what they know in
> contact with those who want to learn;
>
> 3. and to furnish all those who wish to present an
> issue to the public with an opportunity to do so. [7]

To assure some attainment of these purposes; that is, to
guarantee real education, the society would have to provide
four "channels" or learning exchanges, each of which would
contain one of the four resources needed for real learning:
things, models, peers, and elders. [8]

> <u>Things</u>: the first type of learning exchange would be
> a reference service to educational things or objects. In
> contact with objects, which the schools presently shut out,
> the student could learn their real nature and his own and
> his relation to them. Technology could be used to simplify
> rather than complicate objects, and could also be used to
> build instruments to aid in the investigation of objects, and
> ultimately could be used to build "networks" or links in and
> amongst the four channels.

> <u>Models</u>: the second type of exchange would be a ref-
> erence service for the swapping of skills between those who
> possessed them and those who did not, without any regard
> for certification.

> <u>Peers</u>: the third type would be a reference service
> for the matching of peers so that a student could engage with
> his fellows in a learning project.

> <u>Elders</u>: the fourth and last type would be a reference
> service for educators at large, one sub-class of whom
> would create and operate the four channels; a second sub-
> class of whom would guide all age groups in using the chan-
> nels; and a third sub-class of whom would undertake diffi-

cult exploratory intellectual journeys (i. e., research). This liberation of access to things, skill-models, and skills, peers and elders will mean the disestablishment of the schools, the end of their infallible authority over educative processes.

This, the problem of the schools as Illich sees it, and his solution to the problem, is the heart of his theory, his social philosophy in a nutshell. It is necessary to admit that there are real problems in the schools and, that Illich's deschooling of culture may be part of the answer, if not the answer. There is much historical, social, economic and psychological evidence for the essence of his observations. "Schooling" has been oversold in many respects, and one only has to look at the machine of American graduate education, turning out tens of thousands of Ph. D. 's unemployable in their fields, to see that many have bought an empty poke. Something is very wrong in the schools when one can secure its ultimate product and can use that product very little for one's self and not at all for one's society.

Well, the librarian may ask, what implications does all of this have for my public library? I have been in charge of neither the schools nor the overall society. What are my sins? Surely not those Illich imputes to the school. I have not encouraged learning by stages, I have not attempted a monopoly on learning, and I have not forced learning, for library use is not compulsory under the law. Rather I have gone in many cases as far as my society will allow in promoting Illich's aims. I have acted as a reference service to put people in contact with those objects called books, and through books I have referred library readers to skill models and peers and elders. I have certainly maintained an exchange between this latter class, elders or educators, and my readers. Also I have catered especially to self-motivated learners and to seekers after information practical to life. Where have I sinned?

No one would dispute the fact that most public librarians have done a great deal of what Illich recommends. But perhaps part of the public library problem is that librarians feel that they have done enough, that there is not much more they could do. Yet it seems to me they could do more. They could more actively fight for Illich's first goal of "real" education, i. e., for providing all who want to learn with all reasonable available resources at any time in their lives. Public librarians do not by any means serve all of

the population, but only about ten percent of it on a regular
basis. Regular users among the young are largely students,
and among the adults they are largely professionals, according to Mary Lee Bundy. [9] Service to these groups makes
the public library the close ally of both the school system
and the capitalist-industrial society that Illich attacks. Service to these small groups (first cited in Berelson's The Library's Public in 1949 and most recently asserted in the
February 15, 1974 issue of Library Journal by Joseph Sakey)
makes the library a rather definite ally of the "Establishment."

    Secondly, public libraries do not serve all patrons
equally at any time of their lives: they do not tend to serve
"young adults" well, [10] they serve the housewife rather
poorly, and they hardly serve the poor and the aged at all.[11]
And thirdly, public libraries do not provide all of the available resources for learning that they might reasonably be
expected to provide. They, of course, can not be expected
to provide all learning resources unless taxpayers furnish
the money for librarians to buy the world. However, it does
seem reasonable, insofar as the librarian claims the province of the preserver and distributor of the recorded word,
that the library might possess more of a variety of resources in the most basic communications media. After all,
books are only a small fraction of the devices men have for
communicating. Yet only they are the central focus of most
public libraries. The supply of tape recorders, cartridges,
projectors and films (the most moving medium, with no pun
intended, of this century), television kinescopes and television sets (for watching, say, The Forsyte Saga or The Electric Company or Free to Be You and Me), sizable record
collections and phonographs, and facilities for making cheap
reproductions of documents in demand, are abysmally inadequate in most public libraries. Public libraries as a
class of institutions certainly provide few other "objects for
learning" than books, and those they provide largely to an
educated well-to-do middle class. [12]

    The librarians' record in achieving the first goal of
an Illich kind of education is not very impressive, and
leaves no room for self-satisfaction. Of course, it must be
admitted that librarians have never attempted such an
achievement. Thus my object is not to fault them there,
but only to ask the question, now that Illich has suggested
it: shouldn't it be the libraries which are striving to provide
all who want to learn with all of the available media re-

sources at any time in their lives? And can the libraries
accomplish this goal if schools continue to hold a monopoly
on education? Can libraries accomplish this goal if more
and more money is dumped into "schooling," only to have
less and less left over for institutions like the public library, institutions which could be truly open and educative,
in which more and more people might learn for themselves?
Can a public library, which could be open to all, really accomplish anything at all in competition for money with public
grade and high schools, which serve only some of the young?
According to John Holt, "In most places the schools are
probably twenty to fifty times as large as the library and
spend twenty to fifty times as much money."[13] Should not
this kind of imbalance be changed?

And as long as questions are being asked, should librarians in any substantial way attempt the achievement of
Illich's second and third goals of a real educational system?
As far as the second goal is concerned, public libraries do
not now put those who want to share what they know in contact with those who want to learn it, with two weak exceptions: one, there is little evidence of education by skill
models or peer groups except for a few feeble efforts at
"discussion" groups for neighborhood problems or best-
sellers; two, the only evidence of people contacting people
in a regularly consistent way in the library is through the
medium of books, readers contacting authors--and here librarians' detachment is considerable despite the continual
condemnation of impartiality and indifference from Berelson
to Bundy. Public librarians unfortunately tend to make the
reader's contact with the author too much of a "do-it-your-
self" project.[14] Is "impartial service" possible for the librarian who genuinely cares about books, people, and their
relationship to one another? Shouldn't the public library,
for example, with the greatest advertised collection of directories in an area, be bringing, on a regular basis, people
in need of information to those who can help?

Illich's third goal, the furnishing all who wish to
present an issue to the public with an opportunity to do so,
has been attempted to some degree by the public library.
Library rooms have frequently been opened to local groups
and societies under very liberal conditions. But the abilities of such groups to reach the public from "block" clubs
may be the exception. Should the library be making more
means available for local groups to reach the public: type-
writers, mimeograph machines, electronic recording devices,

photography equipment and the like? And should the public
library be more actively aiding local groups to research and
acquire the information they wish to take to the public?
Should the public library develop a permanent public forum?

Illich's educational goals may or may not suggest to
public librarians some sins of omission. I think they should
at least provide a little self-doubt and questioning.

It is another of Illich's ideas, however, the one about
the "hidden curriculum," that I think suggests more serious
and unfortunate problems for librarians. To be blunt, I
think this idea points to some definite acts, perhaps sins of
commission on the part of public librarians in general. What
hidden structure, what implicit unfounded values and attitudes
of the library, constitute a course of instruction for the regular library user? I would suggest but a few as grounds
for further reflection amongst all of us.

What does the almost exclusive distribution of books
by public libraries imply? Does it suggest that librarians
are aware of the value of other media? Does it suggest that
librarians are aware, à la McLuhan, of the dangers of a
reading-only approach to reality?

What does the academic and industrial classification
of knowledge in libraries say about their school and business
commitments? What does the absence of a focus on the categories most people focus on (i. e., men, women, love, sex,
sustenance, shelter, war, life, death) say about libraries'
concern for most people, and their way of thinking? What
do displays on "Book Week" and whaling, and not on a war
which badly crippled the nation (and its libraries), and not
on sex education while eleven and twelve year olds "magic-
ally" conceive, and not on racism while that idiot Archie
Bunker drivels on Saturday after Saturday, demonstrate about
librarians' courage, conviction, and sincere desire to serve
the public interest? What does the neutral serve-yourself
approach to information tell the reflective reader about the
public library's concern for the kind of information it dis-
tributes? What do the patrons themselves, white, alert,
well-dressed, neat, orderly, crowding into the modern sub-
urban library on Saturday afternoon, imply about public library service? What does emptiness of the ghetto library
on the southern-end of a nearby city tell us? Features such
as these make up the obvious "hidden curriculum," the implied values of the public libraries. If one analyzes the less

obvious "hidden curriculum," say the book selection policies,
what does one conclude? What values does the employee
situation suggest, when one finds non-whites nearly nowhere,
when one finds few women at the top of the top libraries,
when one finds miserable salaries at the bottom? Do librarians care about themselves?

The public library should amend the unfortunate elements in its "hidden curriculum," first for its own salvation,
and second for the salvation of people most in need of salvation. It has to look to its own salvation, before some
public officials, unhappy for personal or political or moral
motives with their libraries, take courage and inform their
public how much it is costing the many to serve the few.
The public library must make amends as soon as possible to
have the public "on its side" in time. This is more and
more true as federal money is withdrawn and libraries are
forced to rely on local revenues. But more importantly, it
must help those most in need, those already most cheated by
the society, the elderly, the black, the Indian, the Spanish
American, the poor, the young, those outside "The Establishment. "

To make the change the public library must rid itself
of its cool concentration on things, on I-it relationships in
the words of Martin Buber, and must think about developing
some greater sense of people, some I-Thou relationships.
Librarians must decide to begin to build their libraries as
information and life-education centers for all. [15] They will
have to decide, to choose to undertake the job, for only they
can make effective library innovations. [16] They will have to
focus the library on humanity. The National Commission on
Libraries and Information Science will not. They will have
to make the library what Illich calls a place for reference
service directories and the storing of learning objects, they
will have to bring people together and give them the stuff to
learn, they will have to make the library the information
center for all ages and with all resources. Only they, the
individual public librarians, in regional, district, local or
mobile libraries, can finally determine, however much or
little they be aided by the community, what variety of services will achieve the purpose of serving people. A librarian
hardly needs to limit the public library institution for want
of alternatives, given the many suggestions made in recent
years. Whatever techniques, devices, and services the librarians choose, however, Illich implies they have the choice
of only a single role. If a librarian be a person of good

conscience then he or she must choose the role of <u>ombuds-</u>
<u>man</u> between people and the source of the means of <u>learn-</u>
<u>ing.</u> 17

    The librarian in a public institution must choose, be-
cause, as Illich implies and Buckminster Fuller states, human beings for tens of thousands of years have complained
about a host of social evils. Now men and women of good
will who are aware of the whole panorama of these ills, who
are aware of how very long they have been with us, know
that for the first time the major powers at least have the
wealth and technological know-how to do something about
many of these evils. Those of good will must choose to
actively compel the major governmental and industrial
powers, and must actively help those powers to use their
wealth and know-how to begin to ameliorate the evils of the
human conditions. Or else they must allow the major
powers to misuse their wealth and know-how, they must admit their good will is nothing more than a hollow show, and
they must accept themselves as moral cowards. There is
no middle ground. There is no reason to delay decision,
there is every reason to make one. Which way will the
public librarian go? Let me suggest that Illich offers some
persuasive reasoning for choosing the humane course.

Notes

1. Woolf, Robert P., <u>The Ideal of the University.</u> Boston:
    Beacon Press, 1969. An excellent reflection on the
    function of the university, by a Columbia University
    philosophy professor.

2. Illich, Ivan, <u>Deschooling Society</u>. New York: Harper
    and Row, 1971.

3. Illich, Ivan, "The Alternative to Schooling," <u>Saturday</u>
    <u>Review</u>, 54:44-48 and 59-60, 19 June 1971.

4. Schrag, Peter, "Ivan Illich: The Christian as Rebel,"
    <u>Saturday Review</u>, 54:14-19, 19 June 1971.

5. Schrag, <u>op. cit.</u>, p. 18.

6. Holt, John, "The Little Red Prison," <u>Harper's</u>, 244:
    80-82, June 1972.

Communication and Education   361

7. Illich, Ivan, "Education without School: How It Can Be Done," The New York Review of Books, 15:24-31, 7 January 1971.

8. Ibid., p. 29.

9. Bundy, Mary Lee, "Metropolitan Public Library Use," Wilson Library Bulletin, 41:950-961, May 1967.

10. Edwards, Margaret A., "The Urban Library and the Adolescent," in The Public Library in the Urban Setting. Leon Carnovsky, ed. London and Chicago: University of Chicago Press, 1968, p. 70-77.

11. Bundy, Mary Lee, "Urban Information and Public Libraries: A Design for Service," Library Journal 97:161-169, 15 January 1972.

12. Monat, William R., "The Community Library: Its Search for a Vital Purpose," ALA Bulletin, 61: 1301-1310, December 1967.

13. Holt, op. cit., p. 81.

14. Berelson, Bernard, "The Myth of Library Impartiality: An Interpretation for Democracy," Wilson Library Bulletin, 13:87-90, October 1938.

15. Campbell, H. C., "Effects of Metropolitanism on the Public Library," in Leon Carnovsky, ed., The Public Library in the Urban Setting. Chicago and London: University of Chicago Press, 1968, p. 30-40.

16. Monat, op. cit., p. 1309.

17. Braverman, Miriam, "In Touch: Connecting the Library's Resources to the Ghetto," Wilson Library Bulletin, 43:854-857, May 1969.

Part IV

THE SOCIAL PREROGATIVE

SOCIAL RESPONSIBILITY AND LIBRARIES*

Arthur Curley

INTRODUCTION

Like so many other concepts which frustrate our
yearnings for simplicity, "Social Responsibility and Libraries" is a complex topic with at least two major facets. First,
of course, there is the slippery matter of what the term "social responsibility" really means--if anything--and what implications it contains for the policies and practices of libraries. But, second, there is the fascinating subject of the
library world's reaction to the concept, apart from definition,
since it entered the annals of library thought and debate during the 1960's. In fact, it may be suggested that a dialectical gavotte has gone on between the two facets: introduction
of the term ... initial reactions based on varying definitions ... attempts at definition ... reactions based on varying interpretations ... reactions to the reactions ... drawing
of party lines ... multiple definitions of the concept to justify personal viewpoints ... reactions to the entire concept
based on only one of its many definitions ... continuous evolution of concept and reactions as the term "social responsibility" is flung back and forth between groups, which sometimes are fighting over what the term means or should mean
and sometimes are fighting over deeper social and political
differences to which the term has come to have a symbolic
relationship. Some approve or oppose the concept, others
simply approve or oppose those who approve or oppose.

*Reprinted by permission of the author and publisher from
Advances in Librarianship, Vol. 4, 1974, pp. 77-101. Copyright 1974, Academic Press, Inc.

DEFINITIONS

Definition seems, at first, a simple task. The
American Library Association's Committee on Organization
suggested, in 1968, that "social responsibilities can be defined as the relationships that librarians and libraries have
to nonlibrary problems that relate to the social welfare of
our society" (American Library Association, 1970d, p. 29).
Two difficulties are immediately apparent here. First, this
is not a definition of social responsibility, but simply a
statement of relationship; a precise definition of the social
responsibilities of libraries and librarians would have to
spell out the nature of that relationship, not merely offer
the truism that it exists. The second difficulty here is centered in the term "nonlibrary." It has been the contention
of many proponents of social responsibility that the social
issues to which they want librarians to address themselves
are library issues.

The Subcommittee on Social Responsibilities of the
Activities Committee on New Directions for ALA (ACONDA)
noted that the social concerns of librarians ranged from library service to the disadvantaged to international relations,
and concluded in its January 1970 report that "whatever is
meant by Social Responsibility, it was clearly a primary
concern" (American Library Association, 1970d, p. 29).

The ACONDA subcommittee identified "two conflicting
definitions" of social responsibility held by members of the
American Library Association. "The first, " said the subcommittee, "is traditional, conservative and variously
phrased: 'The function of a library is to have factual material on both sides of the question. The library is a reservoir for information, and our business is to conserve it
and wait till our users require its contents. The library is
a source of ideas, not a promoter of them. A library's social responsibility is to answer the information needs of its
users and to be responsible to those needs is a librarian's
foremost duty, and, therefore his chief social responsibility'. " The second definition, according to the subcommittee, "is considered radical, new, activist" (American Library Association, 1970d, p. 29). But the subcommittee then
goes on to suggest that this second definition can best be
summed up by the statement of the Committee on Organization, which is cited above but which bears repeating: "Social
Responsibilities can be defined as the relationships that librarians and libraries have to nonlibrary problems that re-

late to the social welfare of our society" (American Library
Association, 1970d, p. 29). The subcommittee was prepared
to gloss over the vagueness of this definition, presumably
since its members (George Alfred, A. P. Marshall, and
Shirley Olofson) were clear in their own minds as to just
what the nature of that relationship should be, and urged that
ALA "embrace this latter definition and carry programs forward to support it." "We believe that debate is no longer
necessary. The time has come for action," they added
(American Library Association, 1970d, p. 29). Well, if so,
the imperative fell largely on deaf ears--for the debate had
hardly begun.

But should this surprise us? It is, after all, not
really just the nature of social responsibility that has been
at the heart of debate but the very nature of libraries themselves. The argument is not over the relationship of libraries to nonlibrary problems, but over a definition of the
library's role in society that is broad enough in scope to encompass concern with a far greater variety of social, political, and economic factors than has traditionally found a
hallowed place on the milestones of library literature. This
may seem like semantic hair-splitting, but semantic confusion has added countless hours to the debate on this subject.
If one accepts the assumption that social responsibility refers to nonlibrary problems, then one has already placed
serious obstacles in the path toward a socially responsible
definition of the role of libraries. The definition put forth
by the Committee on Organization may seem "radical, new,
activist" to some, depending on their interpretation of the
nature of that relationship (I doubt that the Committee ever
intended it as such); but vagueness of the concept has at
times contributed to a mistaken notion by others that anything
which is radical, anything which is new, or anything which
is activist--is, ipso facto, "social responsibility." The
waters surrounding this concept have been further muddied
by a perverse failure to differentiate between the social responsibilities of a library, those of a librarian, and those of
a library association. It is important to distinguish between
social responsibility and the social responsibility movement,
but at the same time to appreciate the cause and effect relationship between the two. In the late 1960's, there developed in the American library world a flying phalanx of
youth, youth cultists, aging radicals dormant since the thirties, large numbers of camp followers, and a handful of
genuine idealists--all rallying around the cry "social responsibility." Few took the trouble to define what the term

really meant, and this may even be fortunate, for its very
vagueness enabled it to serve as an umbrella for a multi-
plicity of important causes. Library service to the disadvantaged, minorities recruitment, moral stands on social and
political issues, cooperation with other social agencies, re-
ordering of priorities, meaningful defense of intellectual freedom and its practitioners, spring-cleaning for many a cob-
web-infested library, the bum's rush for limitations on
access to libraries--each cause derived energy and support
from participation in the movement and each in turn contributed further to the momentum. Many achievements were
real and will have a lasting impact on how we define the
purposes of libraries. But what held the movement together
was not blind acceptance of some dogmatic definition of social responsibility; it was rather a shared sense of idealism,
derived largely from factors outside the library world, and
the common wish to translate ideals into realities. In his
novel Chimera, John Barth (1972, p. 56) suggests in the
Scheherazade sequence that "the key to the treasure, is the
treasure. " Idealism was the key to the social responsibility
movement. The idealism that characterized the search for
a definition is of far greater value to the progressive evolution of librarianship than any finite definition could possibly
be. If we seldom agree on a single definition of the role of
libraries, how can we expect to agree on a single definition
of a concept which goes to the very heart of that role? In
fact, it has been the claim of many "social responsibility"
apologists that our definitions of the library's role have been
too static, that responding to changing social needs is the
very essence of social responsibility. The responsive and
responsible library is itself an evolving concept, embracing
many abstract principles and values, and "social responsibility" is one of those evolving abstractions.

ROOTS

Tradition

       The term "social responsibility" makes its official
debut as a heading (or rather, subheading: Librarians--So-
cial Responsibilities) in the index, Library Literature, in
1968. "Libraries and Social and Economic Problems" began
to appear there in 1964. And while the triumphal entrance
of these terms certainly does signify the emergence of a new
social concern on the part of librarians (or at least that
segment of our profession with pretensions of literacy), it

would be absurd to suggest that immaculate conception has
occurred. A variety of factors, peculiar to the 1960's, both
within and without the library field, contributed to this
parentage, but there are other seeds of earlier origin. Few
students have survived stints at library school without passing through some course such as "The Library as a Social
Institution. " Admittedly, the social philosophy of an Andrew
Carnegie would receive a reception somewhat less than enthusiastic from the so-called "Young Turks" of the social responsibility movement, but it can hardly be claimed that libraries in America were oblivous to any social role until it
turned up on their doorsteps in the mid-1960's. There may
have been suffocatingly patronizing and chauvinistic attitudes
behind many of the "upward mobility" pronouncements on the
role of libraries in nineteenth- and early twentieth-century
America, but do we not sense similar attitudes behind the
"services to the disadvantaged" efforts so central to the "social responsibility" concept of the 1960's? The "people's
university" is a descriptor no longer in heavy circulation,
but the social attitudes it represented are not really all that
different from those which prompted the "libraries to the
people" slogans of the recent past, only of a different age,
but closely related to progressive social philosophy of that
age. And when it comes to "reaching out, " it is doubtful
that many librarians of today have surpassed the efforts of
Joseph L. Wheeler and Margaret Edwards, who brought the
Enoch Pratt Library out onto sidewalks and street corners
all over Baltimore nearly fifty years ago--and without a federal grant, to boot (Coplan and Castagna, 1965, pp. 135-162;
Dennis, 1964). Their ideals, and those of others who
shared their outlook, have exerted a profound influence on
generations of libraries and librarians, and it is highly
questionable whether the library world would have been even
as receptive as it was (pathetically inadequate though many
of us consider that response to be) to the social challenges
of the sixties, were it not for the roots put down by such
socially responsible predecessors. It is a tragic irony of
the public library movement in America that our origins and
history are so steeped in noble ideals, yet the policies and
practices of our institutions are so often drab, repressive,
trivial--and unrelated to those ideals. But, then, the nation's "glorious experiment, " of which our libraries are off-
shoots, has also picked up considerable tarnish since its
idealistic beginnings.

Intellectual Freedom

        The traditional concern of librarians with the prin-
ciple of intellectual freedom also served to pave the way for
the social responsibilities movement of the sixties. For a
start, it represents at least one area in which librarians
have never claimed to be "neutral"--that blissful state, the
potential loss of which has time and time again been suggested as the inevitable and disasterous consequence of librarians' saying "boo" about racial injustice, military mania,
and other such national pastimes, which, in the opinions of
some librarians, cannot be ignored by a socially responsible
profession. Many librarians, who looked initially with dis-
favor upon the idea of the library profession's taking stands
on political and social issues, were forced to admit, when
remembering the consequences for intellectual freedom and
libraries during the McCarthy era, that the actions of our
government and the sociopolitical climate in our country can
have major effects upon the functioning of libraries and upon
the fundamental principles for which they stand. The opening wedge, here, was significant--as was the timing. Growing public opposition during the mid-1960's to the escalating
military action in Southeast Asia drove successive administrations in Washington toward greater governmental secrecy,
suppression or harassment of dissent, and efforts to manage the news. The seriousness of this threat to freedom of
opinion and expression became such that librarians could no
longer remain silent. And the inescapable realization that
the country's desperate military involvement had led to this
climate of intolerance and paranoia provided a bridge which
led to the further realization by many librarians that the war
itself was, indeed, an issue for librarians--and, if the war,
then possibly other social issues as well. To the extent to
which the social responsibility debate has really been a battle
between idealists and pragmatists, progressives and conservatives, again the precedent of the profession's concern with
intellectual freedom helped prepare the way. A debate of
long standing has centered around interpretations and rewordings of the Library Bill of Rights (American Library
Association, 1970a, p. 63), the role of the American Library
Association in defending the principles of intellectual freedom
as well as those librarians who are attacked for doing so,
and the appropriateness of loyalty oaths and other such "nonlibrary" issues for the attention of the profession. Efforts
during the sixties by advocates of social responsibility to
establish intellectual freedom as the first priority of the
American Library Association were greeted warmly by li-

brarians who had struggled for years to translate the profession's pious statements on the subject into meaningful realities. (The ALA's Office on Intellectual Freedom was first proposed forty years before its eventual creation.)

Civil Rights

The early 1960's were a period of radical change in our national character, a new decade of optimism and excitement ushered in by the inauguration of President John Fitzgerald Kennedy, a period of determined attack on long-neglected social ills with widespread expectation of success: and, most significantly, the period in which that extraordinary movement, which so recently had seemed just a few isolated instances of southern Blacks' refusing to sit in the back of the bus, developed a furious momentum and exploded on the national scene. The impact of Martin Luther King, Jr., and the Civil Rights Movement propelled the country into a frenzy of social responsibility and social protest that seemed headed toward virtual revolution. Even librarians were unmoved. A serious case could be made for the proposition that without the impetus of the civil rights movement there might never have been a student rebellion, a Ralph Nader, an ecological consciousness-raising, conceivably not even an antiwar movement (at least not one of the proportions actually attained), and certainly no social responsibility movement in the library world.

Interestingly, the centrality of intellectual freedom seems to have played some role even in the response of the library profession in the matter of civil rights. As in other areas, the attitude of the American Library Association was similar to that which has brought so much abuse of late on the head of traditional liberalism: commendable principles, but infinite patience. Just as "access" has been a key term in matters of intellectual freedom, so it was in matters of racial equality. Lip service had long been paid to the "without regard to race, religion, or national origin" shibboleths. But mounting pressure for more forthright attacks on racial discrimination led to the commissioning by ALA's Library Administration Division of the seminal "Access to Libraries" study (International Research Associates, 1963), in response to recommendations made at the 1961 ALA Annual Conference in Cleveland. It was expected, of course, that the survey results would administer yet another tongue-lashing to all those bigoted Southerners, but the report was to con-

front librarians with a finding that was soon to stick in the
throats of many northern Americans: social prejudice, particularly of a de facto nature, is not a Southern monopoly.
First aired (in the form of unfortunately incomplete "high-
lights") at the 1963 Chicago Conference (Access to Public Libraries Study, 1963; American Library Association, 1963a,
b), the survey results, compiled by International Research
Associates (1963), appeared to document discrimination in
branch location and quality in several northern cities.   Intense abuse was heaped on the report by those whose toes
were being stepped on (American Library Association, 1964b),
and, in hallowed ALA tradition, the report was subjected to
restudies and analyses by committees for the next four years.
What seemed like an attempted whitewash at one stage was
rejected by angry members, led on by Verner Clapp (Moon,
1966, pp. 3617-3619).   A reshuffled committee, under the
chairmanship of Keith Doms, finally presented at the 1968
Conference an impeccably fair and balanced appraisal, finding some fault in the research methods but also substantiat-
ing many of the findings (American Library Association,
1968).   By 1968, of course, revelations of de facto discrimination had lost some of their shock value, but the Access
study and the emotions it aroused helped prod the social consciousness of the Association.

The "Statement on Individual Membership, Chapter
Status, and Institutional Membership" (American Library
Association, 1962), which was passed at the 1962 Conference
in Miami Beach, set the stage for a most influential development.   What came to be known as the "Miami Beach" statement, specifically denied chapter status in the American Library Association to state associations which discriminated
on racial grounds in membership requirements.   The result
was the withdrawal from ALA by several Southern state
chapters.   The nondiscrimination requirement was extended
to "any library or other organization" at the 1965 Conference
(American Library Association, 1965), under pressure from
Eli Oboler, an early and outspoken antiestablishmentarian
and champion of civil rights.

One of the decisive thrusts in the social responsibility
movement (then still an embryo) occurred as a delayed-re-
action result of the Miami Beach statement at the 1964 ALA
Conference in St. Louis.   It was the week in which the Civil
Rights Act of 1964 was signed into law.   And as the week
drew to a close with the droning recitation of committee reports at the traditionally dull Friday morning membership

session (there was only one membership meeting at conferences in those days), there suddenly appeared at a micro-
phone an articulate and determined Black librarian from
Savannah, E. J. Josey, to protest the participation by officers
and staff of ALA in conferences of state associations that
were barred from chapter status and whose meetings Mr.
Josey himself and other Black librarians were not allowed to
attend.   From that moment on, ALA membership meetings
would never be the same again.   The auditorium came to life.
Long lines formed at microphones.   Debate was intense and
protracted, but kept on course by an exceptional presiding
officer, President Frederick Wagman, who would five years
later become the first chairman of ACONDA (the Committee
on New Directions).   In what has since emerged as a powerful weapon of conservative forces in ALA, opponents of the
Josey motion sought not to defeat it but to refer it to committee so as to safeguard the Association from "precipitous
action. "   Finally, the delaying tactic was defeated and a
tightened motion was produced, moved by Mr. Josey and
seconded by Eric Moon (in whose writings as Editor of Library Journal, 1959-1968, can be found many of the earliest
and most persuasive calls for social responsibility).   The
motion that "all ALA officers and ALA staff members should
refrain from attending, in their official capacity or at the
expense of ALA, the meetings of any state associations which
are unable to meet fully the requirements of chapter status
in ALA" was adopted overwhelmingly (American Library Association 1964b).   An important symbolic victory for social
responsiblity had been won, and from Kiel Auditorium there
emerged an aroused body of librarians determined to increase
the voice of membership in ALA and to push the Association
in more socially responsible directions.

The War on Poverty

While idealism was a driving force of no small consequence in bringing about an important shift in the service
patterns of American libraries during the sixties, there was
another factor of possibly greater influence: money.   Efforts
to "reach out" to nonlibrary users can be found in a samp-
ling of virtually any period in American library history. The
early example of Joseph L. Wheeler has already been mentioned.   Coplan and Castagna's The Library Reaches Out
(1965) provides numerous other examples.   But, somehow,
these commendable efforts usually seemed to be unalterably
tied to traditional patterns of service and to be relying pri-

marily on evangelism for the cause of reading. Two instances of a different approach achieved lonely prominence in
the early sixties: New Haven's "Community Center" approach,
pioneered by Bloss (1964), which broke down traditional distinctions between the role of branch libraries and that of
other recreational or social community agencies; and Brooklyn's plan to appoint "community coordinators, " to serve as
liaison with ghetto-neighborhoods, library staff, whose chief
responsibility would be to become a part of the community
and to relate to its people (Moon, 1964). But even this
imaginative program struggled along for several years with
only one coordinator (Hardy Franklin), and when others were
added with the help of an LSCA (Library Services and Construction Act) grant, the continuance of the program seemed
annually in jeopardy with neither guarantee from the federal
government of funding renewal nor willingness of the city to
accept the cost of "reaching out" as a municipal responsibility. But a "war on poverty" was being launched by Great
Society architects in Washington. While most public libraries continued to serve the same middle-class patrons with
whom they had always felt comfortable, federal money was
flowing at torrential rates into new agencies that were spring-
ing up all around to administer community action programs,
model cities programs, job corps, and economic opportunity
programs. It began to occur to librarians of conscience
that those ghetto residents at whom such programs were
aimed were also entitled to library service. It occurred to
others that there just might be money in the idea, but federal
funds seemed available only to projects sponsored by a complex variety of community agencies--and such cooperative
political ventures were for the most part alien to the operating styles of American librarians. The breakthrough came
in 1965, when a spokesman for the Office of Economic Opportunity (OEO), speaking at the ALA Conference in Detroit,
suggested that OEO was now prepared to fund directly projects planned by libraries to reach ghetto residents, but that
they were interested primarily in innovative demonstration
projects, using new methods, new kinds of staff, and new
types of service (Berry, 1965).   (The New Haven experiment
was cited as a favorable example.) Overnight, seemingly,
librarians discovered "the disadvantaged. " It would be an
injustice to suggest that the promise of money was alone responsible for the explosive rate at which "service to the disadvantaged" programs sprang up in the late sixties. But it
certainly did help.

So central to the popularly held concept of social re-

sponsibility did this aspect of service become that ACONDA's
subcommittee on Social Responsibility was led to complain:
"As recently as 1968, a list of articles on social responsibility in ALA publications reflected this overriding concern
with library service to the disadvantaged as the primary definition of social responsibility. In a list of over fifty articles
fully 80% concerned themselves with library service to the
disadvantaged.... Library service to the disadvantaged is
definitely one of the major social responsibilities that face libraries and librarians at this time, and ALA will have to
commit itself to this fact and work to help its members solve
this problem.... What is now considered controversial is
the demand that ALA demonstrate a sense of responsibility
on many other issues" (American Library Association,
1970d, p. 30). One of ACONDA's recommendations called
for the establishment of an Office of Social Responsibility at
ALA headquarters (American Library Association, 1970b, pp.
9-10). The thinking behind this proposal was that the library
profession (and ALA in particular) has been slow to adapt to
changing social needs and that an Office, such as the one
proposed, could be concerned with continuing research into
the potential relationships of libraries to changing conditions
and issues in our society. It was an effort to devise a
mechanism to speed up the response time of the profession
to unpredictable social issues of the future. But when the
proposal finally reached the floor of the 1970 ALA Conference
in Detroit, the council and membership promptly proceeded
to change the title of the Office from "Social Responsibility"
to "Library Service to the Disadvantaged" (Berry, 1970, p.
2617). The profession's confusion as to just what "social
responsibility" is has served as a dragging anchor on the
ability of librarians to respond to the radical social changes
of the sixties.

Persistent doubts about the sincerity of librarians'
concern for "the disadvantaged" are difficult to dispel. The
very choice of term suggests a lack of the basic human empathy for which social responsibilitarians have called. The
1970 report of ACONDA's Social Responsibilities subcommittee
is again appropriate: "A startling occasion when librarians
finally woke up to their true social responsibility, was, unfortunately, at the prodding of another arm of government.
The Federal government's War on Poverty captured the imagination of the nation and woke us all up to our responsibility.
Like other institutions, libraries followed this lead and began
to think of the poor and the disadvantaged and manifested
(with the aid of Federal money) a concern for the disadvant-

aged and poor around them. Programs were instituted,
routines changed, people hired, a new look given to many library programs. This was, clearly, a great social responsibility, and many libraries rose to the occasion (although they
relied almost solely on federal funds to do this). Here was
a case of an institution recognizing an obligation, often two
generations behind the presentation of the original debt, but
recognizing and assuming responsibility nonetheless. The library suddenly discovered these people (mostly Black) whom
they were to serve. In many cases they discovered that they
were surrounded by these people, and had ignored them for
years and, in turn, had been ignored, primarily because they
had clung to the traditional reservoir theory of social responsibility, and sat back complacently and expected the
people to come to them.... The bulk of library programs
geared to library service to the disadvantaged were federally
financed. This source of money is slowly drying up. When
it is cut off, will we allow the programs to die, and once
again ignore the masses of disadvantaged? It would seem so.
The communities served have still not reached a state of
political effectiveness where they can demand proper, self-
tailored library services and be sure of getting [what they
ask for]. The libraries must rethink and reallocate their
traditional sources of income to continue to support these
programs" (American Library Association, 1970d, pp. 29-30).

The Youth Movement and the War

        The 1950's, the placid Eisenhower years, were a time
of somnolence on the American campus. A silent generation
of students poured its energies into dating, football games,
and the minimum of study, bluff, and ghost-written term
papers needed to carry off the diploma that would ensure the
security of a junior executiveship in the temples of business.
One read with incomprehension of students in Caracas or La
Paz mounting rebellious protests over social or political
issues. That could certainly never happen here.

        The Civil Rights movement changed all that, too. Or,
at least it began the process of change to which the war in
Southeast Asia would later add an explosive catalyst. Youth
is a time of maximum susceptibility to idealism. In fact,
the sternest test for idealism is the passing of youth. Exposure to the intellectual stimulation of the university atmosphere, at a time in life at which one does not yet feel
a rigid sense of vested interest in "the way things are now,"

can create a strong potential for receptivity to an articulate
call for change or social justice.   The moral imperatives of
the Civil Rights movement and the stirring eloquence of Martin Luther King, Jr., drew thousands of students to the freedom rides, protest marches, and voter registration drives in
the South.   (Idealism apart, who else but students can take
a summer off or a year's leave without serious financial
loss?)   Even students who stuck to the campus found it
harder and harder to suppress the suspicion that all was not
right in America.   The writings of Thoreau and Gandhi
gained in campus popularity.   Social consciousness was on
an upswing, and liberal white America was developing a guilt
complex as the Civil Rights movement spread northward. For
a time, the sense of hope and apparent prospects of measur-
able social change prevailed.   Much of that was shattered by
the death of Dr. King.   The lid was off.   No successor
possessed the stature to hold in check the mounting impatience of increasingly militant young Blacks for redress, now,
of three hundred years of injustice.   A sense of impatience
was spreading to white youths as well.   Cracks appeared in
the facade of America's patient liberalism.   The war, of
course, completed the process.   Military conflict means
something quite different to young people of draft age than it
does to anyone else.   From 1965 on, opposition accelerated
among all age groups to a war that was becoming more and
more clearly a governmental blunder, an imperialistic and
even racially motivated atrocity, a drain on the financial and
moral resources of the country at a time when it had just
barely launched what once promised to be the greatest attack
on poverty and inequality in the nation's (or any nation's) history, and an affront to the entire structure of humanistic
values by which we had thought we lived.   It is hardly surprising that the vanguard of the antiwar movement was to be
found on America's campuses or that this shared concern
served to bind the growing youth movement into a force of
near-revolutionary potential.

        Someone had to be blamed for everything that had gone
wrong with America.   And to the student generation, it was
pretty clearly the fault of the people who run America: everybody over thirty, the Establishment.   Many adults, of course,
do not feel part of the Establishment, and for a time the
youth movement had considerable sympathy and outright support from people over thirty, who had to agree that the
country certainly did seem to be lurching toward disaster.
Since their generation lacked any easy solutions perhaps these
kids and their revolutionary values really were right.

A new generation of young librarians, who had been
in college or even just in library school during the sixties,
imported this revolutionary zeal into the library field and
quickly moved to the nerve center of the new social responsibility movement to demand radical changes in library service. The clear proof of their emergence was seen by anyone
who attended the 1969 ALA Conference in Atlantic City. The
young librarians possessed dynamism and idealism, which
few older members of the profession could match. As they
demanded, and sometimes got, concessions from librarianship's "establishment" for which older liberals had long
pleaded in vain, many a senior professional was compelled
to fall in line (sometimes enthusiastically, sometimes grudg-
ingly) behind their leadership: not leadership of the profession, that is--such vested interest is not so readily sur-
rendered--but leadership of the progressive movement for
change whose ideals had come to be labeled "social responsibility. "

THE SOCIAL RESPONSIBILITIES ROUND TABLE

Establishment

The year 1968 was a momentous and turbulent one in
the United States, and few librarians attending the ALA Conference in Kansas City, during June, could doubt that this
was so. The tensions of an American presidential election
year had been painfully heightened by the shocking assassi-
nations of Martin Luther King, Jr. , and Robert Kennedy, the
intensity of the antiwar movement, which had virtually driven
President Johnson from office, and forebodings of what was
shortly to take place on the streets of Chicago during the
Democratic National Convention. Virtual revolution was in
the wind, and even librarians felt compelled to abandon
"business as usual" and confront the havoc all about them.

Dorothy Bendix and Kenneth Duchac had some months
earlier conceived the idea of a mechanism within the American Library Association that could serve as a forum for librarians concerned with the heightening pressures of social
issues. They secured petition signatures and forwarded to
ALA's Committee on Organization (COO) a formal request
for establishment of a Round Table on Social Responsibilities.
The Committee, in keeping with tradition, calmly promised
to set in motion (slow motion, that is) the rusty gears designed to cope with demands for something new (Kansas City

Conference, 1968, pp. 830-831). But this was not the year
in which to counsel patience. Mr. Duchac (1968) took his
appeal directly to the membership, and for all practical purposes his eloquent presentation gave birth right then and
there to the instrument that was to become the principal vehicle of the social responsibility movement. No article on
this subject could fail to quote at some length from that
speech. "We are concerned, " said Mr. Duchac,

> that the ALA, in its routine functioning in the
> many layers of its structure, all too infrequently
> addresses its talents and manpower to the major
> issues which affect our society, our government,
> and the world of 1968. Of course, much of the
> Association activity must always be concerned with
> nuts and bolts.... There are notable activities in
> the Association which do attack the library's role
> in meeting critical social problems, largely activi-
> ties carried on by a small number of committees
> in the areas of poverty and the constitutional
> guarantee of free speech.... Despite these worthy
> activities, inquiries, and studies, it is our judg-
> ment that they are not enough expression of con-
> cern in this critical time--in this year in which
> two commanding national figures have been assas-
> sinated in our increasingly violent country;--in this
> year in which the old politics refuses to hear the
> party's members and in which the political power
> structure is not responsive to the overwhelming
> evidence of social decay and incipient revolution;--
> in this year in which an American military adven-
> ture, which has already cost us the lives of more
> than 25, 000 young men, which has bludgeoned the
> economy and our senses of international responsi-
> bility and morality, has pursued an undeclared war
> which has perhaps irreconcilably divided our
> people;--in this year in which prestigious institu-
> tions of higher learning have faced the unbridled
> hostilities of students, faculty, and administration
> as a result of a breakdown of communication over
> substantive issues;--in this year in which looting
> and burning of inner cities may be a prelude to a
> black and white civil war.
>
> One need not have the wisdom of Solomon to know
> that the events of this year, unprecedented in our
> history, are indices of a force of change which is

accelerating at such a colossal rate and with such
a burning intensity that we as a people and a nation
are in a condition where intransigence is replacing
flexibility, and in which extremes of action--of an-
archy or fascism--are possible, even probable, for
the first time in over 100 years.

It was the request of our petition that ALA provide
an outlet for expression of libraries' and librarians' concerns on these issues--race, violence,
war and peace, inequality of justice and opportun-
ity--by creating a Round Table on the Social Responsibilities of Libraries, whose purpose would
be to provide a forum where responsible membership discussion can take place, to examine current
library efforts to face issues, and to propose action
programs to the Association.

By the action of COO a decision on establishment
of the Round Table is effectively delayed for six
months, maybe a year. These issues cannot wait
that long to surface in a bold and visible way in
the activities of the Association.... We hope that
the membership concurs in our judgment that a
condition of urgency exists in this regard.

The membership did agree, overwhelmingly. Council
was told to demand an answer from COO before the end of
the conference week (Kansas City Conference, 1968, p. 831),
and the Round Table proceeded to meet, in confident anticipation of eventual official status, with Kenneth Duchac as interim president (Moon, 1968, p. 2800). (One of the most
effective speakers at that first meeting was a young Black
librarian of impressive intelligence and foresight: Robert
Wedgeworth, who became Executive Director of the American
Library Association in 1972.)

The Social Responsibilities Round Table had been
founded by librarians of some standing in the profession,
moderate liberals for the most part, many of whom had
stood up with E. J. Josey at that decisive St. Louis Conference four years earlier, and some of whom had been exert-
ing pressure on the conscience of the profession since much
earlier than that. But a cadre of younger activists would
soon seize the helm. A loosely structured meeting of the
Round Table was held at the Drexel Institute, Philadelphia,
in September of 1968, to lay plans for the future. But, as

many of those present were becoming immersed in calm dis-
quisitions on the definition of social responsibility, others insisted "there has been enough talk, it's time for action"
(Schuman, 1969). Unsure of exactly what kind of action to
take, the acquiescent gathering invited a group of New York
City librarians present to form a pilot regional group. They
did so, organizing rapidly in a geographical area of so many
librarians, meeting frequently in casual Greenwich Village
restaurants or each other's apartments, and soon became
deeply involved in producing bibliographies, fact sheets, and
position papers for public consumption on the racially sensi-
tive school decentralization controversy then raging in New
York. By the time of the 1969 ALA Midwinter meeting in
Washington, a loose alliance was already forming between
members of the New York group and action-oriented, predominantly young librarians from other metropolitan areas
(Philadelphia, Pittsburgh, Washington-Baltimore). The location of that year's ALA midwinter sessions contributed a
heavy representation of East Coast librarians, among whose
younger elements there already existed close ties from recent association at library school. Strategy sessions ran almost continuously, and the sense of commitment among these
atypical conference attendees (for those days, that is) so impressed many of the original SRRT leaders that they agreed
among themselves to take a back seat and let the leadership
be assumed by the younger activists. (In effect, the latter
were already exercising the only leadership evident.) De-
monstrating from the start that SRRT (which was finally given
official status by unanimous action of the ALA Council that
week; American Library Association, 1969c, p. 6) was not
destined to become just one more dull library group, members shouted down formal structural proposals, preferring to
let people volunteer for jobs--by which process an organizing
committee emerged with Bill DeJohn as its chairman. Another step had been taken toward the generational confronta-
tion that would take place that summer at the Atlantic City
conference.

Congress for Change

      Although the new leaders of SRRT were unquestionably
young, they were nearly all practicing librarians, and the
median age in the full body of SRRT members was well above
that age of such mystical significance that year: thirty. But
an even younger movement, which would exert a decisive influence on SRRT, was beginning to coalesce. Organized by

James Welbourne and Andrew Armitage, young library school
faculty members, the Congress for Change was a call to dis-
affected library school students across the country to come
together as a driving wedge to force radical changes in library school curriculum. "Libraries to the people" was
their unifying slogan. Far more militant in style and forceful in demands than most of the emerging regional SRRT
groups, the Congress moved front and center in the social
responsibility movement. Threatening an all-out assault on
ALA, and a boycott if change did not take place, the Congress met in Washington for three days (and nights) before
the ALA conference (Congress of Change, 1969), "rapping"
around the clock, grinding out manifestos, and generating a
momentum of idealistic fervor, which swept into Atlantic City
on Sunday, June 22, 1969, the opening day of the eighty-
eighth annual conference of the American Library Association.

Atlantic City

        Pressing social issues may arouse the idealistic seg-
ment of our profession, but association politics provided the
initial bond which fused a mass movement on the eve of the
Atlantic City Conference. Nervous about the increasing demands by membership (since the St. Louis Conference) for a
major voice in determining ALA policy and well aware of the
constitutional provision permitting membership to overturn
actions of the Council, the Executive Board and the conservative Constitution and By-Laws committee had come up with
a proposal, to put a ninety-day limit on this power (American Library Association, 1969a, p. 140). (Ninety days is a
hopelessly inadequate time in which to organize such a move.)
However, the "Ninety-days amendment" would have to be
passed by membership. This attempt to stifle opposition
aroused the irritation of even moderate members, pushing
them toward accommodation with the younger activists, whose
claims that the "establishment" could not be trusted seemed
borne out by this latest action. The number of "No on 90"
buttons, which began to appear on conferees' lapels, gave
evidence that an effectively organized lobbying effort had been
carried out by SRRT leaders and that the governing element
of ALA was about to be handed an embarrassing defeat. In
the face of this, the Executive Board withdrew the amendment (American Library Association, 1969b, pp. 65-66) and
SRRT forces had won their first battle without a struggle.

        Since the Congress for Change had no official status

in ALA, it had no convenient platform from which to launch
its proposals. SRRT officers solved this problem with
characteristic contempt for red tape by adopting the resolutions of the Congress in toto and, as an ALA Round Table,
laid plans to present them to membership (American Library
Association, 1969d, pp. 3-4).

      That membership meeting was to turn into one of the
most traumatic marathons our staid association has witnessed. What had once been a brief formality at the end of
each conference to rubberstamp bylaws rewordings over-
spilled its prealloted time at this conference by some ten
hours. Hotly debated resolutions included proposals for reform of library school curricula, new ALA election procedures, platform statements by candidates for office, completely open meetings, imposition of sanctions against libraries that violate the Library Bill of Rights, roll call votes by
Council, aggressive recruitment of minorities, boycotting
Chicago (site of the 1968 Democratic Convention), defense
funds and other support for defenders of intellectual freedom,
backing for community control, and opposition to the anti-
ballistic missile program and to the war in Vietnam (American Library Association, 1969b).

      The social responsibility movement had accelerated,
seemingly overnight, from quiet pressures for gradual reform to a strident demand for virtual revolution. The impatience of the SRRT forces had been clearly signified by
the title and contents of their membership program, "The
failure of libraries: A call to action" (American Library
Association, 1969b, pp. 66-68). The conservative opposition,
whose unease was already evidenced by the number of security guards in attendance, dug in its heels. While many
a middle-aged radical and young reactionary were in evidence, battle lines did separate largely according to age
group. And being novices to parliamentary procedures, the
young reformers frequently found themselves maneuvered into
battles over referral to committee, semantic amendments to
amendments, motions to table (and even adjourn), and a
series of other filibusters. So incensed were many older
members by the seemingly disrespectful demeanor of the
"young rebels"--their contempt for traditional values and
authority, their long hair and short skirts, their uninhibited
lifestyles, their disdain for the wisdom of their elders--that
they opposed their very presence at microphones to interrupt the "business" of the association by the insertion of
"issues" (Berry, 1969, pp. 2731-2732).

Of course, the majority of members, steeped in the
profession's liberal traditions, were prepared to acknowledge
the right of the young activists to have their say. Many
moderates did show signs of dismay that so little gratitude
was exchanged for the granting of this privilege. Others,
while not quite prepared to open the floodgates to precipitous
action, did seem to sense that ALA and the profession itself
just might be the primary beneficiaries of this injection of
new life: this forced reassessment of the purposes of libraries and the priorities of ALA, this demand for a renewed
commitment to ideals.

NEW DIRECTIONS

ACONDA and Post-ACONDA

The response of the American Library Association to
these demands for change was drawn from the traditions of
organizational survival and adaptation: creation of a committee. For the fifth time in its near-century long history,
ALA authorized the establishment of a high-level "activities"
committee to take a look at the big picture and make far-
reaching recommendations. A unique feature was built into
this body by the membership assembled at Atlantic City, reflecting a general recognition of generational conflict. The
Activities Committee on New Directions for ALA (ACONDA)
was to be made up of "six old and six young" members, the
younger ones to be nominated by the Social Responsibilities
Round Table and the Junior Members Round Table (American
Library Association, 1969b, p. 72). (The age factor was
never defined and was quickly forgotten; fortunately, since
two of SRRT's three representatives were "over thirty. ")
To some of the activists, ACONDA was a shabby ploy to co-
opt the social responsibilities movement, to others it seemed
a potential vehicle for change.

This Committee on New Directions was charged as
follows: "To recognize the changes in the interests of ALA
members and provide leadership and activities relevant to
those interests. To reinterpret and restate the philosophy
of ALA in order to provide a meaningful foundation to the
organization--a foundation which is capable of supporting a
structure and program which reflects the beliefs and priorities of the profession. To determine priorities for action
which reflect the desires and needs of the members of ALA
and to reexamine the organizational structure of ALA and

all its committees, divisions, and round tables with the object of eliminating those units of the organization which are superfluous or irrelevant" (American Library Association, 1970b, p. 1; 1970c, p. 7).

Chaired first by Frederick Wagman, and later by Katherine Laich, ACONDA seemed broadly representative of the profession. The fact that this was probably illusory, and that progressive elements dominated the committee, is suggested by the extraordinary fact that the seemingly diffuse group was sufficiently convinced of the possibility of change to produce a report of some substance within six months' time (American Library Association, 1970c). The rest of the Association was not so ready to be pushed into action, however. In fact, after the committee had held extensive open hearings on its first report (American Library Association, 1970c) at the 1970 ALA midwinter conference in Los Angeles and proceeded to submit a final report (American Library Association, 1970b) at the annual conference in Detroit that summer--as it was specifically instructed to do by membership--it was confronted at the first session of that conference by a movement to remove its report from the agenda and to defer any possible action on it for at least another year. Although the report survived the agenda battle, debate throughout the week on "whether to act" exceeded consideration of the report's substance, and no action of any consequence was taken until the Dallas Conference of 1971 (American Library Association, 1971).

By 1970, the country had already begun to show clear-cut signs of exasperation with proponents of radical change. Finally having to accept the notion that something is basically wrong with the country, the "Middle-Americans" and the self-styled silent majority and the hardhats found it a short jump to the conclusion that what is wrong with America is those who keep saying that something is wrong. So, just as the social revolution of the sixties had spurred on the social responsibility movement within the library field, so the decisive swing of the national pendulum to the right at the start of the seventies produced a parallel backlash among librarians. To the dismay of social responsibilitarians, our profession does seem doomed to follow, rather than lead, the national mood. The conservative opposition's strategy of seeking delay, rather than outright defeat, seems in retrospect a clever tactic, since an idea whose time has come may soon find that the time has passed--and with it any chance for meaningful change.

ACONDA had little difficulty in gaining support for its
list of "new priorities": Social responsibilities; Manpower;
Intellectual freedom; Legislation; Planning, research, and
development; and Democratization and reorganization of the
Association (American Library Association, 1970b, pp. 1-4).
Adoption of principles is one thing, action programs to support them something else. By 1970 and 1971, ACONDA had
become for many a symbol of demands for change in an age
that apparently wants a respite from change. And SRRT had
become, in many eyes, a front for the counterculture. But,
despite delaying tactics, many ACONDA proposals had gained
sufficient momentum to squeak through (American Library
Association, 1971, p. 76). ALA did finally acknowledge that
taking stands on social issues is consistent with its purposes, support for recruitment and intellectual freedom and
services to the unserved have increased, and with the election of an entirely new governing body of the Association in
1972 the stage has been set for a new phase in the movement for social responsibility.

And Now ...

As suggested at the outset, the term "social responsibility" has represented both a concept and a movement. As a movement of mass appeal, it is a thing of the
past. At the very moment when the profession showed signs
of shedding old skins--at that extraordinary conference in
Atlantic City--the movement was already beginning to weaken
at the seams. The very vagueness of the term "social responsibility, " which had enabled it to serve as an umbrella
for so many loosely related causes, was seized upon by
opponents. Efforts to focus the profession's attention on social issues were attacked as threats to the neutrality of li-
braries--when recognition of the need for institutions to remain neutral was precisely the motivation of many who
sought expression through their professional Association,
which is under no such compulsion to remain impartial.
And, as vague generalities evolved into more rigid positions,
the one movement became several. Despair at the failure
of their colleagues to respond to the urgency of the social
crises of the sixties caused many an activist to abandon the
profession entirely. In fact, a moment's pause to ponder
the rapid deceleration from that idealistic pinnacle of the
Atlantic City conference prompts the shocking suggestion that
Allen Ginsberg's (1965, p. 1) drastic epitaph for an earlier
age, which begins "I saw the best minds of my generation

destroyed, " is not without applicability to our own generation
of the sixties. But, primarily, as the country backed away
from its earlier commitment to social change, so did the library world.

The total membership of the library profession is
broadly representative of the makeup of the rest of the
country, and its receptivity to change ebbs and flows, reflecting the general temper of the times. The librarians'
social responsibility movement of the sixties clearly paralleled a similar movement in the nation at large. Numerous
other professions--architecture, medicine, law, social work,
even notable segments of the business community--had similar experiences in this same period. The SRRT forces have
frequently been labeled "new left. " But Joseph W. Kraus
(1972), in a recent article on "The Progressive Librarians'
Council, " spawned by the volatile years 1939-1944, demonstrates that much that was considered "left" in those years
has become "center" or even "right of center" today. So
will many tenets of the social responsibility movement if its
advocates do not lose sight of their goals during this period
of contraction.

The concept of social responsibility was not invented
in the 1960's. It simply came of age then. Idealistic librarians have long sought to propel their profession toward
people-oriented service, toward a courageous commitment to
intellectual freedom that goes well beyond lip service to
principle, toward tearing down regulatory and psychological
barriers to access, toward attitudes of true human empathy
and respect for the needs of all segments of society (which
is the real basis of "reaching out"), toward a recognition of
the interrelatedness of libraries with a broad spectrum of
social forces and the need for librarians to address themselves to issues which relate to the social and humanistic
values which libraries claim to serve--if that claim is to
have substance. The social responsibility movement of the
1960's provided a major thrust in that direction. SRRT continues to occupy a vanguard position as a conscience of the
profession. The tangible achievements may seem small in
the light of earlier hopes. But the relative inertia of libraries can sometimes work toward surprising ends; for,
once started toward "new directions, " they resist pressures
for change of direction. Libraries today have come to accept responsibilities that were foreign to them a decade ago;
the number of students emerging from library school today
with stimulated senses of social responsibility has increased

appreciably; the infusion of idealism gained from the social
responsibility movement will provide momentum for some
time to come. And the concept of social responsibility will
remain alive in the consciences of those librarians who refuse to confuse the routine functions of libraries with their
social purposes, the housekeeping business of the American
Library Association with the ideals to which it should commit its energies. Can libraries change the world? Hardly.
At least, not alone. But in contrast to the often cynical and
materialistic values of our age they do stand as tangible symbols of a belief in the nobility of human aspirations and the
possibility of social progress. Mass movements are fickle.
These ideals--for which "social responsibility" came to be a
slogan of our times--are constant.

References

The Access to Public Libraries Study (1963). American Li-
    brary Association Bulletin 57, 742-745.

American Library Association (1962). Statement on individual
    memberships, chapter status, and institutional mem-
    bership. American Library Association Bulletin 56,
    637.

American Library Association (1963a). Membership Meeting.
    American Library Association Proceedings 1963, 41-
    50.

American Library Association. Library Administration Di-
    vision (1963b). Membership Meeting. American Li-
    brary Association Proceedings 1963, 88-90.

American Library Association (1964a). Membership Meeting.
    American Library Association Proceedings 1964, 22-
    32.

American Library Association. Library Administration Di-
    vision (1964b). Report on the Study of Access to
    Public Libraries. American Library Association Bul-
    letin 58, 299-304.

American Library Association (1965). Membership Meeting.
    American Library Association Proceedings 1965, 14-
    18.

American Library Association. Council. Special Council Committee on Freedom of Access to Libraries (1968). Final Report. American Library Association Bulletin 62, 883-887.

American Library Association (1969a). ALA Committee reports. Constitution and Bylaws. American Library Association Proceedings 1969, 140-144.

American Library Association (1969b). Annual Conference, Atlantic City. American Library Association Proceedings 1969, 45-85. (Also published in American Library Association Bulletin 63, 915-964.)

American Library Association (1969c). Midwinter Meeting. American Library Association Proceedings 1969, 5-25.

American Library Association. Social Responsibility Round Table (1969d). "Business Meeting [Minutes] ALA Conference, Atlantic City, New Jersey, June 26, 1969." (Mimeograph copy.)

American Library Association (1970a). "Policies, Procedures, and Position Statements," 2nd ed. American Library Association, Chicago, Illinois.

American Library Association. Activities Committee for New Directions for ALA (1970b). "Final Report." American Library Association, Chicago, Illinois.

American Library Association. Activities Committee on New Directions for ALA (1970c). "Interim Report" [January]. American Library Association, Chicago, Ill.

American Library Association. Activities Committee on New Directions for ALA. Subcommittee on Social Responsibilities (1970d). Report, January 1970. In: American Library Association. Activities Committee on New Directions for ALA. "Final Report," pp. 29-31. American Library Association, Chicago, Illinois. [Also in the Committees Interim Report: American Library Association (1970a).]

American Library Association (1971). Annual Conference, Dallas. American Library Association Proceedings 1971, 49-100. (Also published in American Libraries 2, 804-835.)

Barth, J. (1972). Chimera. Random House, New York.

Berry, J. (1965). Poverty Programs. Library Journal 90,
    3196-3205.

Berry, J. (1969). The new constituency. Library Journal
    94, 2725-2739.

Berry, J. (1970). ALA was the subject. Library Journal
    95, 2613-2622.

Bloss, M. (1964). Responding to manifest needs. Library
    Journal 89, 3252-3254.

Congress for Change (1969). American Library Association
    Proceedings 1969, 58-62. (Also published in Amer-
    ican Library Association Bulletin 63, 931-936.)

Coplan, K. and Castagna, E. (1965). The Library Reaches
    Out. Oceana Publications, Dobbs Ferry, New York.

Dennis, D. D. (1964). Joseph L. Wheeler. Library Journal
    89, 2941-2943.

Duchac, K. F. (1968). A plea for social responsibility.
    Library Journal 93, 2798-2799.

Ginsberg, A. (1956). Howl, and other poems. City Lights
    Pocket Bookshop, San Francisco, California.

International Research Associates (1963). Access to Public
    Libraries. American Library Association, Chicago
    Illinois.

Kansas City Conference; growing pains and generation gaps
    (1968). American Library Association Bulletin 62,
    817-864.

Kraus, J. W. (1972). Progressive Librarians' Council.
    Library Journal 97, 2351-2354.

Moon, E. (1964). A day in Bedford Stuyvesant. Library
    Journal 89, 3689-3693.

Moon, E. (1966). Echoes from Miami Beach. Library
    Journal 91, 3615-3624.

Moon, E. (1968). Business--not quite as usual. Library
    Journal 93, 2797-2809.

Schuman, P. (1969). Social responsibility--a progress re-
    port. Library Journal 94, 1950-1952.

General References

Bendix, D. (1970). When is a social issue a library issue?
    Wilson Library Bulletin 45, 43-61.

Brown, E. (1971). Library Service to the Disadvantaged.
    Scarecrow Press, Metuchen, New Jersey.

Christian Science Monitor. (1968). Libraries That Care.
    Christian Science Publishing Society, Boston, Massa-
    chusetts. (Reprint.)

Curley, A. (1970). ALA identity crisis. Library Journal
    95, 2089-2090.

Curley, A. (1972). The forest and the trees. Library
    Journal 97, 990.

DeJohn, W. (1971). Social responsibilities: what it's all
    about. American Libraries 2, 300-302.

Forsman, C. (1970). Up against the stacks. Synergy 9,
    No. 28, 6-14.

McDonald, J. (1970). How social responsibility fits the
    game of business. Fortune 82, (Dec.) 104-106, 131-
    133.

Moon, E. (1964). Two stars from Georgia. Library
    Journal 89, 2919-2921.

SOME INSIGHTS INTO ACCESS:
THE PROBLEM OF PRISON LIBRARIES*

Agnes M. Griffen

The doors define the limits within which we must work. Prison. The doors. Stand and wait. Clicks and crashings of steel. Hard metal against hard metal. Waiting. Standing. Monotony, with a rhythm. I am in jail. I am in prison.

Other times I have been in better places. There were no walls. Or there were only fences. But still the doors. Always somewhere the locked, barred, steel-enforced doors. To keep me in. To keep the world out. To separate. To "rehabilitate," "correct," "educate"--to shut me out. A better place--but still a prison.

So all I have is me. I am alone. My world is gone, fallen apart, my children scattered, my loving stopped, my world cut off. And always there are the doors. Everything here shuts me out. All I have is me, and I hate it. I hate. Period.

SIX AXIOMS

In order to talk about access, we must understand about the doors, where they are, who controls their opening and closing, and how we, as librarians, can open them. But, in order to understand about the doors, we must talk about politics. I use the term as meaning the methods or tactics involved in managing a state or government, or, in a broader sense, how a person functions as a "political

*Reprinted by permission of the author from Proceedings of the University of California Extension, Santa Cruz, Workshop on Library and Information Services for Prison Populations, March 2-3, 1973.

animal" opening or closing doors within an organization. For
if a librarian who dares set foot inside a prison would prefer survival to being eaten alive, it is absolutely essential
that she understand: a prison librarian must be a political
animal. She must have the appropriate survival skills, as
well as the ability to pacify and conquer all the wild beasts,
both staff and resident variety. She must be able to control that hating/loving beast that she carries inside herself.
For we must also understand that "the defects of the correctional system" upon which we hope the library service
we provide will have some impact, "reflects our own collective defects, or the failures of our society, " and "changing
the correctional system must begin with understanding and
changing ourselves as individuals. "

        Let me begin by talking about institutions. What is
said about prisons and jails can also be applied to other
types of institutions: to mental hospitals, "schools" for the
retarded, even to the public library as an organization.
There are certain basic facts about the institution called the
prison. I hope these statements which I throw out to you
as axioms or hypotheses of a theory of institutional library
service, will be helpful. If not, tear them up and write
your own.

        (Please excuse my mixed metaphors and incomplete
analogies. I have been visiting prisons and talking to people
in prisons. If my language takes on a wild, undisciplined
jungle quality, well, it is appropriate!)

Axiom One

        Each institution is an island. Isolated from the main
stream of society, it has developed its own peculiar species
of flora and fauna, its own alternative life style, its own
rules, its own rhythms, its own power structure, and its
own political process. The librarian's first task is to understand all these factors. Only then can she even begin to
think of developing a library program adapted to the realities as well as the information needs of the people within
that institution.

Axiom Two

        The librarian's role in the institutional setting is to

explore, define, and <u>negotiate</u> the specific functions of library service appropriate to that institution, and this must
be done with all groups of users or potential users within
the institution.   These groups include <u>all</u> the institutionalized: the prisoners, the custodial staff, the treatment staff,
and the adminstration.   The librarian who neglects or does
not take into account any one of these power groups during
the task of designing a library service delivery system for
the institution, jeopardizes the entire program.   This does
not mean that librarians cannot set priorities of service.
All it means is that any one of these groups can subvert,
obstruct, or kill <u>any</u> library program through direct or indirect means, including the most deadly method--apathy.

<u>Axiom Three</u>

        The only <u>effective</u> method of gaining support for li-
brary services from <u>all</u> the power groups is to give good
library service to all of them.   Good service will be that
which provides the information that will meet the actual needs
of the people no matter which group they belong to.   The
skill which is specifically required is the ability to demonstrate the usefulness of information resources to the individual, whether his function is to learn a trade, to develop
himself personally, to guard the hallway, to write up the
case, to defend the budget to the next layer of the bureaucracy, or just to do time.   If you can do this <u>one time</u> for
at least a few individuals within each power group, you will
be off to a good start.   If you are really smart, you will
make sure that you do this for the most <u>influential</u> individuals within each group.   Don't misunderstand me--I do not
mean that the librarian serves <u>only</u> these individuals at the
expense of all the rest.   I mean that she makes sure that
potential allies know through experience what the value of
the library is, in terms of meeting their own information
needs.   These allies will be helpful in support of any ongoing program.   For above all, in order to survive in the institutional setting, the librarian must have allies, yet she
must avoid being contaminated.   In order to make allies,
the librarian must overcome the negative or apathetic attitudes toward libraries that are common to the institutionalized, and the best way to do this is to provide a positive
experience.

Axiom Four

It takes a certain kind of person to explore and define functions appropriate to the islanded population, to negotiate alliances and agreements, to survive and then to achieve! An effective institutional librarian, i. e., one who does not get eaten alive, must have these characteristics:

a. She must be highly sophisticated (or at least naturally intuitive) about political processes, including organizational psychology and management.

b. Adaptive, or to put it negatively, manipulative, or have the ability to act as a catalyst or change agent without appearing to do so. That is why we need to recruit ex-cons.

c. More concerned with the goals of library service than with the means. That is, she must be able to sweep established librarianship-type rules and controls out the door. She must be able to fight the urge to control as a fetish common to the institutionalized. (This is a paradox, because it seems to negate everything I have said about the need to manipulate. Perhaps that skill must be reserved for the performance of administrative duties only.)

d. Open to new information that can change her mind, i. e., one who values reading, one who continually reexamines what is going on in the world. This is an absolute necessity for survival, for an institutional setting is full of insanity. She must keep in touch with reality.

e. Patient, with superb sense of timing, or the ability to wait out certain situations in which to make a move at the wrong time would be to destroy all the gains made so far. Don Horowitz, the Senior Assistant Attorney General for the State of Washington, put it this way, "A life style of justice ... in the correctional area requires one thing above all and that's endurance. Guts. Long-term guts." (A symposium on Prisons and Parole, published by Seattle Crime Prevention Advisory Commission, 1972).

Axiom Five

Any advance in institutional librarianship hinges on
the effectiveness of the person, not on the appropriateness
or nicety of the program alone. A librarian may have the
ability to write a neat proposal, to develop an understandable rationale, etc., but without a liking and concern for
people, a modicum of maturity, strong emotional security,
and highly developed communicative skills, she will never
achieve much, though she may survive.

Axiom Six

All of the foregoing may be seen as a description of
a microcosm of the world of library service delivery systems. These postulates may also be applied to any library.
While the closed institutional setting provides an exaggerated
situation (everything is more closely linked so everything
has a more immediate impact upon each interdependent factor), it could serve as a superb training ground for testing
and refining the kind of people that librarianship desperately
needs--people who know how to fight for the freedom to
read against all the subtle and not-so-subtle pressures now
threatening the right of the people to know. Where better
could we teach the realities of censorship, the necessity of
political involvement and action and compromise, the requirements of strategic and tactical planning, the methods
of developing services to meet human needs, than in the
prison library? And since it is unwise for anyone to remain
in an institutional setting for more than three years (at the
most, five) for the perils of institutionalization are real,
what better training position can we find within the field?
... And after all, is not the world itself a prison for too
many people?

LIBRARIANS AND THE FIRST AMENDMENT
AFTER NIXON*

Nat Hentoff

Although civil libertarians disagree on many issues--
I, for example, am known inside the ACLU as a chronic
dissenter from particular policies of that body--nearly all
would concur that until the Nixon Administration was diverted
by its own desperate struggle for survival, the Nixon years
have been characterized by the most systematic attempt by
government in American history to subvert the Bill of Rights,
certainly including the First Amendment.

By September, 1971, W. Bradford Wiley, speaking as
chairman of the Association of American Publishers, was
saying: "It is a critical fact that we are now faced with defending the First Amendment. Nothing like this has happened since the days of Joseph R. McCarthy."

Equal Time for Hitler?

For one of many illustrations, the Administration had
become the first in American history, in the Pentagon
Papers case, to try to exercise prior restraint on the press.
Starting in 1969, moreover, the then Vice President, Spiro
Agnew, had been zealously bastinadoeing segments of all
media--print, television, radio--as being unworthy of trust,
a view which, until Watergate, appeared to be enthusiastically supported by a sizable percentage of the citizenry at
large.

In corollary moves to ensure what Pres. Johnson
might have called "consensus" journalism, the Administra-

*Reprinted by permission of the author and publisher from
Wilson Library Bulletin, May 1974, pp. 742-747. Copyright 1974 by The H. W. Wilson Company.

tion most persistently attacked what it considered to be its
most effective critics. CBS News was a special target, and
in 1971, its head, Richard Salant, observed mordantly that,
in order to deal with diverse government complaints, "We
now have more lawyers than we have reporters. "

The climate was such during the end of Nixon's first
term that when I visited a public library in Philadelphia
where an exhibit had just been arranged concerning the Hol-
ocaust, the librarian responsible for what was indeed a
strikingly instructive panorama of books and photographs
told me indignantly that a city official had complained to her
superior that the exhibit was not "balanced. "

"My God, " she said, "am I really required to give
Hitler equal time ?"

Teeter-totter Reporting

"Balance" was an Administration shibboleth in those
years, an attitude that filtered down to local administrations
and private groups which insisted that while they certainly
were not in favor of censorship, they were dedicated to in-
suring that "balanced" views became the norm in newspapers, on television, in libraries, and wherever else ideas
were being expressed and exposed.

At a symposium on the conundrum of "balancing" during this period, Richard Salant speculated, rather wearily,
"Suppose the English governor had told Tom Paine that he
could go ahead and publish all he liked, but at the back of
his pamphlets he would have to allow the governor's assistant to guarantee that the pamphlet had given the other side.
That would have preserved Tom's right of free speech, but
far from being an implementation of the First Amendment,
it would have been just the opposite. You would have to
consider it a restriction upon speech if, in order to print a
broadside, Tom Paine had to present not only his views but
also those of someone arguing on the other side. "

Book publishers were also affected by the "chilling
effect" of the Nixon Administration. After Senator Mike
Gravel had inserted the Pentagon Papers into the record of
a meeting of a subcommittee he headed, a man I know was
asked by Gravel to see what publishing interest there might
be in what later came to be known as the Gravel edition of

those papers. Two large New York-based trade houses expressed initial interest, but upon reflection drew back. "Why go looking for trouble with the government?" an editor of one of the houses told me in explanation.

A university press was then approached and expressed keen interest, but its lawyers warned the editor-in-chief that the university, which depended on government contracts for much of its research funds, felt it would be wiser if its press arm dropped the project.

Government Harassment

Finally, Beacon Press, a publishing firm owned by the Unitarian Universalist Association, agreed to publish the Gravel edition of the Pentagon Papers. I will not recount all the details of the subsequent harassment to which Beacon Press was subjected, but it should be noted--even recent history having a tendency to blur as we are continually, multidimensionally bombarded with "new" news--that seven days after the October 22, 1971, publication date of the Gravel edition, FBI agents, acting on instructions of the Justice Department's Internal Security Division, went to the bank in which the Unitarian Universalist Association had its accounts, and took away with them all of the church's records--not only those of Beacon Press. Included were copies of each check written and each check deposited by the church group between June 1 and October 15, 1971.

Throughout the country, every member of the Unitarian Universalist Association who had sent a check to the church during those months had chilling reason to believe that he or she was now in the FBI's files. "This kind of treatment," said Robert Nelson West, chairman of the Association, "is a way of striking at a denomination with respect to its present and potential membership and with respect to the contributions on which a denomination depends for its very existence."

And contributions did go down for some time thereafter. Beacon Press itself, its resources decimated by legal fees and other costs of protecting its First Amendment rights against its government, had to cut down on the number of titles it published until just this year, by which time the firm had more or less recovered.

Library Rights Threatened

    Nor have libraries, in recent years, been immune to
pervasive assaults on the First Amendment which are more
ominous than even the wave of fear Joe McCarthy rode in
the 1950s. That saturnine senator, after all, was not acting
with the full powers of the executive branch of the government. For a time, he did indeed intimidate the executive
branch, but he was not able to command at will agents of
the FBI and of other government bureaus. In recent years,
it has been presidential power itself that many of those
choosing to exercise their First Amendment rights have had
to deal with.

    I am reasonably sure, for instance, that readers of
this journal recall that, as the Executive Board of the ALA
declared in July 1970, "the Internal Revenue Service of the
Treasury Department has requested access to the circulation
records of public libraries in Atlanta, Georgia, and Mil-
waukee, Wisconsin, for the purpose of determining the identity of persons reading matter pertaining to the construction
of explosive devices. "

    The Executive Board of the ALA went on to say that
"the efforts of the federal government to convert library
circulation records into 'suspect lists' constitute an uncon-
scionable and unconstitutional invasion of the right of privacy
of library patrons and, if permitted to continue, will do ir-
reparable damage to the educational and social value of the
libraries of this country. "

    Properly, constitutionally, the ALA advised its mem-
bers to resist this breach of confidentiality of its circulation
records.

    Then there was a series of incidents in which the
Government recalled certain of its publications from deposi-
tory libraries. The ostensible reasons were that a particular document had been released by "mistake" or that the
government agency involved was so constricted financially
that it couldn't afford to provide copies of certain documents
to depositories. Often no reason at all was given. Actually,
the operative reason for these arbitrary recalls of government documents very much appeared to be that a government
official had decided they were "controversial. "

    An especially vivid illustration of government intru-

sion into the professional--and constitutional--responsibilities
of librarians was the case of Zoia Horn, which has been
amply documented in previous issues of the Wilson Library
Bulletin. When she, then chief of public services at the library of Bucknell University, refused to testify at the Harrisburg "conspiracy" trial of Father Phil Berrigan and five
others, she was jailed. The Government, in preparing its
case against the defendants at that trial, had shown considerable interest in the books which informer Boyd Douglas
had borrowed from the library so that he could more effectively infiltrate anti-war groups at Bucknell.

Zoia Horn's statement at the time--one of the most
significant, I think, in the history of the chronic battle for
intellectual freedom in this country--is no less germane
now:

> I love and respect this country too much to see a
> farce made of the tenets on which it stands. To
> me it stands on freedom of thought; but govern-
> ment spying in homes, in libraries, and universi-
> ties inhibits and destroys this freedom....

But, as in many of its other "conspiracy" cases
which were manifestly contemptuous of First Amendment
rights of freedom of association and of speech, the Government lost the Harrisburg case. Furthermore, its attacks
on the press, on publishing houses, on diverse dissenters,
have diminished during the past year because of the devastating impact of Watergate and attendant revelations on the
government's own credibility. No other Administration in
American history has lost so much of the trust of its citizenry.

Nixon's Disquieting Supreme Court Legacy

Those of sanguine temperament might conclude, therefore, that just as the furiously damaging windstorms un-
leashed by Joe McCarthy eventually subsided, so now we are
again at the start of a relatively tranquil period during
which civil liberties, including those protected by the First
Amendment, are no longer much in danger.

The evidence to the contrary, unfortunately, leads
me to postpone any libations to a "new era" of the flowering
of American freedoms just in time for the Bicentennial cele-

bration.   Even if Nixon is impeached and convicted by the
Senate; or, failing that resolution of his disintegrating last
term, even if Nixon endures until 1976, too crippled by
Watergate to continue his subversion of the Bill of Rights,
the Nixon Administration has left a disquieting and active
legacy.

There are his four appointees to the Supreme Court
who, with Byron White and sometimes Potter Stewart as
swing votes, have placed William O. Douglas, the fiercest
defender of Americans on the Court, into the position of being an all too frequent dissenter to the Court's majority
opinions.

It is the Nixon Court, in Miller v. California and
Paris v. Slaton (1973), that has led us into a new thicket of
confusion and much potential censorship with regard to "obscenity. " Previously, a book, film, or any form of expression had to be utterly "without socially redeeming value" to
be held obscene.   In the 1973 case, the Court changed the
rules of that murky game by narrowing the operative definition of obscenity.   A work is protected by the First Amendment only if it has "serious literary, artistic, political or
scientific value. "

What does "serious" mean?   And to whom?   Compounding the confusion is the Court's holding that each "community" (the geographical area meant by "community" remains unclear) can define for itself which allegedly "obscene"
works are sufficiently "unserious" to be banned.   As each
State, encouraged by the Court, passes its own obscenity
laws--with counties, cities, and towns quite possibly also setting up their own codes--the consequences to "Freedom to
Read" outside and inside libraries are likely to be far from
salutary.

It is still William O. Douglas's opinion (Byrne v.
Karalexis, 396 U. S. 976, 1969) that "the First Amendment
bars all kinds of censorship.... To impose a regime of censors requires, in my view, a constitutional amendment. 'Obscenity' is no exception. "

It will be a long time, I am afraid, before Justice
Douglas's viewpoint on this issue prevails in this country.

Abridging the Right to Know

The Nixon Administration has also bequeathed us a
continuing inclination by government officials--more often
State and local these days than federal--to circumscribe the
press. When the Nixon Court held, in 1972, in the case of
Earl Caldwell (and other allied cases) that a journalist does
not have a clear First Amendment right to protect the confidentiality of his sources, the Court gave license to local
district attorneys and other officials to go after journalists
engaged in investigative reporting of government corruption,
among other areas of news that the public has "the right to
know. "

An investigative reporter who cannot guarantee confidentiality to his sources is severely hampered in both imple-
menting his First Amendment rights and the First Amendment rights of the citizenry to know what's going on. The
Reporters Committee for Freedom of the Press, on whose
steering committee I serve, is currently involved in nearly
thirty cases around the country in which a reporter has refused to give up his sources.

Nor have the pressures, greatly intensified by the
Nixon Administration, for "balance" in radio and television
disappeared. Recently, Dick Cavett was forced by ABC-TV
to postpone an already taped, and quite mild, discussion with
such radicals of the 1960s as Tom Hayden and Abbie Hoff-
man until he inserted the convictions of avowed conservatives
in the program.

NBC, meanwhile, is engaged in expensive litigation
with the FCC because that government agency has ordered
the network to "balance" its account of how badly many pension plans actually work out. In a footnote to its decision
against NBC, the FCC's staff, ironically, conceded that the
program at issue--a 1972 documentary, "Pensions: The
Broken Promise"--had opened up new investigative territory.

> For years prior to the broadcast of Pensions,
> [the footnote said], neither NBC nor the other net-
> works, to the best of our knowledge had telecast
> any program dealing extensively with private pen-
> sions. There was little discussion in any general
> circulation print media and no widely circulated
> books on the subject. In fact, there was no ap-
> parent public discussion, much less controversy,

apart from that of a relatively small number of
experts, businessmen and government officials who
take a professional interest in the subject. There
had been hearings in the last Congress on the subject, but NBC was breaking new ground journalis-
tically, on a subject about which the public, as
that time, had little knowledge.

Nonetheless, the FCC held that NBC had to give more
time to those who defend the virtues of private pension plans
as they now operate.

As NBC's lawyers have pointed out, if the FCC's decision is confirmed by the courts, television journalists will
be forced "to engage in a kind of thinking and practice which
has nothing to do with journalism. It would impose, as well,
a variety of other less obvious sanctions--[among them] the
inhibiting effect upon television journalists and producers of
being obliged to justify to their superiors and to the [Fed-
eral Communications] Commission the work they have done
.... The issue is not alone whether television journalism will
be too bland; it is whether it will be free enough not to be
bland. "

Enforced Fairness

At issue here is the Fairness Doctrine, a concept of
mandatory "balancing" of television content that has been
strengthened by the Nixon Court. Justice Douglas, who believes that television journalists should have the same full
First Amendment rights to which print reporters are entitled, has said of the Fairness Doctrine: "It put the head
of the camel inside the tent and enables administration after
administration to toy with TV or radio in order to serve its
sordid or its benevolent ends. "

Nonetheless, with Nixon having thoroughly politicized
the FCC and having appointed four justices of the Supreme
Court who support, in varying degrees, the concept of "balance" in television news, the Fairness Doctrine--with its
inhibiting effects on our most powerful means of communi-
cation--is likely to be with us for some time to come.

Not only networks are affected. Louis Seltzer, President of WCOJ, a 5,000-watt radio station in Chester, Pennsylvania, has pointed out that "as a practical matter, I

know that the Fairness Doctrine has served to muzzle this
station for 25 years.   An example: we aired only one or two
of a well-produced series put out by the Anti-Defamation
League of the B'nai B'rith on 'The Radical Right.'   Why?
Simply because airing these programs would open the floodgates to a paranoid response from the 'nut' groups....   True,
we could refuse to run the reply programs on the basis of
their patent untruth, but this would cost us a $10,000 lawsuit
up to the Supreme Court of the United States and even then
there would be a possibility of losing....   This station is
not small, but it is not that large.   We have neither the time
nor the money to devote to such Joan-of-Arcian causes. "

          I would point out to Mr. Seltzer that the First Amend-
ment is for "nut" groups too; but to require "balanced" time
for their views does indeed have a potential effect similar to
what would happen at publishing houses if each book released
advocating a particular viewpoint had to be "balanced" by a
book supporting a contrary view.

          Or, as Benjamin Franklin said when he was publishing
a newspaper, "My publication is not a stagecoach with seats
for everyone. "

An Ill Omen

          The fall of the Nixon Administration--or its existence
until 1976 in a state of near-paralysis--will also not automatically remove pressure for censorship of books, including the removal of books from libraries.   As any issue of
the Newsletter on Intellectual Freedom (a publication of the
ALA Intellectual Freedom Committee) demonstrates, attempts,
often successful, at "cleansing" libraries of "immoral" or
"un-American" books and magazines, continue no matter what
administration is in power.   The climate does worsen when a
particularly repressive administration is in office because the
signal thereby goes out from Washington to would-be censors
throughout the country that savaging the First Amendment is
being officially encouraged.   And that kind of stimulus to
excise books lasts for some time after such an anti-civil-
libertarian administration as that of Richard Nixon has lost
much of its own power to itself pursue its penchant for suppression.

          I don't have the space to cite even a cross-section of
current efforts at censorship, but a particularly ominous

portent has been reported in the July 1973 issue of the Newsletter on Intellectual Freedom:

> Parents of a Princeton City School District student,
> Joyce E. Carroll, brought suit in Common Pleas
> Court because of damages allegedly suffered when
> she read Trips: Rock Life in the Sixties, a book
> assigned by her eighth-grade music teacher. The
> parents contend that Trips exposed her to 'promis-
> cuous group sex practices, ' a side of modern life
> from which her parents tried to protect her, and
> that the book 'confused her and put her in the mid-
> dle of an antithesis between the values her par-
> ents had taught her and the school's apparent
> values. ' ... Included among the defendants are the
> district superintendent, the principal of Princeton
> Junior High School, the teacher who made the
> assignment, and the supervisor of the school li-
> brary where the girl obtained the book. Reported
> in Cincinnati Enquirer, March 21. (Emphasis
> added: N. H.)

Speaking Out

I do not intend, in this article, to advise librarians and other readers of this journal how best--through their
professional organizations and in other ways (such as through
working with ACLU affiliates)--to counter the continual thrust
of both public and private efforts to restrict the freedom to
read.   I do think, however, that there ought to be much
more continuous, specific discussion among librarians of the
most effective ways in which they can help protect our common First Amendment.   But as an outsider, I am not sufficiently informed as to how well or how poorly the ALA and
other cadres of librarians are meeting this persistent problem.   My sense of the dynamics of politics, however, indicates to me that librarians could make their First Amendment views much more strongly heard--not only among themselves but also to those who depend on libraries for free information and for freedom of information.

For instance--and I ask this out of not knowing
rather than rhetorically--how many librarians and representatives of librarians are in frequent contact with local, State
and federal legislators to press for laws which will help re-
generate the First Amendment (such as "shield" bills to

protect reporters)? And how active are librarians in trying
to reverse anti-libertarian legislation and administrative practices that have been successfully lobbied for by the censors
and putative censors who are always among us?

Finally, I also believe that more librarians ought to
question themselves to discover the extent to which they
agree, individually and organizationally, with Justice Douglas'
contention that "the First Amendment bars all kinds of censorship." (Emphasis added).

A Fig Leaf for Everyone

A couple of years ago, an old friend, Maurice Sendak,
telephoned me. He was in a quandary of indignation. A few
months before, In the Night Kitchen had been published. Sendak had expected some attempts to remove the book from libraries since the boy at the falling center of this sempiternal
Sendak fantasy is quite naked. This would not have been a
novel experience for Sendak. He'd been censored before.

What Sendak had not expected with regard to In the
Night Kitchen, however, was that some librarians had colored
in clothes for the boy-hero of the book before allowing the
work to be on the shelves. The furor over the book is well
documented in library literature. It was already in enough
trouble from non-librarians. Mothers asked, "If nudity is
acceptable in a kindergarten children's story, how can we
teach our children that Playboy ... is not acceptable?

I would presume that Renaissance paintings included in
art books used in the schools should, by that logic, immediately have fig leaves affixed to them.

First Amendment: No Exceptions

More recently, in the March 1974 issue of the Newsletter on Intellectual Freedom, I was again made aware that
some librarians are themselves deficient in their understanding of the First Amendment:

'A book in elementary school libraries in Cedar
Rapids Community Schools will be removed from
general circulation because it is 'a classical example of sexist literature limiting aspirations,'

according to Robert Foley, director of media and
materials. The offending book is I'm Glad I'm a
Boy, I'm Glad I'm a Girl. 'The decision to remove the book from general access was made by
the reconsideration committee of the Parent-Teacher
-Student Association, composed of four members of
PTSA, two teachers, one librarian, and three
senior high school students.' (Emphasis added).

The First Amendment, however, does not prevent
"abridging the freedom of speech, or of the press, " except
for sexism. It prevents, or at least is intended to prevent,
the prohibition of any point of view.

Until librarians really understand that, they will not
be able to fully understand the necessity for combating all
attempts to censor, whether by government or by private
forces.

My suggestion, however presumptuous, is that librarians' associations start scheduling sessions at their meetings
during which they will be able to ask themselves whether
they entirely subscribe to the First Amendment--or are only
part-time upholders of partial freedom of expression.

BLACK BOOK REVIEWING:
A CASE FOR LIBRARY ACTION*

Ann Allen Shockley

More books by and about blacks are being printed
than ever before in publishing history. An article, which
appeared in the June 1971 issue of Sepia magazine entitled
"The Black Book Boom, " estimated $60,000,000 as the cur-
rent retail value of black books being published. Needless
to say, it is now more. A modicum of these are distributed
by small, newly established black publishers. The effects of
this deluge of black materials on libraries and librarians are
both devastating and frustrating.

To attempt to purchase all books on black themes now
streaming off the presses, no matter how much material is
needed to fill in gaps and support Black Studies programs, is
virtually impossible. Limited budgets, the need to balance
the book collection, relevancy of the materials, and quality
are all factors that have to be taken into consideration.

The criterion for establishing a good basic black book
collection should be quality. The task of discarding quickie
books on blacks from the ones that promote honest scholarship and present meaningful literary insights into the black
experience is indeed an important one.

In order for librarians to be selective in buying books
by and about blacks, they should familiarize themselves with
the few available tools for selecting these materials. In applying professional knowledge to book selection, librarians
can either examine the book if a copy is available and time
permits, or read reviews about the book. For reviewing purposes, librarians can rely on the standard basic tools such
as Choice, Library Journal, American Libraries, Booklist,

*Reprinted by permission of the author and the American Li-
brary Association from College and Research Libraries, January 1974, pp. 16-20.

and other journals. It is tragic to note, however, that few
of these references give even a minimum amount of attention
to reviewing books by and about blacks.

A few noted and established black writers--James
Baldwin, Julius Lester, Ernest J. Gaines, John Edgar Wide-
man, John A. Williams, and Ronald Fair--are reviewed in
the white book media. These authors are published by major
white publishers who can and do exert influence on the book
reviewing hierarchy. Yet other black authors, who are writing on a comparable if not higher level, are not reviewed in
these journals.

The revolutionary novel by Sam Greenlee, The Spook
Who Sat by the Door, was a bestseller in London, and ended
up a bestseller when it finally appeared in this country. When
Greenlee was questioned about where it had been reviewed
during a lecture at Fisk University on April 22, 1971, he replied that only the Johnson City, Tennessee, Chronicle had
bothered to review it. Further search showed the book was
noted in Jet magazine, but not reviewed.

Books by black authors do not get the attention of the
reviewing channels for various reasons: 1) some reviewers
do not think the books are worthy of reviewing; 2) space limitations exist for reviews; 3) the books are judged of no interest to readers of the publication; 4) publishers do not
press for reviews; and 5) the books are not sent to be reviewed. The underlying reason, however, was aptly pointed
out by black librarian and publisher of Broadside Press,
Dudley Randall, who blames it on racism in the reviewing
media. In the much publicized and discussed article, "Why
Minority Publishing?" which appeared in the March 15, 1971,
issue of Publishers Weekly, he noted that books by black
Pulitzer-prize-winning Gwendolyn Brooks were widely reviewed
when published by Harper. But her recent book, Riot, published by Broadside Press, had been received with almost
total silence. Okechukwu Mezu, publisher of Black Academy
Press, in the same article agreed that his main problem in
the book reviewing media was its failure to review his books.

Although white publishers may retort that they too have
the same problem, it is not of the same magnitude. The
hard fact is that whites control reviewing services and publications. There is no doubt that these sources are powers
which repress and influence the dissemination of black reviewing information.

In the twilight of this gray picture tinged with racism, where can librarians turn to obtain reviews and announcements of books by and about blacks, both scholarly and popular? Publishers Weekly does not strain to announce titles by Broadside Press, Third World Press, Third Press, Drum and Spear, Afro-Am, and other minority publishers. Librarians should be able to find reviews in Book Review Digest. This widely-used compilation should seemingly review black titles that are under consideration for purchasing. But what does Book Review Digest index? It purports to index reviews of current fiction and nonfiction in selected periodicals. Unhappily, the Digest does not list one black periodical for indexing in its array of selected titles.

This raises questions. Who makes the selection of periodicals for reviewing? In the prefatory note, Book Review Digest states that it is done by subscribers' votes. Who are the subscribers? Don't the subscribers, certainly libraries, realize the importance of black periodicals and journals in this age?

To qualify for inclusion in Book Review Digest, a work of nonfiction must have received two or more reviews, and for fiction, four or more reviews in the selected journals. Thus, if only one white selected journal reviews one book of black fiction or nonfiction, that book will not qualify for inclusion. As black titles and books by black authors are not extensively reviewed in white reviewing publications, it is obvious that few will reach Book Review Digest.

The Book Review Index, first published by Gale during 1965-68, is a guide to current reviews of books. Four black publications are indexed. These are the Journal of Negro Education, Journal of Negro History, Negro Digest (now Black World), and the Negro History Bulletin. The Journal of Asian Studies is indexed but not the Journal of African Studies.

One can find review information and announcements on black materials primarily in black publications and services designed for disseminating this information. Unfortunately, many librarians have not resorted to using the sources: some lack knowledge about them; sometimes libraries do not subscribe to them; and a few are professionally indifferent and negligent.

One bibliographic service that lists and annotates books by and about blacks (current and reprints) is the Bibliographic

Survey: The Negro in Print, published in Washington, D. C.,
with Beatrice Murphy as managing editor. This service began in May 1965, and many libraries subscribe to it. The
service lists nonfiction, fiction, books for young readers,
periodicals, paperbacks, and reprints. The publishing policy
states: "Its purpose is to inform and let the reader form his
own opinion. "

As librarians are aware, in book selection a decision
for purchasing cannot be effectively made from a book annotation. The book might sound interesting and be needed for
the collection, but it might not meet the criteria for occupancy on a library shelf. There might be another work on
the same topic better written, more timely, and treated by a
more knowledgeable author. The Bibliographic Survey is valuable for book news, but not for reviews.

There currently is one pertinent index for locating reviews on books although slow in publication. The Index to
Selected Periodicals, published by G. K. Hall since 1950, indexes black periodicals and journals. There is a subject
listing in the Index under "Book Reviews. " The entries include the name of the author, title of the book, name and
date of the periodical in which the review appeared, and the
reviewer. With more and more black publications coming
into being, the publishers in the 1971 Annual Index to Periodical Articles by and about Negroes, published in 1973, have
broadened the scope to include "significant Black journals
which are either not indexed or incompletely indexed elsewhere. " Eight new titles have been added.

A new index, Black Information Index, was an out-
growth of the subcommittee on Negro Research Libraries, an
extension of the COASTI Task Group on Library Programs of
the Committee on Scientific and Technical Information, which
had its maiden printing in 1970. To date, four issues have
been published. Whether this index will remain in print is
questionable. The publication, now in limbo, scanned over
eighty newspapers and journals, major white ones included,
providing current information and news about black people.
Book reviews are one of the forty-one categories listed. Here
the entry is under the title of the book. The author is listed
next, with bibliographic information, the name of the reviewer, and location of the review.

The most current listing for black book reviews is the
Black Books Bulletin, which is published quarterly by the In-

stitute of Positive Education in Chicago, Illinois. The Black
Books Bulletin has an attractive format, and contains critical
reviews of books by and about black people on all subjects.
There is a list of current, annotated books, news from black
publishers, and reviews about children's books.

After locating reviews of these books, the kinds of
periodicals in which they appear and the reviewers must be
examined. Frequently, book reviews published in periodicals
other than professional library journals do not help librarians
with book selection. Some simply describe a book, others
are geared for a particular reader interest, and some are
intended to promote an author, or book sales.

When reading reviews about black titles in a black
publication, something should be known about the publication
itself. How is the periodical slanted toward black nationalism
or moderation; black middle-class orientation; scholarly or
popular?

Next, special attention should be given to the reviewers. Are most reviews of books by black authors favorable
because the reviewers are biased, realizing that black authors
have too long been ignored in publishing circles? Do they
feel obligated to help the brothers and sisters? Do the reviewers lean toward the left and totally disregard a good
scholarly work or excellent piece of literary writing because
they do not personally agree with the author's point of view?
Conversely, are the white reviewers of titles by black authors
racially influenced, too critical in comparison with other
works on the same subject by white authors and heedless of
the unique black experience in American life that has nurtured and limited the author's insight, ability, and experience?

There are black journals which publish excellent book
reviews by knowledgeable black as well as white scholars and
researchers in various academic fields. The reviews are
extensive, well-written, and many take the form of an essay.
The number of reviews vary each issue, possibly because of
space limitations.

The Journal of Negro History, issued quarterly by the
esteemed organization of the Association for the Study of
Afro-American Life and History, which has pioneered in the
publishing of black history since 1916, averages fifty book
reviews a year on historical and related topics. Its companion

publication, the Negro History Bulletin, geared for elementary
and secondary schools, as well as for universities and colleges, is published eight times a year.   Approximately two to
four reviews are published in each issue.

        Literary quarterlies of black academic institutions and
organizations present quality reviews.   The prestigious College Language Association journal reviews over sixteen publications a year.   Announcements are included of recent black
publishers' books, and of works by and about blacks. Phylon,
a publication of Atlanta University, reviews books under the
caption "Literature of Race and Culture." The number of
reviews has dwindled somewhat in the past year and vary
from one to two, and in a few instances, none.

        Freedomways, published by Freedomways Associates,
Inc., reviews approximately sixteen books a year.   The outstanding feature of this quarterly is its extensive, annotated
list of recent books in all subject areas.   This list sometimes
numbers over 150 titles per issue.   Full bibliographic information is given and additional titles on similar subjects or
themes are pointed out in the annotations.   These features
are of special interest to librarians.   The Black Scholar,
published monthly except for July and August by the Black
World Foundation, publishes one to two reviews per issue.

        The laudable little magazine, Black World, carries
about two to three reviews monthly.   Often, however, it does
not fully identify the reviewers.   The notes on books and
writers are valuable for information on black writers, publishing news, and literary perspectives.   The librarian seeking reviews of black titles should be able to distinguish a review from a mere description or blurb as those that appear
in the popular, slick Ebony and Essence, and news magazine,
Jet.

        The problem of finding good, reliable reviews about
books by and about blacks is important to librarians.   Presently, publishers are dashing off at an astronomical rate inferior works with black themes.   Many are slipshod, pseudo-
scholarly works published to cash in on the black bonanza by
instant black experts while the demand is heavy.

        In glancing through new titles, it is apparent that an-
thologies are now in vogue and leading the lists.   The rash
of anthologies which some editors have published are collections with almost repetitious titles, making it more confusing

to librarians. These are evidenced in such collections as:
A W. E. B. DuBois Reader, edited by Andrew G. Paschal, and
W. E. B. DuBois: A Reader, edited by Meyer Weinberg; Black
Drama: An Anthology edited by William Brasmer and Domi-
nick Consolo, and Black Drama Anthology, edited by Woodie
King; and The Black Soldier, edited by Jesse J. Johnson,
and The Black Soldier, edited by Jay David and Elaine Crane.

Collections of biographies are also repetitive in con-
tent. For example, both books, Negroes of Achievement in
Modern America by James J. Flynn, and Black Profiles,
edited by George R. Metcalf, have chapters on Roy Wilkins,
Thurgood Marshall, Martin Luther King, Jr., James Howard
Meredith, Medgar Wiley Evers, and Jackie Robinson.

Frequently, similar chapters excerpted from books are
used in different collections. In Melvin Drimmer's work with
the grossly misleading title, Black History: A Reappraisal
(which is a collection of articles rather than a firsthand appraisal), a chapter is included on "The Background of the Harlem Renaissance" which appeared in Robert A. Bone's classic
The Negro Novel in America. The same chapter is repeated
in Eric Foner's America's Black Past: A Reader in Afro-
American History. Other writers who have written on the
background of the Harlem Renaissance could certainly be included in collections; but they are ignored by slovenly editors
out to make a quickie publishing name by capitalizing on books
by and about blacks.

If librarians, both black and white, learn to be more
selective in purchasing titles by or about blacks and let the
publisher know their criteria, perhaps then publishers will
become more selective in printing works that librarians can
point to with professional pride as excellent sources for research or reader interest on blacks. In order to do this,
librarians must let the publishers know that they are aware
of the current mass publication of inferior works, repetitious
subject matter, and misleading titles. Publishers must be
made to realize that librarians are not going to rush blindly
to purchase any book with the word black in the title for
Black Studies programs and collections without any professional inquiry.

Black librarians, in particular, must be hypercritical
and more vocal in evaluating books on black themes and by
black authors. Even though a book is by a black author and
is about blacks, they must ask if it really gives true insight

into black life or black scholarship. These librarians, above all, should be thorns in the side of the white publishing establishment. They should work more closely with black publishers in selecting books relevant and true to the black experience. More black librarians should be invited to review books for white publications and also for black ones, particularly in the juvenile and young adult fields.

Now is the time for the library profession to pressure the book reviewing media to index black publications and to review more books by and about blacks. These should include those published by black publishers. Librarians must contribute to the free flow of black information and influence media in the book publishing establishment.

Today, the black man is being exploited in book publishing. The Indian appears to be next in line, and possibly later, the Chicanos, Puerto Ricans, and alas, even the Eskimos, and librarians will be continuously beleaguered with a flood of miscellaneous print.

Librarians, face the challenge and act! Soon we may be like the tired, old black farmer in the classic joke, who had labored so long and hard under the hot sun, that finally one day, he dropped his plow in the middle of the dusty field, looked up to the sky and said: "Oh, Lawd, ah'm so tired, ah think ah done been called to preach!"

THE MARGINAL MAN*

S. Simsova

When Lester Asheim during his travels experienced a "culture shock" and on coming home a "culture shock in reverse, "[1] he was for a brief period of time in the position of a "marginal man." His experience was a mild form of what to others can come as a severe stress, particularly if their condition of "marginality" is permanent. An overseas student with a rather traumatic past once admitted to me that she suffered from nightmares and was surprised when I could describe her nightmare to her almost picture by picture. It was my own nightmare and I could reassure her that with luck it will leave her when the process of acculturation has reached a certain stage. There is curious similarity in the reactions of migrants to their new environment no matter what geographical area they originally come from. [2] There are differences in the intensity of the experience due to the individual's psychological make up and to some external factors associated with the migration, both in the old and new country. A displaced person will suffer more stress than a voluntary migrant; a person whose socio-economic status is not affected by the migration will settle down more easily than one who has to take a job below his former status.

The term "marginal man" was invented by E. V. Stonequist[3] and used among others by R. E. Park who wrote an introduction to Stonequist's book. [4] According to Stonequist a marginal man is " ... one who is poised in psychological uncertainty between two (or more) social worlds: reflecting in his soul the discords and harmonies, repulsions and attractions of these worlds. "

Marginality can be brought about by other factors such as marriage or class mobility without involving migration.

---

*Reprinted by permission of the author and The Library Association from Journal of Librarianship, January 1974, pp. 46-53.

This paper, however, is going to be limited to the problems of marginality in immigrants.

The world population is not static and has never been. The history of individual countries could be written in terms of successive waves of migration. The Romans in Britain were marginal men and so were the Huguenots. Some migrations have an innovating function (colonizing), others a conserving function (flight), some are forced (refugees), others voluntary (brain drain). [5]

There is a variety of personal motivation on the part of the individual. Among the immigrants we can find the settler who decided to break with the past permanently, the colonist to whom the home values will always be superior, the political idealist for whom the new country will be just a platform from which to continue his work on the problems of the old country, and finally the opportunist. [6] The attraction of the new country may be seen in terms of security, economic conditions, political ideology, opportunities for individual development.

The condition of marginality is influenced by the individual's relationship to the country left behind as well as to the receiving country. From the viewpoint of the old country, the migrant can be a hero, a pioneer or a renegade. He may be expected to perform a service to his old country by bringing back goods (migrant workers) or knowledge (overseas students). The expectations of his old country about his return or non-return may conflict with his personal wishes. In some cases the returning native[7] is subjected to a further shock by feeling a stranger in his old country and this new experience of marginality accelerates his adjustment to his new country.

From the viewpoint of the new country, the immigrant may be welcome and invited (technical expert), merely tolerated, or sympathetically received (refugees, victims of disasters).

The marginal man who finds himself in the no-man's-land between two groups may find that the company of other marginal men suits him best. An ethnic group, composed of natives of the old country within the new country, serves as a transitional group for him in his process of acculturation.

Ethnic groups aim at institutional completeness: the

network of organizations and informal social relationships
which develops inside an ethnic group permits and encourages
its members to remain within it for all their primary relationships and some of their secondary relationships. [8]   In his
choice of the baker and the grocer, the builder and the den-
tist, the immigrant will show a preference for his own ethnic
group.

The degree of the institutional completeness of ethnic
groups is influenced by the differentiating social and cultural
attributes (e.g. language, religion), by the degree of mobility, and by the level of resources and skills among their
members. [9]   Immigrant press, schools, libraries aim at
strengthening the institutional completeness.

Taft sees the world as a pattern of cultures[10] and a
similar pattern of ethnic groups on a smaller scale can be
observed within the confines of one country.   "A culture is
valuable to its group because it embodies the way of life that
group supremely values.   It includes in the broadest sense
all the accomplishments which a group has thought worthy of
preservation, defence, and even propagation. "[11]

The personality of the individuals who compose the
group is influenced by the culture.   According to Park personality is the subjective aspect of culture. [12]   The relationship between personality and culture explains generalizations
that are made about the so-called national character.   The
attribute of nationality in the way a person perceives himself
is normally in the background.   In the marginal man, however, it becomes prominent. [13]

A marginal man is not marginal until he experiences
the conflict of the two cultures as his personal problem. This
is a shock to him and for a time he suffers from a double
consciousness.   He becomes estranged from both cultures and
frequently also from the transitional group (the company of
other marginal men).   Stonequist describes him as "dépaysé,
déclassé, déraciné. "[14]

This cultural conflict is bound to have an effect on the
personality of the individual.   Park lists among the likely
manifestations of the conflict " ... family disorganization,
delinquency and functional derangements of the psyche. "[15]

The individual's psychological reaction to marginality
does not always become pathological, though there is a higher

than average incidence of mental illness among migrants. Within the bounds of normality, the following broad trends can be observed: excessive self consciousness and race consciousness, feelings of inferiority, and hypersensitivity. Depending on personal make-up the marginal man will either take refuge in withdrawal or over-compensate by hyperactivity. Individuals who make their mark on the world are often marginal people.

Marginality brings also some desirable results such as greater insight, self-understanding, and creativity. [16] Because of his in-between situation, the marginal man may become an acute and able critic of the dominant group and its culture. [17]

The intensity of the marginal man's psychological reaction varies from individual to individual. Stonequist describes it as follows: " ... at a minimum it consists of an inner strain and malaise, a feeling of isolation or of not quite belonging ... at the other extreme the mental conflict becomes a disorganizing force. "

The degree of discomfort varies from simple insecurity, to stress and trauma. [18] A mild form of this phenomenon is home sickness. As Mezey says in his paper: "Homer's description of Ulysses weeping and rolling on the floor at the thought of home, and the psalmist's record of lamentations by the waters of Babylon, are the best-known early echoes of psychological symptoms during migration."[19] In its pathological form the stress is manifested as suspicion and paranoid trends, anxiety and depression, and somatic complaints.

The stress situation resolves itself eventually in acculturation defined by Taft as "the process through which immigrants and natives acquire common values. "[20] It is a two-way process which involves the individual and his ethnic group on the one hand and the receiving country on the other and, as at the heart of each culture is its value system, the value systems of both are modified in the process. [21]

When two cultures meet, various processes can result ranging from a negative reaction (conflict, expulsion), over a neutral conflict-preventing one (just letting alone, segregation) to various positive relationships (acculturation, accommodation, assimilation). The benefit of the relationship can be one-sided (exploitation) or both-sided (symbiosis). [22]

The culture of the majority group is not static. It enriches itself and undergoes a change with each individual who is successfully acculturated. The end product of the American "melting pot" theory is supposed to be a standard American, but even in the "melting pot" the brew varies from day to day according to the ingredients.

The policy of cultural pluralism which encourages the individual to find his identity through his ethnic group produces a healthier society than the policy of universalism. A universalistic society expects the immigrants to accept all the basic roles of the society in the political and occupational fields and to identify with its fundamental values. [23] Acculturation is then seen as a process not of acquiring common values but of accepting the native system of values.

The rate of adjustment according to Zubrzycki is affected both by the predisposition to change on the part of the immigrant group and by the attitude of the receiving community. [24] On the part of the immigrants the factors influencing the rate of adjustment are: the circumstances and motives of immigration, the extent to which they identify themselves with the cultural values and patterns of the receiving community, the institutional factors operating within the immigrant group, and the degree of economic and political security in the country of immigration. The attitude of the receiving community is influenced by the cultural affinity of the immigrant group, by factors of political and emotional nature, and by agencies such as the press, organizations, trade unions and government.

Libraries and Acculturation

One can include libraries among the agencies which exert influence in the process of acculturation. Libraries are important both for the strengthening of the institutional completeness of the minority group, mentioned earlier, and for helping with the process of acculturation. It is doubtful that both functions could be performed by the same library and so perhaps there is a need for immigrant libraries (such as the Polish Circulating Library) working side by side with public libraries.

For the individual the process of acculturation falls into two stages: [25] the initial period of subjective feeling of relief, lessening of tension, even exaltation. This is followed

shortly afterwards by a period of "psychological arrival" in
which difficulties of a practical nature have to be faced, new
customs to be learned. This is a difficult period and is frequently accompanied by somatic ailments. The initial exaltation is gone and often there is a lack of vertical adjustment.
The immigrant has to find his place somewhere between the
two extremes of exaggerated acceptance of the majority culture and a withdrawal into himself and his group. If he is
feared by the receiving group as a "stranger, " then the rate
of his adjustment is slowed down by external factors.

The succession of exultation and scepticism in the attitudes of migrants has been described in research literature
as a U curve or W curve. [26]

The acculturation of immigrants is a slow and painful
process which stretches over two or more generations. The
second generation in particular suffer from marginality, though
from a different form of it than their parents. They are natives of the country and are neither "dépaysé" nor "déclassé. "
Their own form of cultural conflict consists in a clash between a loyalty to their parents and the culture they represent and a loyalty to friends. The symptoms of the conflict
are the same as those of their parents: in cases of malad-
justment they suffer from delinquency and personality disorganization.

The experience of marginality is common to all immigrants. It would be interesting to speculate what effect it has
on their characteristics as readers. I do not think that we
can find a common pattern of reading needs for all immigrants
as attitudes to reading depend on the personal circumstances
of each individual. The problems of immigrants as readers
therefore range from illiteracy to the no less acute problems
of the immigrant intellectual.

From a subjective viewpoint immigrants tend to retain
the same attitude to reading as before migration: the illit-
erates and semi-literates tend to manage without and among
the educated the degrees of need for reading vary. In some
cases migration brings about an increased rate of reading:
the individual who solves his problems by withdrawal will read
more in his own language to reinforce his old cultural patterns. The hyperactive individual will read more in the new
language to be able to get on faster.

Motivation from outside will also influence the immi-

grants' reading. Society will encourage them to learn the
new language and, in case of illiteracy, to learn to read.
The second generation provides another source of encouragement to their parents. Some immigrants will read in the
new language to keep pace with their children.

The second generation usually prefer to read in a language of the schools which, in most cases, is the language of
the new country. If they do not turn against their parents'
original culture, they should be enabled to explore it in the
language which comes easiest to them. Many problems of
second generation marginality could be avoided if the children
of immigrants were encouraged in this exploration.

Although the needs of each individual vary greatly, it
is possible that on closer scrutiny the members of an ethnic
group show a pattern. We know very little about this problem and as a first step we should compile an inventory of the
reading and communication needs of all ethnic groups and
then shape our public library services accordingly.

It is quite possible that the public library should not
carry the full weight of the service to immigrants. Co-operation and joint planning with other types of institutions
could ensure a good service to all categories of immigrants.

On the one hand there are the institutions of the ethnic
groups themselves. Side by side with an inventory of the
needs of the ethnic groups, we should also have an inventory
of the group's own services meeting its own needs. Self-help
should be encouraged because it answers the hankering which
is characteristic of the marginal state, the hankering after
institutional completeness. The public library would act as
a mediator arranging contact between individuals and their
institutions. There is a further practical reason for this
approach: a public library cannot be expected to buy a comprehensive stock in the languages of all its readers (although
multi-lingual stock is quite common in Scandinavian public libraries). Deposit collections or postal service to individual
readers are preferable.

On the other hand there is the specialized need of the immigrant intellectual. A public library cannot cope with the special
demands for material on the country of origin and the readers in
question have to turn to scholarly libraries for their research
material. Even there they are not always lucky, though in recent
years, with the increased interest in area studies, comprehen-

sive research collections on other countries are being built. The institutions of the ethnic group cannot cope with this demand (though often they try to do so). Some form of cooperation and sharing of resources would be an advantage.

Finally, institutions outside librarianship such as education, social services, literacy campaigns, broadcasting, should be surveyed to see what work there is relevant to the reading of immigrants.

Conclusion

To sum up: it is difficult to generalize about the reading needs of immigrants. All they have in common is the more or less painful condition of marginality. It is in their interest and in the interest of their host society that they be treated with sensitivity and understanding to help them with their process of acculturation. Each group and each individual has different needs the complexity of which should be understood by librarians. To help librarians with the understanding of this complex situation, and to help them with their planning of the services, an inventory of needs for each ethnic group should be compiled.

Acculturation is a two-way process and, although it seems that services to immigrants are planned on the basis of the stronger helping the weaker, it is ultimately the library service which benefits: it is enriched by the process of acculturation.

References
(for bibliographical details see reading list below)

1. Asheim, L. Librarianship in the developing countries. University of Illinois Press, 1966. p. 2ff.

2. Kaye p. 202.

3. Stonequist.

4. Park (1950).

5. Petersen.

6. Park, R. E. and Miller, H. A. Old world traits transplanted. Harper, 1921. p. 83ff.

7. Adamic, L. The native's return. Harper, 1934. p. 363.

8. Gordon p. 34.

9. Breton.

10. Taft and Robbins p. 127.

11. Taft and Robbins p. 126.

12. Park (1950) p. 358.

13. McClintock.

14. Stonequist p. 83.

15. Park (1950) p. 369.

16. Gordon p. 57.

17. Stonequist p. 154.

18. Boder, D. P. I did not interview the dead. University of Illinois Press, 1949. p. xviii-xix gives a traumatic index to evaluate cases of extreme social stress in displaced persons.

19. Mezey p. 246.

20. Taft and Robbins p. 126.

21. Taft and Robbins p. 126.
    Kent p. 239.
    Zubrzycki (1958) p. 74.

22. Taft and Robbins p. 137.

23. Eisenstadt p. 259.

24. Zubrzycki (1956) p. 76ff.

25. Kaye p. 203ff.

26. Khoshkish p. 179, p. 185.

424   Library Lit. -'74

Some Theoretical Perspectives on Migration

Migration in General

Geisert, H. L.   Population growth and international migration.   G. Washington Univ. Press, 1962.

Petersen, W. "A general typology of migration." Am. Soc. Rev.
23 (3) June 1958, 256-266.

Taft, D. R. and Robbins, R.   International migrations: the
immigrant in the modern world.   Ronald Press Co.,
1955.

The Marginal Man

McClintock, C. G. and Davis, J.   "Changes in the attribute
of 'nationality' in the self-percept of the 'stranger'. "
J. Soc. Psych. 48, 1958, 183-193.

Park, R. E.   Race and culture.   Free Press, 1950.   (Collected papers vol. I.) Part IV. The marginal man.

Stonequist, E. V.   The marginal man: a study in personality
and culture conflict.   Scribner, 1937.

Acculturation

Eisenstadt, S. N.   The absorption of immigrants: a compar-
ative study based mainly on the Jewish community in
Palestine and the State of Israel.   Routledge, 1954.
Ch. 8. Conclusions.

Herskovits, M. J.   Acculturation: the study of culture contact.   J. J. Augustin, 1938.

Kaye, V. J.   "Immigrants' psychology: reactions caused by
environment. "   Revue de l'Université d'Ottawa, 28 (2)
April-June 1958, 199-212.

Mezey, A. G.   "Psychiatric aspects of human migrations. "
Int. J. Soc. Psych. 5 (4) Spring 1960, 245-260.

Zubrzycki, J.   Polish immigrants in Britain: a study of adjustment.   Nijhoff, 1956.

Ethnic Communities

Breton, R.   "Institutional completeness of ethnic communities and the personal relations of immigrants. "
American J. Soc. 70(2) 1964, 192-205.

Gordon, M. M.   Assimilation in American life: the role of
race, religion and national origins.   OUP, 1965.

Redfield, R.   The little community: viewpoints for the study
of a human whole.   Uppsala University, 1955.   (Reprinted by Univ. of Chicago Press, 1960.)

Zubrzycki, J.   "The role of the foreign-language press in
migrant integration. "   Population Studies 12 (1) July
1958, 73-82.

Intellectual Migration

Kent, D. P.   The refugee intellectual: the Americanization
of the immigrants of 1933-41.   Columbia Univ. Press,
1953.

Khoshkish, A.   "Intellectual migration: a sociological approach to 'brain drain'. "   Cahiers d'histoire mondiale,
10 (1) 1966, 170-197.

Refugees

Chandler, E. H. S.   The high tower of refuge: the inspiring
story of refugee relief throughout the world.   Odhams,
1959.

Proudfoot, M. J.   European refugees 1939-52: a study in
forced population movement.   Faber, 1957.

Schechtman, J. B.   The refugee in the world: displacement
and integration.   Yoseloff, 1963.

EPILOGUE

A COMPUTER ANALYSIS OF
LIBRARY POSTCARDS (CALP)*

Norman D. Stevens

Introduction

        In addition to its other programs, The Molesworth In-
stitute[1] has for some time been engaged in a massive effort
to collect picture postcards of libraries throughout the world.
These cards have been collected for a variety of reasons--
including some aesthetic and personal interests--but primarily
to support the research programs of The Institute. Two projects involving the use of these cards have been described in
an earlier report. The first involves the use of a Hinman
collator to identify the common features of library buildings
in an effort to design the perfect library building. The
second involves a consideration of the use of laser beams,
and other advanced techniques in the field of microminiaturi-
zation, to develop programs for the solid state transmission
of books and readers from one library to another. [2]

        The second project mentioned above is still in the
planning stages, but some rough preliminary design studies
have been completed. It appears, on the basis of work to
date, that a much more highly developed technological state
of the art will have to be achieved before that effort can be
sustained. The first project has been proceeding along the
lines originally described and much useful work has been accomplished. It appears now, however, that the work of that
project will largely be supplanted by the work of the project
described in this paper. A final report on the Hinman collator project will be issued in early 1975 by the team of
architects and librarians that has been conducting it.

*Reprinted by permission of the author and publisher from
Journal of the American Society for Information Science,
September-October 1974, pp. 332-335. Copyright 1974 by the
American Society for Information Science, 1155 16th St.
N. W. , Washington, D. C.   20036

Cataloging and Classification

   In attempting to achieve the preliminary organization
of the material for the Hinman collator project certain problems of cataloging and classification were encountered. After
some thought a new system of organization was designed
which not only assisted materially in that project but has, as
was indicated, led to its demise.

   When our collection numbered only a few hundred cards
no system was needed. However, the vast accumulation of
cards over the past five years has led our librarians into a
variety of efforts to arrange and classify this collection which
now numbers over 5, 000 cards. We did initially utilize a
standard library system (see Fig. 1 for a sample of the record produced) but unfortunately Bliss, Cutter, Dewey, the
Library of Congress classification, U. D. C., and the Anglo-
American Cataloging Code all proved to be totally inadequate
for our specialized needs.

```
Bingham, H.F., pub.   ·

      Ashby town library, Ashby, Mass.
Exeter, N.H., Frank W. Swallow, n.d.

      colored postcard   13.5 x 9 cm.

      Unused.




      1. Libraries.   2. Ashby, Mass. - Libraries.

I. Ashby Town Library
                             The Molesworth
Z733.A34              O    Institute - Postcards
```

Fig. 1. Early Catalog Record

   For a time we felt that Ranganathan was on the right
track and we attempted to develop a system, known as PAL
(Postcard Analysis of Libraries), based on his work. Although we employed him as a consultant and hired two Indian
librarians who had been trained by him, we soon found that
staff turnover, and more especially the aging of existing
staff, resulted in a significant variation in indexing levels.
The main difficulty lay in establishing concisely the personality facet of this material. Despite intensive training efforts

tests showed that as we attempted to retrieve material for
our research projects we were obtaining a poor recall/pre-
cision ratio (57. 2%/32. 8%). This effort was subsequently
abandoned for that reason.

We then reverted to our initial, somewhat primitive,
system which incorporated a combination of alphabetical arrangement by place, a cross-reference file by type and name
of library, human memory, and visual scanning of the file.
Tests showed that this gave us a high recall ratio (97. 3%)
but a low precision ratio (2. 7%). Given the nature of our
projects and the then relatively small size of our file, about
1523 cards, this seemed to be satisfactory.

In early 1971, however, our file underwent a tremendous growth in a short period of time as a result of new interest in a variety of projects relating to it. This interest
was sparked by Miss Cecily Cardew who had joined our staff
in late 1970 as a special research associate and fellow. Her
interest grew, in part, out of the work she was conducting
in connection with her doctoral program in librarianship and
architecture at Lord Howe University.

New Technologies

Miss Cardew began to investigate the possible applications of computer technology to the organization of this file.
Preliminary discussions with our library and programming
staffs were encouraging. Next discussions were held with
several outside consultants, including Lawrence Clark Powell,[3]
who had previously expressed an interest in this area. It
was then concluded that there was indeed an enormous amount
of information on these cards that pertained, either directly
or indirectly, to library architecture and history, and that
computer processing of that information was feasible. A
preliminary work sheet (see Fig. 2) was developed and programs were written to test this hypothesis. Approximately
200 cards were then encoded into a machine readable data
base and a series of tests were run.

As a result of those discussions and tests we next organized a month-long planning conference, known as Project
INNREX (Information Retrieval Experiments), which was held
in Rockport, Mass., from August 2 to September 3, 1971.
This conference, which brought together a small group of our
own staff and outside library and computer experts, resulted

```
┌──────────────────────────────────────────────────────┐
│ 10 Name of Library ──────────────────────────────     │
│ 20 Place ──────────────────────────────────────       │
│ 30 Postcard                                            │
│     31 Size (in cm.) ─────────────────────────         │
│     32 Date ──────────────────────────────────         │
│     33 Publisher ─────────────────────────────         │
│     34 Color ─────  or 35 Black & White ──────         │
│     36 Used ─────   or 37 Unused ─────────────         │
│ 40-44 Exterior ─────  or 45-49 Interior ──────         │
│ 50 Type of Construction ──────────────────────         │
│ 60 Type of Library ───────────────────────────         │
│ 70 Architectural Style                                 │
│     72 Carnegie ──────────────────────────────         │
│     74 Modern ────────────────────────────────         │
│     76 Other ─────────────────────────────────         │
│ 80 Other Distinguishing Features ─────────────         │
└──────────────────────────────────────────────────────┘
```

Figure 2. Preliminary CALP Work Sheet

in an intensive discussion of file organization, the basic objectives and goals of the project, the utility of the information, how the relevant information could best be encoded, and technical feasibility. It was concluded, for example, that in addition to architectural information the proper analysis of the details on these cards would enable librarians and social historians to study, for example, the relationships of dogs, and other animals, to libraries. Future technical options, including the possible development of an optical scanning device which would enable us to directly encode the information, were also discussed but it was agreed that the project should move forward as rapidly as possible utilizing existing technology. At the conclusion of the conference a statement of goals and objectives and a detailed work plan were adopted.

After the conference the research and programming staff of The Institute, under the direction of Miss Cardew, developed a series of eight work sheets for the encoding of the information from the cards. These cover the following major categories: (100) the postcard (color, manufacturer, size, etc.); (200) philatelic information (cancellation, place-date-time of cancellation, stamp, etc.); (300) message (person to whom card is addressed, library related/non-library related, etc.); (400) library (architect, date, name, place, etc.); (500) basic building facts (other past or present uses,

shape, size, type of construction, etc.); (600) specific exterior features of the building (chimneys, ivy, lightning rods,
porticos, pediments, signs, swag, weathervanes, etc.); (700)
exterior features not part of the building (animals, cannons,
flagpoles, flowers, means of transportation, other buildings,
people, shrubs, statues, trees, etc.); and (800) interior
views (animals, area of library, books, bookstacks, furniture,
library equipment, lighting fixtures, other accoutrements,
people, plants, etc.). (See Fig. 3 for an example.) In addition, programs were written in FORTRAN to run on our IBM
360 Model 67 configuration computer. We now have on-line
capability and have three IBM 3275 cathode ray terminals
which enable our research staff to carry out their research
analyses. Unfortunately our programming techniques are
somewhat unique and we believe that documentation of techniques and programs only leads to a lack of imagination on
the part of our programmers. We are unable, therefore, to
make our data base or programs available to other interested
institutions. We are willing to utilize our programs and to
develop new programs, at no charge, at The Institute for
qualified researchers. A limited number of fellowships are
available to support such researchers while they are at The
Institute.

```
600 Specific exterior features of the building
     603 Air conditioners _____
     606 Awnings_____
     609 Billboards _____
     612 Chimneys _____
     615 Clocks _____
     618 Cupolas _____
     621 Dome _____
     624 Doors _____
         624.03 Number _____
         624.06 Locations _____
         624.09 Shape _____
         624.12 Size _____
         624.15 Open _____  or 624.18 Closed _____
     627 Flagpoles _____
         627.03 No Flag _____
         627.06 Flag _____
             627.08 Number of stars and stripes _____
```

```
┌─────────────────────────────────────────────────────┐
│ 630 Gargoyles _____    │
│ 633 Inscriptions _____   │
│ 636 Ivy _____   │
│ 639 Lightning rods _____   │
│ 642 Lights _____   │
│ 645 Pediment _____   │
│ 648 Pillars _____   │
│    648.03 Corinthian _____   │
│    648.06 Doric _____   │
│    648.09 Ionic _____   │
│    648.12 Other _____   │
│ 651 Porches _____   │
│ 654 Porticos _____   │
│ 657 Signs _____   │
│ 660 Steps _____   │
│ 663 Television antennas _____   │
│ 666 Towers _____   │
│ 669 Weathervanes _____   │
│ 672 Windows _____   │
│    672.03 Number _____   │
│    672.06 Locations _____   │
│    672.09 Shape _____   │
│    672.12 Size _____.   │
│    672.15 Open _____ or 672.18 Closed _____.     │
│    672.21 Stained glass _____.   │
│    672.24 Shades _____.   │
│       672.27 Open _____.   │
│       672.30 Closed _____.   │
│ 675 - 699 Other information _____.   │
└─────────────────────────────────────────────────────┘
```

Fig. 3. Final CALP Work Sheet

Preliminary Analyses

To date we have encoded the 5,000 postcards currently in our collection and have done a number of analyses. One of the more interesting indicates that only ten cards show a dog, either in or entering a library, while ten interior views include moose heads, which would seem to confirm the impression that most libraries have for a long period of time systematically discriminated against dogs. Another analysis shows that the most frequent library related message on these cards is, "I haven't yet read all of the books here. Ha! Ha!" This tends to demonstrate that library-related humor is of a very low level. Some efforts have been made to determine the growth rates of ivy on the exterior of libraries. While preliminary indications seem to show a somewhat faster rate of growth for Carnegie libraries, our research has been hampered by the lack of comparative information for other public buildings.

Future Activities

Those analyses are, however, apart from our main objectives. The major objective has been to analyze the architectural information in an effort to determine the requirements of the ideal library building and to identify those features which distinguish one type or style of building from another. Some of the elements of the ideal building have tentatively been identified (e. g., the length and nature of the inscription on the exterior of the building) but indications are that we will need to analyze another 7,000 cards in order to more definitely establish that and other requirements. Some library types (e. g., Early Carnegie-Eastern) have also been tentatively identified but here, again, additional analysis of a larger number of cards will be required. At our current rate of progress, and given the continued acquisition of raw data at a reasonable rate, it appears that CALP will run until at least 1982. By that time we believe that the data which we will have analyzed will enable The Molesworth Institute to issue a comprehensive and definitive report describing the various components of the ideal library building and defining a number of types of buildings. This report will be most useful if library buildings are still being constructed in anything approximating the design elements of the period 1900-1920 since the bulk of our information comes from that time.

Notes

1. Stevens, N. D. "The Molesworth Institute, " ALA Bulletin 57:75-76 (1963).

2. _____, "Molesworth Institute Revisited, " ALA Bulletin 63:1275-1277 (1969).

3.   Powell, L. C.   "Any Postcards, " <u>Library Journal</u> 87:
     2960 (1962).

NOTES ON CONTRIBUTORS

Wilfred ASHWORTH is Chief Librarian, the Polytechnic of Central London.

John BALNAVES is Principal Lecturer in Librarianship at Canberra College of Advanced Education, Australia.

Sanford BERMAN is Head Cataloger, Hennepin County Library, Edina, Minnesota.

Arthur CURLEY is Director, Montclair Public Library, New Jersey.

Dennis FLANAGAN is Editor of Scientific American.

Leon N. FLANAGAN is Regional Coordinator, Northern Inter-related Library, Pawtucket, Rhode Island.

William C. FREDERICK is Professor of Business Administration at the University of Pittsburgh, Graduate School of Business.

Daniel GORE is Library Director, Macalester College Library, St. Paul, Minnesota.

Agnes M. GRIFFEN is Assistant Director, Tucson Public Library, Arizona.

Ethel L. HEINS became Editor of The Horn Book Magazine on October 1, 1974.

Margaret HUTCHINSON is Librarian, Venable School, Charlottesville, Virginia.

Raymond JACKSON is Assistant Professor, College of Business, Southeastern Massachusetts University, North Dartmouth, Massachusetts.

Peter JORDAN is Lecturer, Leeds School of Librarianship, England.

Toyo S. KAWAKANI is Assistant Head, Education Library,
    Ohio State University.

Jean Holtz KAY is Architecture Critic for The Nation and
    an editorial commentator for Boston's Educational TV
    network.

Janice M. LADENDORF is a librarian who is studying towards
    her Ph. D. at the University of Minnesota.

Manuel D. LOPEZ is Reference Librarian and Bibliographer
    at Lockwood Memorial Library, S. U. N. Y. at Buffalo.

Judith McPHERON is Reference Librarian, Oklahoma County
    Libraries.

Daniel MELCHER, former President of the R. R. Bowker
    Co., is now a consultant to publishers.   He is also
    the originator of the Montclair Reading Project.

Donald G. MERCER is with the Public Service of Canada.

Roger E. MICHENER serves with The Committee on Social
    Thought at the University of Chicago.

Mildred MYERS is Librarian and Lecturer in Business Ad-
    ministration, University of Pittsburgh, Graduate
    School of Business.

Paul A. NAPIER is Head of the AV Department, The George
    Washington University, Washington, D. C.

Jeanne OSBORN is Professor, School of Library Science,
    University of Iowa.

Leonard RAPPORT is Deputy Director of the records ap-
    praisal staff at the National Archives.

Dorothy J. SCHMIDT supervises a junior high school and two
    elementary school libraries for Community Consoli-
    dated School District 93, Carol Stream, Illinois.

Ann Allen SHOCKLEY is Associate Librarian and Head of
    Special Collections, Fisk University, Nashville, Ten-
    nessee.

S. SIMSOVA, born in Czechoslovakia, now teaches at the

School of Librarianship, The Polytechnic of North
London, England.

Annette D. STEINER is Acting Head, Special Collections, The
George Washington University, Washington, D. C.

Norman D. STEVENS is Director, The Molesworth Institute,
Storrs, Connecticut.

Gordon WILLIAMS is Director, Center for Research Libraries, Chicago.

Rupert C. WOODWARD is University Librarian, The George
Washington University, Washington, D. C.

Wilbur ZELINSKY is Head, Department of Geography, Pennsylvania State University, University Park, Pennsylvania.